Music, Cognition, and Computerized Sound

Music, Cognition, and Computerized Sound

An Introduction to Psychoacoustics

edited by Perry R. Cook

The MIT Press
Cambridge, Massachusetts
London, England

This book was set in Helvetica and Melior by Graphic Composition, Inc. and was printed and bound in the United States of America.

Library of Congress Cataloging-in-Publication Data

Music, cognition, and computerized sound: an introduction to psychoacoustics / Perry R. Cook, editor.
  p. cm.
Includes bibliographical references and index.
ISBN 0-262-03256-2 (hc : alk. paper)
  1. Music—Acoustics and physics. 2. Psychoacoustics. 3. Music—Psychological aspects.
I. Cook, Perry R.
ML3805.M8814   1999
781'.11—dc21   98-16783
                                                                                CIP
                                                                                 MN

Contents

Introduction

.

This book is an introduction to psychoacoustics, specifically geared toward those interested in music. It covers both basic concepts and some brand-new research, and can be used as a textbook for introductory courses at the college sophomore level or above. The book is also suitable for independent study by people interested in psychology and music. The individual chapters are designed to be "interesting reads" as individual units on particular topics. The goal is to capture the interest of readers who are new to the topics, and provide references for those wishing further research. The lecture nature of the book lends well to classroom teaching, with the 23 chapters providing material for one or more lectures each. Further aids for the instructor or reader include sound examples on compact disc, appendices of laboratory exercises, sample test questions, and thought problems.

The course that was the genesis for this book has been offered at the Stanford Center for Computer Research in Music and Acoustics (CCRMA, pronounced "Karma") since the 1980s. The book and its authors owe a tremendous debt of gratitude to CCRMA, and to the teaching assistants who contributed lab exercises, test questions, and chapters. Persons who have served as teaching assistants for the CCRMA course throughout its history include Perry Cook, Brent Gillespie, Sile O'Modhrain, and Craig Sapp.

Special thanks to Dan Levitin for providing editorial help in addition to contributing his own chapters. Thanks to Mary and Liz Douthitt for proofreading and lots of other help. Most thanks of all go to John Pierce, without whose help, guidance, and encouragement this book would have never come into being.

A brief outline of the book follows. Chapters 1 and 2 introduce the basic physiology and functions of the ear and the auditory sections of the brain. Chapter 3 defines and introduces cognitive psychology, and sets the tone for many of the remaining chapters. Chapters 4–7 introduce and develop the basic metrics, analysis tools, and analysis techniques necessary to define, measure, and differentiate such concepts as frequency and pitch, intensity and loudness, spectrum and timbre. Chapter 8 introduces, by example, some of the incredible capabilities of our auditory system. It also discusses which attributes of sound are, and are not, important for perception. Chapter 9 introduces the acoustics and physiology of the voice, one of the most fundamental (we've all got one) and flexible musical instruments. Chapter 10 develops the concept of auditory scene analysis, the ability of the auditory system to identify and sort out individual sounds in a complex texture of audio events. Chapter 11 covers the acoustical bases and perceptual roles of resonances and anti-resonances, particularly in the voice. Chapter 12 discusses the multiple levels of perception, specifically for the voice, which goes beyond basic acoustics to include context, lexicon, and motor articulation. Chapter 13 covers attributes of pitch, explaining such things as octave equivalence by separating chroma (scale degree) from height (absolute spectral frequency). Chapter 14 covers historical, physical, and perceptual aspects of tuning systems and scales. Chapter 15 covers higher-level cognitive organizations of tuning and scales, and introduces a number of psychoacoustic experiments on the topic. Chapter 16 talks about the causes, musical uses, and importance of both intentional (vibrato) and unintentional deviations in pitch. It also discusses noise components in the voice. Chapter 17 Talks about human ability to remember, identify, and produce musical attributes. Perfect pitch, memory for tempo, and memory for rhythmic patterns are discussed. Chapters 18 and 19 introduce the mechanisms, functions, and importance of the sense of touch in music. Chapter 20 surveys and discusses issues related to auditory perspective. Chapter 21 discusses the importance of non-linearity in musical acoustics. Chapter 22 surveys the storage and reproduction of music and sound from a historical and technical perspective. Chapter 23 concludes the book with a description of experimental methods in psychoacoustics, including a typical student project for a course taught from this text.

The lecture nature of the book comes from the fact that as the course developed, faculty and graduate students at CCRMA presented lectures on their particular areas of interest and expertise. I first took the course as a graduate student in electrical engineering, then served as teaching assistant for the course the next two years. After finishing my Ph.D. I became a research associate at CCRMA, and one of my responsibilities was the supervision and coinstruction of the Cognitive Psychology for Musicians course. Other students-turned-teachers coming out of the course include Brent Gillespie and Dan Levitin, both of whom contributed chapters to this book. The variety of authors and areas of expertise represented in this book is impressive indeed. Brief biographies of the authors follow.

John Chowning was the founding director of the Stanford Center for Computer Research in Music and Acoustics (CCRMA). With the help of Max Mathews at Bell Labs, CCRMA was able to secure the software necessary to set up a computer music system at Stanford in the 1960s. John is the inventor of FM sound synthesis, which is used in the Yamaha X family of music synthesizers, the best-selling synthesizers in history. Each of the pieces John has composed has demonstrated something profound, musically, technically, and about the human perceptual system. His work on synthesis of the voice, simulation of space and moving sound sources, and the "details" of sound synthesis has informed and inspired countless composers and engineers.

Perry R. Cook served as a research associate, technical director, and acting director of Stanford CCRMA. He was also senior research scientist for Media Vision Technologies, and has consulted for numerous computer and media companies. He is currently assistant professor in the Department of Computer Science at Princeton University, with a joint appointment in music. His research has included work on singing voice synthesis, musical instrument synthesis by physical modeling, real-time controllers for computer music, and psychoacoustics.

Brent Gillespie has studied both mechanical engineering and performance piano. While at Stanford CCRMA, he worked on computer simulation and haptic (touch) display of the grand piano action, as well as other topics involving haptic display for music, assistive technologies for the handicapped, and remote manipulation. Brent is now a postdoctoral fellow at the Laboratory for Intelligent Mechanisms (LIMS), Northwestern University, Chicago.

Daniel J. Levitin has studied music and psychology. His work in the area of memory for musical attributes has caused him to review and reevaluate much of the literature on perfect pitch and auditory memory, and his thesis proposed new theories on various musical skills and competencies. Dan has also worked as a record producer, and has some gold records to his credit. He is a prolific writer, having published hundreds of articles in popular and music industry publications, in addition to his scholarly publications on topics in psychoacoustics and psychometrics. Dan is now a cognitive psychologist at Interval Research Corporation and a visiting scholar/ lecturer at Stanford CCRMA

Max Mathews, known as the "Father of Computer Music," has been involved in the study of sound, communications, and music since his days at Bell Laboratories in the 1950s. Max wrote the first generalized computer language for computer sound and music synthesis. He has created instruments and controllers for computer music, and has written many papers and books on the central topics in this volume. The graphical MIDI processing language, MAX, is named in his honor. Max retired from Bell Labs in 1987 and brought his lab, wisdom, and inspiration to Stanford CCRMA, where he is now an emeritus professor.

John Pierce is one of the best-known engineers of all time. He has written many books on such diverse topics as the physics of waves, information theory, the science of musical sound, and even some science fiction under the pseudonym J. J. Coupling. John was Max Mathew's supervisor at Bell Labs, and has taken an active interest in music research throughout his career, which has spanned the era of vacuum tubes (on which John is considered an expert) and the transistor (a name coined by John for the Bell Labs invention that was to revolutionize our lives). John was director of the Telstar project, and recently was honored with the Draper Award, from the National Academy of Engineering, for his contributions to telecommunications.

Roger Shepard is on the faculty of the Stanford Department of Psychology. His work in the areas of human perception, thought, and creativity are well known and highly regarded. His sketches and drawings showing various optical illusions, and his relation of those cases of visual illusion and ambiguity to similar phenomena in audition (and also taction) not only have informed many of the modern theories on perception but also have inspired composers and artists. Roger was recently awarded the National Medal of Science for "research which provides insights into the nature of mental processes that previously had been considered impossible to study."

1 The Ear and How It Works

Max Mathews

1.1 Structure of the Ear

In this chapter we will introduce the structure and function of the ear. We will also talk about some of the other physical aspects of how sound gets into our ears, such as the effects that the head and shoulders have on what we hear. The outer ear or pinna (plural pinnae) leads to the middle ear's auditory canal or meatus. The auditory canal terminates at the eardrum, or tympanic membrane. Beyond the eardrum is the inner ear, which contains the hidden parts of the ear, encased in bone. The complicated structure is hard to see or to understand in photomicrographs of actual dissected specimens. We will rely on schematized drawings that depict the shapes and relations of the various parts of the ear. Even here we are in difficulty, for few diagrams give typical dimensions.

The schematized drawing of the ear in figure 1.1 shows the semicircular canals, three liquid-filled passages that are associated with equilibrium rather than hearing. They tell us about the orientation of the head, cause us to get dizzy when they are malfunctioning, and cause some of us to get seasick when the head, body, and eyes undergo motional disturbances. The three little bones of the air-filled middle ear, which are attached to the eardrum, excite vibrations in the cochlea, the liquid-filled inner ear. It is in the cochlea that the vibrations of sound are converted into nerve impulses that travel along the auditory nerve, the *eighth nerve*, toward the brain. The purpose of the auditory canal is to guide sound waves to the eardrum. The pinna acts as a collector of sound from the outside world and also as a directional filter, as will be discussed later. Other body structures outside of the ear also affect the sound that reaches the inner ear.

1.2 Acoustic Shadows and Filters

The intensity of a sound wave in the auditory canal is proportional to the intensity of the sound wave that approaches the listener. It also depends on the direction from which the sound wave comes.

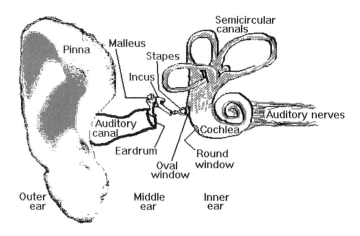

Figure 1.1   The outer, middle, and inner ears (not to scale).

The shoulders can reflect the sound wave toward the pinnae. The head can cast an acoustical shadow. The "guiding" effect of the convolutions of the pinna increases with increasing frequency, and at high frequencies it rises and falls with frequency. The effects of the pinna, the head, and the shoulders become significant only when the wavelength of the sound wave is comparable with the dimensions of the structures. Each shoulder is about 6 inches wide. The head is approximately an 8-inch sphere. The height of the outer ear or pinna is around 2 inches.

Sound moves through the air as a travelling wave with a velocity of 1128 feet (344 meters) per second. The wavelengths of sinusoidal sound waves of various frequencies and musical notes are shown in table 1.1. Middle C on the piano keyboard (traditionally located closest to the first letter of the brand name above the keyboard) is C4 and has a frequency of 261.6 hertz (Hz; cycles per second). Each doubling or halving of frequency is called an "octave," and causes the index number to go up or down by 1. Thus the C above middle C is C5, and has a frequency of 523.2 Hz.

From the tabulated values we would expect an appreciable influence from the shoulders and the head above the pitch of A6. We would expect pinna effects to be most important above a pitch of A8 (although no musical instrument normally produces a fundamental pitch this high). However, in most musical sounds much of the overall energy is contained in harmonics (integer multiples) of the fundamental frequency. Thus, reflections, shadowing, and guidance effects will occur at frequencies two octaves, three octaves, or even further above the actual pitch frequency.

Table 1.1 Musical pitch, frequency, and wavelengths

MUSICAL PITCH	FREQUENCY (HZ)	WAVELENGTH (IN.)
A2	110	123
A3	220	62
A4	440	31
A5	880	15
A6	1,760	7.7
A7	3,520	3.8
A8	7,040	1.9

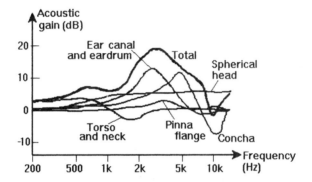

Figure 1.2 The acoustic effects of various body structures as a function of frequency. Sound is from 45 degrees off center in front of listener. (Modified from E. H. G. Shaw, 1974, *Handbook of Sensory Physiology,* vol. 5/1. Berlin: Springer, fig. 11.)

Computations have been made concerning variation with frequency of the ratio (measured in decibels, dB) of sound pressure at the eardrum to sound pressure in the wave approaching the listener. Figure 1.2 shows the outcome of such a calculation for a wave approaching from 45 degrees off center. The curve labeled Total shows the total variation with frequency, plotted in dB as a function of frequency. The other curves show the parts of the effect attributable to various structures of the body and outer ear. The concha and the pinna flange are separate parts of the pinna. We may note that many of the interesting effects happen between 2000 and 5000 Hz, with the total peak at around 2500 Hz.

The influence of the head in shadowing the ear from the sound source is important in judging left or right, particularly for high-frequency sounds. The disparity in time of arrival at the two ears is more important. Changes in the disparity by 20 or 30 microseconds (millionths of a second) can produce noticeable changes in our judgement of the angular position of a sound source.

1.3   The Pinnae and Auditory Canal

The frequency-dependant effect of the pinnae on the intensity of sound in the auditory canal is important in judging whether a sound comes from ahead or behind; it is crucial in judging the height of a source in the median plane (a vertical plane that divides the head into left and right halves). If you fold down the tops of your ears, you will notice that it becomes difficult to discern the position of a sound source.

The externalization of a sound source (the sense that the sound comes from some point outside the head) is ordinarily absent in listening through headphones, which give us only a sense of left and right. Some degree of externalization can be obtained with headphones by recording the two stereo channels from microphones located in the two auditory canals, or even in the auditory canals of a dummy head with typical pinnae.

The auditory canal is a little over an inch (2.54 cm) long and a quarter of an inch (0.6 cm) in diameter, and leads from the pinna to the eardrum. If we regard the auditory canal as a quarter-wave resonator (this will be discussed more in later chapters), the ratio of sound pressure at the eardrum to sound pressure at the outer opening of the canal will be greatest at a frequency around 3000 Hz. From this alone, we can deduce that the maximum sensitivity of the ear to sound should be around 3000 Hz.

1.4   Inside the Ear

The eardrum vibrates in response to sound. For us to hear this vibration, it must be transferred from the air-filled outer and middle ears to the fluid-filled cochlea, which is "stiffer" (has a higher impedance) than air. Transfer of vibration is effected through the leverage of a chain of three little bones or *ossicles,* the *malleus* (hammer), the *incus* (anvil), and the *stapes* (stirrup).

The chain of little bones can be stiffened and the transfer of vibration decreased by the contraction of the *stapedius* muscle. This provides a gain control that gives some protection to the inner ear, because loud sounds cause a contraction of the muscle and a reduction in the sound transmitted to the cochlea. This *stapedius reflex* gives some protection against steady sounds, but no protection against very intense, very brief sounds, such as a gunshot.

Figure 1.1 shows the cochlea as a coiled, snail-shell-like structure. Its actual size is about that of a pencil eraser. Vibration is transmitted into the cochlea by the stapes driving the flexible membrane that covers the oval window. Below the oval window is the round window, which also is covered with a flexible membrane; the function of the round window will be discussed later. The auditory nerve (*eighth nerve,* or *spiral ganglion*) comes from the cochlea, carrying *afferent* nerve impulses toward the brain, as well as some *efferent* nerve impulses from the brain into the cochlea. The function of the cochlea is to convert the vibration of sound into nerve impulses in the auditory nerve. The details of the way it carries out this function can be modified by pulses reaching it from the eighth nerve. Let us now consider the structure and function of the cochlea.

The cochlea is a long, narrow, three-and-a-half-turn coiled passage surrounded by bone. The passage is about 35 millimeters (mm) (1⅜″) long. The diameter of the passage (around 2 mm, or ⁵⁄₆₄″) varies somewhat with distance from the basal, oval-window end, being least at the apical end. Figure 1.3 shows a cross section at some place along the tube of the cochlea. From this figure we see that the cochlear passage is divided into three parts:

1. The *scala tympani* stretches from the oval window at its basal end to the apical end. The oval window is driven by the stapes at the basal end. The apical end is the end at the small termination of the coiled cochlea.
2. The *scala vestibula* stretches from the round window at its basal end to the apical end.
3. These two scalae are connected at their apical end by a passage called the *helicotrema* (not shown in figure 1.3).

The *scala media* lies between the other two scalae, and is closed at both the basal and the apical ends.

All three scalae are filled with fluid. The fluid in the scala media is different from that in the other two, and the difference in composition makes the scala media fluid (*endolymph*) about 80 millivolts positive with respect to the *perilymph* that fills the other two

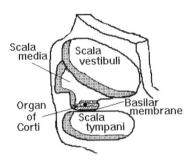

Figure 1.3 Cross section of the cochlear ducts.

scalae, and also with respect to the bony tissue of the cochlea. This potential difference plays a part in the excitation of nerve pulses.

The actual production of nerve pulses takes place in the *organ of Corti*. At the bottom of the organ of Corti is the *basilar membrane,* which separates the scala media from the scala tympani. The basilar membrane vibrates in response to sound, and that vibration causes vibration in some of the 3500 inner hair cells with respect to the *tectorial membrane* that lies on top of them. This relative motion produces nerve pulses that are transmitted toward the brain by the eighth nerve. There are also three rows of outer hair cells whose functions are different. They respond to nerve pulses coming toward them *from* the brain via the eighth nerve.

1.5   Details of the Cochlea

To understand hearing, it is important to understand the way in which the basilar membrane responds to the vibrations of the stapes pushing the oval window in and out. This mechanical aspect of the cochlea is made more obvious by "unrolling" the cochlea and its basilar membrane into a tapered tube, as shown in figure 1.4. The basilar membrane divides the tapered cochlea into two passages that are joined at the right end by the helicotrema. The upper passage, which starts at the oval window at the left or basal end, represents the scala tympani. The lower passage, which starts at the round window at the left, represents the scala vestibuli. The scala media, closed at both ends, is not shown.

We may regard the fluid in the cochlea as incompressible. In figure 1.4 the oval window is shown at the top, and the round window at the bottom, of the basal end of the cochlea. If the oval window is pushed in slowly, the round window will bulge out slowly as fluid

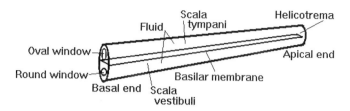

Figure 1.4 An unrolled view of the cochlea. Fluid volume is constant. If the stapes pushes the oval window in, the fluid pushes the round window out.

passes through the helicotrema slowly, so that the total volume of the fluid remains constant.

What happens if we push the oval window in quickly? The springy basilar membrane is pushed down, the oval window is pushed out, and constant volume is maintained without motion of fluid through the helicotrema. In fact, when the oval window is pushed in suddenly, the deflection of the basilar membrane is a wave that travels from the oval window toward the helicotrema. As in an ocean wave or a sound wave, there is no actual flow of liquid from the basal to the apical end. Rather, deflection of the basilar membrane at one point causes a subsequent deflection of the adjoining part of the basilar membrane, and so on.

Suppose we excite the oval window with a steady sine wave. Figure 1.5 shows deflection vs. distance at successive times, moving rightward. We see that as the wave on the basilar membrane travels from left to right, it slowly increases in amplitude, peaks, and then rapidly decreases in amplitude. In essence, the wave of this particular frequency can't travel beyond a certain "cutoff point" on the cochlea. As it approaches this place, the wave slows, the amplitude increases, and the power of the wave is absorbed. A wave of that frequency can't travel beyond the cutoff position. This cutoff phenomenon is important because a wave of high frequency can't mask (or hide) a wave of low frequency, while a wave of low frequency can mask a wave of higher frequency.

The dashed lines in figure 1.5 designate the envelope of the wave as a function of distance along the cochlea, the highest (or lowest) amplitude as the wave passes. Figure 1.6 shows the envelopes of waves along the cochlea for various frequencies. We see that the basilar membrane acts as a filter in which the maximum response to a sinusoidal sound wave moves further to the right as the frequency of the wave is decreased. Thus, the basilar membrane excites different hair cells for sufficiently differing frequencies.

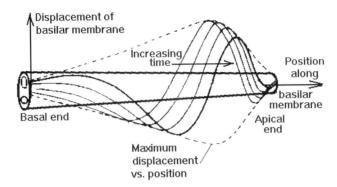

Figure 1.5 Progressive basilar membrane deflection vs. distance for a 200 Hz wave. The dashed curves show the envelope, the maximum upward and downward deflection, as a function of position along the basilar membrane. (Modified from G. von Békésy, 1960, *Experiments in Hearing*. New York: Wiley, fig. 12–17.)

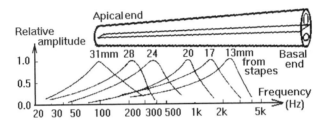

Figure 1.6 The envelope or maximum deflection as a function of distance along the basilar membrane for sinusoidal excitation at the oval window of various frequencies. (Modified from G. von Békésy, *Experiments in Hearing*. New York: Wiley, 1960, fig. 11–49.)

What happens when a sound consists of two frequencies that aren't widely separated, so that some hair cells are excited by both sinusoids? We hear beats. If the two frequencies are a few cycles apart, what we hear is like a single sine wave of rising and falling intensity. As we increase the frequency difference, we hear a vibrating, somewhat harsh sound. If we make the frequency difference large enough, we hear the two sinusoidal sounds clearly and separately.

Thus, we can explore the frequency resolution of the cochlea by listening to pairs of sine waves and varying their frequency separation. Or, at a given frequency, we can add to a strong sine wave a weaker sine wave of different frequency whose intensity is some number of dB less than that of the strong sinusoidal signal. For each frequency separation we can ask, "How much weaker [in dB] must we make the weaker signal in order that it be masked [not heard] in the presence of the stronger signal?" In this way we can obtain *masking curves* for different frequency separations. A *critical band-*

width is the bandwidth within which two sinusoidal signals interact, or mask one another. It should be possible to relate the masking curves to curves of response vs. distance, such as those of figure 1.6. Measurements of critical bandwidth indicate that the curves of figure 1.6 aren't narrow enough. The curves of figure 1.6 are based on early work of Békésy (work that won him the Nobel Prize). Békésy measured cochlea extracted from corpses. More recent data from experiments on living animals show that the curves in living creatures are much sharper, or more narrow-band, than Békésy's data indicate.

Much effort has been devoted to mathematical models of waves traveling along the basilar membrane. Such models are intended to take into account the stiffness of the membrane, which decreases from the basal end to the apical end, the mass of the fluid in which the membrane is immersed, and losses along the membrane. No model fits the data satisfactorily at any signal level. Moreover, a model that fits a dB vs. frequency curve fairly well at one sound level fits worse at other sound levels.

It is now believed that at low levels the outer hair cells act like little muscles and actually add energy to the traveling wave to make up for mechanical losses in the basilar membrane. Indeed, in some forms of tinnitus (ringing in the ears) the ringing can be picked up with a sensitive microphone placed near the ear—in such a case the loss has been more than compensated for, and some part of the basilar membrane oscillates.

The fraction of energy added by the outer hair cells is thought to be controlled by nerve signals carried to the outer hair cells by the auditory nerve. In effect, there is a gain control that reduces the response of the ear to sounds that send strong signals up the auditory nerve toward the brain. This gain control is much faster-acting than the stapedius reflex.

1.6 Concluding Remarks About the Ear

While not all details of the precise functioning of the ear have been fully worked out, several things are clear.

The basilar membrane of the cochlea performs a frequency analysis; a given place along the basilar membrane responds most strongly to a sinusoidal vibration of a particular frequency. While a sound of one frequency can mask a sound of a nearby frequency, it cannot mask a sound of widely separated frequency. Lower-frequency sounds can mask sounds of higher frequency, but higher-frequency sounds cannot mask sounds of lower frequency.

Sounds widely separated in frequency are heard separately. Sounds separated in frequency by less than a critical bandwidth interact to produce beats or harshness.

The ear provides two sorts of gain control so that we can hear sounds over a range of intensity of around 120 dB. One gain control is the slow-acting stapedius reflex. The other is provided through the three rows of outer hair cells.

References

Békésy, G. von. (1960). *Experiments in Hearing*. New York: Wiley.

Pickles, James O. (1988). *An Introduction to the Physiology of Hearing*. Second edition. San Diego: Academic Press.

Pierce, J. R. (1992). *The Science of Musical Sound*. Revised edition. New York: W. H. Freeman.

2 The Auditory Brain

Max Mathews

2.1 Nerves and the Brain

Figure 2.1 shows a motor neuron type of nerve cell, with the cell body located at the right end. Small fibers called *dendrites* radiate from it. Fibers from other nerve cells terminate on the dendrites at tiny *synaptic* knobs, and pulses from these other nerves can cause the firing of the nerve cell. Other types of nerve pulses can act to inhibit the firing of a nerve cell. A long fiber called an *axon* leaves the cell body. The axon of this motor nerve cell terminates at the left end, near a motor cell in some muscle.

2.2 Electrical Behavior of Nerves

The human body is a good conductor of electricity, except for the skin when it is dry. You could test that the body is a good conductor by grabbing a pair of high-voltage terminals, but please don't. A safer experiment would involve touching the terminals of a small 9-volt battery to the back of your hand, then licking the terminals. The dry, dead skin on the back of your hand keeps current from flowing efficiently, while your wet tongue is a much better conductor.

With some exceptions, we can say that all of the bodily tissue outside of nerve cells is at a common electrical potential, positive with respect to the interior of nerve cells. In its resting state, the inside of the neuron is approximately 50 millivolts negative with respect to the tissue outside the neuron. A chemical reaction involving sodium and potassium ions maintains this difference of electrical potential. When the nerve cell fires, the voltage changes momentarily, and a positive (relative to the usual negative bias) electrical pulse travels along the long axon of the nerve cell. The membrane that surrounds a resting nerve cell is ordinarily a nonconductor, but this insulator can break down, allowing current to flow. Such a breakdown can spread, and turn into a nerve pulse.

The axon of a nerve cell can be very long, for axons terminate at sites throughout the body, including the fingers and toes, while the cell bodies of all nerves lie in the central nervous system, in various

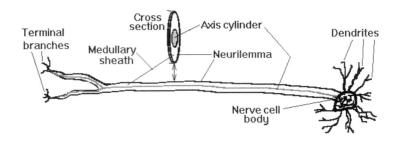

Figure 2.1 A motor neuron.

parts of the brain, or in the spinal cord. Long axons, and even some types of short axons, are coated with a fatty insulating layer or medullary sheath called *myelin.* This conserves energy and speeds propagation along the axon.

As a nerve pulse travels along a long axon, it must be boosted occasionally. Interruptions in the myelin coating spaced around a millimeter apart are called the *nodes of Ranvier.* These interruptions in the insulation put the sheath of the nerve into contact with the surrounding positive tissue. When a nerve pulse reaches an interruption in the fatty insulation, the nerve sheath breaks down electrically and energy is added to the passing nerve pulse. Thus, the nerve pulse traveling down a long axon is repeatedly regenerated, which keeps its intensity and shape essentially constant as it moves along the axon.

2.3 Propagation Times in Nerves

The electrochemical pulses travel down a neuron fairly slowly, compared with the speed of electromagnetic waves (300 million meters per second) or even the speed of sound waves in air (334 meters per second). The velocity increases linearly with the diameter of the axon. For an axon diameter of about 2 microns (a micron is a millionth of a meter or a ten thousandth of a centimeter), the conduction velocity is around 10 meters per second. For an axon diameter of 20 microns, the conduction velocity is about 120 meters per second.

An organist plays pedals with his feet, plays keys with his hands, looks at music and other musicians with his eyes, and listens with his ears. The control and perception for all of these are located in his head, which is up to 2 meters from his feet. It can take a fifth of a second for a message from the organist's head to reach the muscles of his foot. The organist must compensate for this time difference. This is so well learned that the organist isn't even aware of doing it. But it is clear that in a rapid musical passage the organist must "tell his foot what to do" before the note is played; he can't make corrections in any one note on the basis of what he currently hears. This is true of other instrumentalists as well, and we will discuss more of this later in the book.

In this part of the book we are mostly interested in the nerves of the inner ear. Figure 2.2 shows two distinct types of nerves that are found in the cochlea, an inner hair cell (left of figure 2.2) and an outer hair cell. The hairs that make physical contact with vibrations of the basilar membrane are shown at the top. The nerve endings that innervate the hair cells are shown at the bottom. The inner hair cells are innervated by afferent fibers that send pulses toward the brain; the outer hair cells are innervated by efferent fibers that bring nerve pulses to the hair cells from the higher parts of the auditory system.

2.4 Inner and Outer Hair Cells: Nerve Signals in the Ear

Let us consider the inner hair cell first. The area at the bottom, between the axon and the body of the hair cell, is called a *synapse*. The inner hair cell itself is a sort of specialized nerve cell. It is charged to the negative potential characteristic of a nerve cell. When the inner

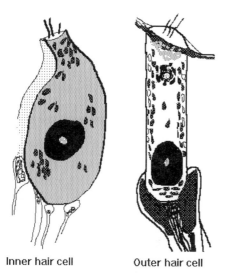

Inner hair cell   Outer hair cell

Figure 2.2   Inner and outer hair cells.

hair cell is activated mechanically by a disturbance of the hairs at the top, the potential falls, and the connecting nerve axon is stimulated and fires. The pulse travels and is transferred to whatever cell body lies higher in the auditory system than the hair cell from which the nerve axon came.

When such a pulse reaches the next cell body, that cell body fires. The firing is propagated along the nerve axon to another synapse. There the nerve pulse will cause another cell body to fire, sending a pulse along another axon toward the higher levels of the brain.

Thus, you can have a chain of nerve cells set off by the firing of a hair cell. And that's basically how messages get from the ear to the higher levels of the auditory system.

By means of its many dendrites, the body of a nerve cell can receive impulses from many other nerve cells. Some impulses tend to make the cell fire; others *inhibit* or tend to block firing. Inhibition is very important in neural processing.

The outer hair cells of the inner ear are motor cells. They add energy to the vibration of the part of the basilar membrane to which they are mechanically coupled. They act as a "negative resistance," counteracting the energy losses in the process of vibration. The amount of negative resistance can be decreased by nerve pulses from the upper auditory system. The outer hair cells are part of an automatic gain control that reduces the relative vibration in response to intense sound waves. This tells us about interactions between the specialized cells of the inner ear and the cells of the upper auditory system.

In discussing the processing of pulses in the upper auditory system, it is important to know something about what nerve pulses look like. It is hard to look at pulses on single nerve fibers, but people have done it. They can stick a tiny electrode inside a nerve cell, or even inside an axon. Then they stimulate the nerve and watch the voltage.

In the records of firings shown in figure 2.3, the erratic horizontal bars are noise. The narrow upward spikes are nerve cell firings.

Immediately after firing, a nerve cell goes into a refractory state. It cannot fire again until its charge has been built up by a chemical readjustment inside the cell body. After the end of the refractory period the cell can fire again, either spontaneously or when stimulated by the firing of another nerve cell, or in the case of an inner hair cell, when the hairs are wiggled.

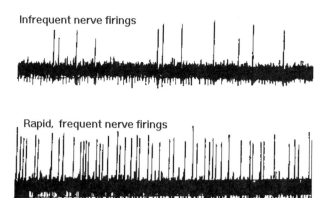

Figure 2.3 Nerve firings. (From Brink, Bronk, and Larrabee, 1946.)

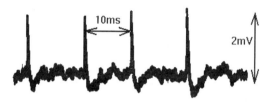

Figure 2.4 Nerve firings, finer time scale. (From J. Pickles, 1988, *An Introduction to the Physiology of Hearing,* 2nd ed. London: Academic Press. Courtesy G. Leng.)

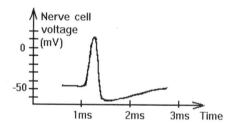

Figure 2.5 Details of a single nerve firing.

Figure 2.3 is a rather broad-scale look at nerve pulses. In figure 2.4 we see firings of an auditory nerve on an expanded time scale. There is a negative charge, then a positive pulse, then a return to a negative state.

Figure 2.5 is a further expansion of a nerve firing. It shows the bottom portion of a single pulse, sitting at approximately −45 millivolts. The cell fires and the pulse rises sharply. The voltage then drops below the value it had before firing. During the refractory period the voltage gradually rises again, until after 0.5 millisecond to 1 millisecond, depending on the nerve, the cell is once more capable of firing. The time marks below the pulse waveform are 1 millisecond apart.

2.5 Rate and Place Theory of Pitch Perception

The refractory period of the nerve seems curiously long, for musical sounds rise and fall hundreds to many thousands of times a second. A single nerve cell cannot capture the time variation of such sounds, for it cannot follow their rise and fall. But hair cells tend to fire at a certain point in the waveform of the mechanical motion that excites them. So if many hair cells fire as a result of a sound wave, the number firing in any very short time can reflect the wave shape of the exciting sound. That is, one cell cannot fire each cycle of a fast waveform, but if a few cells fire each time the wave comes around, the frequency of the waveform is represented.

Basically, nerve pulses aren't fast enough to encode the exact waveform shapes of musical sounds. There must be other mechanisms for responding to the details of the rise and fall of musical sound waves. Various mechanisms have been proposed. I will not try to settle the question entirely here, but I will point out some of the proposed mechanisms.

One proposed mechanism is called the *place theory* of how we encode musical sounds. It goes along with what we have learned about the cochlea. You will remember that figure 1.6 showed that various frequencies cause maximum vibration at various places along the cochlea, the high frequencies at the basal end near the oval window, and the low frequencies farthest toward the apical end. And different nerves go to different parts of the basilar membrane to pick up the pulses caused by vibrations in different places.

Frequency dependence can be seen in the patterns of firing of various fibers of the auditory nerve. Figure 2.6 shows tuning curves (or threshold firings) for different fibers of the auditory nerve of a cat. The hearing of the cat is close enough to ours that we would expect similar behavior in the human being. The plots are of the least signal (in dB) that can cause a noticeable increase in firing rate versus frequency (in Hz). Curves are shown for fibers centered on six different frequencies. For each frequency, curves for two different fibers are shown. This shows that different fibers centered on the same frequency behave almost identically.

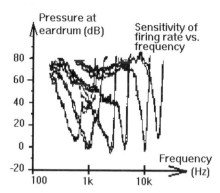

Figure 2.6 Tuning curves from nerve firings of a cat. (Modified after M. C. Liberman and N. Y. S. Kiang, 1978, "Acoustic Trauma in Cats," *Acta Otolaryngologica* suppl. 358: 1–63.)

In figure 2.6 we are looking at curves that are different from the curves we saw in chapter 1, curves of excitation versus distance along the basilar membrane of the cochlea for a signal of constant frequency. We might attribute the shape of the curves of figure 2.6 entirely to the relative amplitudes of vibration along the basilar membrane caused by a sinusoidal signal of constant frequency. This could be so if an X dB increase in signal strength caused an X dB increase in intensity of vibration of the basilar membrane. But for strong signals it doesn't. To get an X dB increase in vibration, we must increase the signal by more than X dB.

2.6 Efferent Nerves and Cochlear Response Curves

We noted earlier that there is a long-term gain control due to the stapedius reflex and a short-term gain control due to the action of the outer hair cells. The curves of figure 2.6 are plots of firings versus pressure at the tympanic membrane. An automatic gain control, which reduces the effect of high-intensity signals in causing vibration of the basilar membrane, will make the curves steeper than curves for a constant sensitivity to vibration. The sharpness of the curves of figure 2.6 is consistent with our ability to discriminate frequency. We can discriminate the frequencies of two signals that are about 0.30 percent different. The rather broad band-pass filters we saw in plotting vibration along the basilar membrane against frequency would probably not do that. The sharper neural frequency responses to a single sine tone of constant level are more in line with our ability to discriminate frequency. That would be particularly true if we notice that the right sides of the response curves of figure

2.6 are very steep, and if we use the steep high-frequency cutoff as our means of discrimination.

So far we have discussed the anatomy of the ear and the excitation of the eighth nerve. The eighth nerve is just the entrance to the vestibule of the brain. What goes on in the auditory pathways is much more complicated and less understood. But it is fascinating.

2.7 The Auditory Brain

Figure 2.7 shows the brain and a blowup of the functional mapping of part of the auditory cortex. I used to think of the brain as a three-dimensional object, but it is more nearly proper to think of the various regions of the brain as two-dimensional, highly convoluted surfaces. The functions of the various parts of the brain appear to be spread out over a crumpled two-dimensional surface, that of the gray matter. The gray matter is cell bodies. The surface of the brain contains the endings of cells whose axons lie under that surface, and interconnect various regions on the surface. Anatomically, it is possible to communicate between any two parts of the surface of the brain through axons that lie under the surface.

The various structural features of the auditory system, all the way up to and including the auditory cortex, are *tonotopically* organized. In figure 2.7 a portion of the auditory cortex is mapped out. We find that if we increase the frequency of a sine wave, the excitation on

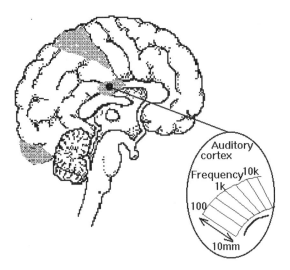

Figure 2.7 The brain and the tonotopic mapping of the auditory cortex.

the cortex moves along a curved path that runs up and to the right. Such movement with frequency is true of a number of auditory structures. There is something fundamental about frequency in the response of the brain to sound, right up to the highest level, the auditory cortex.

Figure 2.8 represents nerve pathways between the eighth nerve and the auditory cortex of the brain, drawn like a wiring diagram. Let us look at the lower-left corner, which shows fibers of the eighth nerve going from the cochlea to the *cochlear nucleus.* The heavy dots denote cell bodies. The junction point in the cochlear nucleus is where the first synapse occurs. The axons end near the cell bodies of other cells, and cause those cells to fire. Beyond the cochlear nucleus the pathways continue, and become harder to follow. Eventually you reach the *auditory cortex,* the highest part of the auditory brain.

2.8 Interaural Timings

It is interesting to consider how we identify and separate the sounds coming into our left and right ears. We know that we can make very good comparisons of sounds coming into the left and right ears because of our directional hearing, our sense of left and right. The accuracy of such left and right judgments corresponds to an accu-

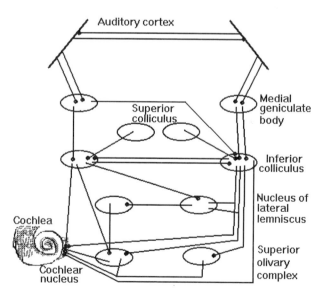

Figure 2.8   Neural network from cochlea to auditory cortex.

racy of some 10 microseconds in comparing the nerve pulses from the left and right ears. Yet the length of the nerve pulses themselves is closer to 0.10 millisecond, which is 10 times as long. This accuracy of comparison to a small fraction of the pulse length is amazing, yet perhaps our strongest cue as to the location of a source of sound is the interaural time difference.

Another thing that helps us to determine the direction of a sound source is the interaural intensity difference, because a sound coming from the left side of our head travels less far in getting to our left ear than to our right, and thus is louder in our left ear. One final thing that helps us determine the location of a sound source is the differences in spectral coloration of that sound that we perceive in our two ears. Recall from figure 1.2 that the various structures of the body, particularly those of the ear, cause different frequencies to be increased or decreased in amplitude. These effects will be different in the two ears, and our brain can use that information to make decisions about the direction of the source of that sound. For example, a sound coming from the right side of our head will be spectrally brighter in the right ear and less bright in our left ear, due to the high-frequency absorption caused by our (roughly) spherical head and by the effects of the horn-shaped concha.

References

Carterette, E. D., and M. P. Friedman, eds. (1978). *Handbook of Perception.* Volume IV, Hearing. New York: Academic Press.

Pickles, James O. (1988). *An Introduction to the Physiology of Hearing.* Second edition. San Diego: Academic Press.

Schubert, E. D. (1980). *Hearing, Its Function and Dysfunction.* New York: Springer-Verlag.

Stevens, S. S., ed. (1951; fourth printing 1962). *Handbook of Experimental Psychology.* New York: Wiley.

3 Cognitive Psychology and Music

Roger Shepard

3.1 Cognitive Psychology

What does cognitive psychology have to do with the perception of sound and music? There is a long chain of processes between the physical events going on in the world and the perceptual registration of those events by a human observer. The processes include the generation of energy by some external object or event, the transmission of the energy through the space between the event and the observer, the reception and processing of the energy by the observer's sensory receptors, and the transmission of signals to the brain, where still more processing takes place. Presumably, the end result is the formation of a representation in the brain of what is going on in the external world. The brain has been shaped by natural selection; only those organisms that were able to interpret correctly what goes on in the external world and to behave accordingly have survived to reproduce.

The way we experience all events in the world, including musical events, is the result of this process of interpretation in the brain. What is happening inside the eye on the surface of the retina, or on the basilar membrane in the ear, is of no significant interest whatsoever, except insofar as it provides information from which the brain is able to construct a representation of what is going on in the world. True, the signals from the receptors are generally the only source of information the brain has about what is actually going on in the external world, so it is important to understand the workings of the observer's eyes and ears. But what goes on in those sensory transducers has relatively little direct correspondence to the final representation experienced by the observer, which is the result of extensive further processing within the observer's brain.

Sensory psychophysicists and psychologists study what goes on in the sensory transducers, and the eye and ear appear fundamentally quite different in function and behavior. There are many things specific to a particular sensory organ, and they must be studied and discussed independently. In contrast, cognitive psychologists are principally interested in the final internal representation. If the internal representation is to be useful, it must correspond to events in the real world. There is one world to be perceived, and all of the senses provide information to the observer about that world. Therefore, a confluence should emerge from the processing in the brain, regardless of whether the input is from the visual, auditory, or some other sensory modality. This chapter will point out some general principles of perception and cognition that, though similar for vision and audition, are directly relevant to the understanding of music and music perception.

Figure 3.1 demonstrates that internal representation can indeed be quite different from the physical stimulus on the retina. Two tables are depicted as if in different orientations in space, but stating that there are two tables already makes a cognitive interpretation. The figure actually consists only of a pattern of lines (or dots) on a two-dimensional surface. Still, humans tend to interpret the patterns of lines as three-dimensional objects, as two differently oriented tables with one larger than the other. If one were able to turn off the cognitive representation of "tables in space," one would see that the two parallelograms corresponding to the tabletops are of identical size and shape! Verify this with a ruler, or trace one parallelogram (tabletop) on a sheet of tracing paper and then slide it into congruence with the other. The fact that it is difficult to see the two tabletops abstractly as simple parallelograms, and thus to see them as the same size and shape, proves that the internal representation in the brain is quite different from the pattern present on the sensory surface (retina). We tend to represent the pattern of lines as objects in

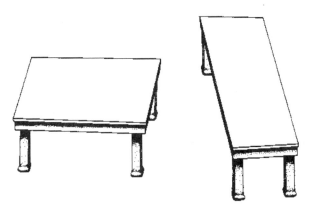

Figure 3.1 Things are sometimes different than they appear to be. Use a ruler to measure the tops of these two tables, specifically comparing the short ends and the long ends.

the external world because evolution has selected for such representation. The interpretation process in the brain has been shaped to be so automatic, swift, and efficient that it is virtually unconscious and outside of our control. As a result, we cannot suppress it even when we try.

3.2 Unconscious Inference

Hermann von Helmholtz (born 1821) made more contributions to the understanding of hearing and vision than perhaps any other individual. In addition to his fundamental contributions to physics and to physiology, in cognitive psychology he is known for his formulation of the principle of *unconscious inference*. Figure 3.2 illustrates the principle of unconscious inference. Our perceptual machinery automatically makes the inference to three-dimensional objects on the basis of perceptual cues that are present in the two-dimensional pattern on the retina. Cues—particularly linear perspective—support the inference to the three-dimensional interpretation, but the inference is quite unconscious.

Many retinal cues enable us to construct a three-dimensional representation from purely two-dimensional representation input. Following are a few examples of these cues:

Figure 3.2 Unconscious inference is at work in this picture. Even though both "monsters" are exactly the same size (measure them with a ruler), the perspective placement makes the chaser look bigger than the one being chased.

Linear perspective. Converging lines in a two-dimensional drawing convey parallel lines and depth in three dimensions. This is evident in the rows of stones in figure 3.2.

Gradient of size. The elements of a uniform texture decrease in size as they approach the horizon. This is evident in figure 3.2, where the stone patterns get smaller in the receding tunnel.

Aerial perspective. Objects in the far distance appear lighter and blue (for the same reason that the sky appears light and blue).

Binocular parallax. Each of our two eyes receives a slightly different image, and from these the brain is able to make quite precise inferences about the relative distances of objects. This is particularly true for objects close to the observer.

Motion parallax. Movement on the part of the observer changes the images on each retina, and the differences between successive viewpoints is used to infer distances, just as in binocular parallax.

It is interesting to note that in general we have no notion of the cues that our brains are using. Experiments have shown that some of the cues can be missing (or intentionally removed); but as long as some subset of these cues is still available, the observer sees things in depth and can make accurate judgments about the relative distances and placements of objects. Even though the examples printed in this book are just two-dimensional drawings, the important thing to remember is that all images end up entering our retinas as two-dimensional images. We use unconscious inference to make sense of the real world just as we use it to interpret drawings, photographs, and movies.

The use of the term *inference* does not imply that the cognitive processes of interpretation are mere probabilistic guesses, although situations do occur in which the number of cues is reduced to the point where unconscious inference may become a random guesslike process. James Gibson, a perceptual psychologist at Cornell University, emphasized that under most circumstances (when there is good illumination, we are free to move about with both eyes open, and our spatial perception is completely accurate and certain), the information is sufficient to construct an accurate representation of the disposition of objects in space. Gibson referred to this as *direct perception,* as contrasted to *unconscious inference.* The two can be reconciled by the fact that complex computation must go on to process the information coming into the sensory systems, and most of that computation goes on unconsciously. The information is integrated in order to give very precise information about what is going on in the world, not random guesses based on fragmentary information.

3.3 Size and Loudness Constancy

Objects in the world are, in general, of constant size; but the image of an object on the retina expands and contracts as the object moves closer and farther away. What has been important for us and for our ancestors has been the ability to perceive objects as they are, independent of their distance from us. This is known as *size constancy*. Figure 3.3 demonstrates this principle.

In the auditory domain, *loudness constancy* is a direct analog of size constancy. If an instrument emitting a sound of constant output is moved farther away, the intensity that reaches a listener decreases. This is because the wave fronts emanating from the instrument are spherical in shape, and the surface area of a sphere increases with the square of the radius. The energy from the instrument is uniformly distributed over this spherical surface, and hence the intensity reaching the listener decreases with the square of the distance from the instrument to the listener. Not surprisingly then, if the amplitude of a sound is decreased, the sound may seem to come from farther away. But we could alternatively experience the source as decreasing in intensity without moving farther away. Similarly, a visually perceived balloon from which air is escaping may

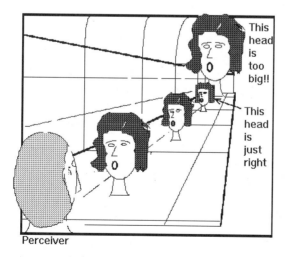

Figure 3.3   Size constancy. The head closest to the perceiver is the same physical size on the page as the "too-big" head farthest from the perceiver.

appear to be receding into the distance or simply shrinking in size. Other cues besides size or loudness may determine whether the change in the external world is in the size or the intensity of the source, or in its distance from the observer.

The intensity of a musical source can be decreased by playing the instrument more softly. There are accompanying changes in timbre, however, that are different from a simple decrease in amplitude. The higher-frequency components of the sound tend to increase and decrease with the effort exerted by the musician, an amount that is not proportional to the lower components of the spectrum. Thus, spectral balance as well as overall amplitude provides cues to the intensity versus distance of a source.

In our normal surroundings, there are surfaces around us that reflect sound, causing echoes or reverberation. In general we have little direct awareness of the reflected sound reaching us via these paths, but we use the information in these reflected waves to make unconscious inferences about the surroundings and sound sources within those surroundings. The reflections tell us, for example, that we are in a room of a certain size and composition, and give us a sense of the space. We receive a signal from a sound source within the room, then some time later we receive signals via the reflected paths. If a sound source is close, the direct sound is relatively intense, and the reflected sounds occur at decreased intensity and later in time. If the sound source moves away, the direct sound decreases, but the reflected sound remains roughly constant in intensity. The time difference between the arrival of the direct and the reflected sounds also decreases as the source recedes. By unconscious inference, the intensity ratio of direct to reflected sound, and the time delay between the direct and reflected sound, are used, along with other cues, to determine the distance and intensity of a source.

3.4 Spatial and Temporal Inversion

Some of the correlations in the world are so common that we have developed special machinery for their interpretation. If a familiar pattern is transformed in some way, even though all of the information is retained intact, then that pattern will not be interpreted in the same way by a human observer because our machinery is "wired" to interpret the information only in its usually encountered form. Consider the simple transformation of rotation. Figure 3.4 shows a number of presentations of the same face. Because we are attuned to perceiving faces in their usual upright orientation, the upper and lower rows of shapes shown in the figure are perceived as being of two different faces rather than as one face in two orientations. We tend to make the interpretation that is consistent with a standard face, in which the eyes are on the top and the mouth is on the bottom. Developmental studies have shown that up to a certain age, children are equally skilled at interpreting faces either right-side up or upside down, but with increasing age the skill at interpreting faces right-side up continues to increase after the ability to interpret inverted faces levels off. Eventually the right-side up exposure becomes so great that the perception dominates. We develop an impressive ability to recognize and to interpret the expressions of right-side up faces—an ability not yet matched by machine—but this ability does not generalize to upside-down faces, with which we have had much less practice.

An analog of this spatial inversion in the visual domain is a temporal reversal in the auditory domain. In normal surroundings, we receive direct and reflected sound. We generally do not hear the reflected echoes and reverberation as such, but make the unconscious inference that we are hearing the source in a certain type of space, where the impression of that space is determined by the character of the reflected signals.

It is curious that the addition of walls and boundaries, essentially limiting space, gives the sense of spaciousness in audition. In a purely anechoic room (a specially constructed space that minimizes

Figure 3.4 Turn this page over and you still will see faces right-side up. After infancy, we become more tuned to seeing faces right-side up, and thus must try hard to see the "frowning" faces as being upside down.

reflections from the walls, floor, and ceiling) we get no reverberation, and thus no sense of space. In vision, too, if an observer were in space with no objects around, there would be no sense of the space. Gibson pointed out that we do not perceive space but, rather, objects in space. In audition, we need surfaces to give us the sense of the space they define.

The ears can hear the direction of the source by comparing the differences between the arrival times and intensities at the two ears. The ears can similarly process differences in times and amplitudes of reflected sounds, and infer the source locations implied by those reflected sounds. In this way, we auditorally identify a sound source and a number of *virtual sources,* or copies of the sound source in virtual locations that lie *outside* the space actually enclosed by the walls. Figure 3.5 shows a sound source, an ear, and a few reflected sound paths. Only the first reflections (those that reflect from only one wall in going from the source to the listener) are shown, but there are many important second, third, and so on reflections. Figure 3.6 shows the same sound paths as direct paths from virtual sources. It is clear why reverberation gives the sense of space, with virtual sources distributed over a large space outside the room. The same sense of space can be experienced visually in a room (such as a barbershop or restaurant) with large mirrors on opposite walls.

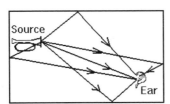

Figure 3.5   Many reflected acoustic paths in a room.

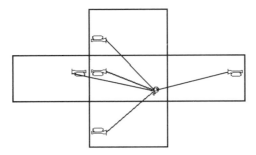

Figure 3.6   The same paths, shown as direct paths from "virtual sources."

There is a fundamental time asymmetry in the reception of direct and reflected sounds. All reflected sounds reach the listener *after* the direct signal. This is a manifestation of the second law of thermodynamics: in the absence of external energy input, order tends to go over into disorder. The direct sound may be orderly, but the randomly timed reflected copies of that sound appear to become random, with a momentary impulse decaying into white noise over time. Our auditory processing machinery evolved to process echoes and reverberation that follow a direct signal; it is ill-equipped to deal with an artificially produced case in which the echoes precede the signal.

Similarly, a resonant object, when struck, typically produces a sound that decays exponentially with time. Because of its unfamiliarity, a note or chord struck on a piano (with the damper lifted) sounds quite odd when played backward on a tape recorder. The sound suggests an organ more than a piano, slowly building up to an abrupt termination that gives no percussive impression. Moreover, if the individual notes of the chord are struck in rapid succession rather than simultaneously, their order is much more difficult to determine in the temporally reversed case than in the normal, forward presentation.

A sound of two hands clapping in a room is quite natural. In a normal-size room, the listener will hardly notice the reverberation; but in larger rooms it becomes noticeable, and the listener may think of the sounds only as indicating a large room, not a long reverberation. Completely unnatural sounds be can be created by mechanical manipulations using tape or a digital computer. A sound can be reversed, then reverberation added, then the resultant sound can be reversed. This generates a sound where the reverberation precedes the sound, but the sound itself still progresses forward. Speech processed in this fashion becomes extremely difficult to understand. This is because we are used to processing speech sounds in reverberant environments but are completely unfamiliar with an environment that would cause reverberation to come before a sound.

3.5 Perceptual Completion

Another fundamental principle of perception is called *perceptual completion*. Sometimes we have incomplete information coming into our sensory systems. To infer what is going on, we have to do some amount of top-down processing in addition to the normal bottom-up processing. We must complete the information to determine the most probable explanation for what is occurring in the real world that is consistent with the information presented to our senses. All of us can think of familiar examples of this from our own experience with camouflage, both in nature; with animals, insects, and birds, and in the artificial camouflage worn by humans. There are also many examples from the art world of the intentional use and manipulation of ambiguity and camouflage. Most famous perhaps are paintings by Bev Doolittle, such as her "Pintos on a Snowy Background," which depicts pinto horses against a snowy and rocky mountainside. Because of the patterning of the brown and white horse hair on the pintos, it is not easily distinguished from the background of brown rocks and white snow.

It is difficult to program a computer to correctly process ambiguous visual stimuli, because computers do not have the kind of real-world knowledge that humans have gained through evolution and learning. This knowledge allows us to make reasonable inferences about what is going on in the world, using only partial information. Figure 3.7 shows two (or more) objects, with one of the objects apparently covering part of the other object. The most probable explanation for the alignment of the objects is that the bar is one object that extends continuously under the disk. It is also possible that there are two shorter bars whose colors, alignments, and such just happen to coincide as shown in figure 3.8. But the simpler explanation is that it is a single bar. Research with young infants has shown that they, too, are sensitive to this type of environmental context, and if the disk of figure 3.8 is removed to reveal two bars, the infant registers surprise (as measured by breathing and heart rate increases). We will discuss more on early infant studies later in this chapter.

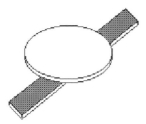

Figure 3.7   Continuation. We would normally assume one bar beneath the disk.

The Italian psychologist Gaetano Kanizsa has come up with a number of interesting examples of perceptual completion or *subjective contours*. Figure 3.9 demonstrates this phenomenon: it is difficult not to see a white triangle located at the center of the figure, although no such triangle actually exists. In the external world, the most probable cause for the improbable alignment of the objects is that a white triangle is lying on top of these objects, covering some and partially masking others.

This phenomenon can also be demonstrated in the auditory domain. Al Bregman has demonstrated this with sinusoidal tones that sweep up and down in frequency. These tones are interrupted with blank spaces, which cause quite obvious perceptual breaks. When the gaps are masked with bursts of white noise—just as the gaps in the inferred solid bar of figure 3.8 are masked by the disk—the listener makes the inference that the sinusoidal sweeps are continuous. The resulting perception is that a smoothly sweeping sinusoidal sound is occasionally covered up by noise bursts, not that the parts of the sinusoidal sound are actually replaced by bursts of noise, which is what is happening in the signal. The same thing can be done with music: the gaps sound like they are caused by a loose

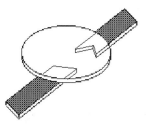

Figure 3.8 Another possible explanation of figure 3.7.

Figure 3.9 More continuation, and some symmetry.

connection in a circuit somewhere; but when the noise bursts fill in the gaps, the illusion is that the music continues throughout.

3.6 The Gestalt Grouping Principles

According to Max Wertheimer, one of the three principal founders of Gestalt psychology, Gestalt principles of grouping are used by the brain when parsing sensory input into objects in the world, especially when information is incomplete or missing altogether. Following are the Gestalt principles of grouping, which are all based on Helmholtz's concept of unconscious inference.

Proximity. Things that are located close together are likely to be grouped as being part of the same object. Figure 3.10a shows the principle of grouping by proximity.

Similarity. When objects are equally spaced, the ones that appear similar tend to be grouped as being related. If objects are similar in shape they are most probably related. (See figure 3.10b.)

Symmetry. Because random unrelated objects in the world are not expected to exhibit symmetry, it would be most improbable for unrelated objects to exhibit symmetric relationships. Figure 3.10c shows principles of both symmetry and similarity.

Good continuation. If objects are collinear, or arranged in such a way that it appears likely that they continue each other, they tend to be grouped perceptually. Figure 3.10d shows the principle of good continuation.

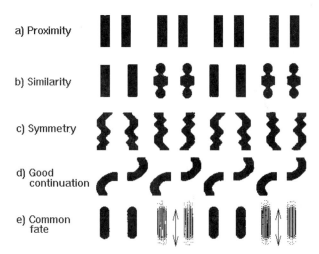

Figure 3.10 Gestalt grouping principles.

The principles of proximity, similarity, symmetry, and good continuation are considered *weak* principles of grouping, and are often used when the information is incomplete or noisy, or the perceiver has little to go on except the sensory input.

The principle of *common fate* (figure 3.10e) is much stronger. Common fate dictates that objects that move together are likely to be connected. In the world, it is extremely improbable that two things move in a perfectly correlated way unless they are in some way connected. For example, figure 3.11 shows a field of dots, and figure 3.12 shows another field of dots. If figure 3.12 is superimposed over figure 3.11 and moved back and forth, the face shape emerges from the random field of dots, made apparent by the fact that the dots that compose the face move together, and the others do not move.

Demonstrations of auditory common fate typically involve common onset time, common amplitude modulation, and common frequency modulation. One such example involves the grouping of partials and harmonics of a source: we are able to isolate the voice of a speaker or the musical line of a solo instrument in a complex auditory field. The task of isolating a sound source is essentially one of grouping the harmonics or partials that make up the sound; this is done by grouping those partials by the principle of common fate. The partials tend to move in ensemble, in both frequency and amplitude, and are thus recognized as being part of one object. Individual voices, even though they may be singing the same note, exhibit microfine deviations in pitch and amplitude that allow us to group the voices individually. This will be discussed in more detail in chapters 16 and 20.

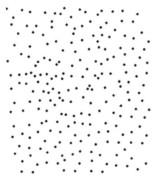

Figure 3.11 Common fate: some "random" dots. Photocopy figure 3.12 onto a transparency sheet, then lay it over figure 3.11. Slide the transparency slightly back and forth, and you will see a woman appear from the field of dots.

Figure 3.12   Some "random" dots. See figure 3.11.

Chowning's examples in chapter 20 will demonstrate grouping sound sources by common fate. One such demonstration involves a complex bell-like sound consisting of many inharmonic partials. The partials were computer-generated in such a way that they can be grouped into three sets of harmonic partials, each making up a female sung vowel spectrum. When the three voice sets are given a small amount of periodic and random pitch deviation (vibrato), the bell sound is transformed into the sound of three women singing. When the vibrato is removed, the three female voices merge again to form the original bell sound. This is another example of how common fate influences perception of sound.

As will be discussed in Chapter 16, there are styles of singing in which the vibrato is suppressed as much as possible. Such singing has quite a different effect than typical Western European singing; when the singers are successful in suppressing the vibrato to a sufficient extent, the chorus sound is replaced by a more instrumental timbre. The percept is not one of a group of singers but of a large, complex instrument.

The grouping principles discussed here are actually "wired into" our perceptual machinery. They do not have to be learned by trial and possibly fatal error, because they generally hold in the real world. For example, Elizabeth Spelky did work with early infant development and found that the principle of common fate is used by very young infants. She presented infants with displays of three-dimensional objects and moved some of them together. The infants registered surprise (measured physiologically) when they were shown that the objects that were moving together were not actually parts of the same object, but were artificially caused to move in synchrony. The infants were thus making an unconscious inference based on common fate and good continuation.

We have seen how the Gestalt grouping principle of common fate applies in both vision and audition. In later chapters we will explore how some other Gestalt principles—those of similarity and proximity, for example—might apply to auditory stimuli, and in particular to musical events.

References

Bregman, A. S. (1990). *Auditory Scene Analysis: The Perceptual Organization of Sound.* Cambridge, Mass.: MIT Press. An excellent overview of many grouping principles in audio.

Flavell, J. H., and E. M. Markman, eds. (1983). *Cognitive Development.* New York: Wiley. A good book on general cognitive development, including early infant development.

4 *Sound Waves and Sine Waves*

John Pierce

4.1 Sound and Sine Waves

We are immersed in an ocean of air. Physical disturbances—snapping the fingers, speaking, singing, plucking a string, or blowing a horn—set up a vibration in the air around the source of sound. A sound wave travels outward from the source as a spherical wavefront. It is a *longitudinal* wave in which the pulsating motion of the air is in the direction the wave travels. In contrast, waves in a stretched string are *transverse* waves, for the motion of the string is at right angles to the direction in which the wave travels.

How fast does a sound wave travel? If the air temperature is 20 degrees Celsius, a sound wave travels at a velocity of 344 meters (1128 feet) a second—a little faster at higher temperatures and a little slower at lower temperatures. Sound travels in helium almost three times as fast as in air, and longitudinal sound waves can travel through metals and other solids far faster.

The sound waves that travel through the air cause components of our ears to vibrate in a manner similar to those of the sound source. What we hear grows weaker with distance from the source, because the area of the spherical wavefront increases as the square of the distance from the source, and the power of the source wave is spread over that increasing surface. What actually reaches our ears is complicated by reflections from the ground and other objects. In a room, much of the sound we hear comes to our ears after being reflected from floor, walls, and ceiling.

The vibrations of musical sound are complicated, and the charm of musical sounds lies in their complexity. But most old-time discussions of musical sounds and most old-time experiments with sound waves and with hearing were carried out with a rare and simple sort of sound wave, a sinusoidal wave. How can such discussions and experiments have any relevance to the complicated sounds of music? Chiefly, because the phenomenon of sound propagation in air at intensities encountered in musical performance is a *linear* phenomenon. The undisturbed vibrations of strings or of columns of air are at least approximately linear. Even the vibrations along the cochlea of the ear are close enough to linear for linear systems ideas to be an appropriate guide to thought. What are the characteristics of linear systems? How can sine waves be useful in connection with the complicated sounds of music?

4.2 Linear Systems

Sine waves are important both mathematically and practically in describing the behavior of *linear systems.*

What is a linear system? The amplifier depicted in figure 4.1 illustrates a linear system. Suppose that an input signal or waveform In1 produces an output waveform Out1, and that an input waveform In2 produces an output waveform Out2. If the amplifier is linear, the combined input waveform In1+In2 will produce an output waveform Out1+Out2. The output of a linear amplifier (or of any linear system or phenomenon) for a sum of inputs is the sum of the outputs produced by the inputs separately.

It may be easier to understand if we say that an amplifier is linear if it doesn't produce any distortion. In some real amplifiers there is distortion. We hear things in the output that were not present in the input. Mathematically, a linear system is a system whose behavior is described by a linear differential equation or by a linear partial differential equation. In such an equation the sum of constants times partial derivatives with respect to time and space is equal to 0, or to an input driving function. Some linear, or approximately linear, systems are the following:

A sound wave in air   (linear for musical intensities)
A vibrating string   (linear for small amplitudes)
A vibrating chime or bell   (ordinarily linear)
The bones of the middle ear   (linear for small changes in level)
Vibrations along the basilar membrane of the cochlea   (with some assumptions).

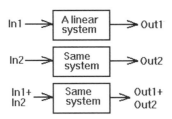

Figure 4.1   A system is linear if the output due to two overlapping inputs is the sum of the outputs to each input separately.

Tam-tams, cymbals, and some other percussion instruments exhibit a clearly nonlinear phenomenon: an upwelling of high frequencies after striking. Smaller nonlinearities in nearly all musical instruments are responsible for subtle but characteristic musical qualities of the sounds produced. But the most obvious features of the sounds of conventional instruments are consistent with an assumption of linearity.

To the degree to which an instrument such as a piano, guitar, bell, or gong is linear, the vibrations it produces can be represented as a sum of slowly decaying sine waves that have different frequencies. Each frequency is associated with a particular spatial distribution of vibrations and has a particular rate of decay. The sound of the wave generated by such a sum of vibrations at different frequencies constitutes a musical tone.

The frequencies of free vibrations of a violin string or the air in a horn predispose the forced (by bowing or blowing) vibrations to have frequencies quite close to those of a free vibration. Skillful bowing of a violin string can give *harmonics,* which are integer multiples of some fundamental frequency. A bugle can be blown so as to produce a rather small number of musical tones, each near a frequency of the free vibration of the air in the tube, again a series of harmonics.

4.3 Sine Waves

Because sine waves, and measurements based on sine waves, are pervasive in musical lore, it is important at this point to become well acquainted with a sine wave. Figure 4.2 shows a swinging pendulum that traces out a portion of a sine wave on a moving strip of paper. A true sine wave lasts forever, with its past, present, and future an endless repetition of identical periods or cycles of oscillation. A sine wave can be characterized or described completely by three numbers: the maximum amplitude (in centimeters, volts, sound pressure, or some other unit of measurement), the frequency in Hertz (Hz, cycles per second), and the phase, which specifies the position when the sine wave reaches its peak amplitude. This is illustrated in figure 4.3.

With respect to phase, we should note that the mathematical cosine function is at its peak when the phase is 0 degrees, 360 degrees, 720 degrees, and so on. The mathematical sine function reaches its peak at 90 degrees, 450 degrees, and so on.

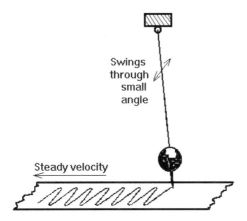

Figure 4.2   A swinging pendulum traces out a sine wave.

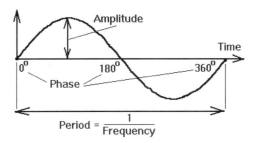

Figure 4.3   Sine waves are described completely by their frequency (or period), amplitude, and phase.

The relative amplitudes of sine waves are often expressed in terms of *decibels (dB)*. If wave 1 has a peak amplitude of vibration of *A1* and a reference wave or vibration has a peak amplitude of vibration of *A2,* the relationship in decibels of vibration *A1* to vibration *A2* is given by

$20 \, log_{10} \, (A1/A2).$ (4.1)

A sound level in decibels should always be given as decibels above some reference level. Reference level is often taken as a sound power of a millionth of a millionth of a watt per square meter. A person with acute hearing can hear a 3000 Hz sine wave at reference level. Reference level is sometimes also taken as a sound pressure of 0.00005 newtons, which is almost exactly the same reference level as that based on watts per square meter.

In many experiments with sound we listen to sounds of different frequencies. It seems sensible to listen to sinusoidal sound waves in an orderly fashion. We will use the diagram shown in figure 4.4 to

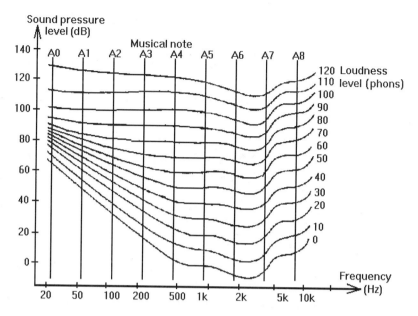

Figure 4.4 The equal loudness curves link combinations of sound pressure level and frequency that are heard as equally loud.

guide our listening. Here frequency in Hertz is plotted horizontally. Nine vertical lines are shown, spaced one octave apart at frequencies from 27.5 Hz (A0), the pitch frequency of the lowest key on the piano keyboard, to 7040 Hz (A8), above the topmost piano key.

The curves shown are equal loudness curves. Along a particular loudness curve the various combinations of frequency and level give sounds that are judged to have the same loudness. The constant loudness curves crowd together at low frequencies. At low frequencies, a small change in amplitude results in a large change in loudness. There is some crowding together at about 4000 Hz.

We can listen to tones at a chosen frequency given by one of the vertical lines at six different amplitudes, each successively 10 dB below the preceding amplitude. This tells us how a sinusoidal sound of a given frequency sounds at six sound levels 10 dB apart. Of course, the sine wave sounds fainter with each 10 dB decrease in amplitude. What we hear depends on the initial sound level, and that depends on the audio equipment and its loudness setting. But, roughly, this is what we hear:

At 27.5 Hz, a weak sound that disappears after a few 10 dB falls in level. The constant loudness curves are crowded together at this low frequency, and a few 10 dB decreases in amplitude render the sound inaudible

At 110 Hz, a stronger sound that we hear at all successively lower sound levels

At 440 Hz, the pitch to which an orchestra tunes, a still stronger sound

At 1760 Hz, a still stronger sound

At 7040 Hz, a somewhat weaker sound. With increasing age people tend to hear high-frequency sounds as very weak, or not to hear them at all.

4.4 Sine Waves and Musical Sounds

One importance of sine waves is that for linear oscillating systems, the overall vibration of a musical instrument can be regarded as the sum of sinusoids of different frequencies. This is illustrated in figure 4.5, which shows several patterns of oscillation of a vibrating string.

In the vibration at the top, the deviation of the string from straightness varies sinusoidally with distance along the string. The center of the string vibrates up and down, with a sinusoidal displacement as a function of time, and the oscillation falls smoothly to 0 at the ends. At any instant the variation of displacement with distance along the string is sinusoidal. We can think of the oscillation of the string as corresponding to a traveling sine wave of twice the length of the string, reflected at the fixed ends of the string. We

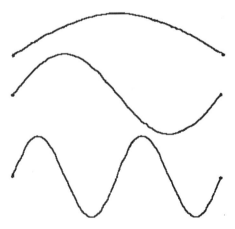

Figure 4.5 Some modes of vibrations of a stretched string. Different modes have different numbers of loops: from top to bottom, here, one, two, three. The frequencies of vibration are proportional to the number of loops.

can describe this pattern of oscillation as having one loop along the string. Below we see patterns of vibration with two and three loops along the string.

In agreement with the original observations of Pythagoras as interpreted in terms of frequency of vibration, the frequencies of the various patterns of vibration are proportional to the number of loops along the string. Thus, if f_0 is the frequency for vibration at the top of figure 4.5, the frequencies of vibration shown lower are $2f_0$ (two loops) and $3f_0$ (three loops). Other "modes" would have frequencies of $4f_0$ (four loops), $5f_0$, and so on.

Ordinarily, when we excite the string by plucking or striking, we excite patterns of vibration at many different frequencies that are integers (whole numbers) times the lowest frequency. In one period of duration, $1/f_0$, the various other *harmonic* frequencies of oscillation, corresponding to two, three, four, five, and so on loops, will complete two, three, four, five, and so on oscillations. After the period $1/f_0$, the overall oscillation will repeat again, "endlessly" in an ideal case of no decay in amplitude.

We have considered various aspects of sine waves that we hear. Wavelength is an aspect of sinusoidal sound that is associated with a sound wave traveling through air. The wavelength of a sinusoidal sound is sound velocity divided by frequency. As noted in section 4.1, the velocity of sound in air is 344 meters/second (1128 feet/second). In table 4.1, wavelength is tabulated for various frequencies (and musical pitches). We see that in going from the lowest key on the piano, A0 (frequency 27.5 Hz) to A7 (the highest A on the keyboard (frequency 3520 Hz), the wavelength goes from 41 feet (12.5 meters) to 0.32 foot (0.1 meter). Actual musical tones include harmonics whose wavelengths are much shorter than that of the fundamental or pitch frequency.

For some musical instruments (including some organ pipes and the clarinet), the sounds produced contain chiefly odd harmonics of a fundamental frequency. This happens whenever one end of a tube is closed and the other end is open. If f_0 is the fundamental frequency of a closed organ pipe, the chief frequencies present are f_0, $3f_0$, $5f_0$, $7f_0$, and so on.

We can represent the sustained sound of a musical instrument by a sum of sine waves with many harmonic frequencies. But we hear the sound as a single musical tone with a pitch that is given by the *pitch frequency*, the frequency of which the frequencies of all the partials are integer multiples. The pitch of a musical sound de-

Table 4.1 Musical notes, frequencies, and wavelengths

NOTE NAME	FREQUENCY (HZ)	WAVELENGTH (FT.)
A0	27.5	41
A1	55	20.5
A2	110	10.25
A3	220	5.1
A4	440	2.56
A5	880	1.28
A6	1760	0.64
A7	3520	0.32

pends on the simple harmonic relation among the many frequencies present. The musical quality of the overall sound depends in part on the relative intensities of the various harmonics, and in part on how they are excited initially (the *attack* quality of the sound). (We will discuss the topics of pitch and quality further in later chapters.)

4.5 Fourier Analysis

Most musical instruments produce sounds that are nearly periodic. That is, one overall cycle of the waveform repeats, or nearly repeats, over and over again. Looking at this in another way, traditional musical tones, of the voice or of an instrument, are periodic, or nearly periodic. Hence, it is pertinent to consider the general qualities of periodic sounds. Any periodic waveform can be approximated by a number of sinusoidal components that are *harmonics* of a *fundamental frequency.* That fundamental frequency may or may not be present in the sound. It is the reciprocal of the period of the waveform measured in seconds.

This is illustrated in figure 4.6 by three approximations of a sawtooth waveform. In approximating a sawtooth waveform we add harmonic-related sine waves whose frequencies are f_0, $2f_0$, $3f_0$ and so on, and whose amplitudes are inversely proportional to the frequencies. Three sine waves give a very poor approximation to a sawtooth. A better approximation is given by 6 sinusoidal components, and a still better approximation by 12.

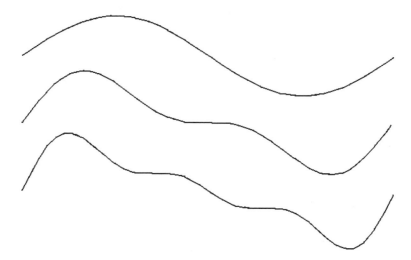

Figure 4.6 Representation of a sawtooth wave as the sum of one, two, and three sinusoids.

A true sawtooth waveform is a succession of vertical and slanting straight-line segments. A Fourier series approximation to a true sawtooth waveform that uses a finite number of harmonically related sine waves differs from the sawtooth waveform in two ways. In a gross way, the approximation gets better and better as we include more and more terms. But there is a persistent wiggle whose amplitude decreases but whose frequency increases as we add more and more terms. We will see later that the ear can sometimes hear such a wiggle, as well as a pitch associated with a true sawtooth waveform. Remember, from the equal loudness contours, that we can hear only up to a given frequency, so if we add enough harmonic sinusoids to our approximation of any wave, we can get perceptually as close as we like.

A fitting of the sum of harmonically related sine waves to a periodic waveform is called *Fourier analysis.*

Mathematically, the Fourier series transform is defined by the equations

$$v(t) = \sum_{n=-\infty}^{\infty} C_n e^{j2\pi nt/T} \tag{4.2}$$

$$C_n = \frac{1}{T} \int_{-T/2}^{T/2} v(t) e^{j2\pi nt/T} dt. \tag{4.3}$$

These describe the representation of a periodic time waveform v(t) in terms of complex coefficients C_n that represent the phases and amplitudes of the harmonic sinusoidal components (4.2), and the expression for finding the coefficients C_n from the waveform signal $v(t)$ (4.3). The coefficients C_n are found by integrating over the period (T) of the waveform.

What about waveforms that aren't periodic? The equations

$$v(t) = \int_{-\infty}^{\infty} V(f)e^{j2\pi nt/T} df \qquad (4.4)$$

$$V(f) = \int_{-\infty}^{\infty} v(t)e^{j2\pi nt/T} dt \qquad (4.5)$$

give expressions for an arbitrary, nonperiodic waveform in terms of a complex sound spectrum $V(f)$ that has frequencies ranging from minus infinity to plus infinity, and an integral that, for a given waveform $v(t)$, gives the complex spectral function $V(f)$. Such an overall resolution of a complete waveform into a spectrum is of limited use in connection with music. For example, we could in principle find the spectrum of a complete piece of music. This would tell us very little that we would care to know. Today, most Fourier analyses of waveforms are performed by computer programs, using a discrete definition of the Fourier transform.

It is important to note that a waveform, that is, a plot one cycle long of amplitude versus time, is a complete description of a periodic waveform. A spectrum gives a complete description of a waveform, consisting of two numbers for each single frequency. These two numbers can describe the real and imaginary parts of a complex number, or they can describe the amplitude and phase of a particular frequency component. Conversion back and forth from complex number representation to amplitude and phase representation is accomplished simply.

In plots of spectra of sound waves, the phase of the spectral components is seldom displayed. What is plotted against frequency is usually how the amplitude varies with frequency. The amplitude is often given in decibels. Or the square of the amplitude is plotted versus frequency. This is called a power spectrum.

Is the phase of a Fourier component important? Figure 4.7 shows 4 periods of waveforms made up of 16 sinusoidal components with harmonic frequencies (f_0, $2f_0$, $3f_0$, etc.) having equal amplitudes but different phases. The waveforms look very different. The topmost waveform is a sequence of narrow spikes with wiggles in between. In the center waveform the phases have been chosen so as to make each repeated cycle of the waveform look like a sinusoid of decreasing frequency, also called a chirp. In the waveform at the

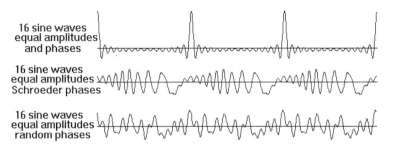

16 sine waves
equal amplitudes
and phases

16 sine waves
equal amplitudes
Schroeder phases

16 sine waves
equal amplitudes
random phases

Figure 4.7   The effect of phase on waveform. Sixteen harmonically related sine waves of equal amplitude make up the three waveforms, with the only difference being phase.

bottom, the relative phases were chosen at random, and the waveform looks like a repeating noise. Although the amplitude spectrum is the same for all three waveforms, the phase spectra are different and the waveforms look very different. These three different waveforms sound different at 27.5 Hz with headphones. At 220 Hz the sounds scarcely differ with headphones. At 880 Hz there is no difference in sound. In a reverberant room, differences are small even at 27.5 Hz.

Partly because we don't listen through headphones, and partly because most pitches are higher than 27.5 Hz, most plots of spectra take no account of phase.

It can be important to know how the frequency content of a musical sound changes with time. Many sustained musical sounds have small, nearly periodic changes of amplitude (tremolo) or of frequency (vibrato). And there are attack and decay portions of musical sounds. As an example of the importance of this, Jean-Claude Risset and Max Mathews found in 1969 that in the sounds of brassy instruments, the higher harmonics rise later than the lower harmonics. This is useful, indeed necessary, in synthesizing sounds with a brassy timbre. How can we present a changing spectrum in a way that is informative to the eye? One way of representing changing spectra is to plot successive spectra a little above and to the right of one another, so as to give a sense of perspective in time. Figure 4.8 shows successive spectra of a sine wave with a little vibrato that shifts the peak a little to the left, then back, repeating this pattern periodically.

There is another way of representing changing spectra, a representation by sonograms (also called spectrograms). This is particularly valuable in studying very complicated sounds such as speech. A sonogram of speech is shown in figure 4.9. The amplitude at a given

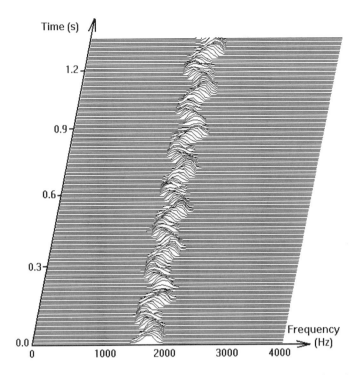

Figure 4.8 A "waterfall spectrum" representation of a sinusoidal sound with a slow sinusoidal variation of frequency with time.

frequency is represented by darkness (pure white represents zero amplitude). Distance from the bottom represents frequency. Time is plotted left to right. The two sonograms are of the same speech sound. In the upper sonogram, resolution is good in the frequency direction—we can see individual harmonic tracks—but it is blurred in the time direction. In the lower sonogram the resolution is good in the time direction—we can see individual pitch periods representing the vibrations of the vocal folds—but it is fuzzy in the frequency direction. Resolution can't be sharp in both directions. If we want precise pitch, we must observe the waveform for many periods. If we want precise time, we must observe the waveform for only part of a period. In general, the product of resolution in frequency and resolution in time is constant. This is a mathematical limitation that has nothing to do with the nature of the sound source.

Fourier analysis, the representation of a periodic waveform in terms of sine waves, is an essential tool in the study of musical sound. It allows us to determine the frequency components of a sound and to determine how those components change with time. Is the waveform or the spectrum better? If you are looking for a weak

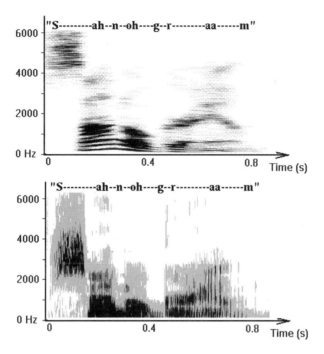

Figure 4.9 Spectrograms in which amplitude or intensity is represented by degree of darkness.

reflection following a short sound (as in radar), the waveform is better. But suppose you want to find the sound of a tin whistle in the midst of orchestral noise. You may have a chance with a spectral analysis that sharply separates sound energy in frequency. You won't have a chance by just looking at the waveform. So both waveforms and spectra are legitimate and useful ways of depicting sounds.

What we actually do in Fourier analysis of musical sounds is to use a computer program, called a fast Fourier transform (FFT). The analysis produces a spectrum that gives both amplitude and phase information, so that the waveform can be reconstructed from the spectrum obtained. Or the amplitude alone can be used in a spectral plot. Of an actual sound wave, we take the spectrum of a selected or *windowed* portion of a musical sound that may be several periods long.

Figure 4.10 illustrates the process of windowing. At the top are a few periods of a sine wave. In the center is a windowing function. This is multiplied by the overall waveform to give the windowed portion of the waveform, shown at the bottom. In analyzing the waveform, a succession of overlapping windows is used to find out

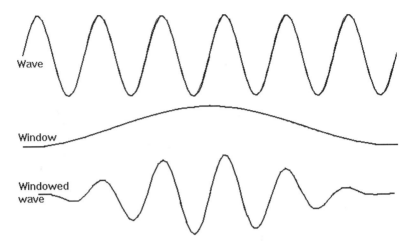

Figure 4.10 Windowed time function. Top, time function, center, time window function, bottom, windowed time function whose Fourier transform is to be taken.

how the spectrum varies with time. This is the way the data were prepared for constructing the waterfall and sonogram plots of figures 4.8 and 4.9.

A strict reconstruction of the waveform from the spectrum obtained from any one window would repeat over and over again, but such a reconstruction is never made. In constructing the variation of the spectrum with time, or in reconstructing the waveform from the spectra of successive windowed waveforms, each windowed waveform is limited to the time duration of the window. Such a reconstruction necessarily goes to 0 at the ends of a particular window, where the window and the windowed waveform go to 0. The analysis of a succession of overlapping windowed waveforms makes it possible to construct an overall spectrum that varies with time, and from this overall spectrum the waveform itself can be reconstructed.

Fourier analysis is a mathematical verity. It is useful in connection with musical tones because the ear sorts sounds into ranges of frequency, and tampering with the sound spectrum has clear effects on what we hear and identify. Consider the sound of a human voice. If we remove or filter out low frequencies, the sound becomes high and tinny, but its musical pitch does not change. If we filter out the high frequencies, the voice becomes dull. Nonperiodic fricative (noise) components of a sound are identified through the higher frequencies of their spectra. If we filter out the higher frequencies, we can't tell *f* (as in fee) from *s* (as in see).

4.6   The Sampling Theorem

Fourier analysis allows us to represent a periodic waveform in terms of sine waves whose frequencies are harmonics of some fundamental frequency, the lowest frequency present in the representation. More generally, any waveform, periodic or not, can be represented by its spectrum, a collection of sine waves. Mathematically, the spectrum and the waveform itself are alternative ways of describing the same signal. We can think of the same signal either as a time waveform or as a spectrum, a collection of sine waves.

All spectral representations of sound waveforms are *band limited.* That is, somewhere along the line all frequency components that lie outside of a prescribed range of frequencies have been eliminated, have been filtered out by a circuit that will pass only frequency components that lie in some delimited bandwidth. In musical applications this bandwidth extends from quite low frequencies to a frequency of tens of thousands of Hertz.

The *sampling theorem* tells us that a band-limited waveform of bandwidth B Hz can be represented exactly, and (in principle) can be reconstructed without error from its amplitudes at 2B equally spaced "sampling times" each second. For example, 20,000 sample amplitudes a second completely describe a waveform of bandwidth 10,000 Hz. In sampling and reconstruction of signals, any component of frequency B+f (f is some frequency) will give rise to sample amplitudes that will produce, in the output after filtering, a component of frequency B−f. This phenomenon of the presence of false frequency components in the output is called *aliasing.*

Figure 4.11 illustrates the process of sampling a continuous waveform. At the top we have a waveform that contains no frequencies greater than some bandwidth B. We sample this waveform 2B times a second and transmit or store successive samples as the amplitudes, represented in the drawing by the amplitudes of the short pulses in the lower part of the figure.

To reconstruct a sampled waveform, we turn each received sample amplitude into a short pulse with an amplitude proportional to the amplitude of the sample. We filter the sequence of pulses with a filter that passes no frequencies higher than B. The filter output is a faithful representation of the original signal that was sampled 2B times a second. For this process to work, the signal that is sampled must contain no frequencies greater than B. That means that a filter with an infinitely sharp cutoff must be used. Finally, the phase shifts of all filters must be strictly proportional to frequency.

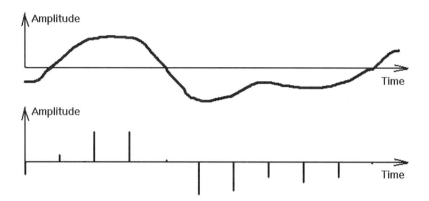

Figure 4.11 A waveform of bandwidth B (upper) can be sampled (lower), and recovered *exactly* from 2B samples (numbers representing the amplitude) per second. The waveform is recovered from the samples by filtering (smoothing).

Such unrealistic filters can't be made or used for many reasons. One involves the time–bandwidth constant described earlier in this chapter. Filters with infinitely steep cutoffs would require infinite time to implement. Since the bandwidth can't be made strictly equal to B, the aliasing components must be reduced somehow. The "cure" is to limit the bandwidth to somewhat less than half the sampling rate, so as to reduce the effect of aliasing rather than to eliminate it entirely. Thus, an actual sampling rate of 44,100 samples a second (the compact disc sampling rate) is used to attain a bandwidth of around 20,000 Hz rather than the ideal bandwidth of 22,050 Hz.

In actual systems employing sampling, the sample amplitudes are represented as digital numbers. The amplitudes are specified by groups of binary digits. As many as 21 such digits are in commercial use (Deutsche Gramaphon). In standard compact disc recording, the accuracy of representation of sample amplitudes is commonly 16 binary digits, which gives a signal-to-noise ratio of around 90 dB.

4.7 Filter Banks and Vocoders

In the compact disc system the whole bandwidth of an audio signal is encoded by means of one set of samples. However, filters can be used prior to sampling to break an audio signal of bandwidth B into N adjacent frequency channels, each of bandwidth B/N, as indicated in figure 4.12. These channels could in principle be separated sharply, but it is also permissible that adjacent frequency bands

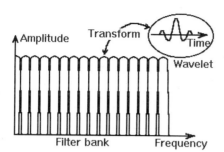

Figure 4.12 A filter bank divides the signal into overlapping frequency bands; the sum of these band-limited signals is the original signal.

overlap in any way such that the sum of the outputs of the overlapping filters gives the original signal.

It turns out that the overall number of samples per second needed to describe an ideal multichannel signal is simply 2B. 2B/N samples per second are allotted to encode each channel of bandwidth B/N. For reasons historical rather than logical, a system that encodes a waveform of bandwidth B into N channels of bandwidth B/N (and then recombines the channels to get the original signal) is called a *phase vocoder.*

We note in figure 4.12 that the filtered channels of successively increasing frequency constitute a spectrum of the signal that depicts the signal as a variation of amplitude and phase in bands with increasing center frequencies. Indeed, the channel signals of a phase vocoder are commonly derived through a process of digital spectral analysis using FFT. In this process, the overall signal waveform is cut into overlapping windowed (as in figure 4.10) segments. The spectrum of each windowed waveform is obtained. Under certain constraints depending on the shape of the window used, the successive spectra describe the original waveform, and the original waveform can be recovered from the successive spectra.

What is gained through the resolution of the overall waveform into a number of narrow-band waveforms that vary with time? In figure 4.13, the waveform in any "channel" (frequency range of the analyzed signal) will look very much like a sine wave whose frequency is the center frequency of that channel, and whose amplitude and phase change slowly with time. This makes it possible to operate on the channel signals in interesting ways.

Suppose, for example, we double the frequency of each channel signal. That is, wherever the original signal goes up and down, we

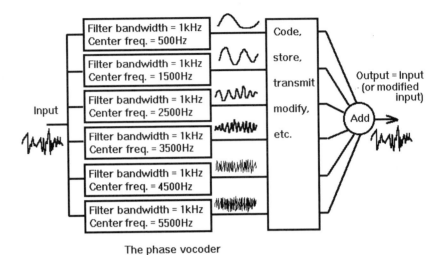

The phase vocoder

Figure 4.13 The phase vocoder splits a signal into bands of equal spacing and bandwidth.

construct a signal of approximately the same amplitude and phase that goes up and down twice. Roughly at least, we double all frequencies in the original signal and shift its pitch upward by an octave. What a fine way to create speech or song of very high pitch! Or, by halving the frequencies, to create speech or song of very low pitch.

Suppose that we delete every other sample in each narrow-band channel. For a fixed final sample rate this will double the speed of the reconstructed signal without appreciably changing its spectrum. Or, if we interpolate samples in the narrow channels, we can slow the rate of speaking or singing.

In the phase vocoder the signal is filtered into overlapping bands of equal bandwidth, as shown in figure 4.12. If the signal were divided into N overlapping bands, but the contour of each higher filter were the contour of the lowest filter stretched out by a constant (2, 3, 4), we would have a representation of the overall sound by *wavelets.*

4.8 Wavelets and the Sampling Theorem

So far, we have assumed that the successive filters are identical in bandwidth and are equally spaced in frequency, as shown in figure 4.13. In that figure the boxes represent amplitude versus frequency for successive filters. Each filter contributes the same fraction to the total bandwidth. If the input to the phase vocoder is a very short pulse, the output of each filter will have the same duration but a different frequency.

Now consider filters such that the bandwidth of the next higher filter is broader than the preceding filter by some constant greater than unity. A simple example of such filters is shown in figure 4.14. In this figure the triangles that represent the response versus frequency of the individual filters are broader with increasing frequency. Each triangle is twice as broad and twice as far to the right as its predecessor. The filters of figure 4.14 are a simple example of overlapping filters in which the contour of the next higher filter is just like that of the preceding filter but is broader by a constant factor greater than 1. Suppose such a bank of filters is excited by a very short pulse. The output of any one of the filters is called a *wavelet.* An input waveform can be represented by a sum of such wavelets, each having an amplitude appropriate to the signal to be represented. The time–frequency relationship is thus more appropriately dealt with in the wavelet filter bank, in that for each higher-frequency filter, the time impulse response is narrower. Thus, the optimum time–frequency trade-off can be approached in each subband.

Representation of musical waveforms by successions of wavelets is related to, but different from, the phase vocoder's spectral analysis, in which waveforms are represented by components that are equal in frequency spacing and in width (in Hz). Wavelets have shown much promise for compression of images, but less promise in audio. The use of wavelets for audio event recognition, however, shows much more potential.

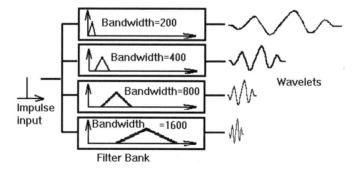

Figure 4.14   A wavelet filter bank. Filters have increasing bandwidth.

4.9 Closing Thoughts

Sine waves and Fourier analysis are powerful resources in all studies of musical sounds. Most musical sounds are produced by linear systems, or by approximately linear systems (freely vibrating strings or columns of air), or by forced vibrations of such systems that reflect their linear nature. Parts of our organs of perception are approximately linear. Higher-level processing, while not linear in itself, reflects the approximately linear processing that is carried out at lower levels.

Analyses based on sine waves are of crucial value in understanding the nature of musical sounds and of their perception. Sine waves, however, are not music. Nor are they even musical sounds by themselves. Rather, they are ingredients out of which musical sounds can be concocted, or through which musical sounds can be analyzed and studied. What we do with sine waves, how we use them, must be guided by the capabilities and limitations of human perception.

References

Bracewell, R. N. (1986). *The Fourier Transform and Its Applications.* Second edition. New York: McGraw-Hill. An advanced book on Fourier analysis.

Chui, C. K. (1992). *An Introduction to Wavelets.* Boston: Academic Press.

———, ed. (1992). *Wavelets: A Tutorial in Theory and Applications.* Boston: Academic Press. Gives more sense of actual application.

Risset, J. C., and M. V. Mathews. (1969). "Analysis of Musical Instrument Tones." *Physics Today,* 22(2): 23–40.

Schafer, R. W., and J. D. Markel, eds. (1979). *Speech Analysis.* New York: IEEE Press. Contains many early papers on speech and on the phase and channel vocoders.

Steiglitz, K. (1996). *A Digital Signal Processing Primer.* Menlo Park, CA: Addison Wesley. An excellent introductory reference to Fourier analysis, sinusoids, and linear systems.

5   Introduction to Pitch Perception

John Pierce

5.1   Pitch

Most musical instruments, except percussion instruments and some bells, have a clear pitch that is associated with the periodicity of the sound they produce. Nearly periodic sounds have nearly harmonic partials. A vibrating string or column of air produces nearly periodic sounds with nearly harmonic partials. One orchestral instrument can be tuned to the same pitch as another by ear, by judging when the two pitches are nearly the same. With greater precision, an instrument can be tuned to the same pitch as another by slowing the beats between the two simultaneous instrumental sounds.

But is pitch just periodicity, harmonicity, or the lack of beats? It is important to note that pitch is a perceptual measure, like loudness and some other terms we will use in this book. A machine that detects pitch would have to match human judgments of pitch. Just making a periodicity detector or a harmonicity detector would get us close, but it would not be enough because there are ambiguous cases where humans would assign a pitch and the machine would not. In this chapter we will look at various quantitative aspects of pitch.

5.2   Pitch and Brightness

In thinking about and experimenting with the pitch of musical tones, we must distinguish the sense of pitch from a sense of brightness or dullness. A sound is bright when its spectrum has many high-frequency partials. Musical tones ordinarily have no partials below their pitch frequency. Hence, tones of high pitch tend to be brighter than tones of low pitch.

Pitch depends on periodicity. Brightness or dullness depends on the distribution of total power between high and low frequencies. At the same pitch, the vowel /i/ (as in "beet") is brighter than the vowel /u/ (as in "boot"). At the same pitch the fraction of high-frequency power is greater in the spectrum of /i/ than in the spectrum of /u/. As another example, the sound of a trombone is brighter

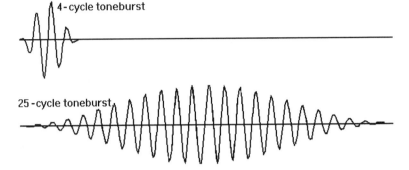

Figure 5.1 The upper tone burst would likely not produce a sensation of pitch, whereas the lower one would.

than the sound of a French horn, because the French horn is played facing away from the listener and the player places his hand in the bell.

A short click made up of low frequencies only sounds dull; a short click made up of high frequencies only sounds bright. Such a difference in brightness may or may not be associated with a difference in pitch. The waveforms in figure 5.1 are sine waves with a raised cosine envelope. The wave at the top is composed of four cycles of a sine wave. It sounds like a click, bright or dull depending on the frequency of the sine wave. It does not give any impression of a musical tone with a pitch. The waveform shown at the bottom has 25 cycles rather than 4. It gives a clear sensation of pitch, though there may also be a little sensation of click. If the number of cycles is made large enough, the "clicky" sensation disappears completely.

As the number of cycles in such a tone burst is increased from four, we begin to experience a sensation of pitch as well as a clicky sensation. Above some tens of cycles the clickiness fades away, and we have a sensation of pitch without click. The number of cycles necessary to give a pure pitch without a click increases somewhat with the frequency of the sine wave, but it lies in the range of tens of cycles. We will return to this sort of tone-burst waveform later.

Periodic waves are essential to the sensation of pitch. But we should keep in mind that a periodic sound wave can have a clear pitch only if it has a sufficient duration measured in cycles or periods.

5.3 Pitch and Partials

Musical tones have a number of harmonic partials whose frequencies are integer multiples of a fundamental frequency or pitch frequency, the frequency of a sine wave that matches the tone in pitch. The pitch frequency, the fundamental frequency (or, more commonly, fundamental), need not be present in the musical tone. In 1924, Harvey Fletcher of Bell Telephone Laboratories observed that for a sound with harmonic partials to be heard as a musical tone, its spectrum must include three successive harmonics of a common frequency. The pitch is given by that common frequency, whether or not it is present in the musical tone.

Orchestra chimes provide a striking example of a musical tone whose pitch frequency is entirely absent from the spectrum. The fourth, fifth, and sixth partials of the flexural mode have frequencies that are approximately the second, third, and fourth harmonics of a tone that just isn't there but is heard as the pitch frequency of the chime.

In the nineteenth century Helmholtz and his followers believed, erroneously, that the musical pitch of a sound is dependent on the actual presence in the sound wave of a sinusoidal component or partial of the pitch frequency. This misled Fletcher in the first of two papers he published in 1924 in *The Physical Review*. These papers recount experiments in listening to a number of instrumental sounds from which the fundamental or pitch frequency had been filtered out by a high-pass filter. Fletcher found that filtering out the fundamental, or even the fundamental and several successive low harmonics, did not change the pitch of the sound. Indeed, the identities of some sounds weren't much changed by the omission of lower harmonics. Instruments could still be easily recognized.

This is in accord with everyday experience. We hear the "right" pitches when we listen to a little radio that has a tiny speaker, which for low pitches puts out negligible power at the pitch frequency even when the pitch frequency is present in the original waveform. The telephone system rests on a frequency response that is not sufficient to carry the fundamental frequency of the lowest male voices, but we still hear voices as basically normal over the telephone. The most plausible and the true conclusion is that eliminating energy at the pitch frequency, and even at several low harmonics of the pitch frequency, doesn't necessarily alter our sensation of pitch.

In his first paper Fletcher proposed that the missing fundamental was re-created by nonlinearities in the mechanism of the ear. He soon abandoned this false conclusion. In the second paper he described experiments in synthesizing musical tones. It was these experiments that led to the assertion stated above, that a tone must include three successive harmonic partials in order to be heard as a musical tone, a tone that has the pitch of the fundamental, whether or not the fundamental is present.

In 1972, Terhardt published a theory of pitch perception, and later worked with others to define a computer algorithm that was capable of matching human pitch judgments on a number of sounds, including speech, bells, and spectra containing only octave partials. He defined a *virtual pitch* characterized by the presence of harmonics or near-harmonics, and a *spectral pitch* corresponding to individual audible pure-tone components. He stated that most pitches heard in normal sounds are virtual pitches, and this is true whether the fundamental is present in the spectrum or not. His algorithm calls for spectrum analysis using the Fourier transform, followed by the identification of important audible sinusoidal components, weighting the components, and allowing for masking effects (some components may cover up others nearby). The weighted sinusoids are then used to form many candidate virtual pitches that are the common divisors, or subharmonics, of the important component frequencies. These subharmonics are then combined and inspected to determine the most likely perceived pitch, and a measure of the saliency (how pitched it will sound, and how likely it is to be selected as the pitch) of that pitch is determined.

The mechanism of human pitch perception is different at low pitches and at high pitches. Fletcher's observations on pitch do not apply at very low frequencies, nor at frequencies well above 1000 Hz. Terhardt defines the crossover from virtual to spectral pitch to be at about 800 Hz, but his method depends on the selection of clear sinusoidal components in the spectrum. At very low frequencies we may hear successive features of a waveform, so that it is not heard as having just one pitch. For frequencies well above 1000 Hz the pitch frequency is heard only when the fundamental is actually present. Fletcher proposed that at high frequencies the pitch is given by the position of excitation along the cochlea, and at low frequencies by a time mechanism.

We should note that we do not sense any discontinuity or abrupt difference in sensation as we play notes from the lowest to the highest musical pitches. For periodic musical sounds, the two mechanisms overlap in frequency range. To investigate them we must tease them out with ingenious experiments.

One interesting experiment is to add successive equal-amplitude harmonics (integer multiples of a fundamental frequency), one by one, to a sinusoidal tone of some fundamental pitch frequency. It is

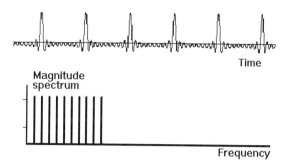

Figure 5.2 If we add successive harmonics to the fundamental frequency of a low-pitched sound, the sense of pitch grows stronger. However, a high-frequency component is also heard, associated with the wiggles between the peaks.

interesting to do this at frequencies of 55 and 440 Hz. One thing that we hear is a gradual reinforcement of the pitch frequency. But, in addition to the constant, low-pitch frequency, we get a sense of a higher frequency. This is most apparent in the 55 Hz tone.

Figure 5.2 shows the overall waveform of 10 successive harmonic cosine waves of equal amplitude. The big − to + excursion of every cycle accounts for a strong sensation of pitch at the fundamental frequency. But the strong wiggles between the peaks tend to create a sensation of a high pitch. It is as if we heard the shape of the wave-form—a strong, low-pitched sound at the fundamental, and a weaker, high-pitched sound corresponding to the wiggles.

That seems to be how we hear sounds when the pitch is low enough. Somehow, the ear follows excursions of sound pressure. In some sense, it counts out the pitch at low frequencies.

We can reduce or get rid of the sensations of frequencies higher than the pitch frequency by choosing the relative amplitudes of the harmonics in a different way. Figure 5.3b shows the waveform for 12 sinusoids with relative amplitudes 1.2, 1.1, 1.0, 0.9, and so on. Figure 5.3a shows the waveform for six successive harmonics with relative amplitudes 1.2, 1.0, 0.8, 0.6, 0.4, and 0.2. The wiggles be-tween the peaks are quite small in figure 5.3b, and moderate in figure 5.3a. The waveform of figure 5.3c contains only harmonics 7–12, with amplitudes 0.4, 0.8, 1.2, 1.2, 0.8, 0.4. We see that this last wave-form has an envelope that goes periodically from great to small with the same periodicity as the other waveforms.

Suppose that at frequencies around 55 Hz and around 440 Hz we listen to sequences of three waveforms, the 12-partial waveform of figure 5.3a, the 6-partial waveform of figure 5.3b, and the waveform of figure 5.3c, which consists of only 5 high partials.

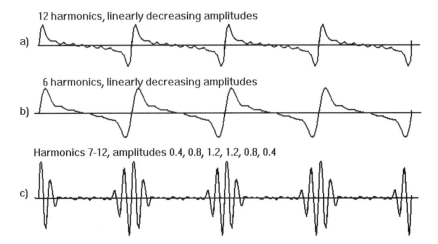

12 harmonics, linearly decreasing amplitudes

a)

6 harmonics, linearly decreasing amplitudes

b)

Harmonics 7-12, amplitudes 0.4, 0.8, 1.2, 1.2, 0.8, 0.4

c)

Figure 5.3 Waveforms with small wiggles. At around 55 Hz all three give the same pitches. Around 440 Hz the first two give a pitch frequency near 440 Hz, but the third gives higher frequencies.

The 12-partial tone includes frequencies from 1 through 12 times the pitch frequency. The 6-partial waveform includes frequencies from 1 to 6 times the pitch frequency. The third waveform is centered around a frequency 9.5 times the pitch frequency, and does not include the pitch frequency itself or any of its nearby harmonics.

What about the perceived pitches of these waveforms near 55 Hz and near 440 Hz? We could explore this question by playing a little tune with the three waveforms. Around 55 Hz we will hear the same tune for all three waveforms, with slightly different timbres. Waveform (c) has a somewhat "sharper" or more raucous timbre than the other two. Around 440 Hz we hear the same tune with waveforms (a) and (b). But with the third waveform we hear bright, faint sounds rather than the "correct" pitches that we get with (a) and (b).

Around 55 Hz the ear can "look at" the first 12 harmonics of the pitch frequency, or at the first 6 harmonics of the pitch frequency, or at harmonics 7 through 12 of the pitch frequency, and see a repetition rate equal to the pitch frequency. Around 440 Hz the ear can get the "right" pitch from the first 12 or 6 harmonics, but it can't get the "right" pitch from harmonics 7 through 12 of the pitch frequency. The time resolution of the ear isn't good enough to follow the envelope of waveform (c). Instead, we get a sound based on the frequencies of all the wiggles, small or large.

Experiments of this sort point strongly to what Licklider (1959) called a "duplex theory of pitch." Experiments supporting two pitch mechanisms have been pursued by Houtsma and Smurzinski (1990). These experiments point strongly to a pitch sensation based on waveform or periodicity for lower frequencies, and to some other mechanism for pitch at higher frequencies.

For waveforms such as those of musical instruments, and for waveforms such as those of figure 5.3, the envelope of the sound wave has the same frequency as the pitch frequency. We need some other sort of waveform to help cast more light on the question of pitch perception.

5.4 Experiments with Tone Bursts

Figure 5.4 shows patterns of tone bursts that are reminiscent of the waveforms of figure 5.1. These tone bursts are sine waves with a raised cosine envelope. In (a) all tone bursts have the same phase, and the fundamental frequency is given by the frequency of occurrence of tone bursts. In (b) every fourth tone burst is the negative of the other three. The four tone bursts constitute one period of the waveform, and the fundamental frequency is one-fourth of the tone-burst rate, that is, one-fourth of the fundamental frequency of waveform (a). This is exactly the same fundamental frequency as waveform (c).

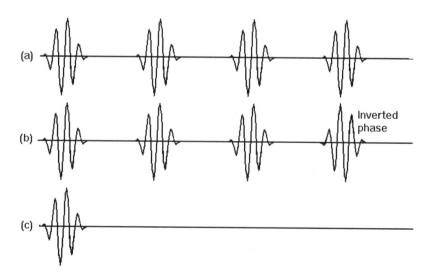

Figure 5.4   Three tone-burst sequences. Top: all tone bursts are the same. Center: every fourth tone burst is inverted. Bottom: one toneburst for each four of (a). At low rates the pitches of (a) and (b) are the same, and c) gives a pitch two octaves lower. At high rates (a) has a pitch two octaves above those of (b) and (c).

Indeed, the amplitude spectrum of (b) is the same as that of (c), but the relative phases of the sinusoidal components are different.

In using such waveforms to investigate pitch, it seems desirable to choose a number of cycles in the tone burst such that an individual tone burst gives no sensation of pitch. Suppose we choose to make the frequency of the sine wave of a tone burst 4000 Hz. By choosing a tone-burst rate for (a) of five tone bursts per second, we can easily hear successive tone bursts. We find that if the tone bursts are 64 cycles long, they give a strong sensation of pitch with no clickiness. However, tone bursts four cycles long give no sensation of pitch; they are strictly bright clicks.

In further experiments we can use 4000 Hz tone bursts that are four cycles long. At sufficiently high tone-burst rates we hear tones whose pitch increases with tone-burst rate. What are the relative pitches of the tone-burst patterns (a), (b), and (c)?

Up to around 300 tone bursts per second, (a) and (b) have the same pitch, which is two octaves above the pitch of (c). At low tone-burst rates the auditory system seems to follow the envelope of the waveform, and we can hear successive tone bursts rise and fall in amplitude. At low rates the auditory system seems to forget all about the preceding tone burst by the time the next one comes along.

At high tone-burst rates, above 1600 tone bursts a second or more, (b) and (c) have the same pitch, which is two octaves below the pitch of (a). The ear cannot distinguish the separate tone bursts in (a) and (b), and must rely on some other criterion or mechanism in judging pitch. Position of vibration along the basilar membrane is a plausible criterion for judging the pitch of high-frequency sounds.

The transition between pitch mechanisms is not abrupt. Up to around 300 tone bursts a second, waveform (a) sounds exactly like waveform (b), and both have a pitch two octaves above that of waveform (c). Above 1600 tone bursts a second, waveform (b) sounds exactly like waveform (c), and waveform (a) has a pitch two octaves higher than (b) or (c). For intermediate rates, waveform (b) gives a sense of two pitches, that of (a) and that of (c). At 640 tone bursts per second, waveform (b) sounds like a reasonably equal mix of the sounds of (a) and (c).

This seems to be conclusive evidence that there are two different mechanisms of pitch perception, a sort of counting mechanism valid at lower frequencies and another mechanism that takes over when the ear cannot "count" peaks in the time envelope of the exciting signal. Plausibly, this high-frequency pitch mechanism relies on the amplitude of excitation along the basilar membrane. The mechanisms appear to be about equally effective at a frequency around 640 Hz. This, which basically agrees with the work of Fletcher, Terhardt, and Licklider, is our overall conclusion about the pitch of periodic waveforms.

5.5 Odd Harmonics Only

Most musical instruments have spectra in which there are both even and odd harmonics. For sounds of low or moderate frequencies, the pitch of such tones is the fundamental frequency, even when there is no component of this frequency in the spectrum.

In the tone of a clarinet, even harmonics are much weaker than odd harmonics. Odd harmonics predominate in the spectra of closed organ pipes.

Digital sound generation enables us to create and explore various types of spectra. For example, we can synthesize sounds with no even harmonics. Will we hear the pitch frequency in the absence of the fundamental frequency? No! Even when the fundamental frequency is present, for sufficiently low pitch frequencies the pitch heard will be higher than the repetition frequency.

Figure 5.5 shows how to demonstrate this. We could first play a tone as shown in figure 5.5 a) with 12 successive harmonics (starting at the first harmonic), with amplitude 1.0 for the first harmonic or pitch frequency, and amplitude 0.7 for each of the 11 higher even and odd harmonics. Then we could play a tone, as shown in figure 5.5 (b), of the same pitch frequency in which each of six successive

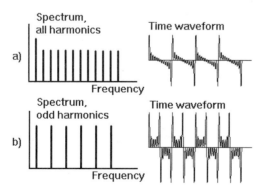

Figure 5.5 Two tones with a similar spectral range, power, and brightness. For a pitch frequency of 880 or 440 Hz the pitches heard are the same. For a pitch frequency of 55 or 110 Hz, the odd harmonic tone has a pitch greater than that of the upper tone.

odd harmonics has amplitude 1.0. The two tones have the same first harmonic, the pitch frequency or fundamental. The widths of the spectra of the tones are similar, so the brightnesses of the tones are similar. The total powers are nearly the same (each harmonic contributes a power proportional to the square of its amplitude).

Suppose the tones are played with pitch frequencies of 880, 440, 220, 110, and 55 Hz. At 880 and 440 Hz the two tones are heard as having the same pitch. At 110 and 55 Hz the odd harmonic tone is heard as having a higher pitch than the successive harmonic tone. When the pitch frequency is low, the loudness of the fundamental and other low harmonics is very much less than that of the higher harmonics. At low enough frequencies the fundamental and some other low harmonics cannot be heard. In the case of odd harmonics only, the frequency separation between successive odd harmonics is twice the pitch frequency. At low pitch frequencies the ear makes a pitch judgment that reflects the distance between the higher harmonics.

5.6 Chimes and Bells

The orchestra chime consists of a number of metal tubes that vibrate transversely after they are struck. The partials of a transversely vibrating tube are not harmonic. But, as we have noted earlier, the fourth, fifth, and sixth partials have frequencies very close to a harmonic series. That series has a pitch frequency that is 4.5 times the frequency of the lowest frequency of vibration, and the seventh partial is close to being the seventh harmonic of this absent frequency. We hear a pitch of this absent pitch frequency based on the presence of close approximations to its second, third, fourth, and seventh harmonics.

Bells in a carillon are used to play tunes. Around the year 1644, the brothers Frans and Pieter Hemony established the classical tuning of carillon bells that gives partials with the frequency ratios shown in table 5.1. We can observe that the significant partials are separated by musical intervals, and that the *Prime, Third,* and *Fifth* form a minor triad. With the exception of the frequencies of the *Third,* all the partials listed are harmonics of the *Hum tone,* which is an octave below the *Prime.*

If the Hemony third were a major third rather than a minor third above the prime, then the prime, third, and fifth would form a major triad, and all listed partials would be harmonics of a tone one octave

Table 5.1   The frequencies of a Hemony bell sound

PARTIAL	RELATION TO f_p, THE PERCEIVED PITCH
Hum tone	$0.5\,f_p$, one octave down
Prime	f_p
Third	$1.2\,f_p$ (a minor third up)
Fifth	$1.5\,f_p$ (a fifth up)
Octave	$2\,f_p$
Upper third	$2.5\,f_p$
Upper fifth	$3\,f_p$

below the hum tone. Might this not result in more pleasing carillon sounds? In 1987 a collaborative effort between the Dutch Institute for Perception in Eindhoven and the Royal Eijbouts Bell Foundry in Asten resulted in the casting of a four-octave transportable carillon of major-third bells. The major-third bell indeed sounds less dissonant than the traditional Hemony bell, and has been received with a good deal of favor.

5.7   Pitch and Unusual Tones

There has been a good deal of work relevant to pitch that makes use of computer-generated sounds. In 1964, Roger Shepard published material on what have come to be called Shepard tones. These tones consist of a number of sinusoidal components an octave apart, with a fixed envelope that goes to zero at low and high frequencies. Figure 5.6 shows the spectral characteristics of Shepard tones.

When we raise the frequencies of the sinusoidal components a semitone, we get the sense of an increase in pitch. This sense of change persists, semitone by semitone, but when we've reached 12 semitones total, we are back where we started. The pitch appears to increase endlessly.

What happens when we raise or lower the pitch by six semitones, half an octave? Some hear the pitch as going up; some, as going down. Raising or lowering the pitch by six semitones gives us exactly the same waveform.

We may note that Shepard tones are somewhat different from musical tones. Though they have many partials, they omit partials other than those an octave apart. Also, there is no lowest partial. As we

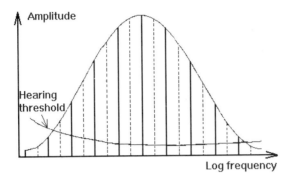

Figure 5.6 Frequency components of a Shepard tone. The envelope goes from left to right, from an inaudible level to an audible level and back down to an inaudible level. A tone has partials separated by an octave. (Modified from Shepard, 1964. Reprinted with permission, © 1964 Acoustical Society of America.)

continually increase the frequency of the octave partials in order to give a higher pitch, a partial will eventually attain audible amplitude, rise in amplitude, fall in amplitude, and sink into inaudibility. There are always more low and high partials available, but they're inaudible due to the imposed spectral envelope and the threshold of hearing.

Successive Shepard tones need not be separated by a semitone. Shepard tones separated by a tenth of an octave can be synthesized as nine equal-amplitude octave partials of a fundamental frequency A0 (27.5 Hz) and of successive fundamentals 0.1 octave, 0.2 octave, 0.3 octave, and so on, to 0.9 octave, then back to A0, and on up again. The sensitivity of human hearing provides the required "attenuation" at low and high frequencies.

Let us consider the pitch of another sort of computer-generated tone. What happens to the pitch of a tone when we double the frequencies of all its frequency components? Jean-Claude Risset has produced tones for which the pitch decreases a little when we double the frequencies of all partials. The tones are made up of successive partials a little more than an octave apart. That is, the ratio of the frequencies of two successive partials is a constant slightly greater than 2. When we abruptly double the frequencies of all partials, the ear hears each frequency component as "replaced" by a partial of slightly lower frequency. The lowest frequency vanishes, and a partial appears with a frequency slightly more than an octave above the previously highest partial. The ear can disregard this disappearance and appearance of partials.

To illustrate this, we could synthesize a tone with nine partials, each successive partial having a frequency 2.1 times that of the preceding partial. When the frequency is shifted from a "fundamental" of 27.5 Hz to a "fundamental" of 55 Hz, the perceived pitch obligingly falls a little.

Risset's tones started with a partial at some plausible and highly audible pitch frequency. The effect isn't as strong or foolproof in this more musical form. Risset also produced tones of ambiguous pitch, in which the pitch heard is dependent on context.

5.8 Concluding Remarks

Our sense of pitch is essential in almost all music. *Pitch frequency* can be related to the fundamental frequency of the sound wave, the frequency of the lowest harmonic or fundamental, whether or not a component of that frequency is actually present in a sound wave. We sense changes in pitch as similar both in notes of low pitch frequency and in notes of high pitch frequency.

There are two mechanisms of pitch perception. One is a sort of counting out of the cycles of a periodic musical tone. This is the dominant mechanism for pitch frequencies below a few hundred Hz. The other mechanism must be based on the place of excitation along the basilar membrane. This mechanism is dominant for pitch frequencies above perhaps 1600 Hz. In between these ranges of complete dominance, both mechanisms operate. For musical sounds, for which the fluctuation of the envelope is equal to the fundamental frequency (which may be present or absent), the mechanisms agree in their estimate of pitch. For tones of low pitch that have odd harmonics only, the pitch may be different from the frequency of the fundamental.

By using computers, tones with peculiar pitch properties have been devised. These peculiar properties do not occur in the tones produced by traditional musical instruments. They are useful experimentally, and may be useful musically.

References

In taking the work of Fletcher into account, it is important to note that he does not discuss his work on pitch in his book.

Fletcher, H. (1953). *Speech and Hearing in Communication.* New York: D. Van Nostrand. Republished in 1995 by the Acoustical Society of America, New York. The republished version, edited by Jont B. Allen, includes a complete bibliography of Fletcher's publications, through which the 1924 *Physical Review* papers and other papers that discuss pitch can be found.

It appears that Schouten was not aware of Fletcher's earlier work, nor were many of his readers. Schouten is responsible for the term *virtual pitch,* used to describe pitch in the absence of the fundamental, as contrasted to the pitch of tones with a fundamental. Of course, no one can separate pitch and virtual pitch while listening to music.

Schouten, J. F., Ritsma, R. J., and B. L. Cardozo. (1962). "Pitch of the residue." *Journal of the Acoustical Society of America,* 134, 1418–1424.

Terhardt's pitch model seems to work well for most signals encountered in music, but does not exactly match human responses on particular types of specially designed tones, such as Risset's tones and the pulse trains described in this chapter. Here are the fundamental Terhardt references:

Terhardt, E. (1972). "Perception of the Pitch of Complex Tones." *Acustica,* 26, 173–199.

Terhardt, E., G. Stoll, and M. Seewann. (1982). "Algorithm for Extraction of Pitch and Pitch Salience from Complex Tonal Signals." *Journal of the Acoustical Society of America,* 71, 679–688.

Risset's paradoxical sounds:

Risset, J. C. (1969). "Pitch Control and Pitch Paradoxes Demonstrated with Computer-Synthesized Sounds," *Journal of the Acoustical Society of America,* 46, 88. (Abstract).

Mathews, M. V., and J. R. Pierce, eds. (1989). *Current Directions in Computer Music Research.* Cambridge, Mass.: MIT Press. Compact disc sound examples for the book are available from the publisher. Chapter 11, "Paradoxical Sounds," by Jean-Claude Risset, is particularly appropriate. Unfortunately, chapter 14, "Residues and Summation Tones—What Do We Hear?," by John Pierce, is erroneous, as are the sound examples.

Other references on pitch perception:

Greenberg, S., J. T. Marsh, W. S. Brown and J. C. Smith. (1987). "Neural Temporal Coding of Low Pitch. I. Human Frequency-Following Responses to Complex Tones." *Hearing Research,* 25, 91–114.

Houtsma, A. J. M., and Smurzynski, J. (1990). "Pitch Identification and Discrimination for Complex Tones with Many Harmonics," *Journal of the Acoustical Society of America,* 87, 304–310.

Licklider, J. C. R. (1959). "Three Auditory Theories." In S. Koch, ed., *Psychology: A Study of the Science,* vol. 1. New York: McGraw Hill.

Nordmark, J. O. (1968). "Mechanisms of Frequency Discrimination." *Journal of the Acoustical Society of America,* 44, 1533–1540.

Pierce, J. R. (1991). "Periodicity and Pitch Perception." *Journal of the Acoustical Society of America,* 90, 1889–1893.

6 What Is Loudness?

Max Mathews

What does "loud" mean? Can you measure it with a meter? How loud is "twice as loud"? In chapters 1 and 2 we considered how the ear and the brain work. In chapter 5 we discussed some fundamentals of pitch perception. Here we will concentrate not on the mechanics of how our sensors work but on how we eventually perceive auditory phenomena. As with the chapter on pitch, we will not consider physically measured things, such as intensity, but rather how we perceive intensity as loudness.

6.1 Equal Loudness Contours

Figure 6.1 shows an important, classical diagram known as the Fletcher–Munson curves. We were first introduced to these curves, which show equal loudness contours for sine wave sounds, in chapter 4. Frequency in Hz is shown left to right, from 20 Hz at the left to over 10,000 Hz at the right. Sounds of different frequencies whose intensities lie along any one of these curves sound equally loud. Along the ordinate (vertical axis) are the actual sound pressures (or intensity) in decibels.

As you can see, some of the equal loudness curves go up and down quite a lot. For example, in order for a soft sound at 50 Hz to sound as loud as one at 2000 Hz, the 50 Hz sound has to be about 50 dB more intense than the 2000 Hz sound. That is an enormous difference of 100,000 times in power.

What this tells us is that our auditory systems are much more sensitive at 2000 Hz than at 50 Hz. You may have noticed that you can barely hear the 60 Hz hum that is present in cheap audio equipment. If the equipment produced the same intensity of "hum" at 2000 Hz, it would drive you out of the room.

If you examine the curves of figure 6.1 a little more closely, you can see that the auditory system is most sensitive at a frequency of about 2000 Hz. Some of the curves show the maximum sensitivity nearer to 3000 Hz. Musically, 2000 Hz is a fairly high pitch; most singers cannot produce a pitch that high. But they might get up to

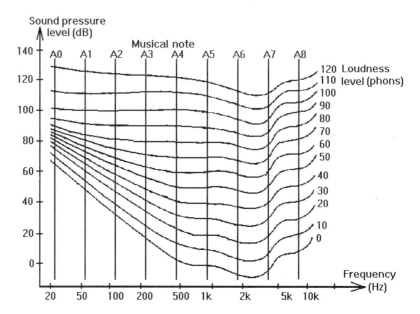

Figure 6.1 Fletcher–Munson equal loudness contours show the intensity at which a sine wave must be presented, as a function of frequency, in order to sound equally loud as sine waves at other frequencies on the same curve.

1000 Hz, and really blast you. Moreover, musical tones of lower pitch have harmonics in the range of 2000 Hz and above, and a part of the loudness of musical tones is contributed by their harmonics.

At low frequencies below 100 Hz, the auditory system is not very sensitive. And at high frequencies of 10,000 Hz and above, it also is insensitive. How fast the sensitivity of the ear falls off at high frequencies depends on how old you are. My hearing (at age 60) falls off very rapidly around 10,000 Hz, whereas most young people can hear sounds up to 15,000 to 20,000 Hz.

Musically, the most important frequencies lie between 100 and 5000 Hz. As discussed in chapter 5, musical tones with pitch frequencies below 100 Hz are heard chiefly through their harmonics. It's amazing how little we lose by eliminating all frequencies below 100 Hz and above 5000 Hz. AM radio stations don't broadcast above 5000 cycles. Small radio sets don't produce much intensity at 100 Hz and below. Lower and higher frequencies do make a difference, however, that we can appreciate in good hi-fi systems.

There are a lot of curves in figure 6.1. What are the differences between them? It's the intensity of the sound. Consider the lowest curve. For this curve, the intensity of sound at the auditory system's most sensitive frequency is 8 dB greater than the threshold of perception at that frequency. This bottom curve is close to the softest sound that the average person can hear at most frequencies.

The number attached to a particular curve is its loudness level in *phons,* defined by the shape of the curve itself. The intensities along the curve, including the minimum intensity, have a common loudness level, specified in the number of phons that labels the curve. These curves are 10 dB apart. What do the decibels refer to? A sound-level meter will read such intensities in SPL (sound pressure level), which is a measure of sound intensity. Sound-level meters are calibrated in SPLs.

If you read a number on a sound-level meter, for sine waves you will get SPLs in decibels above the threshold of hearing. To get the loudness level for a complicated sound such as speech, you must find the loudness level in phons of a sine wave that sounds equal in loudness to the sound you're trying to quantify.

The lower curves in figure 6.1 represent soft sounds. Normal speech sounds are 70 to 80 dB above the levels of the lowest curve. The ambient sound level in a good empty auditorium will be around 30 dB. It takes good sound insulation to get the ambient noise much below 30 dB.

We must remember that the curves of figure 6.1 are for sine waves. Speech and noise have many frequencies. For weak sounds, some frequency components may lie below threshold, so that their power, which is included in the SPL reading, may actually not contribute to the audibility of the sound. In an extreme case, a 20 Hz sound with a 30 dB SPL would be completely inaudible.

At the top of the set of curves, the sounds at 120 dB approach the threshold of pain. That hurts, and is dangerous. If you are exposed to levels like that for very long, you are apt to have damage to your hearing—you'll have what's called a "threshold shift." A little exposure will result in temporary shift, and you can suffer permanent damage through prolonged or repeated exposure. As a matter of fact, sound levels above 100 dB should be experienced with caution, and not for very long.

I once went to a Grateful Dead concert and sat behind the mixing console. The Grateful Dead concerts (and many others) are very carefully controlled by the engineer doing the sound mixing. The musicians don't have anything to do with it during the concert. All the lines from the pickups and microphones lead to the mixing console, which is always at a given location, 80 or so feet from the two towers of loudspeakers on the stage. The mixing console can adjust the levels of all the sounds of the instruments. I watched the sound-level meter during part of the concert. It never went below 100 dB, and it never went above 110 dB. Later, I asked why this was so. I was told that if the level went below 100 dB, the audience got restless. If it went above 110 dB, there was so much feedback to the stage that the performers couldn't play. I didn't ask about hearing damage.

Returning to the curves of figure 6.1, we should note that for soft sounds there is a great difference in the auditory system's sensitivity to different frequencies. The lower curves have a big dip in them. For loud sounds, even for 90 phons, there is much less variation with frequency. There is a moderate amount of variation for sounds of intermediate intensities.

Musically, this variation is important. For one thing, this tells us that if we want a musical instrument to be heard easily, its frequencies should lie between, say, 500 Hz and a few thousand Hz. If you have an instrument that produces low frequencies only, it can't be perceived as loud. If you have a high-frequency instrument, it won't be quite as loud as a midfrequency instrument. To get a very loud sound you need a lot of energy in the frequency range from 500 to a few thousand Hz.

Another conclusion is that when your are playing fortissimo, low frequencies contribute relatively more than in a soft passage. In connection with the things I have covered in this chapter, and in connection with other matters concerning the hearing of sound, I advocate the "I'm from Missouri" approach. You shouldn't believe things unless you can hear them. You should listen to sounds and decide whether or not to believe what you are told. Data are average data, and you weren't included in the averaging. The course I advocate is best carried out by listening to synthesized sounds.

6.2 Synthesizing and Listening to Examples

There are various ways of producing computer-generated sounds, but most are related by the ability to manipulate sine waves in frequency, phase, and amplitude. Some systems allow for control of noise and other characteristics. With computer-generated sounds we can try to confirm what has been said about various features of the Fletcher–Munson (equal loudness) curves. One can adjust the relative intensities of sine tones at 50 Hz and at 2000 Hz until they seem to sound equally loud, and compare the result with the published curves. In such a demonstration it is desirable to be able to see the waveform and a spectrum display, as well as to hear the sounds, so that you're sure about the sound to which you're listening.

In a lecture demonstration I use when teaching the psychoacoustics course, sounds are played at various relative levels in decibels SPL. The level of the sinusoidal sound in the room is adjusted by using a sound-level meter.

The class votes as to which frequency sounds louder. As the level of the 50 Hz sound is increased in steps, from a level equal to that of the 2000 Hz sound to a higher and higher level, the vote finally changes from the 2000 Hz tone sounding louder to the 50 Hz tone sounding louder. The procedure is tried with softer sounds, and can be used with other frequencies as well. The results come out strikingly close to those shown in figure 6.1. But they are not as precise, for the levels are adjusted in 10 dB steps.

The large change in relative intensities is sensible for a demonstration in a room in which the relative intensities at various locations may be different for different frequencies. The data for the curves of figure 6.1 were of course taken with earphones.

Another important demonstration is "How much is a decibel?" I do this at 440 Hz, the A above middle C. This frequency is chosen to avoid changes in intensity that can be caused by varying head position in a real room with resonances (remember that the wavelength of 440 Hz is about 2.6 feet). Successive sounds are played 1 dB apart; the difference in intensity is difficult to hear. Musically, a 1 dB difference in intensity doesn't produce any impact. A 6 dB difference is easy to hear, but not very impressive as a contrast in music. Six dB is a factor of 4 in the intensity or power of a sound, or a factor of 2 in pressure. Twenty dB is a factor of 100 in intensity or 10 in pressure—a pretty big change. Forty dB is a really big change, from barely audible in a "noisy" room to a good loud sound. It is about the largest range of musically significant sound in ordinary circumstances. In a quiet concert hall you can't do much better than 60 dB.

Musically, if you want to make a contrast, you have to do more than just change the intensity of the sound. You have to change the complexity of the sound, and perhaps the harmony. A composer must do more than just change intensity in going from soothing to startling.

Again we must remember that figure 6.1 is for sine waves. Most demonstrations of sounds are for sine waves. The voice, music, and all natural sounds are not sine waves; they are made up of many partials or frequency components, and often of nearly harmonic partials. We must take into account the data we get with sine waves, but we must not let ourselves be misled by them. We have considered the perception of equal loudness, and the perception of more or less loudness. But does it make sense to call one sound twice as loud as another, or half as loud as another, or ten or a hundred times as loud as another?

6.3 What's Twice as Loud?

In order to answer this question, you have to be willing to make a different kind of judgment. This new kind of judgment is harder to make, but if enough people agree, it will be one we can rely on. So far we have talked about listening to two sounds and saying which one is louder, or we have adjusted the level of one of two sounds until the sounds are equally loud.

We can present a sound, and then follow it with another sound that is more intense than the first by some number of decibels. Then we can ask, "Is the second sound more or less than twice as loud as the first?" This has been done both in classroom demonstrations and in controlled research labs. The judgments by vote showed that most people heard a 5 dB more intense sound as less than twice as loud, and most people said a 10 dB more intense sound was at least twice as loud. Thus, somewhere between 5 and 10 dB difference in intensity is twice as loud.

What do researchers find when they carefully run such an experiment with earphones, and repeat it many times with many people? What they find for 1000 Hz sine tones is shown in figure 6.2. At moderate-to-high levels a difference in intensity of around 10 dB doubles the loudness measured in *sones* (the sone is defined as a perceptual comparative loudness relative to a sine wave at 1000 Hz, 40 dB SPL). But at lower intensities, and especially near the threshold of hearing, the loudness in sones increases more rapidly with intensity in decibels. That makes sense, because if you compare a sound you can barely hear with a sound just a few decibels more intense, the latter seems bound to sound much louder.

Figure 6.2 holds only for the frequency 1000 Hz. Curves have been measured and plotted for several frequencies across the audio range but all curves look about the same in shape except for the one at 100 Hz. At high enough levels the curves have a slope of about 10 dB for doubling the loudness. Fletcher, Stevens, and others have

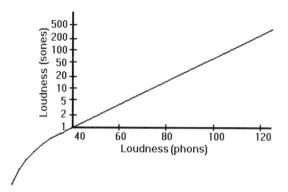

Figure 6.2   Loudness in sones versus loudness level in phons at 1000 Hz.

proposed that in the normal-to-high range, the loudness varies as the third root of the intensity; that would give about 9.4 dB for doubling the loudness, and 10 dB is close enough to this level to be a good rule of thumb. The region of loudness for which this linear variation of loudness versus intensity holds is the region that is of interest in music. In this region we can get, for sine waves, the loudness versus intensity level at any frequency from figure 6.1, the equal-loudness contour.

We have now done two things. We have investigated contours of equal loudness, with each contour labeled in phons. We also have made a scale of relative loudnesses in sones. The equal loudness contours involve only quantities that you can read on a meter, once you have made an adjustment for equal loudness. The relative loudness in sones cannot be read on a meter. It depends on consistent human judgment of what intensity ratio doubles the perceived loudness.

6.4   Complex Sounds

What about more complex sounds? We can adjust the level of a sine wave of some frequency so that the sine wave sounds as loud as some other sound. The loudnesses will not necessarily seem the same if we raise or lower the levels of the two sounds by the same number of decibels. Fletcher's experimental conclusion was that putting the same sound in both ears makes it sound twice as loud as if it were heard monaurally. Experiments also indicate that the loudnesses of two sounds in the same ear add, but only if the sounds are separated enough in frequency so that one doesn't interact with or mask the other.

Some other interesting observations on loudness of spectra, which you could investigate with computer music synthesis software, include the following:

Take one sound that is a single sine wave of, say, 1000 Hz. Let another sound be composed of six sine waves, each with one-sixth the power of that single sine wave. Let the frequencies of the sine waves in the second sound be 500, 1000, 1500, 2000, 2500, and 3000 Hz. The six harmonically related sine waves will sound a good deal louder than the single sine wave of the same total power. See if this is true at many amplitude levels.

Compare the loudness of the six harmonic waves above with a sound composed of six inharmonic frequencies (e.g., 500, 1100, 1773, 2173, 2717, 3141 Hz). Which do you think will be louder?

Reference

Moore, B. C. J. (1989). *An Introduction to the Psychology of Hearing.* Third edition. London: Academic Press.

7   *Introduction to Timbre*

Max Mathews

In prior chapters we've covered some basic aspects of sine waves, spectra, pitch, and loudness. In this chapter we will consider some of the fundamental aspects of psychoacoustic timbre. We'll cover the basis of timbre, but as with our initial examples of pitch and loudness, some of these examples won't seem very musical. They have been simplified so that we can focus our attention on the various factors of timbre.

7.1   Average Spectral Shape

One important timbral factor is the average shape of the spectrum. Just how rapidly does the energy fall off as you go into the higher partials? In musical tones the spectrum is made up of harmonic partials or *harmonics,* but the same thing applies in some sense with inharmonic partials.

Table 7.1 gives the relative amplitudes of successive harmonics of tones for which the harmonic intensity falls off by 0 dB, 3 dB, 6 dB, 9 dB, and 12 dB per octave. This falloff is also sometimes called spectral rolloff or spectral attenuation. Harmonics corresponding to octaves (doublings of the fundamental) are shown in bold. In the first example, column (a), all harmonics have equal amplitude. In example (c) the harmonics fall off at 6 dB per octave. This means that the second harmonic, an octave above the fundamental, is 6 dB below the fundamental in amplitude. The fourth harmonic—up two octaves from the fundamental—is 12 dB below the fundamental, and the eighth harmonic, up another octave, is down 18 dB. The third, fifth, and other harmonics, which are not integer numbers of octaves, have appropriate numbers of decibels. In the last example, column (e), the partials fall off at 12 dB per octave, twice as fast in log amplitude as the 6 dB per octave spectrum.

Figure 7.1 shows the waveforms of the examples from table 7.1, normalized so that they all exhibit the same power (power = sum of squares of samples = sum of squares of harmonic amplitudes). Waveform (a), the 0 dB per octave waveform, is a sequence of pulses

Table 7.1 Fractional amplitudes for 0, 3, 6, 9, and 12 dB per octave attenuation

HARMONIC NO.	(A) 0 dB/OCT.	(B) 3 dB/OCT.	(C) 6 dB/OCT.	(D) 9 dB/OCT.	(E) 12 dB/OCT.
Fundamental ampl.	1.0	1.0	1.0	1.0	1.0
Harmonic 2 ampl.	1.0	0.7079	0.5012	0.3548	0.2512
Harmonic 3 ampl.	1.0	0.5784	0.3345	0.1935	0.1120
Harmonic 4 ampl.	1.0	0.5012	0.2512	0.1259	0.0631
Harmonic 5 ampl.	1.0	0.4484	0.2011	0.0902	0.0404
Harmonic 6 ampl.	1.0	0.4095	0.1677	0.0687	0.0281
Harmonic 7 ampl.	1.0	0.3792	0.1438	0.0545	0.0207
Harmonic 8 ampl.	1.0	0.3548	0.1259	0.0447	0.0158
Harmonic 9 ampl.	1.0	0.3346	0.1120	0.0375	0.0125
Harm. 10 ampl.	1.0	0.3175	0.1008	0.0320	0.0102
Harm. 11 ampl.	1.0	0.3028	0.0917	0.0277	0.0084
Harm. 12 ampl.	1.0	0.2899	0.0840	0.0244	0.0071

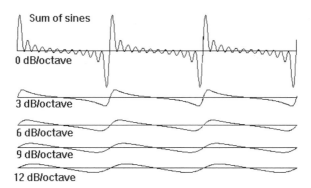

Figure 7.1 Waveshapes for 0, 3, 6, 9, and 12 dB per octave rolloff.

with wiggles in between. If many more harmonics were included, the wiggles would become smaller and the waveform would approach a sequence of very short pulses. Waveform (a) has a very harsh and buzzy sound. The nearest thing to this sound in a musical instrument would be the waveform near the player's mouth (or reed) in an oboe.

Waveform (c) rolls off at 6 dB per octave, and is a sawtooth wave (as discussed in section 4.5). If there were more harmonics, the wave would be nearly a sequence of straight lines. We can look at this as a falling straight line with a discontinuity in magnitude that brings it back up, to fall again. The nearest thing to this in a musical instrument is a bowed string at the point of bowing. The bow pulls the string sideways while they're stuck together, then eventually the string breaks away and slips back. This repeats, causing a sawtooth motion of the string.

Waveform (e), which rolls off at 12 dB per octave, is a lot smoother, and has a smoother sound than the 6 dB per octave sawtooth of waveform (c).

There is no simple geometric description of waveforms (b) and (d), whose harmonic amplitudes roll off at 3 dB and 9 dB per octave, respectively. Their sounds are intermediate between those of the next lower and higher waveforms.

To summarize, the greater the negative slope of spectral rolloff, the smoother the waveform; and the sound becomes less bright and buzzy. The 12 dB per octave waveform is a bland sound. The 0 dB per octave waveform is probably too harsh for musical use. If you were to listen to the sounds in order from (a) to (e), they would sound progressively less bright. It is good to listen to these sounds in sequence and form your own idea of how buzziness depends on the rolloff in decibels per octave.

There are some important points about spectral shape. First, you have to consider the average spectrum before you go on to other timbral factors. This could involve using notions like equal loudness to determine which components of the spectrum are most important. Second, the most musically interesting rates of rolloff are between 3 and 9 dB per octave.

So far we have been considering steady state, truly periodic sound waveforms. We will get to time variations of waveform and spectrum later. Also, the spectra we have considered so far are monotonic spectra; spectra in which the spectrum falls off linearly with increasing logarithmic frequency rather than spectra that both and rise and fall in amplitude as a function of frequency.

7.2 Bumpy Spectra

Monotonic spectra aren't as musically interesting as those with more complex structure. Spectra can have all sorts of bumps. One important class of spectra consists of those that contain formants (spectral peaks). (For more examples, see chapter 9, which examines what are probably the most interesting and challenging spectra with humps [or formants], the spectra of the vowel sounds of song or speech.) In such sounds the envelope of the spectrum has peaks at three principal formant frequencies that are characteristic of a particular vowel.

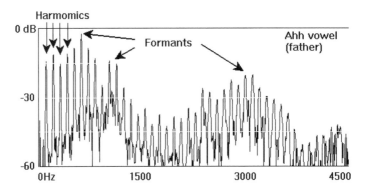

Figure 7.2 Spectrum of vowel sound, showing formants.

Figure 7.2 gives an example. Most important about the voice is that the bumps move around as the speaker/singer forms different sounds by moving his/her mouth.

Some musical instruments also have formants. The violin has many more formants than the human voice, and these are likely related to the tone qualities of the violin. Formants in the violin do not change with time, as those of the voice do. Woodwinds such as the bassoon and oboe have fewer formants than the human voice, but the formants are strong and perceptually important.

You can have formants that, like the formants of vocal vowels, are independent of the pitch of the sound (you can say *ahh* on many pitches, or *eeeahh* on one pitch). Or you can have formants whose positions change with the pitch of the sound.

In most cases the fixed-frequency formants give more interesting timbres than formants that move with pitch. Another way of saying this is that sounds whose formant frequencies are proportional to the pitch frequency have a waveshape that is constant, or almost constant, with pitch. It's just the period that changes with pitch. Sounds with a constant waveshape independent of frequency tend to sound dull, or artificial, as you go up and down in pitch.

7.3 "Holy Spectra"

There is one set of nonmonotonic spectra that have been called *holy* by John Pierce and by me—because we have purposely put holes (missing harmonics) in the spectra in generating such hol(e)y tones.

In figure 7.3 we see one spectrum that has 24 successive harmonics, with a rolloff of 3 dB per octave. In another spectrum the first six harmonics are present: the seventh and ninth are left out, the

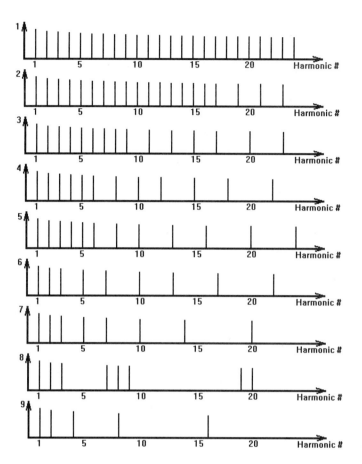

Figure 7.3   Spectra of holy tones 1 through 9.

eleventh and twelfth are left out, and more and more among the higher harmonics are left out.

Why should we want to omit more of the higher harmonics than of the lower ones? This has to do with the critical bandwidth of hearing. The critical bandwidth reflects the frequency-filtering action of the basilar membrane. The critical bandwidth is about 100 Hz at low frequencies; it changes gradually to around 20 percent of the frequency (a musical minor third, or a third of an octave) at higher frequencies. If two sinusoidal components of the spectrum are separated by several critical bandwidths, they don't interact and can be heard separately. But as we move two sinusoidal components closer and closer in frequency, they become hard to disentangle. Moreover, if they lie within a critical bandwidth, they sound harsh.

Except for very low pitches, successive lower harmonics of a musical tone are separated by more than a critical bandwidth and do not interact to produce harshness. But the higher the harmonic number, the closer the harmonic spacing in critical bandwidths. Roughly, above the sixth harmonic the harmonic spacing is small enough to lie within a critical bandwidth and to produce roughness.

What we wanted to do was produce tones with strong high-frequency components giving the tone power and brilliance, while eliminating the harshness associated with a flat or gradually sloping spectrum. To do this, we have lots of high-frequency harmonics. However, when more than one harmonic lies within a critical bandwidth, we remove the harmonic components until no two remain within the critical bandwidth. Holes in the spectrum allow for no two components being within one critical bandwidth. Thus we have a "holy spectrum."

Several such spectra are shown in figure 7.3. These include *holy 7,* in which higher partials are spaced more than a critical bandwidth apart, and *unholy 8,* which has the same number of partials as *holy 7* but the higher partials are deliberately moved close together in groups.

Among musical instruments, the violin tends to approximate such an effect. The coupling between the string and the soundboard rises and falls rapidly with frequency, as shown in figure 7.4. The valleys tend to eliminate higher harmonics that are very close together in frequency.

It is important to listen to the examples of holy spectra of figure 7.3 and form your own judgment of the effectiveness of holy tones. The amplitudes of the spectral components that are present fall off at 3 dB per octave.

These manipulations of spectral components can get rid of a good deal of buzziness. Particularly, compare *holy 7* with *unholy 8,* which

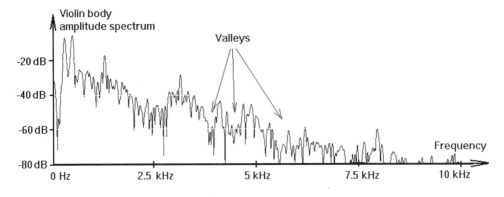

Figure 7.4 Transfer function of violin versus frequency.

has the same number of partials but the higher partials are deliberately moved close together. The effect is there, though not as clear an effect as we had hoped for when we conceived of the idea of holy spectra.

Why do we have several holy tones—5, 6, and 7? The reason is that leaving out partials produces a coloration. Depending on which partials you leave out, you get different colors. One can play tones that have the same amount of "holiness" but sound different because different partials are omitted. Among these I wish to call attention to tones with octave partials (holy 9), which have a distinctive and "octavely" quality. There are other holy tones whose higher partials lie in other musical intervals.

As we leave holy tones, we may note that a similar effect can be obtained in an organ through using a mixture of an 8-foot stop, a 4-foot stop, and a 2-foot stop. The 4-foot (an octave up) and the 2-foot (two octaves up) stops add higher harmonics, at two and four times the harmonic spacings of the 8-foot stop. This also happens in orchestration when an instrument "doubles" another at one or two octaves above.

7.4 Time Variation in Sounds

We often talk of the amplitude envelope of a sound, which is a description of how the amplitude, power, or loudness of a sound varies with time. A sound with an amplitude envelope that rises rapidly and falls slowly with time always gives a struck or plucked sound. In brassy sounds the higher harmonics rise a little later than the lower harmonics. In synthesizing tones, this effect can be implemented by increasing a filter cutoff, or the frequency modulation (FM) index. By using this knowledge, I was able to create an electronic violin that has a brassy tone. By displacing the onset of the harmonics of gong or bell sound, so that the onset of each tone is audibly later than that of the last, one gets what Jean-Claude Risset calls "fluid textures." In pianos the higher harmonics are shifted up a little in frequency by the stiffness of the string. This gives an agreeable and essential wavering sound as the harmonics change relative phase with time.

With a few exceptions, all instrumental sounds have some vibrato and some tremolo. This is due to the coupling of the human performer with the oscillator in these instruments. Vibrato is more important than tremolo. Without vibrato, prolonged sounds don't sound

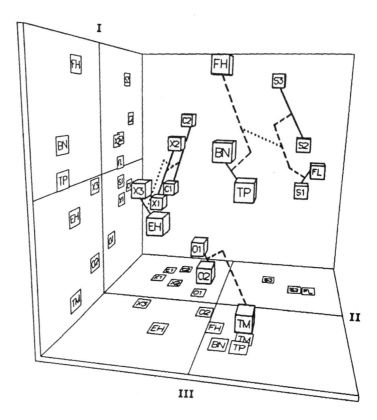

Figure 7.5   Grey's timbre space. Musical instruments are laid out by similarity in three dimensions. Instruments: O, oboes; C, clarinets; X, saxes; EH, English horn; FH, French horn; S, strings; TP, trumpet; TM, trombone; FL, flute; BN, bassoon. (Reprinted with permission from Grey 1976. © 1976 Acoustical Society of America.)

musical. For instance, a sung vowel sound eventually sounds buzzy if it is prolonged without vibrato. A mixture of periodic and random vibrato is necessary to give a musical quality to long tones.

7.5   Concluding Remarks on Timbre

Most dictionaries define timbre as the quality of a sound that distinguishes it from other sounds of the same pitch and loudness. Timbre is therefore a complex phenomenon. All of the quantifiable aspects of a sound go into making up its timbre, most important being the final perception of the listener. A number of systematic studies of timbre perception have been undertaken. They include that by John Grey (1976), who by using a technique called multidimensional scaling, was able to define a "timbre space," as shown in figure 7.5. This allows us to say how close a trumpet is to a trombone, for example.

Many others have looked at aspects of timbre, including David Wessel (1979), who investigated the compositional use of timbre, and Gregory Sandell (1991), who compiled a large database of analyzed sounds for composition and timbre research.

References

Grey, J. M. (1976). "Multidimensional Perceptual Scaling of Musical Timbres." *Journal of the Acoustical Society of America,* 61(5): 1270–1277.

Sandell, G. J. (1991). "Aconcurrent Timbres in Orchestration: A Perceptual Study of Factors Determining 'Blend,'" Ph.D. dissertation, School of Music, Northwestern University.

Wessel, D. L. (1979). "Timbre Space as a Musical Control Structure." *Computer Music Journal,* 3(2): 45–52.

8 Hearing in Time and Space

John Pierce

8.1 Hearing the World

Sight tends to dominate hearing. When we watch home movies or TV, we hear the voices as coming from the characters on the screen, regardless of where the loudspeakers are located. But without visual clues we do sense the direction and even the distance of sound sources.

Imagine stepping down from the porch of your country home on a moonless autumn night. A breeze stirs the remaining leaves of the maple tree above you. Disturbed by your footfalls, some tiny creature rustles in the leaves on the ground. In the distance you hear a car, and from the sounds it makes, you judge that it is not a new car. It turns in at your driveway. You can't really see it—you are blinded by the glare of the headlights—but you hear the crunch of the gravel as it approaches. The car pulls to a stop. You hear the door open. "Hi, John," a voice says. "Hi, Mark," you reply. "Long time, no see."

We think of the world about us as the world we see, but hearing can play an important part in sensing and interpreting what is out there. The blind get along remarkably well by relying strongly on auditory cues. Their world must seem different from ours. We see photos and TV every day, and we regard these as depicting objects and events in a world familiar to us though sight. Indeed, like a camera, the eye has a lens that forms an image on the retina. Our visual world is built by interpreting the two images on our two retinas, and on the way they change as we move our eyes and head.

Bregman (1990) has written at length about the problems of auditory scene analysis. The ear has no lens. The sounds of the world reach our eardrums through two quarter-inch holes in our head. The sound waves that reach these holes are modified by reflections from the torso and the pinnae (outer ears). These modifications change as we move our head. Inside the ear, the sound waves in the auditory canal cause the eardrum to vibrate. That vibration is carried through a network of small bones to cause vibrations in the fluid-filled cochlea. The cochlea sorts them out according to the range of frequency. Some aspects of the time evolution of the oscillations are processed and compared. An example of this would be the comparisons of relative intensities and times of arrival at the two ears, through which we sense the direction of a sound source.

We may hope someday to have a complete and reliable model of human hearing, perhaps attained through guessing at the right neural networks and finding the values of parameters through means at hand. Beyond that, we hope someday to implement, or at least outline, an artificial sense of hearing that will hear as we do, with the same sensitivities and insensitivities that our own hearing exhibits. Then we will be on the road to a true virtual reality.

We do know that research has already disclosed a number of particular examples of things that we do and do not hear. Many of these are recounted in this chapter. It is good for composers and performers to remember them and keep them in mind. It is no use to produce fine gradations of sound that the auditory system cannot hear because of masking or because of the insensitivity of some component of the ear. It can be embarrassing to seek loudness in vain by piling up spectral components that mask each other. The ability of our ears to disregard or group together wanted sounds in the presence of unwanted sounds that could confuse us is essential to our perception of the world through sound.

8.2 The "Cocktail Party Effect"

Figure 8.1 has to do with distinguishing what one speaker is saying when another speaker is talking at the same time. This is easier when the two speakers stand in different locations than when they are in the same place. The ability to follow what one speaker says in the presence of the chatter of many others is called the "cocktail

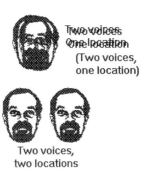

(Two voices,
one location)

Two voices,
two locations

Figure 8.1   Two ears are better than one. We can listen better to one of two voices if the speakers are in different locations.

party effect." This is most easily illustrated to an audience by recording the voice of a single speaker reading different passages of text in succession.

When the different passages of text are simultaneously played at the same level over the same loudspeaker, we may be able to pick up a few words or phrases of one text or the other. It is impossible to follow either when both come from the same location.

It is quite different if we hear one voice from a loudspeaker to the left and the other from a loudspeaker to the right. We can to some degree "tune in" on either speaker, concentrating on the voice, left or right, that we wish to follow.

This "tuning in" is a consequence of the ear's ability to adjust the times of travel in neural pathways from the two ears so that the signals we wish to follow add up, and the interference doesn't. Whether or not we understand all the details of the process, we can see its remarkable consequences in simplified experiments.

8.3   Binaural Masking

Suppose that we use earphones to put various combinations of an identical noise and a sinusoidal signal into the left and right ears, as shown in figure 8.2

In figure 8.2 (a), at the top, the noise and the signal are the same in each ear. The subject cannot hear the signal.

In figure 8.2(b) the noise is the same in each ear, but the sign of the sinusoidal signal in one ear has been inverted (180 degree phase shift). The hearer can now hear the signal despite the noise. Somehow, the sense of hearing manages to make the sinusoidal signals, which arrive at the ears in different phases, add in phase, while the noise doesn't add in phase.

In 8.2(c) noise and signal go to one ear only. The noise keeps the subject from hearing the sinusoidal signal.

In 8.2(d) we have the same noise and signal in one ear as in (c) and the same noise, without signal, in the other ear. The subject can now hear the signal, for the addition of the noise in the other ear has enabled him to "filter" it out. The ear somehow shifts the combined response to the noise in the two ears so as to partially cancel the noise.

Such reduction of masking through binaural effects can be as large as 15 dB at 500 Hz; it falls to 2 or 3 dB for frequencies above 1500 Hz.

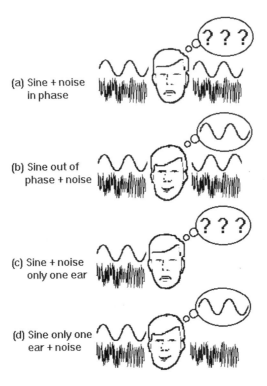

(a) Sine + noise in phase

(b) Sine out of phase + noise

(c) Sine + noise only one ear

(d) Sine only one ear + noise

Figure 8.2 Binaural hearing of a sine wave obscured by noise. If the signal is different in the two ears and the noise is not, it is easier to hear the signal through the noise. With a signal to one ear only, noise in both ears is better than noise to the signal ear only. (Modified from Moore, 1964.)

This ability of the auditory system to shift the relative times at which the signals of the two ears are added is essential to the cocktail party effect.

8.4 The Precedence Effect

In figure 8.2 the "signal" is a steady sine wave, which is unrealistic. A sine wave goes on forever. Noises, clicks, voices, and musical tones have distinct beginnings, and these are essential to the effectiveness of our ability to hear sound from a source in a room that has reflecting walls. In such a room, the combination of many reflected sounds may reach us with greater intensity than direct sound, but that doesn't fool our ears. We hear a sound as coming from the direction from which it first reaches us. This is called the *precedence effect*.

The precedence effect can be demonstrated quite easily, and with startling clarity, as shown in figure 8.3. To do this, the same voice

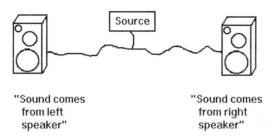

"Sound comes
from left
speaker"

"Sound comes
from right
speaker"

Figure 8.3 When the same signal comes from two loudspeakers, a listener hears it as coming from the nearer speaker. This is not a volume effect but is related to the arrival times of the sounds from the two speakers.

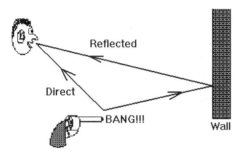

Figure 8.4 A sudden sound arriving both directly and reflected from a smooth wall is heard as having an echo only if the path of the reflected sound is 30 to 40 feet longer than the direct path.

signal is played at the same level from two loudspeakers. The voice asks members of the audience to raise their hands if they hear the voice as coming from the right-hand speaker, and then to raise their hands if they hear the voice as coming from the left-hand speaker.

Typically, those on the left-hand side of the room will hear the voice as coming from the left-hand speaker, and those on the right-hand side of the room will hear it as coming from the right-hand speaker, which is closer to them.

The precedence effect must be one of general sound arrival time rather than of exact waveform, for the behavior described above is unaltered if we reverse the phase of the signal to one of the speakers. Reversing the phase ruins the effectiveness of the stereo system at low frequencies, but the precedence effect persists.

The precedence effect has a long and interesting history that is recounted very well in a paper by Mark Gardner (1968b). One early experiment, described by Joseph Henry in 1849, is illustrated in figure 8.4. A listener hears a sharp sound, such as a hand clap or gunshot, both directly and reflected from a large, smooth wall. When

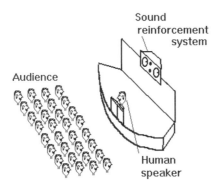

Figure 8.5   If a speaker's amplified voice comes from a speaker more distant from the audience than the speaker's mouth, the audience tends to hear the voice as coming from the speaker's mouth.

the source of the sound is moved away from the wall, at some distance the listener hears two sounds, the original hand clap and its echo. An echo was reported when the difference of distance of the direct sound vs. the source sound reflected from the wall was 30 to 40 feet, or a time difference of 1/40 to 1/30 of a second (25 to 35 milliseconds).

Figure 8.5 illustrates the use of the precedence effect in a public address system. The loudspeaker that emits the amplified voice of the speaker is farther from the audience than the speaker's mouth. Hence, if the amplification isn't too great, the audience tends to hear the speaker's voice as coming from the speaker's mouth rather than from the loudspeaker above, even though the sound coming from the loudspeaker may actually be louder than the speaker's voice. This is also reinforced by the visual cues of the speaker's moving lips and hand gestures.

The precedence effect makes the desired function of two-channel or stereo systems difficult. Ideally, we want a stereo system in which we hear the same source positions as we walk around in the room. But suppose the stereo channels are simply sounds picked up by two separated microphones or by a stereo microphone. The stereo channels will somehow share a component of a complicated sound from a single source. Through the precedence effect we tend to hear the complicated sound as coming from the loudspeaker nearer to us. Thus, we may hear a singing or speaking voice as coming from either the left or the right loudspeaker, even if the voice is located directly in front of us. However, disparities in sound intensity can be used to shift the sound toward the louder source.

Harris (1960) studied this effect with headphones for sinusoidal tones and for low-pass and high-pass clicks. The trade-off in decibels per millisecond time difference varies somewhat with the nature of the signal, so the use of a "left" or "right" centering control in a stereo system somewhat blurs the sense of direction, which is best for a central setting and a listener equidistant from the speakers.

The stereo channels for pop music are commonly obtained from single-channel recordings of individual instruments that are combined ingeniously to give an effect of sound localization or of being immersed in sound. One very simple way to assure a sort of immersion in sound is to filter out successive regions of the frequency spectrum and send alternate sections of the spectrum to the two stereo channels.

Various sorts of experiments give various critical time intervals that we can compare with the 50 or 60 milliseconds characteristic of the precedence effect, and the 30 or more milliseconds necessary for the perception of echoes. Rasch (1979) found that if players are not more than 30 to 50 milliseconds apart, they are perceived as playing "together." Hirsch (1959) and Patterson and Green (1970) found that when two half-second tones of different frequencies are played in succession, the order (low–high or high–low) can be heard if the time separation is more than about 20 milliseconds. But Patterson and Green also found that one can distinguish the difference in sound of a waveform played forward or backward for waveforms as short as 2 milliseconds. And, in estimating the direction of a sound source, Brian Moore (1989) showed that we can sense differences in direction that correspond to changes in relative time of arrival of the sound at our ears of as little as 10 or 20 microseconds.

The time range of some 50 to 60 milliseconds over which the precedence effect ties reflected sounds together without echo is comparable with our ability to hear differences in the time succession of musical notes rather than to our ability to make use of time differences in judging the direction of a sound source, or our ability to hear differences in the structure of short waveforms. It appears that the auditory system uses time disparity in different ways for different purposes.

8.5 Reverberation

Strong, discrete reflections of sound give echoes, which are a most objectionable phenomenon in bad concert halls. A multitude of suc-

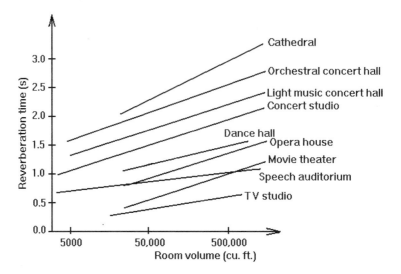

Figure 8.6 Appropriate reverberation times for enclosures of different sizes and purposes.

cessive reflections between walls that are very nearly parallel gives *flutter,* a phenomenon that "puts an edge on" voice and other complex sounds. But a multitude of small reflections that arrive at irregular times and die out smoothly constitute *reverberation,* without which music sounds dull, dry, and weak.

The reverberation in a room or hall is commonly specified by the number of seconds after which the sound produced by a short excitation has decayed by 60 dB. As indicated in figure 8.6, the optimum amount of reverberation for various musical purposes depends on the size of the enclosure and on the nature of the music. Organ music echos majestically through the stony spaces of a medieval cathedral, and so can singing if one doesn't need or want to attend to the words. More reverberation is acceptable in a concert hall than in an opera house, in which we wish to pay some attention to the details of the star's performance.

8.6 A Sense of Distance

Reverberation gives us a sense of some aspects of a room, such as the size and the materials that line the walls. It can also give us a clue to our distance from a sound source. In his book *Experiments in Hearing* (1980), Békésy notes that "In radio broadcasting it is well known that a listener in front of a loudspeaker can judge with considerable accuracy the distance of the speaker from the microphone. The greater the distance, the more reverberant are the sounds, and

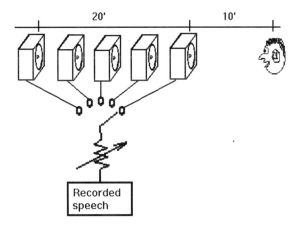

Figure 8.7 Speakers in an anechoic chamber. If intensity at the listener is the same, no matter which speaker the sound comes from, the listener will always judge it as coming from the nearest speaker.

the farther behind the loudspeaker they seem to be." Békésy references four papers published from 1927 to 1935.

Gardner (1968a) experimented with a voice from one of a sequence of visible loudspeakers in an anechoic chamber. As shown in figure 8.7, the speakers lay in the same direction from the listener, but at different distances. The levels at the speakers were adjusted so that the sound intensity at the listener's position was the same, no matter which speaker the voice came from. In the absence of reverberation, the listener always chose the nearest possible source as that of the origin of the voice. From our real-world experience, lack of reverberation means that the source is near the ear.

The addition of reverberation is a common way of controlling the apparent distance of computer-generated sound sources. Chowning (1971) and F. R. Moore (1983) have shown how reverberation and attenuation of high frequencies can be used to give clues to the apparent distance of a sound source. Usually, reverberation at the same level is used for all sound sources. Chowning also showed how the Doppler effect, the shift in frequency of a sound source moving toward or away from the hearer, can be used to give a sense of motion of a sound source.

8.7 Sense of Direction, Left or Right

Reverberation can give us a sense of the distance of a sound source, as well as a grand sense of being immersed in the sound of an orchestra. A sense of direction of a particular source is important in interpreting the sounds that reach our ears. It is through the precedence effect that we are able to sense the direction of a sound source in a closed space with reflecting walls.

In judging the direction of a sound source we make use of onsets or changes in sound that are characteristic of speech, musical notes, or noise. In a reverberant room it is nearly impossible to sense the direction of the source of a persistent sine wave.

Meaningful experiments concerning the effects of frequency on sensing the direction of a single sound source have been made by using clicks with various spectra, such as high-pass clicks or low-pass clicks. Our ability to sense the direction, left or right, of a sound source depends on the relative times of arrival and on relative intensities of the sound reaching the two ears.

The effects of differences in intensity in the two ear canals are greatest for high-frequency sounds, that is, sounds of short wavelength. Such sounds are reflected by the torso and shadowed by the head. The relative sound levels in the two ears depend, to some extent, on the direction that the head is turned. Chiefly the sound in the ear canal aimed toward the source is stronger than that in the ear canal facing away from the source.

The pinnae or outer ears cause a somewhat greater response to high-frequency sounds that are straight ahead than to high-frequency sounds from behind the head.

The relative times of arrival at the two ears are somewhat frequency dependent, but whatever the frequency, the sound arrives earlier at the ear nearer the source.

Experiments by Harris (1960), using headphones, show that there is an inverse relationship between the relative intensities at the two ears and the relative times of arrival at the two ears. This trade-off in decibels per millisecond is somewhat dependent on frequency.

For sounds with broad spectra, binaural localization in a stereo system is best when the two loudspeakers are the same distance from the listener. Through adjustment of the relative intensities of the signals in the two stereo channels, a listener who is not equidistant from the stereo speakers can hear a sound as coming from a point between the speakers, but the sense of direction may be fuzzy.

The accuracy of judgments of left or right can be amazing. Differences of around a degree can be detected. This corresponds to a disparity of only 10 microseconds in the time of arrival at the two ears.

But to get a sense that one musical note is played before or after another, the time disparity must be over a thousand times as great.

The sense of direction can be rendered fuzzy by putting the end of a finger in one ear. This has a greater effect on relative amplitude than on relative time of arrival. Fairly accurate left-or-right judgments can still be made with a finger in one ear.

8.8 Sense of Direction, Up or Down

Suppose someone makes a sound like a click or jingles keys. The location of the sound source is straight ahead of you but variable in height. In this case, there can be no difference in relative intensities at the two ears or in times of arrival. Yet a listener can tell whether the jingling or click comes from high or low. This is true for other sounds with significant high-frequency components.

Batteau (1967) pointed out that if one folds over his/her external ears, he/she completely loses the ability to tell high from low, that is, to localize high-pitched sounds in the median plane. Gardner (1973a) has published an excellent article on localization in the median plane. The chief effects of modifying the pinna occur for frequencies of 4000 Hz and higher.

Batteau thought of the effect of the pinna in terms of reflections of sound, of modifying its time waveform. The same effect can be thought of in terms of the contribution of the folds of the pinna to frequency response. Gardner (1973b) showed the variations with frequency of sound level in the auditory canal. Using a mannequin and a simulated ear, he investigated both a "normal" pinna and one whose convolutions had been occluded with a plasticine plug. He found that the crucial frequency responses appear to lie chiefly above 4,000 Hz.

There is a different effect of apparent height of a sound source in the median plane. Sounds with a strongly high-frequency spectrum can seem to have a source higher than sounds of a lower frequency spectrum.

My two stereo speakers used to be on the floor against the wall of the living room. Standing listeners heard recorded clapping sounds in Paul Lansky's composition "The Sound of Two Hands" (1992) as if the source were four or more feet from the floor, and occasional sounds of lower spectra seemed to come from the floor. This difference in apparent source height persisted when the pinnae were folded over.

8.9 Dummy Heads and Spatial Effects

Whatever spatial effects a two-channel, or even a four-channel, stereo system may provide, it cannot duplicate the entire sound field produced by one or several players in an enclosed space. Can we use headphones to produce in the two auditory canals of a listener the exact sound pressures that would reach the ears of a listener while sitting in a concert hall?

Schroeder, Gottlob, and Siebrasse (1974) addressed this problem by constructing a dummy head with appropriate pinnae and auditory canals. Microphones in the auditory canals provided two channels of sound.

By feeding the signal from the left microphone of the dummy head to a left headphone on a human listener, and feeding the signal from the right dummy microphone to the right listener headphone, we can approximate the signals in the auditory canal of a listener seated in the space in which the recording was made. Does the listener actually "hear" what he/she would have heard in the room?

The effect is better than listening to two ordinary stereo channels with headphones, but it is still not easy to get an adequate sense of a truly external sound source. If you were wearing headphones while listening to binaural signals from a dummy head, you might hear effects such as a nearby sound source behind you, or someone whispering into your ear, or the sound coming from a point within your head. Recording from one's own ear canals is better than recording from a dummy head. Some manufacturers of binaural dummy heads for research and music recording make casts of a specific set of ears, and these manufacturers will produce a binaural head with a custom set of pinnae.

Schroeder, Gottlob, and Siebrasse got more realistic results by using two loudspeakers to produce, at a given head position, the sound intensities that the left and right ears of the dummy head would have "heard" at a given head position. When this is done, the apparent source position can be to the left of the left speaker or to the right of the right speaker. This technique was used in comparing the same recorded performance as it would be heard when played on the stages of various European concert halls.

8.10 Our Perception of Noise

A great deal that is important in the hearing of music has been learned through experiments with sine waves, even though pure sine waves don't qualify as musical sounds. Gaussian noise really isn't a musical sound either, but we can learn important things through studying the perception of noise.

"Gaussian noise" is a sequence of random events smoothed by a special type of low-pass filtering. Suppose that the probability that an extremely short pulse of unit amplitude will occur in a very short time interval dt is $p*dt$. There will be an average number p of pulses per second, but the times of their occurrence will be unpredictable. If we low-pass-filter this sequence of pulses with a filter of bandwidth B, and if the number of pulses per second is large compared with $2B$, the filtered waveform will approach a Gaussian noise.

The bandwidth of a compact disc is around 20,000 Hz. We might think that for a sequence of pulses to be heard as noise, the number of pulses per second would have to be large compared with 40,000 samples per second. What do we actually hear as the pulse rate is increased?

Up to a few tens of pulses per second, we hear separate, unpredictable pulses, as in a Geiger counter. At a few hundred pulses per second we hear an erratic signal, clearly "pulsey," but we can't detect all pulses individually. Above a few thousand (say, 5000) pulses per second, we hear a "smooth" noise. Our hearing runs individual pulses together so that we no longer hear any pulse as a separate event.

This "running together" of pulses is associated with the critical bandwidth of the ear, not with the overall frequency range of hearing. Though differences in time of as little as 10 microseconds are detectable in sensing left and right in binaural hearing, random sequences of pulses run together as smooth noise when the average pulse spacing is around 0.2 millisecond, or 200 microseconds.

8.11 In Conclusion

Unlike the eye, the ear affords no direct image of the world around us. Yet, in addition to our ability to judge frequency and distance, our binaural hearing can give us an amazing amount of help in dealing with that world. Our two ears enable us to listen in a direction, partially disregarding sounds coming from other directions. We can judge vertical as well as horizontal direction of a sound source, even when the initial sound is followed by echoes from the walls of a room. Distinct echoes tell us about reflecting surfaces. A host of small reflections adds a warm quality to the sound, and also tells us

Table 8.1 Discrimination of the ear

Accuracy (just noticeable differences)
Intensity, about 1 dB
Frequency, about 10 cents (0.6 percent)

Bandwidth
Around 20,000 Hz
Critical bandwidth, around f/5 (a musical minor third)

Time resolution
Binaural azimuth, around 20 microseconds (not heard as time order, before or after)
Clicks, around 2 milliseconds (sounds different with different time order, but no sense of before or after)
Musical tones, around 20 milliseconds (sense of before or after)
Playing together (simultaneity), around 30–50 milliseconds
Echoes (clapping, voice), 50–60 milliseconds (precedence effect)

Threshold of hearing
At 3,000 Hz, around 10 watts per square meter for people with acute hearing

Dynamic range
90–120 dB at 3,000 Hz
30–60 dB at 30 Hz

Masking
Around 30 dB, but a complex set of phenomena

something of the distance of the source. Understanding such aspects of sound and our hearing can help computer musicians and composers, both in generating appropriate sounds and in evaluating and using performance spaces.

In exercising the art of music it is good to have a rough sense of some simple limitations of hearing. I have brought together a number of these limitations in table 8.1.

References

Batteau, D. W. (1967). "The Role of the Pinna in Human Localization." *Proceedings of the Royal Society of London,* B168 (1011): 159–180.

Begault, D. (1994). *3D Audio for Virtual Reality and Multimedia Applications* San Diego: Academic Press.

Békésy, G. von (1980). *Experiments in Hearing.* Huntington, N.Y.: Robert E. Krieger. (1st ed. New York: McGraw-Hill, 1960).

Bregman, A. S. (1990). *Auditory Scene Analysis.* Cambridge, Mass.: MIT Press.

Chowning, J. M. (1971). "The Simulation of Moving Sound Sources." *Journal of the Audio Engineering Society,* 199, 2–6.

Gardner, M. B. (1968a). "Proximity Effect in Sound Localization." *Journal of the Acoustical Society of America,* 43, 163–169.

———. (1968b). "Historical Background of the Haas and/or Precedence Effect." *Journal of the Acoustical Society of America,* 43, 1243–1248.

———. (1973a). "Some Monaural and Binaural Factors in Median Plane Localization." *Journal of the Acoustical Society of America,* 54, 1489–1495.

———. (1973b). "Some Single- and Multiple-Source Localization Effects." *Audio Engineering,* 21, 430–437.

Gordon, J. W. (1983). "The Perceptual Synchrony of Attack Times of Musical Tones." *Journal of the Acoustical Society of America,* 82, 88–105.

Harris, G. G. (1960). "Binaural Interactions of Impulsive and Pure Tones." *Journal of the Acoustical Society of America,* 32, 685–692.

Hirsch, I. C. (1959). "Auditory Perception of Temporal Order." *Journal of the Acoustical Society of America,* 31, 759–767.

Lansky, P. (1992). "The Sound of Two Hands." On the compact disc, *Homebrew.* Bridge Records.

Moore, B. C. J. (1989). *An Introduction to the Psychology of Hearing.* San Diego: Academic Press.

Moore, F. R. (1983). "A General Model for Spatial Processing of Sounds." *Computer Music Journal* (Fall) 7, 6–15.

Patterson, J. H., and D. M. Green. (1970). "Discrimination of Transient Signals Having Identical Energy Spectra." *Journal of the Acoustical Society of America,* 48, 121–131.

Rasch, R. A. (1979). "Synchronization in Performed Ensemble Music." *Acustica,* 43, 121–131.

Resnick, S. B., and Feth, L. L. (1975). "Discriminability of Time-Reversed Pairs of Clicks." *Journal of the Acoustical Society of America,* 57, 1493–1499.

Ronkin, D. A. (1970). "Monaural Detection of Phase Difference Between Clicks." *Journal of the Acoustical Society of America,* 47, 1091–1099.

Schroeder, M. R., D. Gottlob, and K. F. Siebrasse (1974). "Comparative Study of European Concert Halls, Correlation of Subjective Preference with Geometric and Acoustic Parameters." *Journal of the Acoustical Society of America,* 56, 1195–1201.

9 Voice Physics and Neurology

Perry R. Cook

9.1 Introduction

Why is the voice important in considering the perception of sound and music? The most fundamental sound-making devices (and musical instruments) available to humans are simple percussion instruments and the voice. For some time now the human race has possessed speech: the ability to convey abstract and complex meanings with sounds produced by the voice. Much of the brain is dedicated to producing and perceiving speech, and much of our experience is so inescapably tied into speech that we naturally filter much of our sensory input through linguistically related thought processes.

We use our speech organ to imitate other humans, animals, and machines. We use it to describe to a mechanic the odd sounds our car is making. We name animals by vocal imitations of the sounds they make: the cuckoo bird, the laughing hyena, the whippoorwill, the bobwhite, and so on. For this reason, much of our musical expression is also linked closely to the vocal organ. We name objects by related sounds: the word "fuzz" both sounds and looks fuzzy, and words such as "smooth" and "round" actually mimic in articulation the textures and shapes they describe. The chapters in this volume on vocal production and perception are intended to provide links between the vocal organ and the perception of sounds in general, and, more specifically, the perception and creation of musical sounds.

In this book, the presentation of the voice covers only those aspects that are important to later discussions. Complex acoustical, physical, and physiological descriptions can be found in other specialized references. In the material presented here, only the physiology and neurology required to give a good sense of the control and perception mechanisms will presented. Simple physical acoustics and physics are used to explain many production and perception phenomena.

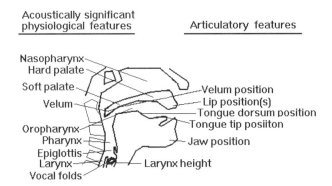

Figure 9.1 Cross-section view of the human head. Acoustically significant features are labeled on the left side, and speech articulators are labeled on the right.

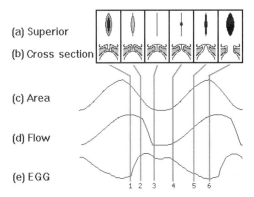

Figure 9.2 Various views of vocal fold vibration, with time proceeding left to right. (a) vocal folds from the top, looking down the throat; (b) cross section as viewed through the neck wall; (c) area of the vocal fold opening; (d) flow through the vocal folds; (e) Electroglottograph (EGG), which measures the electrical admittance between the vocal folds.

9.2 Voice Physiology

Figure 9.1 shows a simple cross-sectional view of the human head, with the acoustically significant features labeled on the left side and the speech articulators labeled on the right side.

It is clear from figure 9.2b that the vocal folds are indeed folds, not cords, as they are often called. The vibration actually takes place in (at least) two dimensions. There is an oval-shaped oscillation as viewed from the top looking down the throat, and a vertical opening and closing motion as viewed from the front, looking inward through the neck wall.

As shown in figure 9.3, the main physiological components that are responsible for control of the vocal folds are the arytenoid cartilage and muscles, to which the vocal folds are attached. These struc-

Vocal fold adduction and abduction

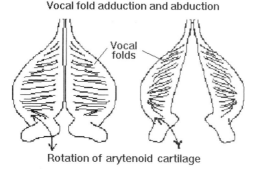

Rotation of arytenoid cartilage

Figure 9.3 Rough drawing of the vocal folds, showing how the rotation of the arytenoid cartilage pulls the vocal folds together (adduction) and apart (abduction).

tures are responsible for bringing the vocal folds together to cause them to oscillate (beat together). This bringing together is called "adduction." Pulling the vocal folds apart, called "abduction," causes the voice source to cease oscillation. These terms can be remembered by their relation to the words "addiction" and "abstinence" (from the Latin *addicere* and *abstinere*).

The vocal folds oscillate when they are adducted, the breath pressure from the lungs forces them apart, and the resulting flow and decrease in breath pressure between the glottal folds allows them to move back together. It was once thought that the brain sent specific instructions to the vocal folds each cycle, to open and close them. This is a flawed notion when viewed in comparison with musical instrument oscillators, such as the lips of the brass player or the reed of the clarinet. The brain of a clarinetist doesn't send explicit instructions to the wooden reed to move each cycle. Both the vocal folds and the clarinet reed oscillate because of basic physics and the constant energy provided by the breath pressure of the player/singer.

The other physiological components that are important to speech will be covered from the standpoint of their functional articulatory use. The main articulators are the following:

- The tongue
- The lips
- The jaw
- The velum
- The position (height) of the larynx.

Most people are fairly familiar with manipulations of their tongue, lips, and jaw in speech, but much less so with the control of their velum and larynx height. The velum is a small flap of skin in the back of the throat that controls the amount of sound and air that is allowed to enter the nasal passages. If you say the sound 'ng' (as in sing) with the back of your tongue as far back as possible, your velum and tongue will touch, and all of the sound will come from your nose.

Control of larynx height allows human speakers to change the effective length of the vocal tract, thus giving a perception of a smaller or larger head on the part of the speaker. The voices of many cartoon characters have a characteristic high tenor quality, produced by raising the larynx. Large, intimidating vocal qualities like that of *Star Wars'* Darth Vader are produced with a lowered larynx. Most people are not aware of their control over larynx height, but when we talk to babies or pets, we often raise our larynx and talk high and fast to show approval or excitement, and we lower our larynx to show disapproval and become more intimidating. Good singers and professional actors with flexible control over their voice can produce a large range of sounds and voices by varying, among other things, the height of their larynx.

9.3   Vocal Tract Acoustics

The vocal folds behave as an oscillator driven by the breath pressure. The force that causes the vocal folds to close, the Bernoulli force, is the same force that lifts airplanes and causes a piece of paper to rise when you blow across it. In the voice, the high flow rate of the air rushing between the vocal folds causes the pressure to drop, and the vocal folds are sucked shut. Different types of voiced vocal sounds (called phonation qualities) are related by how closely the vocal folds are held together. The more tightly pressed together they are, the brighter the sound produced by the vocal fold oscillator. Also, in general, the louder the phonation (higher airflow), the brighter the sound produced by the vocal folds, as shown in figure 9.4. This is due to the increased velocity of vocal fold closure.

The vocal folds are often compared to the reed of the clarinet. There is one important difference between the function and behavior of the vocal folds and the clarinet reed, and thus resulting differences in the behaviors of the clarinet and the voice. Before discussing that difference, some fundamentals about the acoustics of tubes and pipes need to be covered.

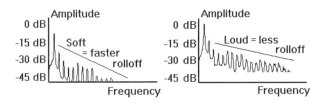

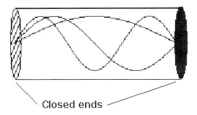

Figure 9.4 Spectra of soft (left) and loud (right) sung tones. The spectrum decreases less with frequency in the loud sung tone, making it sound brighter as well as louder

Figure 9.5 A tube, closed at both ends, and the first three modes of oscillation

As was discussed in section 4.4 for the case of vibrating strings, pipes and tubes also exhibit *modes,* or "favored frequencies" of oscillation. A tube that is closed at both ends is analogous to the vibrating string anchored at both ends. The flow velocity at a closed end must be zero at the end point (no air can flow through the closed end), like the displacement at both ends of a vibrating string. Such points are called "nodes." Any frequency that exhibits the correct nodal pattern (at the end points of a closed tube, for example) will be supported by the tube, and is thus a mode of that tube. Thus, as shown in figure 9.5, the modes of a pipe with two closed ends are integer multiples of a fundamental, which is one half-cycle of a sine wave whose wavelength is twice the length of the tube. A tube that is open at both ends will exhibit the same modes, but with antinodes at both ends.

The fundamental mode can be computed by the simple relationship

$$F_1 = c/l/2, \tag{9.1}$$

where c = the speed of sound (about 1100 feet/second in air) and l is the length of the tube.

Another important analytic result related to modal analysis is the transfer function. The transfer function of a linear system describes what happens to a signal traveling through that system. In our case

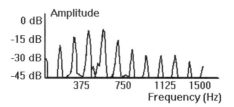

Figure 9.6 Experimentally measured transfer function of a 4-foot tube open at both ends.

the system is an acoustic tube, and our interest is eventually to describe what happens to the waveform coming from the vocal folds as it proceeds through the vocal tract acoustic tube and out through the lips. A common and powerful representation of the transfer function is a graph of gain versus frequency, representing how much a sine wave at each frequency would be amplified or attenuated in going through the system. The most important perceptual features are the peaks in the transfer function, since these are the features to which our ears are most sensitive. The modal frequencies of an acoustic tube exhibit the most gain in the transfer function, with the regions between exhibiting lower gains. The modal resonance peaks in the transfer function are called *formants.*

To investigate resonant formants experimentally, find a tube about 4 feet long, and sing through it. As you sweep your voice frequency slowly up and down, you will find frequencies that are reinforced, or easier to sing, and others that seem difficult to sing. The easy frequencies are the modal formants, or peaks in the transfer function, as shown in figure 9.6.

The oral portion of the vocal tract is essentially a tube that is closed at the vocal fold end and open at the lip end. Assuming that this tube is straight and has uniform shape, the modal solutions are those that exhibit a node at one end and an antinode at the other, as shown in figure 9.7. The modes that satisfy those conditions are all odd multiples of one quarter-cycle of a sine wave, and thus the frequencies are all odd multiples of a fundamental mode F_1, computed by

$$F_1 = c/l/4. \tag{9.2}$$

Using $l = 9$ in. as a human vocal tract length in equation 9.2, the modal frequencies are 375 Hz, 1125 Hz, 2075 Hz, and so on. A transfer function of such a tube is shown in figure 9.7.

The vibrational modes of an acoustic tube that are computed from the end conditions (open or closed) are called longitudinal modes.

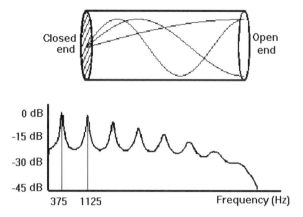

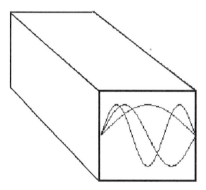

Figure 9.7 Upper: a tube, closed at one end and open at the other, and the first three modes of vibration. Lower: magnitude transfer function of the tube.

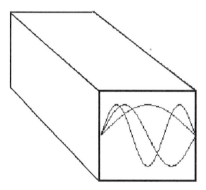

Figure 9.8 The first three cross modes of a rectangular tube. If our vocal tract were in this shape, and 2 in. wide, the frequencies of these first three modes would be 3000, 6000, and 9000 Hz.

The assumption that the longitudinal modes and transfer function are the most significant is based two things: 1) the tube is much longer than it is wide, and 2) the lower frequency modes are perceptually dominant.

The next significant modes would be the cross modes, but how significant are they? For simplicity, if we assume that the tube cross section is a square, as shown in figure 9.8, 2 inches on each side, the cross-modal frequencies, as computed using equation 9.1, are 3000 Hz, 6000 Hz, and so on. Even assuming a 3 inch cross-sectional dimension, the lowest cross-modal frequency is 2000 Hz, which is near the third longitudinal mode frequency of 2075 Hz. The tube diameter in normal speech never approaches 3 in., and thus the first cross mode is always significantly above the first three longitudinal resonances of the vocal tract, which are considered to be the most important for understanding speech.

The modes of an acoustic tube can be changed in frequency by changing the shape of the tube. Some simple rules for modal behavior as a function of tube manipulation are the following:

1. Narrowing the tube at a point
a. Raises the frequency of any mode that exhibits an antinode at that point, and
b. Lowers the frequency of any mode that exhibits a node at that point.
2. Widening the tube at a point.
a. Lowers the frequency of any mode that exhibits an antinode at that point, and
b. Raises the frequency of any mode that exhibits a node at that point.

These rules form the acoustical basis for the human ability to form vowels, and thus our ability to convey information through speech. By changing the shape of the vocal tract acoustic tube, we move the natural resonant frequencies of the tube. The tube acts as a filter for the voice source, shaping the spectrum of the source according to the gain-versus-frequency relationship described by the transfer function.

In the experiment of singing through a 4-foot-long tube, we found that while we could sing any frequency, some were easier to sing and some were harder. The vocal tract is much shorter than 4 feet (for all of the humans I know), and thus most or all of the formant frequencies lie above the frequency of the speaking voice source (about 100 Hz in males and about 150 Hz in females).

In the voice, the vocal folds are free to oscillate at any frequency (within a reasonable range of 50–1500 Hz), and the transfer function acts to shape the spectrum of the harmonics of the voice source. The resulting sound coming from the lips is modified by the vocal tract transfer function, often called the vocal tract filter.

The basis of the source/filter model of the vocal mechanism is depicted in figure 9.9. The voice source generates a complex waveform at some frequency that is controlled by the human speaker/singer. The vocal tract filter shapes the spectrum of the source according to a transfer function determined by the shape of the vocal tract acoustic tube, also under control of the human speaker/singer. The result is a harmonic spectrum with the overall shape of the transfer function determined by the shape of the vocal tract.

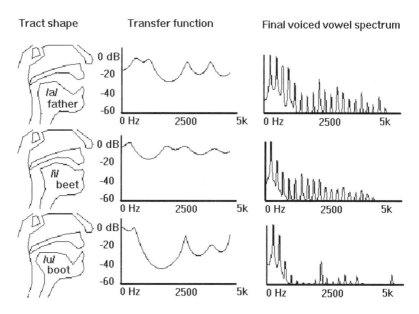

Figure 9.9 Three vocal tract shapes, transfer functions, and voice output spectra.

With what we now know about voice acoustics, we can point out a fundamental difference between the human voice and instruments like the clarinet. In the case of the voice, the source has the ability to oscillate at essentially any frequency, and the vocal tract tube can change shape, grossly modifying the final spectrum coming from the lips. The clarinetist can modify the resonant structure of the instrument by changing the configurations of the tone holes, but the source follows along by oscillating at a new frequency. In such a system, it is said that the coupling between the reed source and bore filter is strong, meaning that the player has trouble controlling the source independently of the filter. In the voice the coupling is weak, so we are able to sing arbitrary pitches on arbitrary vowels, in arbitrary combinations, to make speech and song.

Of course, we are able to make sounds other than vowels, such as nasalized sounds, consonants, and the like. By lowering the velum to open the nasal passage, another tube is opened, another set of resonances becomes active, and a nasalized sound results. Another important phenomenon related to resonance, called cancellation, becomes active when a vocal sound is nasalized. This will be covered in a later chapter.

Many consonant sounds are caused by noise in the vocal tract, as shown in figure 9.10. When a constriction is formed and air travels

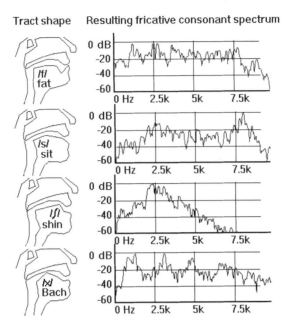

Figure 9.10 Vocal tract shapes and spectra for four unvoiced fricatives.

through it, there is a possibility of turbulence. The likelihood of turbulence increases with increasing airflow, and it also increases with decreasing constriction. The final spectrum of the noise is related to two things: the turbulence itself, and the vocal tract tube downstream from the source of noise.

The high frequency content of the turbulent noise increases with increasing airflow and with decreasing constriction. This is easily tested by forming the sound /s/ (as in sing) and first modulating your breath pressure up and down, then moving your tongue slightly up and down. The effects of the acoustic tube on the final spectrum are described by the same transfer function concept used to express the relationship between voiced vowel sounds. To test this, form a /sh/ sound (as in shift) and move your lips around. You are not changing the turbulence much, just the resonance properties of the tube downstream. Sounds such as /s/ and /sh/ are called *unvoiced fricatives,* and sounds such as /z/ and /v/ are called *voiced fricatives.*

9.4 Voice System Neurology

The two areas of the brain that have well-documented specific speech functions are Broca's area in the frontal lobe and Wernike's

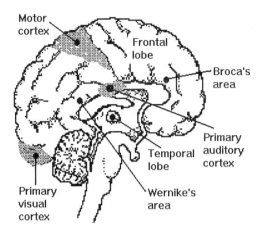

Figure 9.11 Areas of the human brain related to speech and language.

area in the temporal lobe, as shown in figure 9.11. In general, the left half of the brain is dominant for language functions. This is most so in right-handed males, and least so in left-handed females.

Much of what we know about the function of the brain comes from case studies of people who experienced some type of nonfatal brain injury, so we can speak about how an injury to a specific region of the brain causes a specific impairment of function. Brain injuries resulting in speech or language impairments are called *aphasias.* Damage to Broca's area leads to impaired grammatical speech production but relatively unimpaired comprehension. Damage to Wernike's area causes impaired comprehension but possibly fluent speech with grammatically correct inflections. Of course, this specialization is not clear-cut: case studies of injuries are individual and as unpredictable as the accidents that caused the injuries.

Reading seems to piggyback on oral speech production, as shown in some case studies of injuries where phonetic syllabary-based reading (English or the Japanese written language kana) was impaired in addition to speech. In ideographic or pictographic written languages like Chinese or the Japanese kanji, the symbols are related to nonphonetic higher-level concepts (a symbol for the entire concept of sunrise, for example), and thus comprehension can be impaired without affecting reading ability.

A related but different phenomenon of aphasia is amusia, which is a brain injury resulting in impairment of musical ability, either comprehension or production. The French composer Maurice Ravel experienced both aphasia and amusia from brain disease in 1932, and remained both musically unproductive and speech-impaired until his death in 1937. It would seem natural that the brain functions for language and musical processing could be quite closely linked, and indeed they are in many ways. They are quite independent in many other ways, however. The composer Vissarion Shebalin became aphasic from a stroke but composed quite well in his own style for many years thereafter.

Of course the question of ability and competency, both linguistically and musically, has a lot to do with exposure, training, and memory. Chapter 17 will discuss more on the topic of memory for musical events, and case studies of brain injuries as they affect language and musical abilities.

Many interesting distinctions can be found in the processing of language in speech versus music. Sometimes singers perform songs with words in languages with which they are generally unfamiliar, and thus the performance is more like playing an instrument than speaking a language. In these cases the singer is often just rerunning a rehearsed motor program, not spontaneously trying to convey a new abstract meaning to another person on a personal level. Singing has been used successfully as a therapy for persons with profound stuttering disorders; it seems that the rhythm allows the stutterer to form the words more fluently than if the rhythmic constraint were not present. Some aphasics have lost speech but retained their ability to sing songs they knew before their brain injury, and some are even able to learn and sing new songs while unable to speak in a fluent manner.

9.5 Conclusion

We use our voices to communicate with both words and descriptive sounds. A fundamental understanding of how the voice works, both acoustically and neurologically, allows us to study aspects of perception and production of sound later in this book.

References

Gardner, H. (1983). *Frames of Mind: The Theory of Multiple Intelligences*. New York: Basic Books. A reference on brain function in linguistics and music.

O'Shaughnessy, D. (1987). *Speech Communication: Human and Machine*. Reading, Mass.: Addison-Wesley. A good engineering overview of voice analysis and processing.

Sundberg, J. (1987). *The Science of the Singing Voice*. DeKalb: Northern Illinois University Press. An excellent book on singing research.

10 Stream Segregation and Ambiguity in Audition

Roger Shepard

10.1 Introduction

This chapter will discuss some aspects of the perception of musical sounds. Chapter 3 provided some general analogies between visual and auditory perception, covering such things as the Gestalt principles of grouping: proximity, similarity, good continuation, and common fate. Common fate was illustrated with demonstrations in the visual and auditory domains. Other grouping principles can be illustrated, too. For example, one could group a set of tones so that some are closer together than others; the perceptual result is that the closer tones are perceived as "belonging with" the near neighbors. This is an example of grouping by *proximity.* Imagine four tones, equally spaced in time, two of them close in pitch and the other two far apart. The two that are close in pitch will become grouped by *similarity.* If pairs are alternately similar and dissimilar in timbre, such as a pair of trumpet tones alternating with a pair consisting of a vocal vowel and a drum sound, the trumpet pair will group by *similarity.*

The principles of grouping enable us to parse the stream of information entering our sensory systems into sensations associated with discrete objects belonging to the external world. Grouping by common fate is a powerful cue that allows us to form a mental representation of an object or group of objects in the external world. An example in the auditory domain would consist of an alternation between a single pure tone and a complex tone having two components. If two sinusoidal tones are beeps that begin and end at the same time, *common fate* applies; it indicates that the two tones are in some way associated with the same object in the real world. If two things are highly correlated, they are highly likely to have emerged from the same source, whereas if two things are asynchronous, they are likely to be associated with two different objects.

10.2 Apparent Motion

If three tones that are far apart in pitch are alternated slowly enough, you can track a melodic pattern in the sequence. As the sequence is played faster and faster, a point is reached when the three tones no longer make up a melody, and in fact the order of the three tones becomes perceptually indeterminate. The pitches and order remain the same, but with increasing speed it becomes more and more difficult perceptually to make the transitions between the large pitch leaps; you then begin to hear the beeping tones as individual streams. As the speed continues to increase, the percept becomes one of hearing individual groups of beeps, boops, and the like associated with each tone.

This is a general perceptual principle; it is not unique to the auditory perceptual system. The term used for this effect in the visual domain is *apparent motion,* which can be seen in an example where two rapidly alternating dots are perceived as a single dot moving from one location to the other. A general principle that has evolved in our perceptual systems is that objects tend to be conserved; this demonstrates Helmholtz's principle of *unconscious inference.* According to this principle, if there is a stimulus at one position on the retina, the mind constructs whichever process in the world would be most probable, given a particular sensory stimulation. In the case of two alternating dots, the most probable explanation is that one dot is changing location rather than that one dot is dematerializing and another just like it is suddenly materializing in a location different but quite near that of the first. So the principle of object conservation is active in various demonstrations of apparent motion. If the dots are farther apart, you can still get the sensation of motion; but as the speed increases, a point is reached when the motion percept breaks down and you perceive two dots flashing independently. This principle, known as *Korte's third law,* is named after another Gestalt psychologist.

Siegmund Exner, a student of Helmholtz, was the first to demonstrate and systematically study the apparent motion phenomenon. The Gestalt psychologists took up the topic because they were interested in the organizing properties of the brain, that is, how the brain imposes order on sensory stimulation. Visual apparent motion was a particularly nice case to study for the Gestaltists, because there is no actual motion in the experiment or stimuli presentation. There is simply a presentation of one static object, removal of that object, and presentation of another static object. The brain constructs the experience of motion between the two object locations; since no motion is actually present, the visual apparent motion experiment represents a particularly pure demonstration of the organizing principles of the brain as it works to organize and explain the stimuli in accordance with something that might exist in the world.

Korte's third law can be further demonstrated in the auditory domain. When two tones closely spaced in pitch (by 6–13% or a musical minor or major second) are alternated slowly, the pattern is clearly perceived as a melody, that is, there is a clear motion between the two pitches. If the tones are separated farther, say to a musical fifth (50%), as long as the alternation rate is slow enough, the melody or motion percept is retained. A slow rate in this case is about 2 Hz, where one tone is heard every second or so.

If the rate is increased to a medium speed of about 4–5 Hz, the small interval between the two tones is still perceived as a melody, and the large interval between the pairs of tones could be perceived either as a melody or as two independent rhythmic beepings of the two individual tones. If the rate is increased to 8 Hz, the small interval sounds like a musical trill or rapid melodic figure, while the large interval is nearly impossible to perceive as a melody because the two notes segregate into different beeping patterns.

This is analogous to apparent motion in the visual domain in the following way. Remember that when a light is flashed first in one location and then in another, and when the spacing between the lights and the timing between successive flashes is just right, the illusion of motion is created. However, at very rapid rates of alternation no motion is seen because the light flashes segregate into two separate *streams*. Observers report that they can see only rapid flashings of the two lights, and that the lights seem to be flashing independently. Of course, at very slow alternation rates, in both the auditory and the visual domains, no motion is perceived either. If two tones are played in succession, but with a very large time interval between them, we don't hear the two tones as comprising a melody; we hear them as being unrelated, single tones. Similarly, in the visual domain, two lights that flash in very slow alternation do not seem related. Figure 10.1 shows two visual stimuli in two locations,

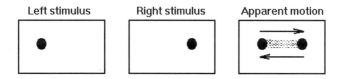

Left stimulus   Right stimulus   Apparent motion

Figure 10.1   If two visual stimuli alternate fast enough, a sense of motion between the two points is formed. The farther apart the two points are, the faster the alternation must be to give the sense of apparent motion.

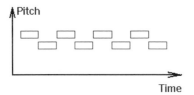

Time

Figure 10.2   Auditory analogy to the apparent motion phenomenon shown in figure 10.1.

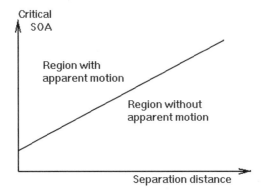

Separation distance

Figure 10.3   Relationship between distance and alternation time for apparent motion, demonstrating Korte's third law.

and illustrates how apparent motion can occur if the two visual stimuli alternate quickly enough.

In figure 10.2, if time increases toward the right, and pitch increases upward, the two pitches would be analogous to the two visual dots. If they are close enough together, one continuous stream is formed. If they are far enough apart, the pattern breaks apart and two separate streams are formed.

Figure 10.3 shows typical data for the visual case demonstrating Korte's third law, including the minimum separation between two dots for which we would perceive a dot moving back and forth. An observer would perceive motion for anything above the line. For anything below the line, an observer would see two dots going off and on independently. The relationship between time and distance is virtually a linear relationship. A similar linear relationship is observed in the data for auditory pitch.

10.3   Pitch, Time, and Amplitude: The Separation Phenomenon

I will later argue that pitch and time are the most important attributes in audition and music. Of course other attributes of tones are also important, such as timbre and spatial location, but most would agree that time and pitch are the most basic. There are fundamental reasons for this that will be discussed later.

One relevant fact is that melodies tend to move in small steps. For example, in a sample of 3000 English folk songs, 68% of the melodic transitions were no larger than one diatonic step, and 91% were no larger than two diatonic steps (minor or major second, with frequencies spaced 6% or 13% apart). The reasons for this are obvious, given Korte's third law: if steps were large and rapid, the melody would not be perceived as a stream but would segregate into separate entities.

An example of this, which occurs in the human voice, is the rapid and rhythmical leaps that take place in yodeling. The singer alternates between the head and chest voice modes of production, and the leaps are large and rapid (often greater than 60% at a 7 Hz alternation rate). The high notes and low notes of yodeling are often perceived as two separate streams.

An example that illustrates this phenomenon involves interleaving two melodies so that the notes of each melody alternate. That is, the first note of melody 1 is played, then the first note of melody 2 is played, then the second note of melody 1 is played, then the second note of melody 2, and so on. If the relative range of the melodies is such that the interleaved patterns contain small leaps, the individual melodies are not recognized, even though they might be quite familiar tunes. As one or the other melody is transposed so that it is farther and farther from the other, a point is reached when both melodies are recognized. The connection from each tone to the next is a function of proximity and time. It becomes easier to identify and connect the alternating tones of each melody when the separation between the notes of both melodies together gets large enough (figure 10.4). This can perhaps be visually effective with two musical scores, one with the two interleaved in the same pitch range, and the other with them separated by an octave and beamed separately.

Dimensions other than pitch can be used to illustrate apparent motion and separation phenomena. Timbre is an appropriate dimension. For example, where a trumpet timbre alternates notes with a violin sound, it is easy to separate the two melodies. If the alternating melodies are both played by only the trumpet or the violin, however, the melodies are difficult to separate. Perhaps more interesting is the case where two streams are separated on the basis of loudness. This can give a paradoxical effect, because two streams that are close

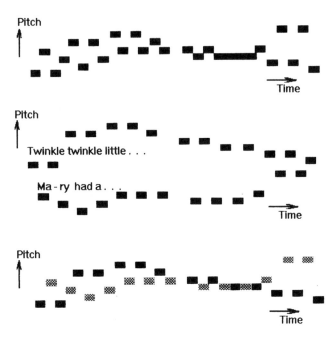

Figure 10.4 (Top) Overlapped melodies cannot be separated even though they alternate in time. (Center) Separation in pitch allows the two melodies to be easily identified. (Bottom) Visually, the melodies can be more easily identified if they are separated in color; in audition this is like separating them in timbre (playing them on different instruments) or volume.

in pitch, and thus hard to separate, can be perceptually "improved" by making one softer than the other. The paradox is that the softer stream is easier to hear in some sense, even though it is made less loud. One usually thinks in terms of making something louder in order to make it more likely to be heard, but in this example something is made easier to hear by making it softer. The visual analog to timbre or loudness is shown in figure 10.4, where making one melody another color makes both easily identifiable.

Warren and Warren (1970) constructed sequences of successive tones of different timbres that are called *Warren loops*. When the tones are separate in timbre, they are difficult to hear as a coherent stream, and tones with the same timbre segregate out from the stream and are heard independently. Further, when repeating sequences of three or four tones are used, the order of the tones becomes difficult to identify. The analog in the visual domain is to present rapidly repeating sequences of different colors: observers are easily able to identify the colors being presented, but are not able to identify the *order* of the colors. A repeating sequence of three suc-

Figure 10.5 A reversible optical illusion.

cessive notes possessing similar timbres might be easy to identify as to the notes and order, while assigning different timbres to the notes might make it more difficult to identify the order of the sequences.

10.4 Ambiguity and Music

When we investigate examples of tone patterns that present the possibility of multiple perceptual results, or can be heard one way or another, the term *ambiguity* is appropriate. Ambiguity in perception means that the same physical stimulus can give rise to different perceptual interpretations on different occasions. In the visual domain, the famous reversible optical illusions are examples of visually ambiguous stimuli (figure 10.5). In such examples, it is virtually impossible to maintain more than one interpretation at once: the image is either two faces or a candlestick; it cannot be both. The stimulus is equally consistent with both interpretations, so both satisfy Helmholtz's principle; however, both interpretations cannot coexist because such things do not occur in the real world. *Sara Nader* (figure 10.6) is either a man playing the saxophone or a woman's face, but not both. The musical example of "Mary Had a Little Lamb" and "Twinkle, Twinkle, Little Star" (figure 10.4) exhibited a pitch spacing at which ambiguous interpretations could exist.

One of the reasons that some kinds of music have a lasting quality is that they contain some inherent ambiguity. Many composers have been aware of this phenomenon, and have constructed music based on these principles. Bach in particular included ambiguity in his compositions. Figure 10.7 shows an excerpt from Bach's Violin Partita (BWV 1004). Melodic leaps of a sufficient size can cause music to be interpreted in different ways. In this Bach example, only a

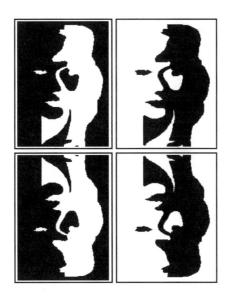

Figure 10.6 Sara Nader: woman or sax player?

Figure 10.7 This section of solo violin music by J. S. Bach shows examples of Gestalt grouping and stream segregation.

single note is played at any given time, but the pitch arrangement and alternation of low with high notes cause multiple submelodic streams to be perceived.

10.5 Shepard Tones

Suppose that one were to construct a complex tone such that all of the sinusoidal components were spaced one octave from each other (so that the frequencies of an A might be 27.5, 55, 110, 220, 440, 880 Hz, etc.). Further, the sinusoidal components of this tone are constructed such that the lowest and highest components have lower amplitudes, and the components in the middle of the frequency spectrum are loudest. Since the components at each end extend beyond the range of hearing, and spectral amplitude is a smooth function that exhibits a broad peak in the center of the frequency range, such a spectrum would be ambiguous in pitch. Some people have come to call ambiguous tones that are constructed in this way "Shepard tones" (figure 10.8). You might remember Shepard tones from chapter 5, but they are particularly applicable here because they help to illustrate a number of musically ambiguous cases. We will use them in chapter 13 to motivate a number of concepts and studies regarding the perception and description of pitch.

The musical note A described above might be perceived as 55, 110, 220 Hz, and so on, and might change from presentation to presentation even for the same hearer. If a listener was presented a tone of this type, followed by another tone exactly halfway between the original tone and the octave above, the second tone might be perceived as above *or* below the first tone.

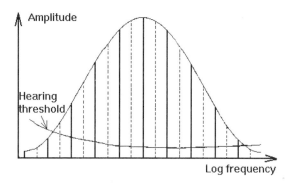

Figure 10.8 Shepard tone spectrum (Reprinted with permission from Shepard 1964. © 1964 Acoustical Society of America.)

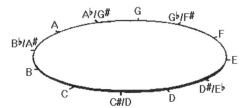

Figure 10.9   With Shepard tones, moving directly across the circle (a musical tritone) is ambiguous as to whether the motion is up or down.

Often a listener who initially perceived the tone sequence as ascending can be convinced to hear it as descending by playing a scale consisting of intermediate tones beginning with the original first tone and ending with the original second tone. Filling in the scale between the two original tones provides direction for the sequence; when the two original tones are presented after the scale, many listeners will then hear them as going in the same direction as the scale. Playing an ascending scale tends to cause listeners to hear the two-tone sequence that follows as ascending.

The tendency to hear a given pair of ambiguous Shepard tones as ascending or descending is a fairly stable attribute of individual subjects. A circle composed of such tones, as shown in figure 10.9, can be used to categorize individual differences in perception of the ambiguous tones because people tend to split the circle along different lines. Diana Deutsch (1992) has shown that such differences are linked to speaking pitch and native language, among other factors.

These discussions of separation phenomona, ambiguity, and Shepard tones demonstrate that apparent motion examples exist in audition and can be quite striking and profound. Visual apparent motion has been studied for a long time. Examples of spatial and temporal presentations where a trajectory is perceived between two dots are well known. However, the notion of apparent motion in pitch space was dismissed by many because it seemed ludicrous that a glissando could be hallucinated between two presented pitches. Pitch was assumed to be a rectilinear attribute. It was argued that a tone could move only up or down, and it should be clear that it traversed the path between. The tones described above make it clear that the apparent motion phenomenon in pitch space is ambiguous; the pitch obviously moved, and obviously ended in a particular place, but could have taken one of two paths. No transition was perceptually synthesized between, but the mental representation allowed only either upward or downward motion to be perceived. The same fundamental laws as Korte's third law apply in this case.

10.6 Conclusion

It should not be surprising that some of the same underlying perceptual principles apply to more than one sensory domain. After all, our sensory systems evolved to respond to stimuli that exist in the same physical environment, regardless of the sensory modality employed. The smell, touch, and sight of a flower work in complementary ways to create a mental representation of the object in the world. And many of us are familiar with the interaction of the senses. Without smelling it first, an apple is often indistinguishable in taste from an onion.

Some differences between the senses are to be expected because of the different ways our sensory transducers pick up the information. The important thing to remember is that our senses of hearing and vision, as well as of taste, smell, and touch, are designed to give us information about the same objects in the physical world.

References

Bregman, A. S. (1990). *Auditory Scene Analysis*. Cambridge, Mass.: MIT Press.

Dawson, M. R. (1991). "The How and Why of What Went Where in Apparent Motion: Modeling Solutions to the Motion Correspondence Problem." *Psychological Review,* 98(4): 569–603.

Deutsch, D. (1992). "The Tritone Paradox: Implications for the Representation and Communication of Pitch Structure." In M. R. Jones and S. Holleran, eds., *Cognitive Bases of Musical Communication*. Washington, D.C.: American Psychological Association.

Kolers, P. (1972). *Aspects of Motion Perception*. New York: Pergamon Press.

Shepard, R. N. (1990). *Mind Sights: Original Visual Illusions, Ambiguities, and Other Anomalies*. New York: W. H. Freeman.

Warren, R. M., and R. P. Warren (1970). "Auditory Illusions and Confusions." *Scientific American,* 233, 30–36.

11 Formant Peaks and Spectral Valleys

Perry R. Cook

11.1 Standing Waves and Resonance

One definition of musical acoustics is that it is a science involved with the production, transmission, reception, and processing (perception) of sound waves in air, wood, and other media. In chapter 9 we discussed and derived the behavior of modes, or resonances of the vocal tract acoustic tube. These modes are the result of standing waves. As shown in figures 11.1 and 11.2, waves coming from a sound source reflect back and forth, and can add "constructively" to make a stationary standing wave of much higher magnitude than the original source wave's magnitude.

The conditions of figures 11.1 and 11.2 are true only because the frequency of the point source was selected to yield a strong standing wave pattern given the spacing of the two walls. This will be the case for all integer multiples of the base fundamental resonant frequency (as we derived in the case of the acoustic tube, open or closed at both ends). However, if we inspect the behavior of the base standing wave frequency multiplied by 1.5 (see figures 11.3 and

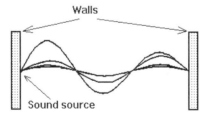

Figure 11.1 Standing wave patterns for source located at left wall, for first four trips across the room.

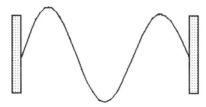

Figure 11.2 Resultant sum of reflected waves of figure 11.1.

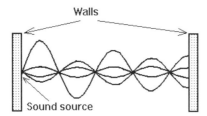

Figure 11.3 Standing wave patterns, source frequency different from figure 11.1.

Figure 11.4 Resultant sum of reflected waves of figure 11.3.

11.4), we see that reflecting waves cancel rather than add, causing a much weaker sound field than in the optimal standing wave case, and even weaker than the original wave emitted by the sound source.

11.2 Destructive Interference, Anti-Resonances

Looking at a simple case of a single point source of sound, a single point receiver (an ear or microphone), and a single boundary like a floor, we can see that the wave coming from the point source has two paths to follow in getting to the pickup: the direct path and the path reflected from the boundary. At certain frequencies these add to create a sound that is louder at the pickup than if the direct sound were the only path, but at other frequencies the two sound paths add in a way that causes them to nearly cancel at the location of the pickup. The phenomena of addition and subtraction of waves are called *constructive interference* and *destructive interference,* respectively. The pickup is said to be at a resonant node in space in the case where the two waves add destructively and there is little sound, and it is at an antinode when they add constructively, causing a louder sound. Figure 11.5 shows a case of destructive interference.

The frequencies causing constructive interference create peaks in the spectrum, like the formants discussed in chapter 9, thus reinforcing those frequencies if they are present in the source signal. The

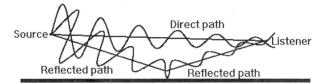

Figure 11.5 Destructive interference.

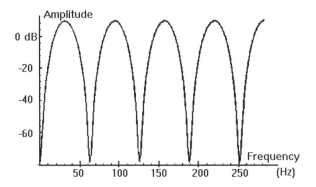

Figure 11.6 Transfer function showing anti-resonances.

frequencies that cause destructive interference create deep valleys, sometimes nearly canceling the sound entirely. These cancellation frequencies are called *anti-resonances*. Figure 11.6 shows a transfer function exhibiting anti-resonances at regular frequency intervals, as might be generated by the conditions of figure 11.5. Anti-resonances arise whenever there are multiple paths from a source to a listener. In real-life acoustical circumstances there are almost always multiple paths, because at least the ground reflection is always present.

11.3 Nasalized Vowels

In the case of the voice, there is one path from the vocal folds to the lip output point only if the velum is raised sufficiently to cut off sound entering the nasal cavities. If the velum is lowered, sound can get out of the head in two (or more) ways: through the lips and through the nose. If bilateral symmetry is not present, then there is actually a discrete path through each nostril, but usually symmetry is assumed. When the velum is open and multiple sound paths are present, anti-resonances appear in the vocal tract transfer function. The anti-resonances are often called *zeroes* by engineers, because

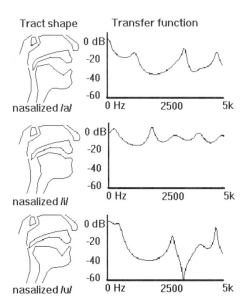

Tract shape   Transfer function

nasalized /a/

nasalized /i/

nasalized /u/

Figure 11.7   Vocal tract shapes and transfer function spectra for three nasalized vowels. Note how the spectra are distorted, compared with the nonnasalized vowels of figure 9.9.

the gain of the transfer function is small (very close to zero) at these frequencies. Engineers also have a term for resonances (formants). Resonant formants are often called *poles,* corresponding to tent poles that hold up the resonant peaks in the transfer function. The regions hanging off to the sides of formants are often called *skirts.* Figure 11.7 shows three nasalized vocal tract vowel shapes and the corresponding transfer functions.

Three vocal sounds that are purely nasal are /m/, /n/, and /ng/, as in mom, non, and sing. Figure 11.8 shows the three vocal tract shapes and transfer functions corresponding to those vocal sounds. Note that the /ng/ spectrum appears to have no zeroes. This is because the velum is lowered and the back of the tongue is raised so far that they join, effectively cutting off the oral path of the vocal tract and leaving only the all-pole (resonance) transfer function of the nasopharynx.

11.4   Resonances and Anti-Resonances in Rooms

In the case of simple resonances, the sounds at certain frequencies are increased in magnitude, but in the case of anti-resonances, the sound can be completely canceled at one or more points in space. The human ear is sensitive to resonances (formants in speech), their

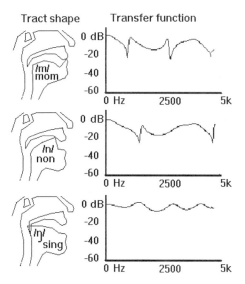

Figure 11.8 Vocal tract shapes and transfer function spectra for three purely nasal vocal sounds.

locations, and especially their movements. The human ear is only weakly sensitive to anti-resonances, which, if an accident, is at least fortunate for us. To convey speech sounds, we move the resonances of our vocal tract around to form formant patterns that are recognized as vowels. When we cause sounds to become nasalized, we manipulate the zeroes in controlled ways, but the zeroes that arise in normal listening situations are not under our control. Try listening to the speech of a friend in a room when he/she is walking around. You will have no trouble understanding what the person is saying although the resonances and anti-resonances are moving profoundly, due to the changing path lengths from his/her mouth to your ears. There are essentially two reasons that we are still able to understand our friend even though he/she and the resultant transfer function zeroes, are moving:

1. The resonances caused by multiple paths in rooms are more dense and move much more slowly than the vocal tract formants.
2. Humans are largely insensitive to anti-resonances.

Anti-resonances often create nearly complete cancellations (zeroes) at certain frequencies, but since we are more sensitive to formant peaks, we hardly ever notice the zeroes, and then only as tonal quality changes rather than as causing us to mistakenly perceive an incorrect vowel.

Table 11.1 Table of male vowel speech sounds and the first three formant frequencies

SYMBOL	REFERENCE WORD	FORMANT 1	FORMANT 2	FORMANT 3
/i/	beet	270	2290	3010
/I/	bit	390	1990	2550
/e/	bet	530	1840	2480
/ae/	bat	660	1720	2410
/a/	father	730	1090	2440
/aw/	bought	570	840	2410
/U/	book	440	1020	2240
/u/	boot	300	870	2240
/L/	but	640	1190	2390
/r/	bird	490	1350	1690

Source: Data from Peterson and Barney (1952).

11.5 Reasonable Formant Ranges

As shown in table 11.1, the location of formant 1 ranges from 270 Hz to 730 Hz, and the location of formant 3 ranges from 1690 Hz to 3010 Hz. Thus the first three formants are confined to the lower 3kHz of the spectrum. It is this fact, and the fact that humans are most sensitive to the frequency range containing the lower formants, that allows us to communicate over telephones, even with a seriously degraded bandwidth of less than 4000 Hz. We can (usually) understand the speech coming over phone lines, even though the full sound "quality" of the speech signal is not transmitted.

As table 11.1 shows, vowel sounds exhibit three formants within the lower 4kHz of the spectrum. If a sound has other than three formants in that range, or one of the three formants lies significantly outside the range of 250 Hz to 3 kHz, we cease to perceive the sound as being speechlike. This is an important fact about human speech perception: the sound must be one that could plausibly be produced by a normal human, or we cease to perceive the sound as being normal human speech.

In chapter 9 we discussed the voice's capability to change pitch and formant locations independently. By manipulating the voice source, we can change the fundamental frequency of the voice, and by moving the tongue, jaw, lips, and so on, we can change the formant patterns. This independence of pitch and formant locations

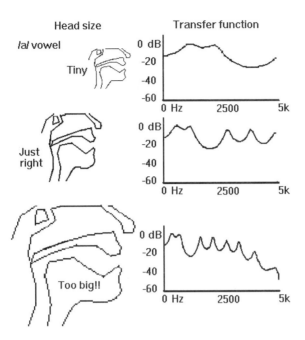

Figure 11.9   Comparison of head size versus vocal tract transfer function.

points to a perceptual phenomenon with which we are all familiar. When a tape recorder or other means is used to speed up the sound of a human speaker, we hear the pitch go up, but the entire spectrum, including all formant positions, shifts upward as well. The opposite effect happens when we slow the tape playback speed: the pitch goes down and all formant frequencies go down by the same amount. Figure 11.9 shows a speaker's head and the accompanying vocal tract transfer function, along with two scaled versions of the same head and transfer function.

When we hear a speech sound that has been *pitch-shifted* upward, we also hear that the formants have been shifted up. The most plausible reason for formants to shift upward, all together, along with pitch is that the person making the speech sound is physically smaller than normal. The speed increase of the tape makes the effect even more pronounced. Remember that if we shorten the vocal tract acoustic tube, all of the resonant modes shift upward proportionally. This causes us to perceive a speech spectrum that has been shifted upward as if it were produced by a tiny-headed human speaker. The small-head sound that arises when a tape is played back at a higher speed is sometimes called *munchkinification* in the recording indus-

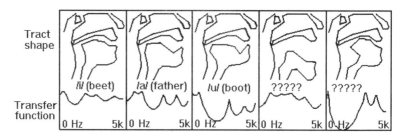

Figure 11.10 Five vocal tract shapes and the resultant transfer functions. The last two shapes are physically impossible, and the transfer functions reflect impossible formant patterns.

try, referring to the diminutive size and voices of the Munchkins in *The Wizard of Oz.* This effect was also used to produce the voices of Alvin and the Chipmunks, with the appropriate perceptual result of speakers (singers) possessing chipmunk-sized heads. If we shift the pitch and spectrum downward, we get an effect opposite that of munchkinification, where the speaker sounds larger than normal. The voices of many villains in cartoons and movies are produced in this manner.

As stated earlier, if more or fewer than three formants exist in the region between 250 and 3000 Hz, the sound is not perceived as speechlike. Figure 11.10 shows five vocal tract shapes and the resultant transfer functions. The first three shapes are physically reasonable, and the sounds are speechlike. The last two shapes are unreasonable, and the spectra show formant patterns that reflect the unreasonableness.

11.6 Human Sensitivity to Formant Frequencies and Bandwidths

Humans are quite sensitive to the locations of the first three formants and the associated vowel sounds. The shape of the resonant formant affects the sound but is not as important for vowel perception as the location. In fact, recognizable vowel sounds can be synthesized by using only three sine waves, one at the location of each of the three speech formants. The shape of a formant immediately surrounding the peak location is often called the Q (for quality) by engineers. A *high* Q formant is peaky, and a *low* Q formant is wide. Figure 11.11 shows a voiced vowel spectrum with normal Q formants, a vowel spectrum with *high* Q formants, and a spectrum with only three sine components located at the formant positions.

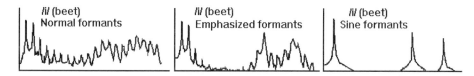

Figure 11.11   Spectra showing normal (left) and emphasized (center) formants for the vowel /i/. The spectrum on the right shows three sinusoids positioned at the formant frequencies. All three of these sounds exhibit an "eee"-like quality, but only the leftmost spectrum sounds natural.

11.7   Some Final Thoughts on Resonance and Anti-Resonance

If we are weakly sensitive to anti-resonances, do we completely ignore their effects? The notches caused by the cancellations of multiple paths all move in a group when any of the path lengths change. We can often hear this ensemble of moving zeroes, and it is commonly used as a recording studio sound effect called *flanging,* named after the discovery of the effect when a recording studio engineer accidentally rested his arm on a tape reel flange, causing the tape to slow down and produce a delayed version of the input signal. The perception of the flanging effect is an example of the Gestalt principle of common fate discussed in chapter 3, where a single moving zero is extremely difficult to discern but a chorus of zeroes all moving together generates a perceptually significant event. There is good evidence that we also use zeroes as extra cues to determine distance and direction of a sound source.

A final topic on formants and formant perception is the *singer's formant.* The singer's formant is responsible for the resonant quality of the voices of trained singers and actors. The singer's formant is actually not a formant at all, but a complex of closely clustered formants. By lowering the larynx, arching the soft palate (velum), and manipulating other articulators in ways to achieve a consistency of sound across all vowels, the third, fourth, and fifth formants are brought into close proximity. This causes a large, broad peak of energy to form in the region between 2500 and 4000 Hz. The location depends on voice type, with bass singers exhibiting the lowest singer's formant location. This broad energy region, when excited by the rich vocal source signal of a singer or actor, causes a ringing quality that allows the person to be heard over great distances and above competing sounds such as an orchestra. When the singer combines the singer's formant with a wide vibrato, as is the case in opera singing (see figure 11.12), the singer can be heard over perhaps as many

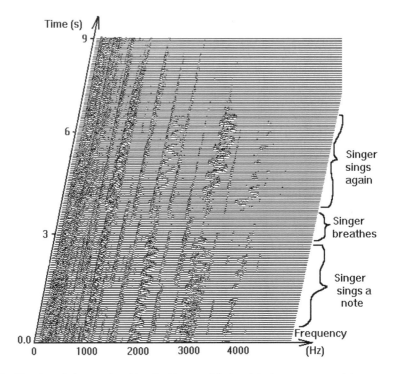

Figure 11.12 The singer's formant is evident in this waterfall plot of the last two notes of the soprano aria "Un Bel Di Vedremo," from Puccini's *Madame Butterfly.* Common frequency modulation of the first three partials allows the fundamental to be picked out visually.

as 100 instruments and 50 other singers. We'll discuss more on the function and effect of vibrato on audibility and intelligibility in chapter 16.

References

Peterson, G. E., and H. L. Barney. (1952). "Control Methods Used in a Study of the Vowels." *Journal of the Acoustical Society of America,* 24, 175–184.

Rossing, T. D. (1990). *The Science of Sound.* Reading, Mass.: Addison-Wesley.

Sundberg, J. (1987). *The Science of the Singing Voice.* DeKalb: Northern Illinois University Press.

12 Articulation in Speech and Sound

Perry R. Cook

12.1 Introduction

This chapter will discuss the effects upon perception of speech articulation, which is the manipulation of the tongue, jaw, lips, velum,
larynx height, and so on, to form speech sounds. The utterance of
familiar words is accomplished through the execution of *motor programs:* rehearsed sequences of muscle control signals stored in the
brain, which can be called up and played back, sometimes at will
and sometimes more automatically. There is strong evidence that
part of our speech recognition system uses these motor programs as
templates for recognizing the gestures that generated the speech
sounds.

Some commonly used phonetic symbols used in this chapter are
listed below.

/i/ eee as in beet	/p/ p as in pop
/I/ ihh as in bit	/t/ t as in tot
/E/ ehh as in bet	/d/ d as in dad
/ae/ aaa as in bat	/b/ b as in bob
/U/ uhh as in but	/g/ g as in gag
/a/ ahh as in father	/s/ s as in soon
/r/ r as in rat	/ʃ/ sh as in shoot

12.2 Spectral Properties of Phonemes

Figure 12.1 shows the time domain waveform envelope of the spoken word "papa." Note the silences corresponding to the two /p/
sounds. The two /p/s are phonetically important, but are essentially
defined by silence with noisy explosions thereafter. Note that the
first noise section is much longer than the second, even though pho-
neticians, and we as human listeners, would define them both as
/p/. Figure 12.2 shows the waveform envelope of the nonsense
word "tata." Note the similarities with "papa," and some subtle differences. The /t/ and /p/ sounds are often confused, especially in
noisy conditions or over a limited bandwidth transmission channel,
such as the telephone.

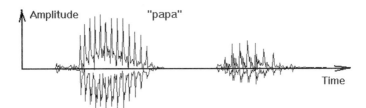

Figure 12.1 Time domain waveform of the word "papa."

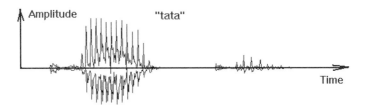

Figure 12.2 Time domain waveform of the word "tata." Note the similarities with the word "papa" (see figure 12.1).

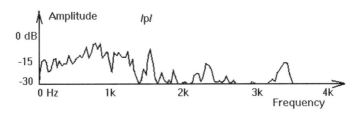

Figure 12.3 Spectrum of the sound /p/.

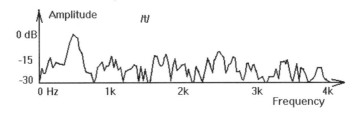

Figure 12.4 Spectrum of the sound /t/.

Figures 12.3 and 12.4 show the spectrum of the noisy explosion corresponding to the /p/ sound and the /t/ sound. Note that the /p/ sound shows more energy in the lower frequencies, and the /t/ sound is distributed more evenly across all 4kHz of frequency range. Given that both sounds are essentially composed of a burst of random noise energy, it is easy to see how they could be confused in noise or in situations with limited bandwidth.

12.3 Production in Perception

We do, however, use cues other than the simple static acoustics of each speech phoneme in order to identify which sound was made. The context within the word and sentence; the meaning of the sentence; which words would make sense in each place; and even other factors, such as how hard a particular possible word would have been to say, affect speech perception. Some of the earliest experiments on vowels and formant perception reached conclusions that point to a production/perception relationship. In a seminal work on vowel production and perception conducted in 1951, Peterson and Barney (1952) included these statements in their conclusions:

a. "... both production and identification depend on previous language experience."

b. "... certain vowels are generally understood better than others, possibly because they represent limit positions of the articulatory mechanism."

The notion that the perceptually significant parts of speech might be the gestures that produce speech sounds, rather than the speech sounds themselves, has been investigated by a number of researchers. Most notable in this field is Alvin Liberman, whose paper "On Finding That Speech is Special" (1982) gave momentum to the so-called *motor theory of speech perception*. Some of the basis for Liberman's work included trying to teach an entirely new acoustic phoneme set to humans. One example of such an alternative set might involve replacing each vowel with the characteristic sound of a melodic musical instrument, and each consonant with a percussion instrument. Liberman found that even though the sounds were acoustically as different as the vowels and consonants we use for speech, humans were unable to learn the new set well enough to recognize even very simple common words made up from the new phoneme dictionary.

Considering that people are able eventually to learn languages with foreign and unfamiliar sounds, sign languages with both word-level and phoneme-level representations, and other such alternative systems of representing speech, Liberman found it odd that people performed so poorly at the task of learning the new acoustic phoneme dictionary he had made up. One plausible explanation was that speech is modularly special, in that the mechanisms in the brain for acoustic speech recognition are so intrinsically tied to the production mechanisms that they are essentially inseparable. The motor programs built for making speech sounds and the inherent limitations on the articulators cause humans to process speech sounds through an elaborate network that resonates with familiar production patterns.

12.4 Ambiguous Sounds: Ba, Da, Ga

Some of the experiments performed to test and verify this theory are based on the voiced consonants b, d, and g. These, like p and t above, are easily confused. In fact, b, d, and g differ most in only one formant trajectory. Figure 12.5 shows the formant trajectories as a function of time for the utterance of the sounds "da" and "ga." Note that the essential difference is in the region above 2kHz, where the third formant sweeps downward in "da" but sweeps upward in "ga."

Due to masking phenomena, the ear is only weakly able to follow the third formant transition after each voiced plosive. This is part of the effect in the examples from section 3.4, where reverberation is evident if played backward, but hardly noticeable in its usual context after the sound. The ear cannot track the third formant trajectory accurately enough to determine unambiguously whether the syllables are "dada," "gaga," "daga," or "gada." If the sounds are played backward, however, the transitions are more clearly different, and the intermediate vowels of /I/ can be heard in the "da" utterance, and of /U/ in the "ga" utterance. Speech sounds abound with such ambiguities, and it is clear that we use more information than simple instant-to-instant acoustical analysis to understand speech.

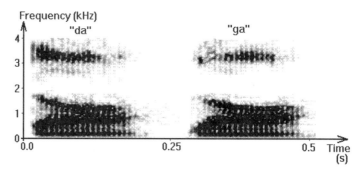

Figure 12.5 Spectrograms of the sounds "da" (left) and "ga" (right). The main difference lies in the trajectory of the third formant, which sweeps downward in "da" and upward in "ga".

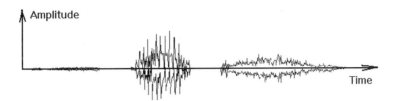

Figure 12.6   Time domain waveform of word constructed by recording "sish," then inserting silence into two points of the word. Most listeners perceive the word as "stitch".

12.5   Pick the Simplest Explanation

A common notion in philosophy, information theory, and many other disciplines is that the simplest explanation is the best. This is known as "Occam's Razor" (after William of Occham, 1285–1349). Human perception processes seem to use this simple guideline. Recall from section 3.5 that the visual processing and perception system assumed that the bar continued beneath the disk, rather than the more complex explanation that there were actually two bars oriented in such a way as to lie on exactly the same line. Figure 12.6 shows a time domain waveform that most English speakers identify as the word "stitch." In actuality the nonsense word "sish" was recorded; then, using a digital editor, blank sound was inserted between /s/ and /I/, and between /I/ and /ʃ/. Some people identify the word as "spich" or even "sdish." Most identify it as "stitch," but not one comes up with the true answer "I'll bet that someone recorded 'sish,' then digitally inserted silence."

Occam's Razor dictates that the simplest explanation is the most plausible, and thus is the correct one. Therefore most people favor the known word that sounds the most like the digitally edited one. The brain decides in favor of the most likely sound uttered, assuming continuity of the articulators. This notion of continuity is central to the articulatory descriptions of speech and gestural descriptions of body motions. Where the waveform, spectrum, and nearly all other descriptions of speech sounds exhibit discontinuities (like "tata" in figure 12.2 above), an articulatory description is *always continuous,* because the articulators are constrained to move smoothly from one point to the next by occupying all states in between.

12.6   Lexical Filtering and Lazy Evaluation

Because of the limited bandwidth of the waveform of figure 12.6 (4 kHz), many people identify the word "sish" as "fish," because the

/s/ and /f/ sounds differ most in the very high-frequency regions. Hardly anyone identifies the digitally edited word as "ftich," however, because no such word exists in English. Many of my friends identify the word as "speech," because they are involved with speech research and the topic is ever in their minds. This points to a layer of linguistic filtering based on lexical (library of known and common words) accessing. People tend to perceive a commonly known word when the acoustical evidence seems a plausible match.

Experiments based on this type of paradigm get more interesting when there are multiple choices for likely familiar words, such as there would be in the case of modifying the word "say" by inserting silence between the /s/ and /Ei/ sounds. In this case there are at least two likely common English words: "stay" and "spay." Depending on the recent history of the perceiver's pets, most people favor the word "stay" for short durations of inserted silence, and "spay" for longer silences. The reason for this is that it takes longer to move the mouth from the shape required to form an /s/ to that required to form a /p/, than from /s/ to /t/. From experiments such as these, it appears that an articulatory component is present in the perception of sounds that have been created or modified in completely artificial ways.

12.7 More on Reasonable Formant Ranges

As discussed in chapter 11, the physical and physiological limits of the articulators determine the space of reasonable formant ranges and sounds that sound speechlike. If formants exceed the realm of reasonable ranges (which would require the articulators to exceed the realm of realizable shapes), the sound no longer is speechlike. Also, if too many formants are present in a sound, we recognize that the sound could not have been produced by a human. Such would be the case if we were to take the sounds of two vowels and mix them together, doing what would be considered a valid interpolation of the spectra or time domain waveshapes. In saying the sound "yah," the articulators move smoothly from the /i/ (eee) shape to the /a/ shape, occupying the spaces between to form the intermediate vowel sounds. The interpolation in this case is in the articulatory domain. One likely vowel trajectory formed in going from /i/ to /a/ is shown below.

/i/	/I/	/E/	/ae/	/U/	/a/
eee	ihh	ehh	aaa	uhh	ahh

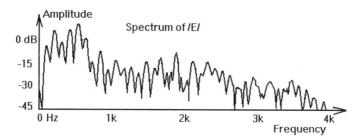

Figure 12.7   Spectrum of the sound /E/, from middle of the utterance /ia/.

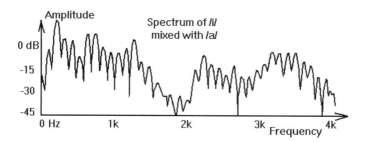

Figure 12.8   Spectrum formed by mixing /i/ with /a/.

This is quite different than a simple *cross fade* or spectral interpolation between the /i/ and /a/ sounds. The spectrum in the central point where both sounds are mixed together looks nothing like the articulatory central point of /E/, because there are essentially six formants active in the region below 3500 Hz. Figures 12.7 and 12.8 show the spectrum of the /E/ sound extracted from the central point of the transition between /i/ and /a/ in the utterance of "yah," and the spectrum of the /i/ and /a/ sounds mixed together.

The physiology and physics of the human vocal mechanism constrain the speed of articulation, and thus also constrain how rapidly changes in speech sounds can be made. The experiment involving "say" with inserted silence is one in which the speed of articulation directly causes the perceived word to change. The time required to go from the /s/ sound to the /t/ sound, involving the same point of constriction on the tongue, is shorter than the time required to go from /s/ to /p/, involving two different points of constriction. If we were to take the "yah" example above and speed up the transition, even though the correct articulatory space interpolation is performed, the sound would still be unnatural when the transition time dropped below the minimum time in which a human speaker could execute the articulatory gestures.

There is even evidence that a level of perceptual filtering is applied that involves selecting the utterance that would have been easiest to say. When presented with cases involving multiple possible nonsense words where there is no lexical significance to the words, and no sentence context to influence the decision, humans tend to "recognize" the utterance that would have been easiest to say. This is a further example of Occam's Razor in perception, in which the definition of simple is actually *laziest, easiest,* or the utterance that would have taken the least effort. An example of this involves using the utterances "ara" and "ala," commonly called VCV utterances (for vowel-consonant-vowel). Short silences placed after the consonants /r/ and /l/ cause the words to be perceived most commonly as "arga" and "alda," likely because the places of articulation are most similar for the pairs /r/ and /g/, and /l/ and /d/.

12.8 The McGurk Effect, and Prosody and Gesture in Perception

One further interesting set of experiments on articulatory perception involves the *McGurk Effect* (McGurk and MacDonald 1976). In these experiments, humans were presented with spoken words from the sets "ba," "da," and "ga"; "bi," "di," and "gi"; and so on. The listeners were simultaneously presented with video images of a human face uttering different words from the same family. For example, the sound of "bi" might be presented simultaneously with the video of a face with a mouth forming the word "gi." Remarkably, the listeners tended to hear a word between the presented audio and visual stimuli. So in the example above involving an audio "bi" and a video "gi," the listener heard "di." The space that best describes the interpolation is the location of closure on the axis running down the vocal tract acoustic tube. "Bi" is formed with a closure at the lip end, "gi" is formed with a closure far back on the tongue, and "di" is formed with a closure that lies between those points of articulation.

A final level of processing in the speech perception process involves prosody: the pitch and emphasis contours that give more meaning to speech. A good example of prosody affecting perception is to utter the sentence "I wish I could go" twice, the first time emphasizing the word "wish" and the second time the word "I." The meanings are clearly different, with the second sentence implying that the person is specifically being restricted from going, while others are not. Obviously, prosody can affect the meaning of the information conveyed by words, but can the perception of the prosody be affected by the words being said? To investigate this question, the utterance of the words "gray ship" can be used. By selectively editing silence into the words, the utterances "gray chip," "great chip," and "great ship" can be formed. Listeners, when asked to estimate the maximum pitch of each utterance, consistently overestimate the pitch of "great ship" and underestimate that of "gray chip." The explanation for this is that "great ship" would likely be said as an exclamation praising someone's ship, and as such would carry higher pitch inflection than the rather boring and potentially nonsense utterance "gray chip."

12.9 Conclusion

The notion of articulation in speech carries over to music in many ways. The concept of *gesture* is important in composition, analysis, and categorization. Picking the simplest, or laziest, or easiest-to-produce explanation for a sound points directly to the idea of idiom, where we find that things that are inherently difficult to play well on a particular instrument do not appear in the majority of music written for that instrument. If a keyboard player uses a MIDI keyboard to play a guitar sound on a synthesizer, often what is "wrong" about the sound is not that the individual notes do not sound like guitar notes but, rather, that the chords used by keyboard players are often impossible to achieve on a normally tuned guitar. If a MIDI score is used to play a trumpet solo using sampled trumpet sounds, the sound is missing not only the smoothness of a real trumpet performance but also the subtle timing variations due to the player's fingers favoring certain transitions over others.

Articulation in music performance and perception is a ripe area for new research. The author hopes that studies of articulation in speech can be used as models for future experiment designs in music.

References

Liberman, A. M. (1982). "On Finding That Speech Is Special." *American Psychologist,* 37 (2): 148–167.

Mattingly, I. G., and M. Studdart-Kennedy. (1991). *Modularity and the Motor Theory of Speech Perception.* Hillsdale, N.J.: Lawrence Erlbaum.

McGurk, H., and J. MacDonald. (1976). "Hearing Lips and Seeing Voices." *Nature,* 264, 746–748.

Peterson, G. E., and H. L. Barney (1952). "Control Methods Used in a Study of the Vowels." *Journal of the Acoustical Society of America,* 24, 175–184.

13 *Pitch Perception and Measurement*

Roger Shepard

13.1 Introduction

As discussed in chapter 3, cognitive psychology deals in part with the problem that what we perceive is not exactly the same as the physical reality of the stimulus. This becomes clear as we talk about pitch, because the perceived pitch is fundamentally connected with the period or frequency of signals, but is not fully described or predicted by fundamental frequency alone. When this fact is applied to pure sine tones, it might be easy to argue that pitch and fundamental frequency are equivalent, but musical signals are not sinusoids, nor are they periodic. So how do we quantify the perceptual attribute of pitch? Is it related to frequency, perhaps the logarithm of frequency, or some other transformation? And how do we go about determining such a thing? Such problems are common in all applications of psychology and psychophysics.

13.2 Logarithms and the Just Noticeable Difference

As we discussed in chapters 5 and 6, the notions of loudness and pitch perception raise questions as to how to quantify and measure such experiences. This is also true in vision, with such attributes as brightness, hue, and saturation. The attempt to quantify such subjective experiences, and many others, started with a physicist named Gustav Fechner (1873). Upon awakening one morning, Fechner had a brainstorm: the perceived quality of a stimulus, such as the redness of an apple, could be something different from the way the stimulus object is specified physically. He subsequently arrived at the idea that the perceived quantity is often a logarithmic transformation of the physical quantity. In reality, the way one measures a perceptual phenomenon directly affects the result. Fechner used the *just noticeable difference* (JND) to do his experiments. Measuring the JND as the minimum physical change detectable by a human observer, and integrating those differences from the point where no change was detected up to a given level, the number of JNDs was used to express the psychological level of a given stimulus. Fechner found that a first approximation to his perceptually measured scales was a logarithmic scale.

13.3   Direct Subjective Assessments

Another point of view that developed later held that there is no reason to believe that the accuracy of discrimination of a stimulus (JND, for example) is necessarily related to the overall perceived magnitude of a stimulus. A principal proponent of this view was S. Smith Stevens, a psychologist at Harvard University, who said that Fechner's methods were comparable with trying to accumulate the error in the position of a needle on a voltmeter to determine where the meter is pointing. Stevens believed that such an accumulation doesn't necessarily have anything to do with voltage, and accumulations of JNDs don't necessarily have anything to do with perceived magnitude. He believed that the way such things should be measured is to acquire direct subjective assessments. Such an experiment might involve presenting a tone and informing the subject that the tone is numbered 30 for loudness. If a subsequent tone seems twice as loud, the subject should label it 60. If it seems half as loud, it should be labeled 15. The responses for successive tones would then be recorded. Stevens found that such experiments yielded quite different results from the cumulative JND experiments.

13.4   The Mel Scale

The details of measuring such quantities are not specifically important here, but I will say that neither of the methods described above yields a "correct" answer regarding pitch. The two methods yield different answers and neither fully describes the complexity of musical pitch. Stevens and others wanted to construct a scale that reflected the *psychological* reality of how people hear musical tones. The result of the experiments was the construction of the *mel scale* (for *melody,* a falsely coined term, given the results of the experiments). The researchers asked listeners to adjust tones so that one tone was "half as high" as another, and other such subdivisions of the frequency range. The reference of 1000 mels was assigned as having a frequency of 1000 Hz. Figure 13.1 shows the mel scale graph and a piano keyboard normalized to mel scale (that is, the keyboard is warped to match steps which are equal "distance" on the mel scale). The keys are closer together at the low end of the keyboard,

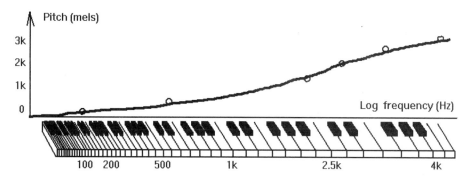

Figure 13.1 The mel scale and a warped keyboard depicting the scale. (After Stevens, Volkmann, and Newman, 1937.)

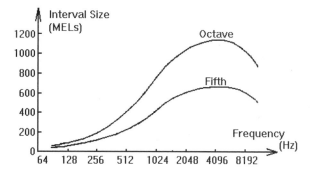

Figure 13.2 Graph showing how musical interval sizes change across the mel scale. (After Stevens, Volkmann, and Newman, 1937. Reprinted with permission of the Acoustical Society of America.)

which undoubtedly shows something about human perception because the results of these experiments were statistically stable and reproducible.

Figure 13.2 shows how interval sizes change across the mel scale. In addition, since pitch is a variable and the results come from human responses, the mel scale shows something about the perception of pitch. It suggests that there are at least two different kinds of pitch: the mel scale measurements and musical (melodic) pitch. What the mel scale does reflect is that the perceived difference between two notes decreases at the extreme ends of the keyboard.

Pitches, and differences between them, are not as clear at low and high frequencies. (This can be verified by playing an interval such as a major second in a few places across the piano keyboard.) What the mel scale fails to recognize in its supposed relation to melody or musical pitch is the fact that there is a *constant* nature to musical intervals, something every musician knows instinctively. A minor third, octave, or fifth is exactly that musical interval no matter where it exists: low, middle, or high. On the actual piano keyboard (which is isomorphic to a log frequency scale, because each time an octave is traversed, the same distance is traversed on a log frequency scale) the fact that musical intervals remain constant in any position is preserved. The distance from C to E, called a major third, is the same on the keyboard and on the log frequency scale, independent of where the individual notes are located on the keyboard or log frequency scale.

13.5 Competence vs. Performance

An analogy can be made here with linguistics. Noam Chomsky (1965) made a distinction between *competence* and *performance* in his theory of grammar and syntax. He noted that many errors in grammar are obvious upon examining transcripts or recordings of actual speech. The grammar that people know to be correct is different from what they actually use in speaking. Such is the competence/performance distinction: the rules may be stored internally, but because our limited brainpower to process and perform speech is overtaxed by long, embedded thoughts, we may get into trouble trying to produce or understand grammatically correct sentences. It is not that grammatical rules are unknown and are not internalized, but rather that limited memory and processing power inhibit the use of these rules. Similarly, the rules that govern musical interval relationships might be known and internalized by musicians, but the limitations of the receiving, producing, and/or processing mechanisms might cause an inability to perceive or produce such intervals at the extremes of the frequency range.

When one listens to a "scale" composed of equal steps on the mel scale, the steps do not sound musically equal at all. The wider spacing at the lower end is especially obvious and, even in the parts of the range where the steps are somewhat close to musical half steps, the scale sounds out of tune in comparison with traditional chromatic scales. A composition played using the mel scale sounds somewhat reasonable in the central range but completely wrong in the higher and lower ranges.

The mel scale is not an appropriate musical scale, but it does indeed capture and describe something important about pitch. Consequently, it is important that musicians and composers understand the mel scale. Concepts related to the mel scale are found in music; for example, the statistically higher number of close intervals in the central frequency range in musical compositions. Musicians and composers intuitively know that pitches are more differentiated in the central range than in the low range. This is not to say that they ignore other parts of the musical scale, but that within the musical scale they select pitches that are consistent with the perceptual discrimination described by the mel scale. The mel scale may also have something to do with brightness of sounds, another qualitative measure similar to pitch.

13.6 Pitch is a Morphophoric Medium

If a psychophysicist wanted to investigate a musical scale system experimentally, a technique different from those used by Stevens and Fechner would be required. Hermann Ebbinghaus (1913), a psychologist who did the earliest experimental studies on human memory, started a tradition that continued for a long time in psychology: removing as much superfluous information from a study or stimulus as possible. Ebbinghaus had subjects learn lists of nonsense words and syllables: he wanted to get away from the complications of materials with intrinsic meaning attached, because things are quite different when one is dealing with meaningful words or sentences.

Similarly, psychophysicists tried to get away from complications by conducting experiments using tones that were quite nonmusical. They therefore used pure sine tones and other sounds that had no standard musical interval relationships. Such experiments might tell a lot about how the ear transduces sound, and how the brain processes some sounds, but they do not tell us much about how the brain processes musical materials. Entirely different principles might come into play when the brain is processing musical sounds than when it is processing sounds that were intentionally designed to be nonmusical. To investigate musical scales, one might present musical tones, perhaps in musical intervals or contexts, so that the principles that emerge are more interesting and relevant to musicians.

Fred Attneave and R. K. Olson (1971) at the University of Oregon were the first persons to make this point forcefully with regard to musical tones and the judgment of pitch. They used simple melodies with which most people are familiar. A few beginning notes were played, then one more note. They then asked if the final note was

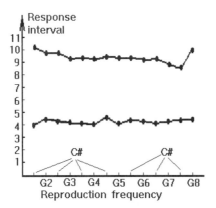

Figure 13.3 Attneave and Olson's subjects' responses to transformations of the NBC chimes. (After Attneave and Olson, 1971.)

appropriate. A variation on this method was that part of the melody was transposed and the subjects had to fill in the missing notes. One of Attneave and Olson's experiments involved the common NBC chimes, consisting of G, E above, then C below E (frequencies 196, 330, 262 Hz). They would transpose the first note and then have subjects adjust one or both of the remaining notes until they felt that the adjusted note(s) sounded correct. What they found was nothing like the mel scale; instead, it resulted in a log frequency scale within the common musical frequency range.

Figure 13.3 shows a plot of the transformations applied by subjects as a function of the transposition of the first note. The plot is linear on a log scale except at high frequencies, where the linear relationship breaks down somewhat. Such a result is important to psychologists who are studying music or language, where different principles apply, than in experiments involving stimuli that contain no inherent meaning. In their 1971 paper Attneave and Olson made the point that there is something fundamental about pitch, as there is about time. There are many other attributes to the organization of sounds—such as timbre, spatial location, and loudness—but the attributes of pitch and time have special importance. Attneave and Olson called pitch a *morphophoric medium,* meaning that it is a medium capable of bearing forms.

Visual space is also a morphophoric medium. For example, if a right triangle is presented in space, the triangle can be moved around and still be recognized as the same triangle. The medium of space is therefore capable of bearing a form that preserves its identity under transformation. Similarly, pitch patterns like simple melodies and harmonies can be moved up and down in pitch and still be recognized by musicians as being the same pattern. For example, a major triad is recognizable in nearly any position on the musical keyboard.

Time is a powerful morphophoric medium. Other dimensions used in music (such as loudness, timbre, and spatial location) are not morphophoric. For example, we have melodies in pitch, but no real analog to melody in loudness. Other structures exist such as accents and rhythms, but they are less recognizable than pitch relationships. If a loudness pattern were constructed that, for example, first went up, then went down, we might recognize that figure if it were transposed in loudness. It would be much more difficult to perceive a subtle change in a loudness pattern than a change of a major triad to minor. The same degree of structural information is not preserved in loudness as it is in pitch and time.

13.7   Dispensable versus Indispensable Attributes

Another type of distinction, made by cognitive psychologist Michael Kubovy (1981), is that of dispensable versus indispensable attributes. Parallels between vision and audition exist here as well, because these are very general cognitive principles; they are not specific to any particular sensory domain. Dispensable and indispensable attributes are parallel to the distinction between mediums that are morphophoric and those that are not.

To illustrate this concept, consider two projectors, one of which is projecting a red spot and one of which is projecting a yellow spot, each in a different location. Each object has two attributes: color and spatial position. Now, suppose that both projectors are instead projecting an orange spot, but still in two different locations. There are still two objects in two different positions, but we have dispensed with the attribute of color. Finally, suppose that the original red and yellow projectors are turned so that they project their individual spots to the same location, so that only a single orange spot is visible. The colors of the two projectors have mixed to make one color that is not present in either of the original two spots, and now the two distinct spots are no longer discriminable. The attribute of spatial position in vision is therefore said to be indispensable, because the eye is incapable of separating out the two individual colored dots, and instead perceives a single orange dot. (Figure 13.4 shows this in black and white.)

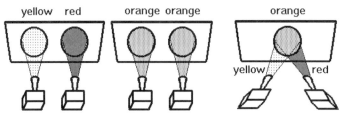

In visual perception, color is dispensable, location is indispensable

Figure 13.4   (Left) Two projected dots, one yellow and one red. Center: two orange dots. (Right) One dot is on top of the other; there are no longer two dots.

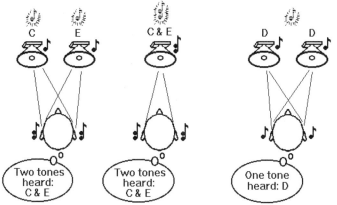

In auditory perception pitch is indispensable, location is dispensable

Figure 13.5   (Left) Two speakers carry two notes. Center: two notes from one speaker. (Right) The same note on two speakers, and there are no longer two notes.

An analogous situation in audition might consist of two loud-speakers, one carrying a musical middle C and the other carrying a musical E above middle C. A subject would respond that one source is on the left, and the other on the right, with the right one being at a higher pitch. If the pitch difference is removed by moving both pitches to musical D, the listener would then likely reply that there is a single source located between both speakers. This would occur because the subject's ears would receive exactly the same input signal; the brain would process this symmetric information and infer that the source location is directly in front. Pitch is therefore an indispensable attribute in audition (see figure 13.5). One might think that pitch in audition is analogous to color in vision because both are frequency-related phenomena. However, the experiment using tones and speakers shows that the two are not analogous, because pitch is indispensable and color is dispensable. If both original pitches of C and E were presented from a single loudspeaker in front of the listener, the two pitches would not blend as did the red and yellow dots, but would still be discriminated as two sounds. This shows that while space is an indispensable attribute in vision, it is a dispensable attribute in audition. The indispensability of space in vision and of pitch in audition are parallel to both of those attributes being morphophoric media. So the analog to visual space is not auditory space but auditory pitch.

13.8   Spaces to Represent Pitch: Chroma versus Height

Attneave and Olson (1971) said that pitch is a morphophoric medium, and as such must be studied differently than it had been studied before. By examining the abilities of subjects to perceive and to produce pitch patterns under transformation, an appropriate representation of pitch can be found. They found that this representation corresponds to the log frequency scale, which is nice in that it preserves musical intervals under transformations (octaves are equal jumps on the log scale, as are fifths, and so on). It also preserves any interval under transformation, such as any arbitrary microtonal relationship. The log scale does not, however, represent the fact that certain intervals are special, such as octaves and perfect fifths. Ethnomusicological studies have found that octaves and perfect fifths seem to be culturally universal; that is, although musical systems and scales of all cultures differ in many respects, they almost always contain an octave relationship, and often the perfect fifth as well. In addition, psychologists have found in studies on humans, and even white rats, that tonal relationships of octaves show increased generalization over intervals slightly less or more than an octave.

If one proceeds up the piano keyboard by sevenths, the pitch height is clearly heard as ascending, but it is also possible to hear a descending sequence. The notes C, B, B-flat, A, and so on form a strong downward chromatic sequence that can be heard with a little imagination. The German physicist Moritz Drobisch (1855) proposed that tones be represented on a helix. This helix, on the surface of a cylinder, places octaves immediately above and below each other. A variant of this structure is the helix shown in figure 13.6. The helix can be recovered by applying multidimensional scaling to human responses, as was done by Carol Krumhansl and R. N. Shepard (1979).

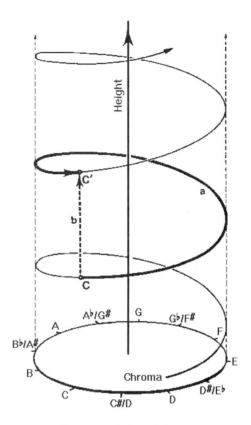

Figure 13.6 A nonlogarithmic pitch helix that clearly depicts octave equivalence.

This concept of pitch organization is what led the author, while at Bell Labs in 1963, to devise tones that are ambiguous in height but unambiguous in pitch—the *Shepard tones* discribed in chapters 5 and 10. Such tones can be made to go upward forever, spiraling up the pitch helix in a barber pole fashion.

The inspiration for generating the circular Shepard tones came from the fact that Max Mathews at Bell Labs had created the first program for generating sounds using the computer. This aroused great excitement, and the author did an experiment using a subdivision of the octave into 10 equal steps instead of the traditional 12. A note's position within the octave is called its *Chroma,* and the *chroma circle* is the base of the helix shown in figure 13.6. The tones were formed by using a symmetrical structure, so that after an octave had been traversed, the ending tone was identical to the beginning tone. Subjects were presented all possible pairs of tones, and asked to judge which of the two was higher. Before the experiment was run, each subject was tested for "tone deafness" by using two sinus-

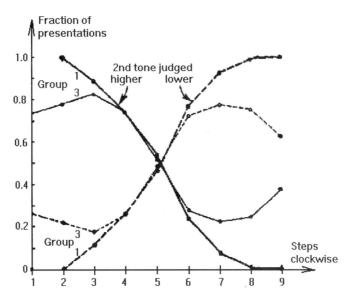

Figure 13.7   Shepard tone responses for groups 1 and 3. (Adapted from Shepard, 1964, reprinted with permission, © 1964 Acoustical Society of America.)

oidal tones. Subjects were grouped as follows: group 1 was categorized as musically astute, group 3 as not astute at all, and group 2 as somewhere in between. Group 1 agreed that tones that are close on the chroma circle appear to ascend when played in a clockwise order.

Figure 13.7 shows the responses of groups 1 and 3 for intervalic leaps around the chroma circle. As the spacing of the interval approaches the tritone, half hear the intervals as ascending and half as descending, with some persisting in an orientation (ascending or descending bias) beyond the tritone. Group 3, composed of subjects who failed the sinusoidal pretest, exhibited the same results except where the tones became very closely spaced; at this point they had difficulty determining which of the two tones was higher.

13.9   Separating Height from Chroma

Tones that are an octave apart have something in common with one another that tones slightly less than an octave apart do not. There is no way to capture this fact on a rectilinear scale of pitch. The most natural way to capture the octave relationship of pitch is to place the pitches on a helix, with the octaves lying on a vertical line. The vertical position on the pitch helix represents what is called *pitch height*. The position within an octave around the cylinder defined

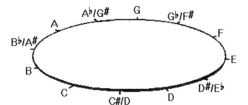

Figure 13.8 A pitch circle.

by the helix is called the *chroma.* Either of these components of pitch can be suppressed. The easiest way to suppress chroma, while leaving height, is to pass noise through a band-pass filter. The center frequency of the band-pass filter determines the perceived height of the sound, but no chroma exists in the sound. Another way to accomplish this is to play all twelve of the chromatic notes within an octave, and then move the octave upward or downward. Like band-passed noise, a sound consisting of all audible octaves of a single pitch—say all Cs—can be passed through a sweeping band-pass filter. The resulting sound has a fixed chroma, but it clearly rises and falls in height.

It is more difficult to suppress height while leaving chroma. One method is related to the Shepard tones. Such tones can be constructed with an ambiguous spectrum, say with harmonics lying only on octaves, and with a spectrum that decreases from a maximum near the center to zero at extremely low and high frequencies. Scales can be played using such tones; after ascending or descending a complete octave, the final tone is located at the same place where the scale began, both literally and perceptually. A tritone constructed using such tones can be perceived as either ascending or descending. Such tones are ambiguous with respect to height but exhibit no ambiguity as to chroma. Why is it that examples using such tones are so strikingly surprising? The most likely explanation is that in the world, height and pitch are almost always linked, and things that ascend in height usually ascend in pitch. Collapsing the helix of figure 13.6 onto the circle of figure 13.8 gives rise to the ability to raise or lower pitch continuously without any net change in height.

This illusion can also be performed with tempo, where pulses occurring at lower rates that are subdivisions of higher-rate tones can be gradually increased in volume while the higher-rate tones are decreased in volume. If all pulses speed up slightly as the volume changes—such that at the same point the slower pulses reach the original speed of the faster pulses, the faster pulses are at zero amplitude—the overall perception is that the pulses are continuously increasing in tempo but never arrive anywhere. The composer Ligeti created tempo illusions in his compositions: the tempo is held absolutely rigid but the percept is that it is slowing down. He accomplished this by placing certain periodic patterns in the melody that are stretched out while overall tempo remains the same. Jean-Claude Risset also constructed examples that effectively combine tempo and pitch illusions.

13.10   Confusing Chroma and Height

If chroma indeed underlies pitch, can a melody be scrambled in terms of height while retaining chroma? If this could be done, would the melody still be recognizable? It would seem that if the listener were able to attend only to chroma and ignore height, the answer would be "yes." Jay Dowling and A. W. Hollombe (1977) and Diana Deutsch (1972), among others, have studied melodies scrambled in this manner. In a typical experiment, they distorted a familiar melody by retaining the chroma but jumping octaves throughout the melody. They found that our perception of melody actually depends quite critically on height as well as chroma, so melodies scrambled in height while retaining chroma are not readily recognized.

Figure 13.9a shows such a melody, and it is quite difficult for even a trained musician to recognize it visually. Figure 13.9b also shows

Figure 13.9   (a) Familiar melody with randomized octaves is harder to recognize visually and aurally than (c) normal or (b) stretched scale version, both of which preserve melodic contour.

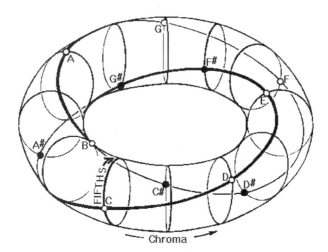

Figure 13.10 A toroid that somewhat captures the relationship between perfect fifths and octaves.

the same melody, scrambled somewhat in height, but its overall "contour" has been maintained, in that upward leaps in the original melody (figure 13.9c) are still upward leaps and downward leaps in the original melody are still downward leaps. The resulting melody is more recognizable than the random height-scrambled melody (See figure 13.9 also for the original melody.) A melody constructed with incorrect chroma, but with the right shape and height contour, can be more recognizable than one that has been completely randomly height-scrambled.

We have examined the special relationship octaves have with each other. The perfect fifth is also quite important perceptually and musically. The helical representation of figure 13.6 preserves the octave relationship but does not capture the importance of fifths. A double helix can be constructed that captures the relationships of the perfect fifths as well as the octaves. This representation has the interesting property that a plane cutting any circle will separate the notes of a major diatonic scale of a particular key from notes not contained in that scale. The diatonic scale tones lie on one side of the plane, and the nondiatonic notes lie on the other side. The toroid of figure 13.10 somewhat captures the relationships of perfect fifths and octaves, but in actuality a five-dimensional space would be required to represent height, chroma, and the special relationships of octaves and fifths, as in the double helix wrapped around a helical cylinder (see figure 13.11).

If you apply multidimensional scaling to individual differences of perception of tone relationships within only a single octave, the re-

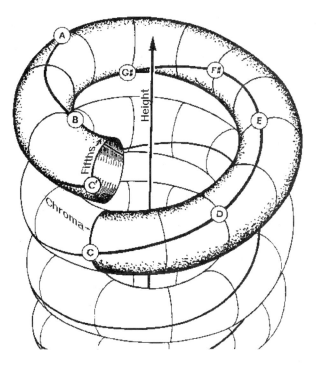

Figure 13.11   Double helix plotted on the surface of a helical cylinder. This captures the octave and perfect fifth relationship better than the simple torus of figure 13.10.

sult is a four-dimensional solution with two dimensions representing the circle of fifths. The other two dimensions are the chroma circle, spread somewhat to represent height within the octave, and rectilinear pitch height. The result is nearly identical to the torus of figure 13.10. The multidimensional scaling method also gives the weights of individual subjects on each of the dimensions. Some subjects seem oblivious to the circle of fifths, whereas those who show weight on the circle of fifths show it in both dimensions. That is, the circle of fifths is complete in its two dimensions; however, if a subject is perceptually sensitive to it, both dimensions come together in a unitary percept.

Based on a clustering solution of the subjects in this test, the subjects basically fall into three groups highly related to musical background and experience. (Note that the terms *musical background* and *experience* do not necessarily imply formal musical training. There is some evidence that musical tendencies are innate, including the possibility of specific genes indicating tone deafness and perfect pitch.) All subjects seemed to respond somewhat to chroma, but musically sophisticated subjects responded most to the circle of fifths. Most musical listeners did not respond much to height.

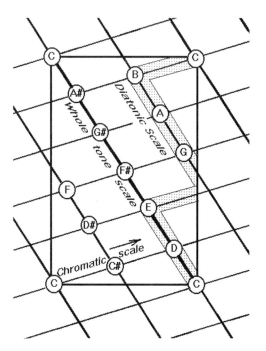

Figure 13.12 Cutting the complex structure of Figure 13.11 and laying it flat results in this surface, sometimes called the "melodic space."

Cutting the torus and unwrapping it into a rectangle yields the map in figure 13.12. Various scales follow the lines indicated on the figure. This figure is often called *melodic space* because melodies most often are comprised of small steps. An analysis of 3000 English folk songs showed that 68 percent of the melodic transitions were no larger than a minor second (half step or whole step), and 91 percent were no larger than two diatonic steps (major third). The concept of melodic space is related to Korte's third law: larger steps require more time to track in a continuous way, and melodies tend to fall apart if large steps are included. This is why melodies that have randomized height are perceptually difficult unless the height can be ignored and only chroma attended.

The Canadian researcher David Huron has done much statistical analysis of songs to look at frequency of small and large leaps, and also the time allowed for the steps. He found that either the ending or the beginning note of a large leap is allowed more time than if the leap is small. This relates to another law called *Fitts's law* (Fitts and Posner 1967), which has to do with production as well as perception. If a person is required to move something between two targets, the distance between the targets, as well as the size of the targets, can be varied. Fitts's law says that the time required to make the transition is proportional to the distance and inversely proportional to the size. This is quite analogous to Korte's law but applies to production of motor actions.

References

Attneave, F., and R. K. Olson. (1971). "Pitch as a Medium: A New Approach to Psychophysical Scaling," *American Journal of Psychology,* 84, 147–166.

Chomsky, N. (1965). *Aspects of the Theory of Syntax.* Cambridge, Mass.: MIT Press.

Deutsch, D. (1972). "Octave Generalization and Tune Recognition." *Perception and Psychophysics,* 11, 411–412.

Dowling, W. J., and A. W. Hollombe. (1977). "The Perception of Melodies Distorted by Splitting into Several Octaves." *Perception and Psychophysics,* 21, 60–64.

Drobisch, M. W. (1855). "Über Musikalische Tonbestimmung und Temperatur." *Abhandlungen Mathematisch Physische Klasse der Koenigliche Sachsischen, Gesellschaft der Wisssenschaften.* 4, 1–120.

Ebbinghaus, H. (1913). "Memory: A Contribution to Experimental Psychology." Mineola, N.Y.: Dover Books, 1964.

Fechner, G. T. (1873). *Einige Ideen zur Schöpfungs-, und Entwickelungsgeschichte der Organismen.* Leipzig: Breitkopf und Hartel.

Fitts, P. M., and M. I. Posner. (1967). *Human Performance.* Belmont Calif.: Wadsworth/Brooks-Cole.

Huron, D. (1994). "Interval-Class Content in Equally Tempered Pitch-Class Sets: Common Scales Exhibit Optimum Tonal Consonance." *Music Perception* 11(3), 289–305.

Krumhansl, C. L., and R. N. Shepard. (1979). "Quantification of the Hierarchy of Tonal Functions Within a Diatonic Context." *Journal of Experimental Psychology: Human Perception & Performance,* 5, 579–594.

Kubovy, M. (1981). "Integral and Separable Dimensions and the Theory of Indispensable Attributes." In M. Kubovy and J. Pomerantz, eds., *Perceptual Organization.* Hillsdale, N.J.: Lawrence Erlbaum.

Risset, J. C. (1986). "Pitch and Rhythm Paradoxes: Comments on Auditory Paradoxes Based on Fractal Waveform." *Journal of the Acoustical Society of America,* 80 (3): 961–962.

Shepard, R. N. (1964). "Circularity in Judgments of Relative Pitch." *Journal of the Acoustical Society of America,* 35, 2346–2353.

Stevens, S. S., J. Volkmann, and E. B. Newman. (1937). "A Scale for the Measurement of the Psychological Magnitude of Pitch." *Journal of the Acoustical Society of America,* 8, 185–190.

14 Consonance and Scales

John Pierce

14.1 Numbers

Men and women sing together in many cultures. Sometimes they sing an octave apart. In close harmony, as in a good barbershop quartet, we feel the impact of carefully sung musical intervals, one shading into another. But tones heard at the same time can interact, producing a noisy or dissonant sound. Such interaction is discussed in a small book written by Reiner Plomp in 1976.

A sinusoidal sound excites a pattern of vibration along the basilar membrane in the cochlea. When two sinusoidal sounds have frequencies separated by more than a critical bandwidth, the patterns of excitation do not overlap, and the sinusoidal sound waves do not interact. The greatest interaction occurs for sine waves whose frequencies are about a quarter of a critical bandwidth apart.

The critical bandwidth is plotted versus frequency in figure 14.1. For frequencies above A5 (880 Hz) the critical bandwidth is about a sixth of the frequency, corresponding to a frequency range of less than a minor third and greater than a whole tone. For lower frequencies the critical bandwidth is larger. It is about 100 Hz at the bottom of the piano keyboard (A0, 27.5 Hz).

If two notes closer than a minor third are played at the same time, we may expect some harshness or dissonance from interaction between their fundamental frequency components, and especially among their harmonics. We may expect a large contribution to dissonance from the interaction of components with frequencies a couple of octaves above the fundamentals of the two tones.

The harshness or dissonance produced by interactions among sinusoidal components is an unavoidable consequence of the structure and mechanism of the ear. Such dissonance may be musically useful; it is unavoidable. The dissonance is larger for some intervals or chords than for others. It is larger for tones with lots of harmonics or overtones than it is for tones with few harmonics. Single tones with many strong, high harmonics can sound dissonant in themselves because of the interactions of successive or nearby harmonics with one another.

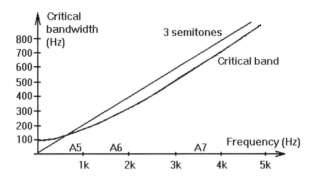

Figure 14.1 The curve shows the width of critical bandwidth plotted against frequency. The straight line represents a musical minor third plotted against frequency.

Table 14.1 The musical mystery of consonant ratios of small integers

1:2	2:3		3:4		4:5	5:6
		(3:4)		(4:5)	3:5	

Note: In classical times these ratios of small numbers used by Greeks were lengths of strings. The modern interpretation is ratios of frequencies

We should keep dissonance in mind in dealing with sounds in which the partials are not harmonic, as in the case of bells or of computer-generated sounds in which the partials are deliberately inharmonic. We should also keep it in mind in connection with conventional musical tones, whose partials are harmonic.

In studying conventional musical intervals we characterize them by ratios of numbers. Table 14.1 illustrates ratios that the Greeks attached to musical intervals. The ratios 1:2, 2:3, 3:4, 4:5, and 5:6 represent the octave, the fifth, the fourth, the major third, and the minor third. The major sixth, 3:5, can be regarded as an interval of a fourth (3:4) plus a major third (4:5).

For the Greeks, such ratios of numbers represented the ratios of lengths of a string of constant mass and tension. We can think of such lengths in terms of the distance from the bridge of a guitar to various fret positions. Thus, halving the length of a string produces a tone an octave higher.

Today we would say that halving the length of a string doubles its frequency of vibration. Here we are in advance of the Greeks, for our association of pitch with the number of vibrations each second fits with aspects of the physical nature of musical consonance.

14.2 Periodicity, Partials, and Intervals

The vibrations of strings, and of columns of air, are nearly periodic. Other nearly periodic sounds include sung and spoken vowels, many animal cries, and the humming of some insects. Periodic sounds are both common and important in nature. It is perfectly reasonable to believe that we have acquired an ability to sense and appreciate the properties of approximately periodic sounds through evolutionary adaptation. Whatever the history of this ability, we deal well with approximately periodic sounds in both speech and music.

We can think of a periodic musical tone in terms of a short waveform repeating over and over f times per second, or we can think of it as the sum of a number of harmonic sinusoidal components, each of which repeats periodically. If the waveform is to be periodic, the frequencies of the partials or frequency components must be integer multiples of a frequency f, which may or may not be present in the actual tone. The partial of frequency f is called the fundamental or first harmonic. It repeats the same number of times a second as the whole waveform does. Its frequency, called the pitch frequency, corresponds to the pitch of the tone; for instance, the pitch of A4 is 440 Hz.

The component of frequency $2f$ is the second harmonic; that of frequency $3f$ is the third harmonic, and so on. A musical tone, which we hear as a single sound, can be thought of as made up of sinusoidal components or partials of many harmonic frequencies.

14.3 Beats and Tuning

Musical tones are periodic. Periodic tones contain harmonic partials whose frequencies are an integer times the frequency of the fundamental. We have noted that consonant musical intervals can be described by the ratios of small integers, for example, 1:2 (the octave) and 2:3 (the fifth). These expressions give the ratio of the fundamental frequency of the lower tone to the fundamental frequency of the higher tone. In any octave, the fundamental frequency of the higher tone is twice that of the lower tone. In any ideal fifth, the fundamental frequency of the higher tone is 3/2 the fundamental of the lower tone.

When we sound two musical tones together, beats occur when any partial of the lower tone has a frequency close to some partial of a higher tone. If we tune one of the tones so as to make the beat rate smaller and smaller, the ratios of the fundamental or pitch frequencies of the beating tones will be given by the ratios of the harmonics of the tones that are beating. Thus, if the second harmonic of the lower tone beats with the fundamental of the upper tone, the tone of higher pitch is an octave above the tone of lower pitch. If the third harmonic partial of the lower tone beats with the second harmonic partial of the upper tone, the pitch frequencies of the lower and upper tones are in the ratio 2:3 and the musical interval is the fifth.

Beats are the chief means for tuning musical instruments precisely. Through a sense of pitch and a memory of intervals, those with musical ability can tune one note of a piano keyboard to approximately the right interval from another note. But it is by beats that the final tuning is made.

In tuning to a tempered scale, the beat will not be set to zero rate; it will be set to some prescribed number of beats per second. After the intervals of a central octave have been tuned, the notes of lower and upper octaves are tuned for zero beat frequency with tones of an adjacent octave.

This means tuning to make the frequency of some harmonic of the higher octave equal to the frequency of some harmonic of the lower octave. However, because of the stiffness of piano strings, the "harmonics" or partials of a piano tone are not quite harmonic; their frequencies depart a little from an integer times the fundamental frequency. Thus, we expect that in a tuned piano the pitches of the tones must depart a little from what they would be if the partials had been truly harmonic. As we see from figure 14.2, the departures are there, though they are a few tens of cents (a cent is 1/100th of a musical half step) at the extremes of pitch.

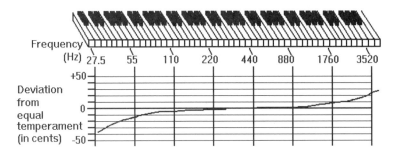

Figure 14.2 Deviations from equal temperament in a piano tuned by beats.

Table 14.2   Stretched spectra and scale examples: harmony and the coincidence of partials

EXAMPLE ATTRIBUTES	PERCEPTUAL RESULT
Normal scale, harmonic partials	harmonious
Stretched scale, harmonic partials	dissonant
Stretched scale, stretched partials	somewhat harmonious
Normal scale, normal partials	harmonious

The stretched partials of the piano strongly support the view that musical intervals are associated with the nature of periodic sounds, but with what aspect of periodic sounds? With some mystic numerological quality of the integers, or with the beating of the partials of several tones sounded together? This is demonstrated by a simple computer-generated sound example, with results given in table 14.2.

In the sound example we play a few bars of a well-known hymn. The music is played with an equal temperament scale. At first the music is played using tones with truly harmonic partials. It sounds harmonious. Then the music is played using tones in which the frequency of the Nth harmonic is increased by a factor:

$$N^{\log_2(2.1)} \tag{14.1}$$

The frequency of the second partial is 2.10, rather than 2, times the pitch frequency. The third partial is 3.241, rather than 3, times the pitch frequency, and so on. Played with these nonharmonic partials, the music sounds awful. Partials of different notes that originally fell near one another now miss disastrously, giving rise to a noisy dissonance.

Suppose we modify the scale that we use with nonharmonic tones whose partial frequencies are given by equation 14.1. The frequencies of successive semitones of the normal equal tempered scale are given by

$$2^{(n/12)} \cdot 440 \tag{14.2}$$

Here n is the number of semitones above A4.

Suppose that instead we take the frequency n semitones above A4 as

$$2.1^{n/12} \cdot 440 \tag{14.3}$$

Then if two harmonic partials of different tones (different values of n) coincide or nearly coincide with the unstretched scale, the corresponding two nonharmonic partials of tones in the stretched scale will coincide or nearly coincide.

We find, as noted in table 14.2, that the piece played with stretched partial spacings according to equation 14.1 and stretched scale according to equation 14.3 sounds harmonious, though slightly different from the piece played with harmonic partials and the normal tempered scale given by equation 14.2. Clearly, the phenomenon of consonance depends on the coincidence of the partials of different tones rather than on the numerological properties of integers.

14.4 Relative Consonance of Intervals

In music the quality of an interval depends on its musical context. A chord from a foreign key sounds out of place, and may appear to be dissonant. The characterization of an interval may also depend on detailed musical training. There is negligible beating between sine waves a tritone apart, yet a musician may characterize a tritone played with sine waves as dissonant simply because he recognizes the interval as a dissonant interval.

Musical intervals played with musical tones have an inherent consonance called tonal consonance. Tonal consonance is generally explained in terms of the separation of partials of the tones sounded together. When partials of two tones sounded together are closer than a critical bandwidth (roughly a frequency ratio of around a minor third, or 1.2) they beat together, and produce a rough or harsh sound. Rainer Plomp has given formulas for calculating the consonance of intervals and chords from the spacings and intensities of the partials that are present.

It is clear that tonal consonance depends both on the spectra of the tones sounded together and on the musical interval between them. Whether or not consonance calculated by formulas agrees exactly with ratings of consonance by musicians, when pairs of partials of two tones sounded together fall in the same critical band, there is dissonance. We noted this in the case of the piece of music in which the spacings of the partials in the tone were stretched but the scale was not stretched. We can observe it in the buzzy, unpleasant timbre of a square wave. The square wave has a dissonant timbre associated

Table 14.3 Superconsonant intervals in which harmonics of upper tone are all harmonics of lower tone

FREQ. RATIO	MUSICAL INTERVAL
1:2	Octave (C–C′)
1:3	Octave + fifth (C–G′)
1:4	Two octaves (C–C″)
1:5	Two octaves + maj. third (C–E″)
1:6	Two octaves + fifth (C–G″)

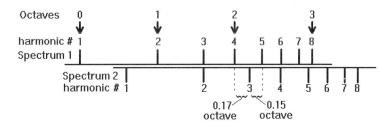

Figure 14.3 First eight harmonics of two tones a fifth apart.

with its strong, closely spaced high harmonics, several of which lie within one critical band.

For some "superconsonant" intervals the harmonics of the upper tone all fall on harmonics of the lower tone, so that they can do no more than intensify the effect of harmonics of the lower tone. Table 14.3 lists some such intervals: 1:2, the octave; 1:3, an octave and a fifth; 1:4, two octaves; 1:5, two octaves and a major third; 1:6, two octaves and a fifth.

Such superconsonant intervals have brighter timbres than the lower tone, but there is little or no harmonic effect. You can easily verify this by comparing a fifth (2:3) with an octave plus a fifth (1:3).

Other sorts of intervals vary in consonance. The fifth is a very consonant interval. As we see in figure 14.3, some of the harmonics of the upper tone fall on harmonics of the lower tone. Other partials are well separated in frequency. In the fifth and other consonant intervals, the frequency components present will all be harmonics of some frequency F, which is lower than (or equal to) the fundamental or pitch frequency f of the lower tone of the interval. This gives a sort of harmonic quality or clue.

Table 14.4 Intervals specified by ratios *M:N*

INTERVAL	M:N	DIVISOR	FREQ. BELOW LOWER FREQ.
Octave	1:2	1	Same
Fifth	2:3	½	One octave
Fourth	3:4	⅓	Octave + fifth
Major third	4:5	¼	Two octaves
Minor third	5:6	⅕	2 octaves + major third

Note: *M* refers to the lower frequency and *N* to the upper frequency. *M* is the ratio of the lower frequency to the common divisor frequency. Also, every *N*th harmonic of the lower frequency coincides with an *M*th harmonic of the upper frequency.

If the ratio of the lower and upper tones is *M:N,* as in table 14.4, the frequency ratio f/F will be M. Thus, for the octave $f/F=M=1$, all frequency components present are harmonics of the lower tone. For the fifth, $f/F=M=2$, and all frequency components present are harmonics of a frequency an octave below the fundamental frequency of the lower tone. For the fourth, $f/F=M=3$, and all frequencies present are harmonics of a frequency an octave and a fifth (1/3) below the pitch frequency of the lower tone. For the major third $f/F=M=4$, and all frequencies present are harmonics of a frequency two octaves (1/4) below the pitch frequency of the lower tone. For the minor third, $f/F=M=5$, and all frequencies present are harmonics of a frequency two octaves and a major third below the pitch frequency of the lower tone.

There is another aspect to consonant intervals. Every *M*th harmonic of the upper tone coincides with an *N*th harmonic of the lower tone. Thus, the larger the value of *M,* the more harmonics there are of the upper tone that do not coincide in frequency with harmonics of the lower tone. Such noncoincident harmonics may lie within a critical bandwidth of harmonics of the lower tone, and hence may produce dissonance. The smaller *M* (the lower component of the interval ratio) is, the less dissonance one expects.

If the spectra of the lower and the upper tones fall off with frequency, and if the upper tone is much higher in fundamental frequency than the lower tone (*N/M* is very large), the spectra of the two tones will not substantially overlap, and we will hear the two simultaneous tones separately.

Table 14.5 Consonance rating of intervals

INTERVAL NAME	NUMBER OF SEMITONES	IDEAL RATIO	DISSONANCE RATING (1–7)
Octave	12	1:2	1.7
Fifth	7	2:3	1.7
Fourth	5	3:4	2.0
Major third	4	4:5	2.0
Major sixth	9	5:3	2.4
Minor third	3	5:6	2.6
Minor sixth	8	5:8	3.0
Minor seventh	10		3.3
Major second	2		3.9
Tritone	6		4.0
Major seventh	11		5.3
Minor second	1		5.7
Minor ninth	13		5.8

Source: Nordmark and Fahlen (1988).

Critical bandwidth as a fraction of fundamental frequency changes somewhat with frequency. The ratio of critical bandwidth to fundamental frequency is quite large for frequencies near the low end of the piano keyboard. Thus, the same interval should be less consonant for low musical pitches than for mid or high musical pitches. This is indeed so, and arrangers are taught never to use a third of a major or minor triad below C2, but to use only the root and the fifth, or octaves.

The general argument is that for intervals whose frequency ratios are of moderate size, the smaller M is, the more consonant the interval, or at least the more likely that the interval is consonant.

This is in agreement with the results of Jan Nordmark and Lennart Fahlen (1988), shown in table 14.5. The tones used consisted of the first six harmonics in equal amplitudes. Degree of dissonance was rated from 1 to 7. Intervals were specified in semitones. In order of increasing dissonance of consonant intervals we have octave (1:2), fifth (2:3), fourth (3:4), major third (4:5), major sixth (3:5), minor third (5:6), and minor sixth (5:8).

Regarding the consonance of "conventional" tetrads, Nordmark and Fahlen (1988) obtained dissonance judgments for a number of such chords. Judgments of the dissonance seemed scattered and not easy to interpret, as shown in table 14.5.

Biard MacGuineas (1992) obtained some data for intervals involving 7, such as 3:7, 4:7, 5:7. Such intervals were judged to be rather dissonant. Could this arise through lack of familiarity? Should triads such as 1:2:3, 2:3:4, 3:4:5, 4:5:6 have greater dissonance, the greater the initial number? Perhaps. Could this have implications for harmony? The triads 1:2:3 and 2:3:4 contain an octave and don't sound at all chordlike. In the case of the other two triads, 3:4:5 is the second inversion of the major triad 4:5:6. The first inversion, 5:6:8, is not of this simple class of triads.

14.5 Beats in Triads of Sine Waves

We have noted that for sine waves there is negligible beating or dissonance when the frequencies are well separated, whatever their ratio. What about three tones sounded together in frequency ratios approximating those of a major triad? Will there be beats when the triad is a little mistuned? Weak but audible beats can be heard for slight mistuning because of a particular nonlinearity in the ear. The nonlinearity produces a *combination tone* from two sine waves of frequencies f_1 and $f_2 > f_1$. The combination tone has a frequency of $f = 2f_1 - f_2$. If f_1 and f_2 aren't too widely separated in frequency, this combination tone can be heard when the tones of frequencies f_1 and f_2 are 20 dB or more above threshold. The ratio of the loudness of f_0 to that of f_1 and f_2 doesn't change markedly with changes in level (Goldstein 1967).

Consider the major triad with frequency ratios 4:5:6. Let us call the lowest frequency $4f_0$ and the successively higher frequencies $5f_0$ and $6f_0$. The frequency produced by the nonlinearity will be $f = 4f_0$, which is simply the lowest of the three frequencies of the chord. This leads one to believe that if we use sine waves for $5f_0$ and $6f_0$, and instead of $4f_0$ we use a tone a few hertz from $4f_0$, we should hear faint beats even at low levels. This is easily verified by using computer-generated sinusoids, whose frequencies can be controlled accurately. However, such beats are of such a low level that they are probably not of musical significance.

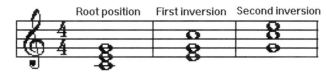

Figure 14.4 Inversions of a triad.

14.6 Rameau and Inversions

The number of intervals of the form *M:N*, where *M* and *N* are integers, is large. Wouldn't it be nice to deal with fewer intervals? That is what Rameau proposed, and musicians have followed.

Suppose we represent all intervals as lying within the octave. Let us feel free to replace either tone of an interval by a tone an octave, or any number of octaves, away. Thus, a major sixth, 3:5, is the same interval as a minor third, 5:6 (with the upper and lower tones interchanged). Applied to triads, our freedom leads to the first and second inversions of the root position (see figure 14.4).

Musicians learn to identify the inversions with the root position chord. In triads, out of any meaningful musical context, people without musical training do not find the inversions similar to one another or to the root position chord (Mathews et al. 1988). Further, we have noted that the interval 1:3 (an octave and a fifth) has little harmonic effect, whereas 2:3 (a fifth) has a striking harmonic effect.

The Autoharp is a stringed instrument used to provide a musical accompaniment in one key. Depressing various buttons on the Autoharp lifts various dampers from the strings, so that stroking the strings produces a chord spread over several octaves. That is, it produces several inversions of the same chord. This sounds fine as a simple accompaniment. In a musical context, inverting a chord is acceptable. Freedom to move the tones of an interval or a chord by an octave simplifies things for both performers and composers.

14.7 Consonant Intervals and Scales

Both consonant intervals and fixed scales are essential to music. As we can see from figure 14.5, we can get all the notes of the scale from triads on the tonic, the subdominant (tonic plus fourth), and the dominant (tonic plus fifth).

However, scales and consonant intervals are incompatible in any exact sense. If we progress from tone to tone by consonant musical intervals, we wander endlessly in pitch. There are a number of com-

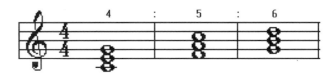

Figure 14.5 Major triads on C, F, and G give all the notes of the C-major scale

Table 14.6 Equations from intervals, scales and temperaments

4V − 2VIII − III = K	(the comma of Didymus, or syntonic comma)	81/80	21.5 cents
8V + III − 5VIII = s	(the schisma)	32805/32768	2.0 cents
12V − 7VIII = p	(the comma of Pythagoris)	521441/534288	23.5 cents
VIII − 3III = d	(diesis)	128/125	41.0 cents
Relations: p = k + s d = 2K − 2			

Note: The pitch "wanders" a little if we go up and down strictly by the ratios of small integers. Exact consonant intervals and scales are inherently inconsistent. For example, going up an octave and down three major thirds results in the "diesis" error of 41.0 cents.
Source: After Lloyd and Boyle (1979).

mon examples of going up and down in pitch by integer ratios and ending up almost, but not quite, where one started. In order to illustrate these, we must associate a few interval names with frequency ratios, such as

VIII	octave	1:2
V	fifth	2:3
III	major third	4:5

We will designate *up four fifths* as 4V, *down two octaves* as −2VIII, and so on. In these terms, various sequences of intervals lead to ratios of final frequency to initial frequency close to, but somewhat different from, unity. Llewellyn Southworth Lloyd and Hugh Boyle (1979) give examples that constitute table 14.6. These are simply well known progressions of consonant intervals; others can be constructed.

The notes of a scale should enable us to sound notes together or to progress from note to note by accepted and useful consonant intervals, or at least by approximations to such consonant intervals. The approximation is necessary if the scale is to have tones of a finite number of frequencies.

The traditional way to represent scales is common music notation with its staff, sharps, and flats. Common notation easily represents the relation of keys. As we go up a fifth to the most nearly related key, we add a sharp, or as we go up a fourth (or down a fifth) to a different most closely related key, we add a flat.

In common notation A-sharp and B-flat do not necessarily have the same pitch. On a piano (or other) keyboard they do. The seven white and five black keys of each octave of the piano can stand for tones of a scale in some key, but they also stand for particular pitches implied in common notation. It is through these pitches that we must approximate intervals whose pitch frequencies are ideally the ratios of small integers.

The pitches of the tones of keyboard instruments are almost universally tuned in equal temperament. The ratios of pitch frequencies of successive keys (white *or* black) are all the twelfth root of 2, approximately 1.05946. This allows perfect octaves, very good fifths and fourths, and not so good major and minor thirds. In equal temperament, the errors in intervals are the same in all musical keys.

Work by L. A. Roberts and Max Mathews (1984) shows that in listening to major triads, some people prefer a "mistuned" third (characteristic of equal temperament) to a just third.

14.8 Pitch Errors in Scales

Pitch errors in scales are errors in ratios of fundamental frequencies. Departures from ideal pitch ratios of small integers are commonly represented in *cents,* or thousandths of an octave (hundredths of a semitone). Table 14.7 gives some relations concerning cents. The pitch ratio of a single cent is approximately $C=1.00057779$.

Table 14.8 shows the pitch in cents for equal temperament intervals and for the corresponding just intervals. Table 14.9 shows errors

Table 14.7 What's a cent? Some relationships

A cent is a frequency ratio C, just slightly greater than unity

$C = 1.00057779$

A cent is 1/1200 of an octave: $C^{1200} = 2.0$

$\ln(C) = \ln(2)/1200$

$C^N = R$

$N \ln(C) = \ln(R)$

$N = \ln(R)/\ln(C)$

Table 14.8 Equal versus just temperament intervals, in cents

INTERVAL	NO. SEMITONES	CENTS, EQUAL TEMP.	CENTS, JUST TEMP.
Fifth	7	700	$\ln(3/2)/\ln(C) = 702.0$
Fourth	5	500	$\ln(4/3)/\ln(C) = 498.0$
Major third	4	400	$\ln(5/4)/\ln(C) = 386.3$
Minor third	3	300	$\ln(6/5)/\ln(C) = 315.6$
Major sixth	9	900	$\ln(5/3)/\ln(C) = 884.4$
Minor sixth	8	800	$\ln(8/5)/\ln(C) = 813.7$

in cents in the tuning of intervals of the white keys of a keyboard (the key of C) for various temperaments.

In the key of C, some just-tuning intervals are correct and some are not. In *Pythagorean,* all fifths and fourths are correct, but minor and major thirds are very bad. In *meantone,* all major thirds are correct in the key of C. In *equal temperament,* the fifths and fourths are nearly but not quite correct, and major and minor thirds have considerable error.

Equal temperament tuning was adopted for pianos around the middle of the nineteenth century. For the preceding two centuries, keyboard instruments had been tuned in meantone temperament.

In meantone temperament the departure of intervals from ideal intervals is different in different keys, and can be very bad in keys with large numbers of sharps or flats. Table 14.10 shows the separation in cents of all tones in a meantone tempered octave. Table 14.11 compares some ideal and meantone intervals. For a major triad in the key of C, the third is perfect and the fifth is 5 cents high. In a major triad in the key of C-sharp, the fifth is only 5 cents high, whereas the third is 41 cents high.

The organ in the Memorial Church at Stanford can be instantly changed to either equal or meantone temperament. Some of its bass chords that sound good in meantone temperament sound throbby and wrong in equal temperament.

As a demonstration, a succession of middle C major tetrads has been synthesized with different temperaments. The stimuli and judgment of consonance are summarized in table 14.12, and are just (very good), meantone key of C (very good), equal (clearly "out of tune"), meantone key of C-sharp (horrendous).

Table 14.9 Intervals and departures from just intervals, in cents

	EQUAL		JUST		MEANTONE		PYTHAGOREAN	
D–F	300	−15.6	294.1	−21.5	310.3	−5.3	294.1	−21.5
E–G	300	−16.6	315.6	0	310.3	−5.3	294.1	−21.5
A–C′	300	−15.6	315.6	0	310.3	−5.3	294.1	−21.5
C–E	400	14.7	386.3	0	386.3	0	407.8	21.5
F–A	400	14.7	386.3	0	386.3	0	407.8	21.5
G–B	400	14.7	386.3	0	386.3	0	407.8	21.5
C–G	700	−2.0	702.0	0	696.6	−5.4	702.0	0
D–A	700	−2.0	680.5	−21.5	696.6	−5.4	702.0	0
E–B	700	−2.0	702.0	0	696.6	−5.4	702.0	0
F–C	700	−2.0	702.0	0	696.6	−5.4	702.0	0
G–D′	700	−2.0	702.0	0	696.6	−5.4	702.0	0
A–E′	700	−2.0	702.0	0	696.6	−5.4	702.0	0

Table 14.10 Frequencies of chromatic meantone scale, middle C to one octave above

NOTE	CENTS	FREQUENCY
C	0	263.1
C-sharp	76	275.0
D	193	294.2
E-flat	310	314.7
E	386	328.9
F	503	352.7
F-sharp	580	367.9
G	697	393.6
G-sharp	773	411.3
A	890	440.0
B-flat	1007	470.8
B	1083	491.9
C′	1200	526.3

Table 14.11 Some ideal and meantone intervals

INTERVAL	CENTS, IDEAL	RATIO, IDEAL	CENTS, MEANTONE	RATIO, MEANTONE
C–E	386	1.25	386	1.25
C–G	702	1.50	697	1.50
C♯–F	386	1.25	427	1.28
C♯–G♯	702	1.50	697	1.50

Table 14.12 Qualitative judgments of middle C major tetrads

Just	Very good
Meantone	Very good
Equal	Out of tune
Meantone, key of C♯	Awful

Meantone is useful only for keys without too many sharps or flats. In the days of meantone temperament, different keys were correctly described as having different musical effects. A composer chose a particular key not only because the notes were higher or lower in pitch but to give a particular flavor to the composition.

With the universal triumph of equal temperament, any rational basis for aesthetic differences in key (except tessitura) vanished, however real or unreal it may have been in the past. Some electronic keyboards can be tuned to a variety of temperaments. This should make it even easier to conduct experiments in temperaments.

The tuning chosen is only part of the story. Except in computer music, the pitch frequency a performer actually plays on a nonkeyboard instrument depends on the player. The performers in a barbershop quartet or a chorus may choose to sing some prolonged and important chords in just intonation, and get back into key, so to speak, while singing shorter notes on less consonant intervals. Paul Hindemith (1969) discusses this in his book *A Composer's World* and in other writings.

14.9 Other Scales

The arguments already presented are consistent with intervals and scales based on periodic tones, and on human ability to learn and to

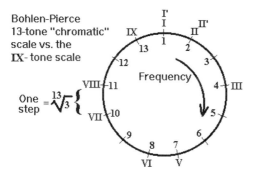

Figure 14.6 Intervals and chords of the Bohlen–Pierce scale.

deal skillfully with periodic tones in terms of rate or pitch, intervals, and scales. What about intervals in the ratios of small whole numbers that can't be approximated on the keyboard? This is a challenge. Unknown to Max Mathews and this author at the time, this question was pursued by Bohlen in a paper published in 1978, and possibly earlier.

The Bohlen–Pierce Scale (Mathews et al. 1988) is one response to this challenge. Figure 14.6 depicts the scale. The Bohlen–Pierce scale repeats every tritave (1:3) rather than every octave (1:2). The tetrad 3:5:7:9 is fundamental to the scale. The intervals of this tetrad are approximated by 13 "chromatic" tones per tritave, successive tones having frequency ratios given by the thirteenth root of 3. The scale itself is a 9-tone subset of the 13 chromatic tones. The scale can begin on any of the 13 chromatic tones, giving 13 keys in all. One modulates from any key to any adjacent key by changing ("flatting" or "sharping") one tone of the nine-tone scale. Composers including Richard Boulanger, Ami Radunskaya, and Jon Appleton have written pieces in the Bohlen–Pierce scale. Some of these can be found on (Mathews 1994).

Dissonance and consonance have been considered in other scales, including scales not based on the ratios of small integers (Pierce 1966; Mathews and Pierce 1980). Sethares (1993) has conducted thorough and effective research in this area.

14.10   Tones with Strange Spectra

Most musical tones are approximately periodic, and the tones we have discussed have harmonics other than the first, the fundamental. Our discussions of intervals and scales have been grounded on these characteristics of musical tones.

The tones of some musical instruments, including orchestra chimes, kettle drums, and carillon bells, have nonharmonic partials as well as a subset of nearly harmonic partials. The nearly harmonic partials are prominent enough to give the tones of these instruments a sense of pitch, of a frequency, missing or present, of which the members of the subset are nearly harmonics. In carillon bells the nonharmonic partials are prominent and add a clangorous sensation to the tone.

While all musical tones have harmonic partials, not all tones with harmonic partials are musical tones in the sense of being adapted to conventional harmony. Sine waves themselves aren't really musical tones. Like a musical tone, a sine wave is periodic, but it has no harmonics. There are vestigial beats between sine waves an octave or other musical interval apart, but such beats are hard to hear. It would be essentially impossible to tune by ear a keyboard instrument that produced sinusoidal tones.

Further, both the pitch and the timbre of piano tones near the left end of the keyboard depend primarily on harmonics rather than on the fundamental, or even on the second harmonic. A 27.5 Hz sine wave is a weak, throbbing tone that does not sound at all musical. At best, sine waves are quasi-musical tones.

In Shepard tones (Shepard 1964) the whole range of pitch is confined to an octave; intervals lying farther than an octave apart do not occur. A Shepard tone has no fundamental, though it does have a lowest audible partial for which the frequencies of all other partials (which are an octave apart) are integer multiples. Shepard tones can be ambiguous in pitch. They do not have certain essential qualities of musical tones. We can imagine novel sorts of harmony and music based on Shepard tones, but such music would be limited compared with that built around musical tones. We can also construct many variants of Shepard tones. For example, we can construct tones in which successive frequency components differ in frequency by a factor of 3 rather than a factor of 2.

Tones other than musical tones are important in unraveling the phenomena of hearing, but they should not be confused with musical tones and the perception of musical tones.

References

Bohlen, H. von. (1978). "Tonstufen in der Duodezine." *Acustica* 39(2): 76–86.

Fischer, J. C. (1975). *Piano Tuning.* Dover, New York. (Repr. from 1st ed., 1907).

Goldstein, J. L. (1967). "Auditory nonlinearity." *Journal of the Acoustical Society of America,* 41, 676–689.

Hindemith, P. (1969). *A Composer's World: Horizons and Limitations.* Gloucester, Mass.: P. Smith.

Houtsma, A. J. M., T. D. Rossing, and W. M. Wagenaars. (1987). *Auditory Demonstrations.* Philips 1126-061. (Compact disc).

Houtsma, A. J. M., and J. Smurzynski. (1990). "Pitch Identification and Discrimination for Complex Tones with Many Harmonics." *Journal of the Acoustical Society of America,* 87, 304–310.

Jorgensen, O. H. (1991). *Tuning.* East Lansing: Michigan State University Press.

Lloyd, L. S., and H. Boyle. (1979). *Intervals, Scales, and Temperaments.* New York: St. Martin's Press.

MacGuineas, B. (1992). "Consonance: Simplicity or Custom?" Center for Computer Research in Music and Acoustics, Music Department, Stanford University. (Unpublished memorandum).

Mathews, M. (1994). *The Virtuoso in the Computer Age.* Centaur CDCM, Computer Music Series vol. 15. (Compact disc).

Mathews, M. V., and J. R. Pierce. (1980). "Harmony and Nonharmonic Partials." *Journal of the Acoustical Society of America,* 68, 1252–1257.

Mathews, M. V., J. R. Pierce, A. Reeves, and L. A. Roberts. (1988). "Theoretical and Experimental Exploration of the Bohlen–Pierce Scale." *Journal of the Acoustical Society of America,* 84, 1214–1222.

Nordmark, J., and Fahlen, L. (1988). "Beat Theories of Musical Consonance." In *Speech Transmission Laboratory, Quarterly Progress and Status Report.* Dept. of Speech Communication and Music Acoustics, Royal Institute of Technology, Stockholm.

Pierce, J. R. (1966). "Attaining Consonance in Arbitrary Scales." *Journal of the Acoustical Society of America,* 40, 249.

————. (1991). "Periodicity and Pitch Perception." *Journal of the Acoustical Society of America,* 90, 1889–1893.

Plomp, R. (1976). *Aspects of Tone Sensation.* New York: Academic Press.

Plomp, R., and W. J. M. Levelt. (1965). "Tonal Consonance and Critical Bandwidth." *Journal of the Acoustical Society of America,* 38, 548–560.

Roberts, L. A., and M. V. Mathews. (1984). "Intonational Sensitivity for Traditional and Nontraditional Chords." *Journal of the Acoustical Society of America,* 75, 952–959.

Shepard, R. N. (1964). "Circularity in Judgments of Relative Pitch." *Journal of the Acoustical Society of America,* 35, 2346–2353.

Sethares, W. A. (1993). "Local Consonance and the Relationship Between Timbre and Scale." *Journal of the Acoustical Society of America,* 94, 1218–1228.

15   Tonal Structure and Scales

Roger Shepard

15.1   Introduction

Concepts such as chroma and height, and the relationships of octaves and fifths, do not tell the whole story of how our scales come into being. Another perceptual phenomenon that affects the structure of musical pitch involves the interpretation of musical sounds that enter the brain. As musical sounds are perceived, especially when they occur in the context of a musical piece, they are related in the brain to a cognitive structure such as a musical scale or, more generally, a tonal structure.

The kinds of scales described by the helical structures shown in chapter 13 are uniform, and nothing in their representation determines any particular reference point. The helix can be translated in any direction and nothing changes. Similarly, there are particular musical scales that exhibit this lack of specific reference point, such as the whole tone scale (as shown in figure 15.1) where all members are equally spaced. Since there is nothing stationary in such a scale, there is no sense of absolute motion. It is interesting that the whole tone scale, when used in orchestration, and specifically in scoring for entertainment, most often is in a context that is fuzzy and nebulous as to reference, such as dreams and underwater scenes. Perhaps the feeling that time seems suspended in dreams, or that gravity is suspended and you can swim around underwater and seemingly not go anywhere, is actually modeled quite well by a musical scale that seems to lack a frame of reference. Such things as musical tension, which give music its dynamic quality, are therefore difficult to portray in the whole tone scale and others like it. To give a sense of absolute motion or reference, one might play certain notes louder, longer, or more often.

A sense of reference is fundamental to musical scales in most cultures. Asymmetry provides this reference, and is therefore a fundamental property of most musical scales. Figure 15.1, for example, shows a plot of spacings between the notes of the diatonic, pentatonic, and whole tone scales. Note that the diatonic scale is composed of two whole steps, then a half step, then three whole steps,

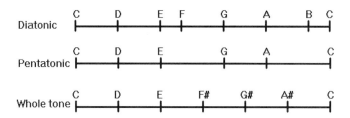

Figure 15.1 Plot of spacings between the notes of the diatonic (top), pentatonic (center), and whole tone (bottom) scales.

then a half step. The pentatonic scale is composed of an asymmetric mixture of whole steps and minor thirds. This asymmetry allows a listener to more easily identify where a tone is located within the scale structure, and tends to emphasize some tones over others.

15.2 Testing Musical Tones in Musical Contexts

The tradition in psychophysics at one time was to attempt to present listeners with the "pure stimulus"—that is, an isolated tone—and then determine the perceptual parameters related to that stimulus. Musical listeners find such an approach unsatisfying—and frankly incorrect—because this approach does not take into account the musically relevant aspects of sounds. An example of this traditional psychophysical approach to testing was the mel scale as determined by S. Smith Stevens, where some height aspect of pitch was measured but the resulting scale did not relate in a fundamental way to music.

The opposite extreme in testing pitch perception is to present musical tones in musical contexts. This was the approach Carol Krumhansl and this author took, beginning in 1979. Our first experiment used sine tones but first presented a musical context (which typically consisted of all the tones of a scale within an octave), followed by a single probe tone. The listener was then asked to judge how well the probe tone seemed to "fit in" with the musical context, rated on a scale from 1 to 7. If the probe tone sounded like it "fit" well with the musical context, it was given a high rating. Using this experimental approach made it necessary to present the musical context many times in order to test the perceptual fitness of the various probe tones.

When this kind of experiment is performed, an increase in individual differences becomes evident. This is because the experiment is aimed at a measurement of musical sensibility rather than a tradi-

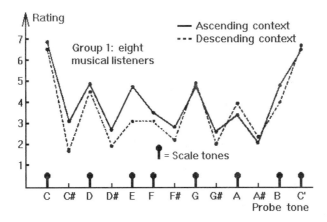

Figure 15.2 Group 1 responses to probe tones in diatonic contexts. (From Krumhansl and Shepard, 1979. © 1979 by the American Psychological Association. Adapted with permission.)

tional, purely objective, psychoacoustic measurement. Like the experiment described in chapter 13, these experiments led to a clustering of three groups: group 1 was musically astute (about seven years of instruction and performance), group 3 was not (no significant instruction or performance), and group 2 fell in between. There were eight members in each group. Figure 15.2 presents the results of group 1 in a plot of the fitness rating of each probe tone selected from all chromatic notes, played after an ascending diatonic scale. Clearly, notes of the diatonic scale show higher fitness than non-scale notes, and notes considered musically important (the tonic and its octave, the perfect fifth, the major third, and the major second) show fitness measures roughly equal to their importance in Western music. The tritone and other tones that are not notes of the diatonic scale show low measures of fitness. One group 1 subject possessed perfect pitch, and could not make judgments based solely on the fitness of pitches because she was aware of the actual note name of each pitch being played. She constantly filtered everything she heard through her music theory training.

Figures 15.3 and 15.4 show the responses of groups 2 and 3. The octave shows a high fitness; other notes of the scale show lower fitnesses. In group 2 there is an interesting difference between descending and ascending contexts. This difference is even more profound in group 3, and the octave importance decreases significantly. As figure 15.5 illustrates, one group 3 subject judged only on pitch height.

Over many studies, the data that show the most pronounced peaks and valleys were the results of studies in which more complex tones

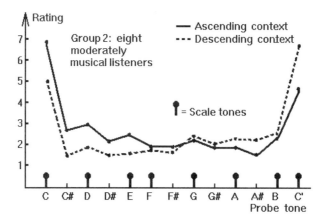

Figure 15.3 Group 2 responses to probe tones in diatonic contexts. (From Krumhansl and Shepard, 1979. © 1979 by the American Psychological Association. Adapted with permission.)

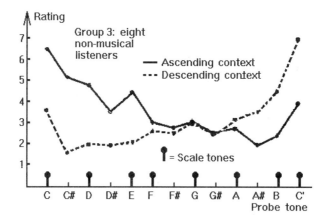

Figure 15.4 Group 3 responses to probe tones in diatonic contexts. (From Krumhansl and Shepard, 1979. © 1979 by the American Psychological Association. Adapted with permission.)

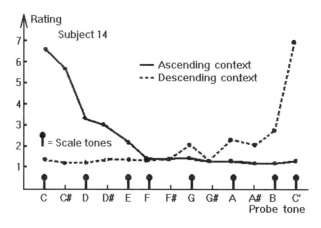

Figure 15.5 Group 3 subject who responded only to pitch height. (From Krumhansl and Shepard, 1979. © 1979 by the American Psychological Association. Adapted with permission.)

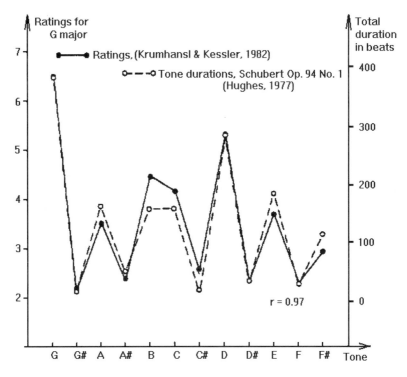

Figure 15.6 Data of Krumhansl and Kessler experiments, compared with an analysis of Schubert's op. 94, no. 1. (From Krumhansl, 1985.)

and/or contexts were used, such as complex timbres rather than sine tones, or a musical passage leading up to a cadence rather than a simple scale. If instead of using a chroma circle to plot the results, a circle of fifths is used, then there is a nearly monotonic decrease from the unison outward. Carol Krumhansl and Edward Kessler (1982) achieved striking results using chord sequences with very sharply defined major or minor keys.

15.3   Scales Are More Than Simple Ratios of Frequency

There is some correlation between the tonal hierarchies derived from experiments like those described above, and purely acoustical descriptions of the intervals. There is more at work, however, than pure mathematical relationships. This was clearly shown by the difference between the major and minor profiles in such experiments. The musical context provided for the subjects clearly influenced the perception of each note of the chromatic scale as to its fitness for that context. Figure 15.6 shows a comparison of Krumhansl and Kessler

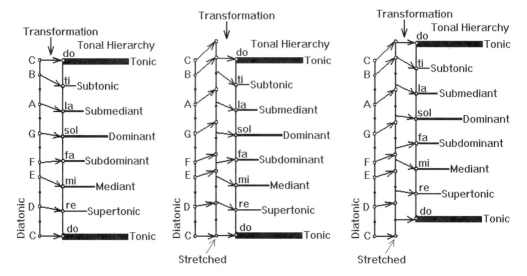

Figure 15.7 (a) Diatonic scale. (b) Stretched scale. (c) Stretched scale.

profiles with data analyzed from Schubert's op. 94, no. 1, concerning the total duration of tones within the chroma circle. The solid line (which represents experimental data) very closely agrees with the dashed line (which represents data extracted from Schubert). Analyses using minor key preferences and note durations showed similar results.

Suppose that we have in our minds a structure of the diatonic scale that can be schematized as in figure 15.1. Our musical scales would have the property that the individual notes are unequally spaced on a log scale (although some people claim that they hear the steps as quite equal). The unequalness allows us to quickly determine the tonic (the root tone, C in figure 15.1). We can also position other tones within the tonal hierarchy, with some tones being more stable than others. The unequal spacing is converted into an unequal weighting or stability measure, assigned to each tone within the cognitive structure. When we hear music, we hear it relative to the structure, so that if a single tone is played, we tend to assign that to tonic and begin interpreting all successive notes as to their position within that hierarchy. For example, a stretched scale can be constructed such that it contains seven notes, like the diatonic scale, but that when the scale is played ascending, it terminates on C# rather than C. (See figure 15.7.)

In figure 15.7(b), each member has been stretched a little, so that unconsciously we adjust as we are hearing, and the C# does not nec-

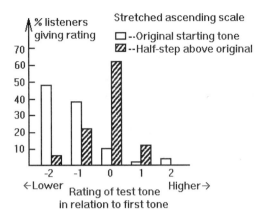

Figure 15.8   Subject responses to stretched ascending scale.

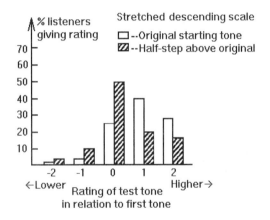

Figure 15.9   Subject responses to stretched descending scale.

essarily sound wrong. If such a scale is played, we adjust our internal concept of the C scale to match the higher tone, as in figure
15.7(c). If we then immediately play the true low C on which the
scale began, the final low C sounds flat. Figures 15.8 and 15.9 show
experimental data from presentations of the stretched scale, followed either by a C or a C#. The C is judged as being flat, whereas
the C# is judged to be correct within the context presented.

15.4   Other Cultures

Beyond the realm of the diatonic scale, one might ask about the
scales of other musical traditions and cultures. A student of mine
went to a remote village in Bali where there was good evidence that

the villagers were unfamiliar with Western scales and music. We employed the context/probe-tone method, using both Western and Balinese scales, and compared the results against the same material presented to Stanford students. We found that in both cultures there were individual differences, but there was also a subset of the Balinese population that tuned into the tonal hierarchy of the Western diatonic scale and yielded similar results.

Different cultures vary widely in the way their scales are constructed, and also in what they deem musical. But studies like those mentioned above lead us to believe that certain properties of the physical world have provided constraints, or guidelines, as to how these scales are constructed and, indeed, how music is heard. Most cultures employ the octave and fifth in their scales, and when presented with the Western diatonic scale for the first time, listeners in other cultures are able to make sense of them.

References

Krumhansl, C. L. (1990). *Cognitive Foundations of Musical Pitch*. New York: Oxford University Press.

Krumhansl, C. L. (1985). "Perceiving Tonal Structure in Music." *American Scientist, 73,* 371–378.

Krumhansl, C. L., and E. J. Kessler. (1982). "Tracing the Dynamic Changes in Perceived Tonal Organization in a Spatial Representation of Musical Keys." *Psychological Review, 89,* 334–368.

Krumhansl, C. L., and R. N. Shepard. (1979). "Quantification of the Hierarchy of Tonal Functions Within a Diatonic Context." *Journal of Experimental Psychology: Human Perception and Performance, 5,* 579–594.

Stevens, S. S., J. Volkmann, and E. B. Newman. (1937). "A Scale for the Measurement of the Psychological Magnitude Pitch." *Journal of the Acoustical Society of America, 8,* 185–190.

16 Pitch, Periodicity, and Noise in the Voice

Perry R. Cook

16.1 Isn't Singing Just Strange Speech?

This chapter will discuss pitch and periodicity in the singing voice. Obviously one of the most important differences between speech and singing is the use and control of pitch. A brief list of the differences between singing and speech follows:

Voiced/unvoiced ratio—The time ratio of voiced/unvoiced/silent phonation is roughly 60%/25%/15% in speech, compared with the nearly continuous 95% voiced time of singing.

Singer's vibrato—Intentionally introduced deviation in the voice pitch. This chapter deals with this topic, as well as unintentional pitch deviations.

Singer's formant—Acoustical phenomenon brought about by grouping the third, fourth, and sometimes fifth formants together for increased resonance. There are also nonlinear phenomena that likely contribute to the increase in spectral information. The singer's formant would be less evident if the glottal source of the singer did not have rich spectral content in this range. Solo singers use the singing formant to be heard, particularly above instruments.

Singer's vowel modification—Intentional and unintentional practices of mutating the vowel sound as a function of pitch for comfort, projection, and/or intelligibility. Some modification in the sound is an artifact of wider harmonic spacing under the vocal tract filter spectrum envelope rather than a spectral envelope change.

Nasal airway use (for Western bel canto, a style of singing)—The pathway through the nose is not used as often as it is in speech. This is caused partly by arching the soft palate (velum) to acquire the *singer's formant*. This mechanism also allows singers to sound much the same whether or not they have a cold.

Average pitch and range of pitch—The average speaking pitch is different from the average singing pitch. The comfortable speaking pitch is often different from the comfortable singing pitch. The range of speaking is determined by the speaker's comfort and emotional state. The singer's range is first determined by physiology and training. For a singer performing a particular musical piece, the range is determined by the composer.

Average volume and range—The average level of the speaking voice is softer than the average level of the singing voice. The dynamic range of singing is greater than that of typical speech. Greater flow rates and greater excursions of the vocal folds imply that the singing system is likely to operate in higher orders of non-linearity.

Singer vocal training—The singer exercises his/her vocal folds regularly in different regimes; thus differences exist between the source signals of singers and non-singers. When asked to phonate loudly, untrained singers (and speakers of loud or angry speech) move toward a pressed (efficient but squeaky) mode of phonation. Good, well-trained singers show no such tendency, and thus present a more consistent timbre across a wide dynamic range. They accomplish this by using vowel modification, and by having increased muscle development and control of the voice source.

Neurology—Some classic studies on head injury document cases of people who are unable to speak but still sing perfectly, and are even able to learn and perform new songs. These and other studies point up the likelihood of different areas of the brain controlling speech and singing.

Statutory—It is unclear at the present time whether singing is protected under the First Amendment to the U.S. Constitution. This part of the Bill of Rights protects free speech, but some recent interpretations have tended toward defining certain artistic performances as non-speech.

This chapter will concentrate on how singers control pitch, how well they can control it, and how the pitch control system behaves in the presence of interference and noise. We will also cover some other aspects of aperiodicity in the voice, specifically noise in the vocal source.

16.2 Pitch in Singing

A feature distinguishing the human singing voice from most other musical instruments, aside from the fact that the instrument is part of the performer, is the lack of a specific reference for pitch. That is, in most instruments, such as brass, wind, and string instruments, there are certain pitches that are produced solely on the basis of the physics of the instrument (and the current state of the tensions in the strings, where applicable). These stable reference pitches are independent of the player. In many instruments, the pitch is quantized, meaning that only certain discrete pitches are playable by the instrument. The best example of this is the piano, where each allowable pitch is associated with one black or white key. Other instruments, like the trumpet, favor quantized pitches, because the resonant peaks in the transfer function of the instrument cause it to tend to oscillate at specific pitches that are the harmonics of the overtone series selected by the valves. The trombone and fretless string instruments like the violin can produce a continuum of pitches, where a smooth sweep in the controls causes the pitch to sweep smoothly as well. There are still reference pitches, such as when the trombone slide is placed at its shortest position or when the violin strings are sounded open.

The voice can produce a continuum of pitches but has no reference pitches. The human *voice player* can approximate a pitch from the feeling and memory of what that pitch feels like, but the instrument is not guaranteed to produce the expected pitch. If the singer has a mental target set for the pitch, and the singer is able to hear his/her own voice, he/she can adapt rapidly to bring the produced pitch into alignment with the target pitch.

There exists no reference, however, such that if all the settings are put in a particular position, the voice always sounds the same pitch. Even singers who possess so-called *perfect pitch* may not be able to produce the correct pitch because of limitations in the production mechanism. They may hear the pitch correctly in their head, but if they are not particularly good vocalists, they may be unable to sing the note they hear. Good vocalists with perfect pitch nevertheless experience large shifts in production capability as a function of the time of day, illness, age, or other factors. If a singer is unable to hear the sound of his/her own voice, the produced pitch can deviate profoundly from the target pitch. A study (Ward and Burns 1978) in which singers (some with perfect pitch) were fitted with headphones carrying a noise-masking signal, showed large production errors when the masking signal was present and the singers were unable to hear their own voice.

When a singer produces a tone, there is always an amount of deviation in the pitch, some intentional and some not. This is true of other instruments in which the player has direct and continuous

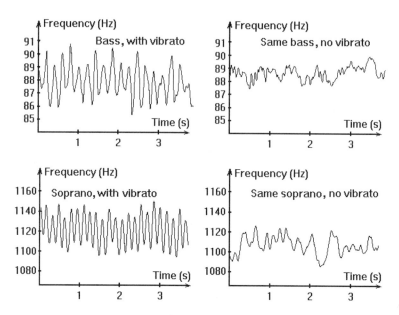

Figure 16.1 Time domain waveforms of a the instantaneous pitch signal of a bass singer (upper) and a soprano singer (lower). The left plots are of vibrato tones, and the right plots are of tones where the singers were instructed to sing without vibrato. A component of vibrato is clearly evident in the soprano "nonvibrato" tone.

contact with the physics of the instrument. Instruments in which this is not the case include the piano and most organs. The player cannot do anything about the instantaneous oscillations on instruments such as these.

In general, the deviations in pitch in the singing voice can be broken into two or three categories. The intentional modulation of pitch, usually for artistic purposes, is called *vibrato*. Vibrato is a nearly sinusoidal frequency deviation in the range of 5–8 Hz. If the instantaneous pitch is treated as a signal, it can be plotted in the time domain and analyzed using frequency spectrum analysis. In the frequency domain, the vibrato appears as a clear sinusoidal spike near 6 Hz. Even when a singer produces a pitch without vibrato, there is usually a small component of measurable vibrato in the signal. Figure 16.1 presents two time domain graphs of instantaneous pitch as a function of time for two singers, a soprano and a bass. Pitch signals both with and without vibrato are shown. Both soprano signals clearly show some vibrato-like fluctuations, even though the singer was intentionally suppressing vibrato in one instance. Figure 16.2 shows the Fourier transforms of the bass vibrato and nonvibrato pitch signals. The spectra show clear peaks in the vibrato region, even on the "nonvibrato" tones.

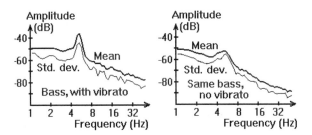

Figure 16.2 Fourier spectra of the pitch signal from figure 16.1. The peak around 6 Hz is the vibrato component. There is still a peak near 6 Hz in the "nonvibrato" tone.

The region above the vibrato peak in the spectrum of the pitch signal is often called the *flutter region,* and the region below is called the *wow region.* These terms stem from tape-recorder specifications. In that context they are to be minimized, because even small amounts of wow or flutter undesirably modulate the recorded signal on tape. It is not necessarily good to minimize them in the voice, however. As a matter of practice these deviation components cannot be controlled much, anyway. In dealing with computer and machine speech and singing synthesis, one soon becomes aware that these components are important, and effort must be spent on making the machine mimic the human qualities of "wow and flutter." The author prefers to remove the negative connotations, and label these two components *drift* and *jitter,* to better represent the causes and effects.

The jitter phenomenon is largely uncontrollable, as in people saying they have the jitters. Consciously trying to control jitter sometimes results in an increase in the activity. As an experiment, try holding your hand directly in front of you, as still as you possibly can. Just being aware that your hand is shaking and trying to stop it causes it to shake more. If you think you hold your hand quite still, drink some coffee or tea, and the jitter phenomenon becomes more obvious. This uncontrollable rapid shaking occurs in the vocal control muscles, causing the pitch of the vocal fold oscillations to vary rapidly.

The *drift* term is borrowed from controls engineering, electronics circuits, and other disciplines. Drift is a slow misadjustment that is usually corrected adaptively by a feedback mechanism. In tracking a satellite, a receiver on Earth might focus in an arc across the sky at the correct velocity to match the satellite. Due to many factors, the receiver deviates slightly from the intended trajectory, and a special sensor circuit indicates that the satellite receiver is not exactly on target. The sensor circuit feeds back to the motor control circuit and instructs it to change its speed to compensate. This process repeats rapidly, resulting in an acceptable tracking of the satellite.

Vocal pitch is controlled in much the same way. The brain sends signals to the articulators to cause the vocal folds to adduct. Once they begin oscillation, the ears detect the vocal sound. The brain deduces a pitch for the sound the ears are hearing and immediately begins sending correction signals to the vocal folds to bring the pitch into alignment. There is inherent time delay associated with receiving the voice signal at the ears, deducing the pitch, comparing that pitch with the intended pitch, and sending the appropriate adjustment signals to the voice source control muscles. This process is repeated continuously, and the resulting voice pitch *drifts* slowly above and below the intended pitch. Drift causes a frequency deviation in the range below 5 Hz.

In general, drift is more easily controlled than jitter. Since drift is related to controlling the perceived pitch of the voice, auditory feedback plays an important role. If the singer is unable to hear his/her own voice well, the amount of drift increases. Since it is difficult to deduce the pitch of very low tones, and the pitch detection process takes longer for low tones, drift increases in the lower voice ranges. Bass singers are slightly less accurate than tenors, but the net result is not as important because the listener cannot deduce the pitch of the bass tones as well as the higher sung tones of the tenor. When singers intentionally impose vibrato, the pitch of the tone becomes more difficult to deduce, and drift increases accordingly. Jitter is largely independent of the auditory feedback process, but does increase slightly in the presence of vibrato. While drift is nearly independent of voice level (unless the voice is so soft that the singer can't hear it), jitter increases with increasing loudness of vocal production and with increasing pitch. Figure 16.3 shows some general relations for drift and jitter as a function of pitch and loudness level, with and without vibrato.

The fact that singers have difficulty removing vibrato entirely brings up a popularly debated question: Do singers train the vibrato in, or does it occur naturally? Does training allow more or less control? The commonly held explanation for vibrato is that it is an entrainment of the jitter mechanism, which occurs naturally in relaxed singing voices. Other opinions abound, but it is fairly clear that in cultures and musical traditions where vibrato is not common, quite different voice qualities are used in singing. Vibrato can be greatly

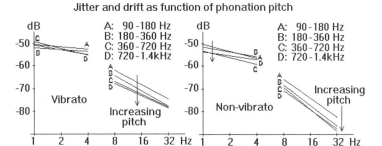

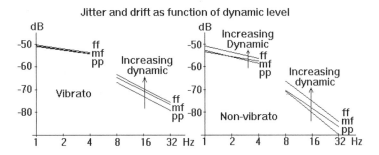

Figure 16.3 Line segment fits to the drift and jitter regions of averaged spectra computed from pitch signals of four singers. In general, jitter decreases with increasing pitch, and increases with increasing dynamic level. Drift is relatively unaffected by pitch and dynamic level in vibrato tones, and exhibits slight dependence in nonvibrato tones.

suppressed by changing the settings of the voice source control muscles affecting larynx height and pitch, and voice quality changes as a result. Training on vibrato seems to have the effect of making the process more automatic, but also more controllable. A study conducted on the effect of delayed auditory feedback on the vibrato of nontrained singers (Deutsch and Clarkson 1959) showed that altered auditory feedback affected the behavior of the vibrato. A later study (Shipp et al. 1984) showed that the vibrato characteristics of trained singers are largely unaffected by distortions in auditory feedback, but the drift component is quite profoundly affected.

As discussed in earlier chapters, anything deviating too profoundly from the normal behaviors we have come to expect in the real world ceases to sound or look natural. Articulatory positions outside those that can physically be formed (or even easily reached) by a human speaker cause sounds that are nonhuman. A synthesized trumpet solo played too fast sounds wrong because a human trumpeter could not have played it.

In the case of vocal vibrato, there are also expected ranges for frequency and amount. The average vocal vibrato lies in the region between 5 and 7 Hz. Anything slower than 5 Hz sounds sluggish, and anything above 7 Hz sounds nervous. The average extent of vibrato in Western singing is ± 2%, and vibrato exceeding ± 4% sounds odd. Drift is normally around 0.5% average deviation. Jitter is about 0.05% at 8 Hz, decreasing to 0.005% at 32 Hz. While these amounts of pitch deviation might seem quite small, if synthetic vocal tones are produced with absolutely no pitch deviation, the listener's auditory system quickly recognizes that no human could produce such a "perfect" tone. Such tones are most often labeled "machinelike." Synthesis with too much drift sounds like the singer is unable to hear or control his/her voice. Synthesis with too much jitter sounds like the singer has a neurological disorder, or has been recorded using an inferior tape recorder.

Besides pitch deviations, there are other aperiodicities in the voice. One is called *shimmer*, which is the deviation in the spectrum (or waveshape) of a vocal tone. We know from our knowledge of vocal tract acoustics that any deviation in vocal tract shape will affect the spectrum. Any deviation in pitch causes the harmonics to move to different locations on the spectral envelope, resulting in a change in the individual amplitudes of the harmonic components. The voice source also deviates in spectrum, adding to the overall result of shimmer.

16.3 Noise in the Voice

Another extremely important aperiodic component in vocal sounds is noise created by turbulence near the voice source. The flow of air through the oscillating narrow slit between the vocal folds creates the possibility for turbulent noise, similar to the way we form consonants such as "s" by creating a narrow place in the vocal tract and forcing air through it. Figure 16.4 shows the time domain waveform and frequency domain spectra of a low tone sung by a bass singer. Note that the spectrum is basically harmonic, but there is a *noise floor* that represents the noisy component of the voice. The waveform is basically periodic but definitely differs in shape from period to period. If you look closely, you can see that the disturbance is larger in some phases of the waveform than others. This is caused by periodic bursts of noise, which occur because of the opening and closing of the vocal folds, and the resulting change in airflow as the folds are rapidly sucked shut.

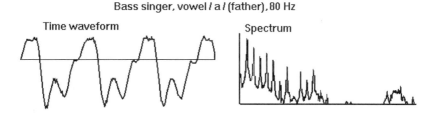

Figure 16.4   Time domain waveform (left) and frequency spectrum (right) of a male vocal tone.

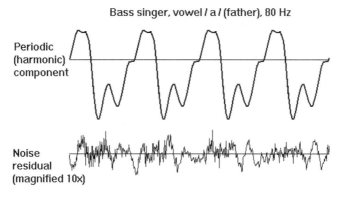

Figure 16.5   Purely periodic component (top) and noise component (bottom) of waveform of male vocal tone shown in figure 16.4. The noise component is amplified 10 times.

Figure 16.5 shows waveforms that are the purely periodic part, and the noisy part, of the waveform of figure 16.4. The splitting of signals in this way into harmonic (or sinusoidal) and noisy parts is called *decomposition*. The noise is called a residual, because it is the residue left when the predictable parts of the signal have been distilled away. Signal decomposition is discussed in more detail in chapter 22.

Much of the research on noise in the voice has focused on abnormally noisy voices, which are sometimes indicative of a pathology or serious illness. Linguists have recently taken more interest in noise in the normal voice, because some of the information in what we say is carried by the *voice quality*, in addition to the pitch, loudness, and words being said. Voice quality is a mixture of the spectral tilt of the voice source, the amount of noise in the voice, and the *flavor* (positions of the formants) of the vowels used. Some of what allows us to identify familiar voices rapidly, often independent of what is being said, is the quality of the speaker's voice. There is quite

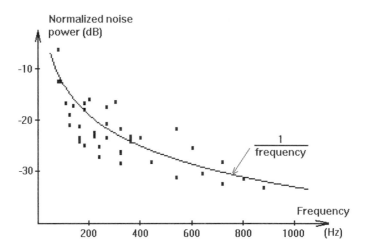

Figure 16.6 Normalized noise power as a function of sung pitch for many singers. The data are close to a 1/*f* dependency.

a large amount of individualism in vocal quality, and that distinguishes the voices of singers as well as speakers. The amount of noise in the singer's voice can be controlled somewhat by the singer, as when creating an excited or whispering singing quality. There is some noise that cannot be controlled by the singer and, as in vibrato, there is always some amount of noise no matter what the singer does to eliminate it. Figure 16.6 presents the results of a study on noise in singer voices, and shows the dependency of vocal noise level on pitch.

16.4 Subharmonics in the Voice

One other type of aperiodicity found in voices is the *subharmonic,* which is a periodic or pseudo-periodic oscillation at a frequency below the intended oscillation frequency. This is sometimes seen in the vocal waveform, and often in the spectrum. Figure 16.7 shows a time domain waveform and a frequency domain spectrum of a vocal tone sung at 340 Hz by a bass singer. There are clear components in the waveform that are more similar every two periods rather than every one, such as the slopes of the peaks of the waveforms.

The subharmonic is clearly seen in the frequency domain plot, with sinusoids visible at 1/2, 3/2, and so on of the frequency of the intended fundamental. If one were to listen to this tone, the subharmonic might not be evident, and the perceived pitch would

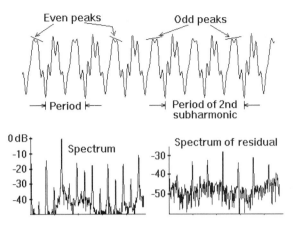

Figure 16.7 Waveform (top) of a male sung tone of 340 Hz. Note the waveform features that occur every two periods. The spectrum of this tone (lower left) shows clear subharmonic components at multiples of 170 Hz. After the components of 340 Hz are removed, the spectrum of the residual (lower right) shows the subharmonic and its odd harmonics.

be 340 Hz. By decomposing the signal into one part that consists only of 340 Hz and all of its harmonics, and another part that is the residual after that harmonic extraction, the subharmonic is easily heard at the pitch one octave below, at 170 Hz. After hearing the subharmonic alone, most listeners report that they can clearly hear the subharmonic component in the original sound. Like noise in the voice, subharmonics have been studied most as a vocal pathology, commonly called *diplophonia* ("diplo" from "two," meaning the waveform looks more similar to itself at two periods than at one).

While studying noise in the singer voice, the author discovered subharmonics more often than expected. This prompted a study in which subharmonics were specifically searched for, using a specially designed decomposition process (Cook 1991). A total of twenty singers were studied, and it was found that all of them exhibited at least one measurable subharmonic. The percentages of tones containing a subharmonic were 33% for all singers, 34% for males, and 32% for females. The percentages by vowel were 34% for /a/, 40% for /u/, and 20% for /i/. The percentages by dynamic level were 10% for soft, 38% for medium, and 20% for loud. As shown in figure 16.8, males exhibited a consistent increase in subharmonic activity with increasing pitch, while the females showed no clear patterns as a function of pitch.

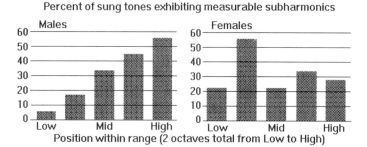

Figure 16.8 Subharmonics exhibited by males (left) and females as a function of position within the vocal range.

16.5 Pitch and Noise in Vowel Perception

As mentioned in chapter 11, vowels sung at high vocal frequencies exhibit ambiguity as to which vowel is being sung. The reason for this is that the harmonics are spaced so far apart that the formants are not obvious. The vocal tract transfer-function spectral envelope is too coarsely sampled to identify the peaks accurately. This is consistent with a fact well known to musicians and composers: that soprano vowels "all sound the same" on high notes above the treble clef staff. One study (Scotto di Carlo and Rutherford 1990) noted that composers who are considered good writers for voice consistently repeat important text on lower pitches if it has been set on high notes. The text is sung on high notes for reasons of musical beauty and line, before or after it is sung on low notes to ensure that the listener knows what is being said.

It has been asserted that pitch deviation, specifically the wide vibrato of singers, allows the perceptual mechanisms to better identify the shape of the spectral envelope. Figure 16.9 shows two harmonics, one on each side of a hidden formant, and the trajectories they trace as they increase and decrease in frequency.

The fact that the lower harmonic increases in amplitude with increasing frequency, while the higher harmonic decreases in amplitude with increasing frequency, might allow the human perceptual mechanism to infer that there is a hidden peak between the two harmonics. While this is plausible, experiments so far have shown it to be untrue in humans. Johann Sundberg (1978) presented synthesized high vocal tones with and without vibrato to listeners, and found no significant difference in vowel recognition. This seems contrary to examples produced by John Chowning (see chapter 20), where the addition of random and periodic vibrato suddenly makes

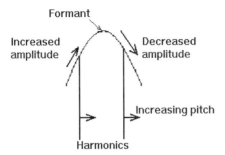

Figure 16.9 A vocal tract formant with a harmonic on either side. As vocal frequency increases, the lower harmonic experiences an increase in amplitude, and the upper harmonic experiences a decrease in amplitude.

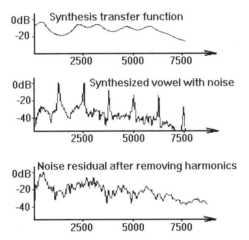

Figure 16.10 Synthesis transfer function (top) and spectrum (middle) of a vocal tone synthesized with noise in the glottal source. After removing the harmonic components, spectral shape is clearer in the residual spectrum (bottom).

a synthesized voice sound clearly vocal and makes the vowel evident. The Chowning tones were synthesized using FM, and no amplitude modulation of the individual harmonics, as shown in figure 16.9, was present. The increased intelligibility in the Chowning tones was likely due to the fact that the complete lack of vibrato made the tones so inhuman that there was no particular notion that there was an underlying vowel to be identified. The addition of human vibrato, drift, and jitter causes the listener to make a categorical shift in perception to hearing the tones as vocal. In the Sundberg experiment the subjects were asked to identify a vowel, which suggested to them that the sounds were vocal-like.

One aspect of aperiodicity that may affect the perception of vowels in high-pitched sung tones is the presence of noise. Figure 16.10 shows a spectrum of a 1250 Hz synthesized soprano tone. Note that the harmonics are too widely spaced to identify the actual spectral envelope, but that the spectral envelope is clearer in the shape of the noise floor. This appears perceptually as a whisperlike component of the sound, in which the vowel is quite evident.

16.6 Conclusion

Any natural sound will have some nonperiodic components. Deviations in the period and noise are present not only in the human voice but also in the sounds of wind instruments, bowed strings, and other instruments. Without components of noise and aperiodicity, synthesized tones sound mechanical. By inspecting these components carefully and noting their behavior across the ranges of pitch and dynamics, we can hope to understand the instruments better and to design better computer-generated sounds.

References

Cook, P. (1991). "Noise and Aperiodicity in the Glottal Source: A Study of Singer Voices." Paper presented at Twelfth International Congress of Phonetic Sciences, Aix-en-Provence, France.

———. (1995). "An Investigation of Singer Pitch Deviation as a Function of Pitch and Dynamics." Paper presented at Thirteenth International Congress of Phonetic Sciences, Stockholm.

Deutsch, J., and J. Clarkson. (1959). "Nature of the Vibrato and the Control Loop in Singing." *Nature,* 183, 167–168.

Scotto di Carlo, N., and A. Rutherford. (1990). "The Effect of Pitch on the Perception of a Coloratura Soprano's Vocalic System." Journal of Research in Singing 13 (2), 11–24.

Shipp, T., J. Sundberg, and S. Haglund. (1984). "A Model of Frequency Vibrato." In L. van Lawrence, ed., *13th Symposium on Care of the Professional Voice,* 116–117. New York: Voice Foundation.

Sundberg, J. (1978). "Vibrato and Vowel Identification." *Archives of Acoustics,* 2, 257–266.

Ward, D., and E. Burns (1978). "Singing Without Auditory Feedback." *Journal of Research in Singing and Applied Vocal Pedagogy,* 1, 24–44.

17 Memory for Musical Attributes

Daniel J. Levitin

17.1 Introduction

What is memory? As with many concepts in psychology, people have an intuition about what memory is until they are asked to define it. When we try to define memory, and break it up into its components, this becomes a complicated question. We talk about memorizing phone numbers, remembering a smell, remembering the best route to school. We talk about "knowing" that we're allergic to ragweed or that we had a haircut three weeks ago. Is this knowing a form of memory? A panty hose manufacturer boasts that its new fabric has memory. What do all these forms of memory and knowledge have in common? How do they differ? Psychology departments teach whole courses on memory. It is thus impossible to say much of importance about the topic in just a few introductory paragraphs, but what follows is a brief overview of some of the issues in memory research. Then we will discuss memory for musical events in more detail.

17.2 Types of Memory

Psychologists tend to make conceptual distinctions among different types of memory. When we talk about different types of memory, an immediate question that comes to mind is whether these different types are conceptual conveniences, or whether they have an underlying neural basis. There is strong neurological evidence that particular memory systems are indeed localized in separate parts of the brain. The hippocampus and prefrontal cortex, for example, are known to play a role in the encoding and storage of particular forms of memory. However, the computational environment of the the brain is massively parallel and widely distributed. It is likely that a number of processes related to memory are located throughout the brain. Further, some of the conceptual labels for memory systems, such as "procedural memory," actually encompass somewhat independent processes that are conveniently categorized together (for pedagogical reasons), but do not necessarily activate a single distinct brain structure. A more detailed discussion of the relation between brain and memory can be found in the book by Larry Squire (1987).

One kind of memory is the immediate sensory memory we experience as image persistence. For example, if you look outside the window on a bright day and then close your eyes, an afterimage stays on your retina for a few moments. This has been called *iconic memory* by Ulric Neisser (1967). We talk about the auditory equivalent of this as *echoic memory:* for a few moments after hearing a sound (such as a friend's voice) we are usually able to "hear" a trace of that sound in our mind's ear. Richard Atkinson and Richard Shiffrin (1968) referred to these immediate sensory memories as being held in a *sensory buffer.*

When you are holding a thought inside your head—such as what you are about to say next in a conversation, or as you're doing some mental arithmetic—it stands to reason that this requires some type of short-term, or immediate, memory. This kind of memory, the contents of your present consciousness and awareness, has been called "working memory" by Alan Badelley (1990), and is similar to what Atkinson and Shiffrin called short-term memory.

Long-term memory is the kind of memory that most of us think of as memory—the ability to remember things that happened some time ago, or that we learned some time ago (usually more than a few minutes ago, and up to a lifetime ago). For example, you might have stored in long-term memory images from your high school graduation, the sound of a locomotive, the capital of Colorado, or the definition of the word "protractor." (Actually, in the latter case, you might not be able to retrieve a definition of a protractor, but rather a visual image of what one looks like; this is also a form of long-term memory.) One of the important features of long-term memory is its durability. That is, we tend to think of long-term memories as staying with us for perhaps an indefinite period of time. We may not always be able to access them when we want (e.g., when you have somebody's name on the tip of your tongue but can't quite retrieve it), but we have the sense that the memories are "in there." This is in contrast to short-term memories, which decay rapidly without rehearsal, and are not durable unless they somehow are transferred to long-term memory. The sensory memory/short-term memory/long-term memory distinction appears to have validity at the neural level.

Psychologists also talk about different types of long-term memory, but it is not clear that these reflect different neural systems. Rather, they are different kinds of knowledge stored in long-term memory. It can be useful to make these distinctions for conceptual purposes. The psychologist Endel Tulving (1985) makes a distinction between episodic and semantic memory. There is something different between remembering your eighth birthday and remembering the capital of Colorado. Your eighth birthday is an episode that you can remember, one that occupied a specific time and place. There was also a time and place when you first learned the capitol of Colorado, but if you're like most people, you can't remember when you learned it, only the fact itself. Similarly, we remember what words mean, but usually not when and where the learning occurred. This is called *semantic memory.* Remembering how to ride a bicycle or tie your shoe is an example of another type of memory called *procedural memory.*

It is also important to make a distinction between *memory storage* (or encoding) and *memory retrieval.* One of the tricky parts about designing memory experiments is distinguishing between these operations. That is, if a subject cannot recall something, we need to distinguish between an encoding failure and a retrieval failure. Sometimes using different retrieval cues can bring up memories that seemed previously unreachable. Current memory researchers use a variety of different methods to study remembering, forgetting, storage, and retrieval processes.

17.3 Working Memory Capacity

George Miller (1956) pointed out that working memory has a limited capacity. The number of pieces of information we can juggle in short-term memory at any one time is between 5 and 9, or what he called "7±2." As a demonstration, try to keep the following series of digits active in memory:

015514804707619

Most people can't keep this many (15) going at once. It is indeed a bit like juggling. But try again, by looking at the numbers when they are rearranged from right to left, as below:

916707408415510

If you're from California, you'll notice that these are the telephone area codes for the northern part of the state. If these are familiar to you, they become grouped—or "chunked," to use Miller's word—

and voilá!—suddenly there are only five pieces of information to remember and it is possible to keep them active in working memory. We will talk more about chunking in chapter 19. As another example, consider the following string of fifteen letters:

FBICIAUSAATTIBM

If you are able to chunk this into the familiar three-letter abbreviations, the problem is reduced to keeping five chunks in memory, something most people can do easily.

What does chunking have to do with music? People who study ear-training and learn how to transcribe music are probably chunking information. For example, in a typical ear-training assignment, the instructor might play a recording of a four-piece combo: piano, bass, drums, and voice. The student's task is to write down, in real time, the chord changes, bass line, and melody. If you have never done this before, it seems impossible. But with chunking, the problem becomes more tractable. Although the chords on the piano each consist of three, four, five, or more notes, we tend to hear the chord as a chord, not as individual notes. Beyond this, musicians tend to hear not individual chords but chord progressions, or fragments of progressions, such as ii-V-I or I-vi-ii-V. This is analogous to seeing FBI as a chunk and not three individual letters. The chord changes can be parsed this way, and if the listener misses something, the part that is there provides constraints the listener can use to make an educated guess about the part that is missing. You can see the role of contextual constraints in reading. It is not hard to guess what the words below are, even though each is missing a letter:

basso_n   cof_ee

17.4   Remembering and Forgetting Details

A common intuition is that the sole function of memory is to preserve the details of different experiences we've had. But there is a large body of research showing that our memory for details is actually pretty poor. Raymond Nickerson and Marilyn Adams (1979) showed people pictures of different pennies (figure 17.1). Americans see pennies every day, but people in the study could not reliably pick out the accurate picture. Similarly, people tend not to have a very good memory for the exact words of a conversation, but instead remember the "gist" of the conversation. What is the function of memory, then, if not to remember events accurately?

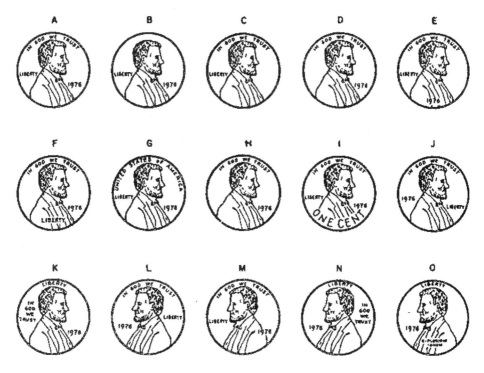

Figure 17.1 Subjects had difficulty identifying the real penny. (Reprinted with permission from Nickerson and Adams, 1979.)

If you think about it, you can see that if we stored and retrieved every detail we encountered every day, we would soon become overloaded with millions of details. When children are first learning language, for example, it is important that they learn to generalize from specific experiences. When a child learns the concept (and the word) "car" as his/her mother points to a car in the street, the child has to somehow disregard the differences among the different cars (the perceptual details) and extract what is common among them. A child who fails to do this, fails to learn the concept of car properly, or to use language properly. That is, the word "car" doesn't apply just to the 1981 Red Honda Accord the child first saw; it applies to objects that share certain properties. This doesn't necessarily mean the perceptual details are lost: the child may maintain a vivid image of the exact car; but the conceptual system of the brain, along with the memory system, by necessity must integrate details into generalizations. In fact, there is a great deal of evidence that memory does preserve both the details and the "gist" of experiences, and we are usually able to access information at the appropriate level.

17.5   Memory For Music

Objects in the visual world have six perceptual attributes: size, color, location, orientation, luminance, and shape. What do we mean by "object"? This definition has been the subject of heated argument among theorists for many years. I propose that an object is something that maintains its identity across changes (or transformations) in these attributes. In other words, as we move an object through space, it is still the same object. If you were to change the color of your car, it will still be your car. Shape is a tricky attribute, because shape distortions can sometimes, but not always, alter an object's identity. For example, as was shown by William Labov (1973), a cup becomes a bowl if the ratio of its diameter to its height becomes too distorted.

A performance of music contains the following seven perceptual attributes: pitch, rhythm, tempo, contour, timbre, loudness, and spatial location (one might add reverberant environment as an eighth). Technically speaking, pitch and loudness are psychological constructs that relate to the physical properties of frequency and amplitude. The term *contour* refers to the shape of a melody when musical interval size is ignored, and only the pattern of "up" and "down" motion is considered. Each one of these eight attributes can be changed without changing the others. With the exception of contour, and sometimes rhythm, the recognizability of the melody is maintained when each of these attributes is changed. In fact, for many melodies, even the rhythm can be changed to some degree and the melody will still be recognizable (White 1960).

To elaborate further, a melody is an auditory object that maintains its identity under certain transformations, just as a chair maintains its identity under certain transformations, such as being moved to the other side of the room or being turned upside down. A melody can generally retain its identity with transformations along the six dimensions of pitch, tempo, timbre, loudness, spatial location, and reverberant environment; sometimes with changes in rhythm; but rarely with changes in contour. So, for example, if you hear a song played louder than you're accustomed to, you can still identify it. If you hear it at a different tempo, played on a different instrument, or coming from a different location in space, it is still the same melody. Of course, extreme changes in any of these dimensions will render the song unrecognizable; a tempo of one beat per day, or a loudness of 200 dB SPL might stretch the limits of identification.

A specific case of transformation invariance for melodies concerns pitch. The identity of a melody is independent of the actual pitches of the tones played. A melody is defined by the pattern of tones, or the relation of pitches to each other. Thus, when we transpose a melody, it is still recognizable as the same melody. In fact, many melodies do not have a "correct" pitch, they just float freely in pitch space, starting anywhere one wants them to. "Happy Birthday" is an example of this. Now, you might object to all this and say that Beethoven's String Quartet in F Major ought to be played in F major, and that it loses something when it is transposed. The timbre of the stringed instruments changes with range, and if the piece is played in C major, the overall spectrum of the piece sounds different to the careful listener. But listeners will still recognize the melody because the identity of the melody is independent of pitch.

A number of controlled laboratory experiments have confirmed that people have little trouble recognizing melodies in transposition (Attneave and Olson 1971; Dowling 1978, 1982; Idson and Massaro 1978). Also, at different times and different places, the tuning standard has changed; our present A440 system is arbitrary and was adopted only during the twentieth century. The absolute pitch of the melody's tones is not the most important feature. It is the pattern, or relation of pitches, that is important.

Note the parallel here with our earlier discussion of generalization and abstraction in memory. One of the reasons we are able to recognize melodies is that the memory system has formed an abstract representation of the melody that is pitch-invariant, loudness-invariant, and so on. We take for granted that our memory system is able to perform this important function. Recent evidence suggests that memory retains both the "gist" and the actual details of experience. But what about melodies? Do we retain pitch details, like the absolute pitch information, alongside the abstract representation? This is an interesting question that we will take up in section 17.9, after first reviewing research on memory for contour, lyrics, and failures of musical perception known as *amusias.*

17.6 Contour

Recall that the term *contour* refers to the shape of a melody when musical interval size is ignored, and only the pattern of "up" and "down" motion is considered. At first, the idea of contour being an important attribute of melody seems counterintuitive. Contour is a relatively gross characterization of a song's identity. However, its utility has been shown in laboratory experiments. There is evidence that for melodies we do not know well (such as a melody we have only heard a few times), the contour is remembered better than the actual intervals (Massaro, Kallman, and Kelly 1980). In contrast, the exact interval patterns of familiar melodies are well remembered, and adults can readily notice contour-preserving alterations of the intervallic pattern (Dowling 1994). Infants respond to contour before they respond to melody; that is, infants cannot distinguish between a song and a melodic alteration of that song, so long as contour is preserved. Only as the child matures is he/she able to attend to the melodic information. Some animals show a similar inability to distinguish different alterations of a melody when contour is preserved (Hulse and Page 1988). One explanation of why the contour of a melody might be more readily processed is that it is a more general description of the melody, and it subsumes the interval information. It is only with increasing familiarity, or increasing cognitive abilities, that the intervallic details become perceptually important.

17.7 Lyrics

The memory of ballad singers and tellers of epic poetry has been the focus of a great deal of recent research. On the surface, their memory capacity seems unbelievable for the amount of detail they can readily access. But Wanda Wallace and David Rubin of Duke University have shown that in fact these performers do not need to rely on remembering every detail, because the structures of songs and poems provide multiple constraints for the lyrics (Wallace and Rubin 1988a, 1988b). These constraints are based in part on rhyme, rhythm, alliteration, melodic emphasis, style, and story progression. As an example of lyric constraints, word phrases tend to have a unique stress pattern, such as weak-strong or strong-weak. Similarly, melodic phrases tend to be characterized by strong-weak or weak-strong patterns of accents. Thus, changing a word sequence could alter an entire line's rhythm.

Wallace and Rubin found that from one telling to another, minor alterations in the lyrics occur within these constraints. In a study of eleven singers performing the same ballad on two different occasions, they found that most of the lyric variations conformed to poetic and semantic constraints of the ballad. For example, many lyric changes are to synonyms or other words that do not affect the meaning, rhyme, or rhythm:

(a)   "Can't you shovel in a little more coal" becomes
(a') "Saying shovel in a little more coal"; or
(b)   "She cried, 'Bold captain, tell me true'" becomes
(b') "She cried, 'Brave captain, tell me true.'"

The lyrics and storyline together provide multiple redundant constraints to assist the recall of a passage. For example, even without music, given the first line of the following rock song, the last word of the second line is relatively easy to infer:

"Well, today a friend told me the sorry tale
As he stood there trembling and turning _____
He said each day's harder to get on the scale."
(From A. Mann, "Jacob Marley's Chain," 1992)

The correct word to end the second line is "pale." Similarly, if one could recall the entire second line except for the word "pale," semantic constraints leave few alternatives. When one adds the contribution of melodic stress patterns, it becomes apparent that our recall of song lyrics is assisted by a number of constraints.

The experimental data corroborate our intuition that the memory representation for lyrics seems to be tied into the memory representation for melody (Serafina et al. 1984). Further evidence of this comes from a case report of a musician who suffered a stroke caused by blockage of the right cerebral artery. After the stroke, he was able to recognize songs played on the piano if they were associated with words (even though the words weren't being presented to him), but he was unable to recognize songs that were purely instrumentals (Steinke et al. 1995).

17.8 Amusia

Amusia is the name given to a broad class of mental deficits, involving music perception, that usually appear after brain damage. The deficits include a sharp decrement in an individual's ability to grasp musical relationships in the perception of sounds, or in the ability to perform, read, or write music. Most amusiacs are capable of understanding spoken language, presumably because their neurological impairment spared the speech centers of the brain. However, in many cases amusia accompanies various auditory and speech disorders, such as the aphasias (the name given to various impairments in the production or perception of speech).

The degree to which music and speech rely on common neural mechanisms is not clear. A wealth of cases have shown clear dissociations between impairments in music and in speech, although there may also be individual differences in the way that music is handled by brains. Indeed, in many cases, amusia and aphasia co-occur. There are some separate brain structures, and some shared structures for processing music and speech. For example, Paula Tallal et al. (1993) found that some children who have trouble learning to speak are unable to process the correct temporal order of sounds. Presumably, if this is a low-level deficit (i.e., a deficit in a brain system shared by music and speech systems), it would also affect the ability to process the order of tones in a melody.

Our current knowledge of the brain's functional architecture is growing rapidly, in part due to advances in neuroimaging techniques. PET (positron-emission tomography), fMRI (functional magnetic resonance imaging), and ERP (event-related potentials) are three such techniques that are allowing neuroscientists to better localize specific brain functions (Posner and Levitin 1997). For example, neuroscientists have demonstrated that there are specific brain anatomies for reading (Posner and Raichle 1994), listening to music (Sergent 1993), mentally practicing one's tennis serve (Roland 1994), calculating numbers (Dehaene 1998), and imagining a friend's face (Kosslyn 1994). Lesions to certain parts of the brain render patients unable to recognize faces (known as prosopagnosia—Bruce 1988; Young and Ellis 1989), although their perception of other objects seems unimpaired. Other lesions cause an inability to read whole words (a type of alexia), although individual letters can still be made out.

Because music performance and perception involve a number of disparate and specialized skills, amusia includes a wide range of deficits. One patient developed an inability to read music note-by-note, but had an intact ability to read whole musical passages. In another case, a musician lost the ability to play the piano (his second instrument) although his ability to play the violin (his first instrument) remained intact. A pianist suffering from aphasia and alexia was unable to read written music or recognize previously familiar melodies; however, her music production abilities were spared, so that she could sing the melody and lyrics to many songs. Following brain damage, an aphasic composer could no longer understand speech but continued to compose without impairment (Luria 1970).

A knowledge of some of the details of brain architecture makes clearer how some of these dissociations can occur. For example, reading music depends a great deal on the integration of spatial and form perception, because the identity of a musical note is determined both by its form and by its position on the musical staff. An established fact in neuroscience is that form perception and location perception follow different pathways in the visual system (Zeki 1993). It is easy to see how musical alexia (an inability to read musical notes) could arise from damage to either of these two visual pathways, since reading music requires perception of both form and position. It is also easy to see that this damage would not necessarily interfere with other musical skills.

A relatively common dissociation is that found between lyric and melodic production. Oscar Marin (1982) reports the case of an aphasic patient who could sing with normal intonation and rhythm, so long as she wasn't required to sing lyrics. Her ability to join lyrics with melodies was totally impaired.

The neurological syndrome called auditory agnosia is a more general and severe perceptual deficit that usually arises from bilateral damage to the temporal lobes, in particular the auditory cortex as shown in figure 9.11 (Heschl's area). Patients with auditory agnosia are unable to organize the sounds in the environment, so that speech, animal sounds, bells, and other noises are perceived as a jumbled, uninterpretable stream of noise. A few cases of purely musical agnosia have been described in which patients are unable to organize music into a coherent percept, although their ability to understand speech and nonmusical stimuli remains intact. The extent to which they can understand the "music" of normal speech (known as "prosody") has not been studied thoroughly. For example, are they able to distinguish a question from a statement if the only cue is a rising contour at the end of the sentence? These remain questions open for study.

17.9 Memory for Musical Pitch and Tempo

To what extent do our memories of music retain perceptual details of the music, such as the timbre, pitch, and tempo of songs we have heard? Do we remember all the details of the piece, even details that are not theoretically important? Specifically, since melody is defined by the relation of pitches and rhythms, it would be easy to argue that people do not need to retain the actual pitch and tempo information in order to recognize the song. However, the music theorist Eugene Narmour (1977) argued that listening to music requires processing of both absolute information (schematic reduction) and relative information (irreducible idiostructural), so the question is whether both types of information reach long-term memory.

If people do encode the actual pitches of songs, this would be something like having "perfect pitch" or "absolute pitch" (AP). If you play a tone on the piano for most people and ask them which tone you played, they cannot tell you (unless they watched your hand). The person with AP can reliably tell you "that was a C#." Some APers can even do the reverse: if you name a tone, they can produce it without any external reference, either by singing or by adjusting a variable oscillator. Those with AP have memory for the actual pitches in songs, not just the relative pitches. In fact, most APers become agitated when they hear a song in transposition because it sounds wrong to them.

It has been estimated that AP is rare, occurring in only 1 out of 10,000 people. However, AP studies tend to test only musicians. There is an obvious reason for this—if you ask most non-musicians to sing an "E-flat," they will not understand. As a term project when I was a student in the Stanford CCRMA psychoacoustics class, I designed a test to determine whether non-musicians could demonstrate AP capabilities. The first test was to determine if non-musicians had an ability to remember pitches over a long period of time—even if they hadn't learned the fancy labels that musicians use. These subjects were given tuning forks, and they were asked to carry the forks around with them for a week, bang them every so often, and to try to memorize the pitch that the forks put out. After a week the tuning fork was taken away, and a week later the subjects were tested on their memory for the tone. Some of them were asked to sing it, and others had to pick it out from three notes played to them. The distribution of the subjects' productions is shown in figure 17.2. Notice that the modal response was perfect memory for the tone, and those who made errors were usually off by only a small amount.

Perhaps, then, absolute musical pitch is an attribute of sound that is encoded in long-term memory. In spite of all the interference—the daily bombardment by different sounds and noises—the subjects were able to keep the pitch of the tuning fork in their heads with great accuracy. A harder test would be to study non-musicians'

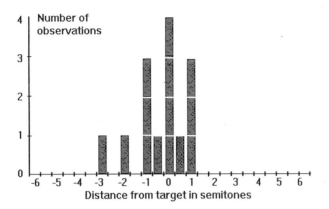

Figure 17.2 Results of pitch memory in non-musicians. The subjects were asked to retain the pitch of a tuning fork in memory for one week.

memory for pitch when that pitch is embedded in a melody. Because melodies are transposition-invariant, the actual pitch information may be discarded once a melody is learned. On the other hand, if somebody hears a melody many times in the same key, we might expect that repeated playings would strengthen the memory trace for the specific pitches.

To test whether people can reproduce the absolute pitch of tones embedded in melodies, I asked subjects to come into the laboratory and sing their favorite rock 'n' roll song from memory (Levitin 1994). The premise was that if they had memorized the actual pitches of the songs, they would reproduce them. It would then be easy to compare the tones they sang with the tones on the original compact disc (CD) version. Rock songs are especially suited to this task because people typically hear them in only one version, and they hear this over and over and over again. Contrast this with "Happy Birthday" or the national anthem, which have no objective key standard, and are likely to be sung in a variety of different keys.

The subjects were mostly introductory psychology students (and a few graduate students), they were not specially selected for musical ability or inability, and they didn't know ahead of time that they'd be participating in a music experiment. After they selected a song, they were asked to imagine that it was playing in their heads, and to sing or hum along with it when they were ready.

The subjects could sing as much or as little of the song as they wanted, and they could start wherever they wanted. The first five tones they sang were analyzed, then compared with the five corresponding tones on the CD. There was no difference in accuracy among the five tones or the average of the five tones. Octave errors were ignored (as is customary in absolute pitch research), and how many semitones they were away from the correct tone on the CD was recorded. Thus, the subjects could deviate from the correct pitch by six semitones in either direction.

Figure 17.3 is a plot of the distribution of the subjects' errors. If subjects were no good at this task, their errors would be uniformly distributed among the error categories. In fact, as the top portion of the figure shows, the modal response was to sing the correct pitch. Notice also that the errors cluster around the correct pitch in a mound-shaped distribution. In fact, 67% of the subjects came within two semitones of the correct pitch. The subjects sang a second song, and the findings were essentially the same (lower portion of the figure). Subjects were also consistent across trials, that is, if they were correct on the first song, they were likely to be correct on the second song. From these data, it appears that these nonmusical subjects have something much like absolute pitch. Instead of asking them to "sing a C♯ or a G," we can ask them to "sing 'Hotel California' or 'Papa Don't Preach,'" and they produce the correct tone. Whether or not they've learned the specialized vocabulary of the musician seems less important than the fact that they have learned to associate a consistent label with a specific tone. This finding has been replicated several times as of this writing (Ashley 1997; Levitin 1996; Wong 1996).

A number of people have wondered if these results might be the product of something other than long-term memory for pitch. If people sing along with their favorite songs, the argument goes, they may have merely developed a "muscle sense" or "kinesthetic sense" from singing the song, and their knowledge of the proper vocal cord tension is driving the results. However, "muscle memory" is a form of long-term memory. All this argument does is specify the subsidiary mechanism in long-term memory that is at work. In addition, it turns out that muscle memory is not very good. W. Dixon Ward and Ed Burns (1978) asked vocalists to sing pitches from memory while being denied auditory feedback (loud white noise in headphones was used to mask the sound of their own voice). The singers were forced to rely solely on muscle memory to produce the requested tones. Their results showed errors as great as a major third, indicating that muscle memory alone cannot account for the precision of performance of the subjects in the sing-your-favorite-rock-song study.

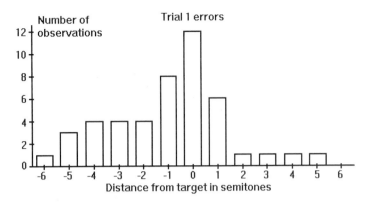

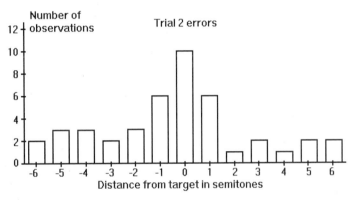

Figure 17.3 Results of pitch memory for the first tone of rock songs. (Upper) Trial 1; (Lower) trial 2.

These data support the idea that long-term memory encodes the absolute pitch of songs, even with a group of subjects in whom AP was not thought to exist. This finding also extends Narmour's theory about the two components required for musical perception, showing that both absolute and relative information are retained in long-term memory. A form of *latent* or *residue* absolute pitch is also implied by Fred Lerdahl and Ray Jackendoff's *strong reduction hypothesis* (1983).

Can a song's tempo be accurately encoded as well? The data collected for the pitch study were reanalyzed to test memory for tempo (Levitin and Cook 1996). The subjects weren't explicitly instructed to reproduce tempo during the experimental session, so to the extent that they did, they did so on their own. Tempo would not necessarily have to be explicitly represented in memory, because a melody's identity does not depend on its being heard at exactly the same tempo every time. Because pitch and tempo are separable dimensions (Kubovy 1981), it is possible that one would be preserved in memory and the other would not.

Some interesting properties of song memory are related to the idea of separable dimensions. When we imagine a song in our heads, most of us can easily imagine it in different keys without changing the speed of the song. This is not how a tape recorder works: if you speed up the tape to raise the key, you automatically speed up the tempo as well. Similarly, we can mentally scan a song at various rates without altering the pitch. If you are asked to determine as quickly as possible whether the word "at" appears in "The Star Spangled Banner," you will probably scan through the lyrics at a rate faster than you normally sing them. This does not necessarily raise your mental representation of the pitch.

In addition, different sections of songs seem to carry "flags" or "markers" that serve as starting points. If you were asked to sing the third verse of "The Twelve Days of Christmas," you might start right on the line: "On the third day of Christmas, my true love gave to me . . ." without having to start from the very beginning. Markers in songs are to some extent idiosyncratic, and depend on what parts of a song are salient, and how well you know the song. Few people are able to jump immediately to the word "at" in "The Star Spangled Banner," but some might be able to start singing it from the phrase "whose broad stripes and bright stars" without having to start from the beginning.

With respect to the other attributes of songs, most people can imagine a song being played loud or soft, being heard in their left ear or right ear or both, being performed inside or outside a large church, and the main melody being carried by various instruments. Most of these things can be imagined even if they have never been experienced before, just as we can imagine a polka-dot elephant, although it's unlikely we've ever seen one.

It is striking to listen to the tapes of nonmusical subjects singing, superimposed on the corresponding passage from the CD. They are only singing along with their memory, but it appears that they hear the recording in their head. Enormous amounts of detail appear to be remembered—the subjects reproduce vocal affectations and stylistic nuances, so that it's hard to imagine they could perform any better if they were singing along with the CD.

It wasn't immediately obvious that people would encode tempo with great accuracy, but the data shown in figure 17.4 suggest that they do. As shown in that plot of subject-produced versus actual tempo, 72% of the subject's productions were within 8% of the correct tempo. How close is 8%? Carolyn Drake and Marie-Claire Botte

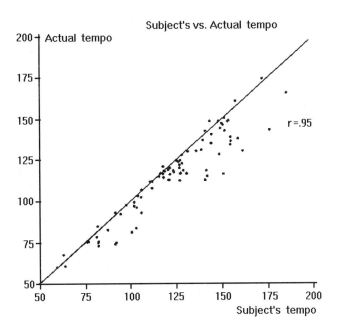

Figure 17.4   Bivariate scatter plot of actual tempo versus produced tempo of rock songs.

(1993) found that the perceptual threshold for changes in tempo (the just-noticeable difference, or JND) was 6.2–8.8%. Thus it appears that people encode tempo information in memory with a high degree of precision.

We have seen that music has a number of different attributes, and that some of these attributes appear to be stored in memory in two forms: a relative encoding of relations and an absolute encoding of sensory features. The precision with which other attributes of musical performances, such as timbre and loudness, are encoded in memory, is the topic of experiments currently under way.

17.10   Summary

The modern view is that memory is distributed throughout various parts of the brain, and that different types of memory engage separate neural structures. Memory for music, just like memory for prose or pictures, probably comprises different cognitive subsystems to encode the various aspects of music. There is a growing consensus that memory serves a dual function: it abstracts general rules from specific experiences, and it preserves to a great degree some of the details of those specific experiences.

Acknowledgments

This chapter benefited greatly from comments by Michael C. Anderson, Gregg DiGirolamo, Gina Gerardi, Lewis R. Goldberg, and Douglas L. Hintzman. I received direct support from a graduate research fellowship from ONR (N-00014-89-J-3186), and indirect support both from CCRMA and from an ONR Grant to M. I. Posner (N-00014-89-3013).

References

Ashley, C. (1997). "Does Pitch Memory Change with Age?" Paper presented at Illinois Junior Academy of Science meeting University of Illinois at Urbana.

Atkinson, R. C., and R. M. Shiffrin. (1968). "Human Memory: A Proposed System and Its Control Processes." In K. W. Spence and J. T. Spence, eds., *The Psychology of Learning and Motivation,* vol. 2, 89–105. New York: Academic Press.

Attneave, F., and Olson, R. K. (1971). "Pitch as a Medium: A New Approach to Psychophysical Scaling." *American Journal of Psychology,* 84, 147–166.

Baddeley, A. (1990). *Human Memory: Theory and Practice.* Boston: Allyn & Bacon.

Bruce, V. (1988). *Recognizing Faces.* Hillsdale, N.J.: Lawrence Erlbaum.

Dehaene, S. (1996). "The Organization of Brain Activations in Number Comparisons: Event Related Potentials and the Additive-Factors Method." *Journal of Cognitive Neuroscience;* 8 (1), 47–68.

Dowling, W. J. (1978). "Scale and Contour: Two Components of a Theory of Memory for Melodies." *Psychological Review,* 85 (4): 341–354.

———. (1982). "Melodic Information Processing and Its Development." In D. Deutsch, ed., *The Psychology of Music,* New York: Academic Press.

———. (1994). "Melodic Contour in Hearing and Remembering Melodies." In R. Aiello and J. A. Sloboda, eds., *Musical Perceptions,* 173–190. New York: Oxford University Press.

Drake, C., and Botte, M.-C. (1993). "Tempo Sensitivity in Auditory Sequences: Evidence for a Multiple-Look Model." *Perception & Psychophysics,* 54 (3): 277–286.

Huxley, P. (1987). "Double Our Numbers." On the Columbia Records album *Sunny Nights.*

Hulse, S. H., and S. C. Page. (1988). "Toward a Comparative Psychology of Music Perception." *Music Perception,* 5 (4): 427–452.

Idson, W. L., and D. W. Massaro. (1978). "A Bidimensional Model of Pitch in the Recognition of Melodies." *Perception and Psychophysics,* 246, 551–565.

Ivry, R. B., and R. E. Hazeltine. (1995). "The Perception and Production of Temporal Intervals Across a Range of Durations: Evidence for a Common Timing Mechanism." *Journal of Experimental Psychology: Human Perception and Performance,* 21 (1): 3–18.

Janata, P. (1995). "ERP Measures Assay the Degree of Expectancy Violation of Harmonic Contexts in Music." *Journal of Cognitive Neuroscience,* 7 (2): 153–164.

Kosslyn, S. (1994). *Image and Brain.* Cambridge, Mass.: MIT Press.

Kubovy, M. (1981). "Integral and Separable Dimensions and the Theory of Indispensable Attributes." In M. Kubovy and J. Pomerantz, eds., *Perceptual Organization.* Hillsdale, N.J.: Lawrence Erlbaum.

Lerdahl, F., and R. Jackendoff. (1983). *A Generative Theory of Tonal Music.* Cambridge, Mass.: MIT Press.

Levitin, D. J. (1994). "Absolute Memory for Musical Pitch: Evidence from the Production of Learned Melodies." *Perception & Psychophysics,* 56 (4): 414–423.

———. (1996), "Mechanisms of Memory for Musical Attributes." Doctoral dissertation, University of Oregon, Eugene, OR. Dissertation Abstracts International, 57(07B), 4755. (University Microfilms No. AAG9638097).

Levitin, D. J., and P. R. Cook. (1996). "Memory for Musical Tempo: Additional Evidence That Auditory Memory is Absolute." *Perception & Psychophysics,* 58 (6): 927–935.

Loftus, E. (1979). *Eyewitness Testimony.* Cambridge, Mass.: Harvard University Press.

Luria, A. R. Tsvetkova, L. S., and Futer, D. S. (1965). "Aphasia in a Composer." *Journal of Neurological Science,* 2, 288–292.

Marin, O. S. M. (1982). "Neurological Aspects of Music Perception and Performance." In D. Deutsch, ed., *The Psychology of Music.* New York: Academic Press.

Mann, A. (1992). "Jacob Marley's Chain," on the Imago Records album *Whatever.*

Massaro, D. W., Kallman, H. J., and Kelly, J. L. (1980). "The Role of Tone Height, Melodic Contour, and Tone Chroma in Melody Recognition." *Journal of Experimental Psychology: Human Learning and Memory,* 6 (1): 77–90.

Miller, G. A. (1956). "The Magical Number Seven Plus or Minus Two: Some Limits on Our Capacity for Processing Information." *Psychological Review,* 63, 81–97.

Narmour, E. (1977). *Beyond Schenkerism: The Need for Alternatives in Music Analysis.* Chicago: University of Chicago Press.

Neisser, U. (1967). *Cognitive Psychology.* Englewood Cliffs, N.J.: Prentice-Hall.

Nickerson, R. S., and M. J. Adams. (1979). "Long-Term Memory for a Common Object." *Cognitive Psychology,* 11, 287–307.

Pavlov, I. P. (1927). *Conditioned Reflexes: An Investigation of the Physiological Activity of the Cerebral Cortex.* London: Oxford University Press.

Posner, M. I. and D. J. Levitin. (1997). "Imaging the Future." In R. L. Solso, ed., *Mind and Brain Sciences in the 21st Century,* 91–109. Cambridge, Mass.: MIT Press.

Posner, M. I., and M. E. Raichle. (1994). *Images of Mind.* New York: Scientific American Library.

Roland, P. (1994). *Brain Activation.* New York: Wiley-Liss.

Schacter, D. (1987). "Implicit Memory: History and Current Status." *Journal of Experimental Psychology: Learning, Memory, & Cognition,* 13 (3): 501–518.

Serafine, M. L., R. G. Crowder, and B. Repp (1984). "Integration of Melody and Text in Memory for Songs." *Cognition,* 16, 285–303.

Sergent, J. (1993). "Mapping the Musician Brain." *Human Brain Mapping,* 1, 20–38.

Squire, L. R. (1987). *Memory and Brain.* New York: Oxford University Press.

Steinke, W. R., L. L., Cuddy, and L. S. Jacobson. (1995). "Evidence for Melodic Processing and Recognition Without Perception of Tonality in an Amusic Subject." Paper presented at Society for Music Perception and Cognition Conference, Berkeley, Calif.

Tallal, P., S. Miller, and R. H. Fitch. (1993). "Neurobiological Basis of Speech: A Case for the Preeminence of Temporal Processing." In P. Tallal, A. M. Galaburda, R. Llinas, and C. von Euler, eds., *Temporal Information Processing in the Nervous System: Special Reference to Dyslexia and Dysphasia,* 27–47. New York: New York Academy of Sciences.

Tulving, E. 1985. "How Many Memory Systems Are There?" *American Psychologist, 40,* 385–398.

Wallace, W. T., and D. C. Rubin. (1988a). "Memory of a Ballad Singer." In M. M. Gruneberg, P. E. Morris, and R. N. Sykes, eds., *Practical Aspects of Memory: Current Research and Issues,* vol. 1, *Memory in Everyday Life.* Chichester, U.K.: Wiley.

———. "'The Wreck of the Old 97': A Real Event Remembered in Song." In U. Neisser and E. Winograd, eds., *Remembering Reconsidered: Ecological and Traditional Approaches to the Study of Memory.* New York: Cambridge University Press.

Ward, W. D., and E. M. Burns. (1978). "Singing Without Auditory Feedback." *Journal of Research in Singing and Applied Vocal Pedagogy,* 1, 24–44.

White, B. W. (1960). "Recognition of Distorted Melodies." *American Journal of Psychology, 73,* 100–107.

Wong, S. (1996). "Memory for Musical Pitch in Speakers of A Tonal Language." Undergraduate honors thesis, University of Oregon, Eugene.

Young, A. W., and H. D. Ellis. (1989). *Handbook of Research on Face Processing.* Amsterdam: North Holland.

Zeki, S. (1993). *A Vision of the Brain.* Oxford: Blackwell.

18 Haptics

Brent Gillespie

18.1 Introduction

In the next two chapters, our focus will shift from the sense of hearing to the sense of touch. Actually, our interests are broader than the sense of touch (taction); they include the sense of body position and motion (kinesthesia) as well. Thus our discussion will cover sensors not only in the skin but also in the joints and muscles. Convenient for us, there does exist one word that may be used to refer to taction and kinesthesia together: *haptics.* These two chapters are about haptics, and especially the role of haptics in music production and perception.

Haptics is a very relevant topic in a book on psychoacoustics. There are many parallels between the studies of psychoacoustics and of haptics, since the two are neighboring branches of the more general field of psychophysics. But more important (given our interest in music), the haptic senses provide the second most important means for observing the behavior of a musical instrument—audition is, of course, the primary means. The player of an instrument, besides hearing it, feels it. While audition carries meaning regarding the acoustical behavior of an instrument, haptics carries meaning regarding the mechanical behavior. This mechanical information is quite valuable to the process of playing or learning to play an instrument, as we shall see.

Take the trio of player, instrument, and listener depicted in figure 18.1. The player, on the left, manipulates the instrument, that is, exchanges mechanical energy with the instrument through one or more (perhaps transient) mechanical contacts. Note that mechanical information flows in both directions between player and instrument. The musical instrument converts this mechanical excitation into sound waves. The listener on the right senses and processes the sound waves to create a mental model of the musical instrument. Perhaps the listener even contemplates a musical idea expressed through the instrument by the player.

Previous chapters have concentrated on the perceptual processes taking place in the listener. We now turn our attention to the

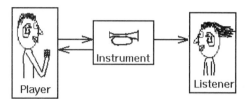

Figure 18.1   The components of musical interaction. A player and an instrument exchange mechanical information, and a listener receives acoustic information.

perceptual processes taking place in the player. In particular, what information regarding the acoustical behavior of the instrument can the player pick up by feeling for the mechanical behavior? After all, every instrument has both an acoustical and a mechanical response, and usually there is a relationship between the two—depending on the sound production physics of the instrument. The player forms a haptic impression of the instrument, much as the listener forms an acoustic impression. Moreover, an instrument's mechanical response may provide clues as to how to modify subsequent manipulations if the player desires a different sound.

Our study centers on the player's haptic senses and associated perceptual processes, but also encompasses the energetic interaction between player and instrument. The information available to the haptic senses is dependent on the player's actions, or how he/she exerts control over the instrument. Indeed, in mechanical interaction, the notion of sensation and control are closely coupled. For example, we shall see that whether haptic perception takes place during active manipulation or during passive stimulation has a large effect on the haptic impression formed. We will therefore delve into the topics of motor control and motor learning while considering the manipulation of musical instruments to make sounds.

Figure 18.1 is a general illustration. If we define music as sound that carries meaning, any device that produces sound under the control of a human player may be considered a musical instrument. Traditional *acoustic* instruments rely on mechanical excitation, in which case the player's control information comes encapsulated in the mechanical energy provided by the player through the mechanical contact. In *electronic* instruments, although production of the acoustical output is from an electrical energy source, modulation of the electrical-to-acoustical conversion is up to the player, and that modulation control is introduced through a mechanical contact. Certain electronic instruments fall outside this description: those that use noncontact transducers to pick up the player's control input. We are interested in the ways in which an understanding of haptics can be used to inform the process of designing electronic musical instruments, and to improve those designs.

The remainder of this chapter comprises a historical overview of the field of haptics and a discussion of the physiology of the haptic sensors. In addition to introducing the important figures in the field, the historical discussion will introduce and organize some subtle but significant concepts, such as the role of intentional movement in haptic sensation. The historical overview also leads into the discussion of sensor physiology, since many of the same subtle concepts must be brought to bear while discussing their function. Chapter 19 will take up the topics of motor control and motor learning.

18.2   Historical Overview

18.2.1   Aristotle

Haptics as an academic discipline dates to the time of Aristotle. To Aristotle, touch was the most essential of the five senses. His treatise *De Anima* (On the Soul), which dates from 350 B.C., discusses each of the five senses in turn. He noted that possession of the sense of touch was the one feature that could be used to distinguish an animal from a plant or an inanimate object. While some animals cannot see or hear, all respond to touch. Aristotle noted the direct correlation between man's superior intelligence and his superior sense of touch. Moreover, when stimuli for the sense of touch are at their extreme, they cause damage to the being itself, whereas extremes of the other senses cause damage only to *well-being*.

Interestingly (in light of modern thought on haptics, reviewed below), there exists a thread tying together the sense of touch and the capacity for movement in Aristotle's work. To Aristotle, features are closely related to function. One may suitably classify an object by describing either its features or its function. Having identified the sense of touch as the distinguishing *feature* of animals, Aristotle associated touch with the accepted *functional* definition of animals: objects that move of their own volition.

Today the close link between motility and haptics is readily acknowledged, both because the mechanical senses are indispensable in the production of movement, and because movement is indispensable in the gathering of haptic information. We will return to this unbreakable link between feature and function, sensation and movement, many times in these chapters on haptics.

Two questions regarding haptics that interested Aristotle persist today. First, is skin the organ of touch or is the organ situated somewhere else, possibly deeper? Second, is touch a single sense or a group of senses? Aristotle provided answers to these questions that are surprisingly insightful, given that he had no knowledge of nervous system physiology. Aristotle maintained that skin is not the organ of touch but, rather, a medium, much as air can be considered the medium for hearing, sight, and smell. He cited the fact that one can feel through gloves, which can be explained only by their being an extension of the medium, the skin. In answer to the second question, Aristotle postulated the existence of more than a single touch sensor, noting that things tangible are marked by several *binarisms,* or pairs of contrasting qualities: hot/cold, hard/soft, wet/dry, and so on. There are many more binarisms in haptics than can be named for the other senses. Since man carries the medium for touch (skin) with his being, he is inclined to group the various binarisms into one sense. If man were to carry an envelope of air, he would tend to group sight, sound, and vision into one sense.

Aristotle was in fact correct from a physiological standpoint, for today we know there are several specialized tactile sense organs embedded in the dermis and epidermis (see section 18.3). With his answer to these questions, Aristotle effectively anticipated much current research on taction that aims to ascertain the mechanical filtering properties of the skin, that is, its transmission properties as a medium for mechanical energy. The question as to the organ of touch may be answered in various ways, depending on the standpoint of the researcher. Even Aristotle acknowledged that "We are unable clearly to detect in the case of touch what the single subject is which underlies the contrasted qualities and corresponds to sound in the case of hearing."

18.2.2 Denis Diderot

In 1749, Diderot (of *Encyclopedia* fame) published his "Letter on the Blind," a fascinating account of tactile perception in the congenitally blind. He laid the foundation for our understanding of *sensory substitution,* that one sense gains in power with use or loss of another. Modern neurological evidence also points to the plasticity of the brain: changes in cortical organization occur with changes in use or type of sensory stimulation. Diderot also wrote on the role of memory and the process of learning in touch, noting that an impression of form relies on retention of component sensations.

18.2.3   Ernst H. Weber

Weber introduced systematic experimental procedures to the study of haptics and the other senses, and is thus considered the founder of the field of psychophysics. His famous law, formulated while investigating cutaneous sensation, was reported in *The Sense of Touch* (1834). *Weber's law* states that one's ability to discriminate differences between a standard and a comparison is a function of the magnitude of the standard. For example, a larger difference is needed to discriminate between two weights when the standard weighs 100 grams than when the standard weighs 20 grams. Anticipating later work in haptics, Weber recognized the role of intentional movement in the perception of hardness and distance between objects.

18.2.4   David Katz

In 1925, David Katz published his influential book *Der Aufbau der Tastwelt* (*The World of Touch*). He was interested in bringing the sense of touch back into prominence, since psychological research in vision and audition had already outstripped haptics research. Although Katz was certainly influenced by the work of his contemporaries who were laying the foundations of Gestalt psychology, he was more concerned with texture and ground than form and figure. Rather than simplicity of the internal response, he was interested in the correspondence of the internal response with the external stimulus. But, consistent with Gestalt thinking, he held that sensations themselves are irrelevant. Rather, the invariants of the object are obtained over time, and an internal impression is formed that is quite isolated from the sensory input.

Katz was particularly interested in the role of movement in haptic perception. Resting your hand against a surface, you may feel that it is flat, but until there is relative movement between your fingertips and the surface, you will not be able to discern its texture. Only with movement do objects "come into view" to the haptic senses. With movement, touch becomes more effective than vision at discerning certain types of texture.

In part to emphasize the importance of movement, Katz proposed that vibration be added as a fifth sensory component of touch. The accepted four at that time were those proposed by Max von Frey in 1894: pressure, warmth, cold, and pain. Katz noted that the pressure sense adapts or dies away without change in stimulus, whereas vibration persists. For example, one does not notice clothes against the body, yet motion of cloth past a fingertip can stimulate the vibration sense indefinitely. Indeed, Katz treated vibratory sensitivity as separate from and superior to pressure sensitivity. Vibration was not simply oscillating pressure. He paired vibration with hearing as dynamic senses, whereas pressure and vision he associated with stationary qualities.

Katz noted that the pressure sense can be excluded by holding a stick, or stylus, between the teeth and moving it across some material: vibrations are still produced and accurate judgments can be made as to the material "touched." Katz's experiments with styli further suggest that touch is a *far sense,* like vision and hearing, contrary to our tendency to assume that it requires direct impression on the skin by an object. Vibration of the earth (felt in our feet) may signal the imminent approach of a train or a herd of wild buffalo. In a real sense, a tool becomes an extension of one's body; the sensory site moves out to the tool tip. These comments further underline the claim that understanding haptics has important implications for the effective use and design of tools (including musical instruments).

Arguably, Katz's most important contribution to haptics research was on the subject of active and passive touch. When a subject is allowed to independently direct the movements of his/her hand, he/she is able to make a much more detailed report of surface texture than when the object is moved under his/her passive fingertips. Rather boldly, and with much foresight, Katz proposed an altogether different kind of organ for the sense of touch: the hand. By identifying the hand as the seat of haptic perception, he emphasized the role of intentional movement. He essentially coupled the performatory function of the hand to its perceptual function. By naming an organ that includes muscles, joints, and skin, he coupled the kinesthetic sense to the tactile. In certain instances, he claimed, two hands may be considered the organ of touch just as two eyes may be considered the organ of vision.

18.2.5 Geza Revesz

Revesz was particularly interested in the development of haptic perception in the blind, and especially the coding of spatial information. According to Revesz, haptic recognition of objects is not immediate, as it is in vision, but requires constructive processing of sequentially acquired information. In haptics, the construction of the whole is a cognitive process that follows perception of parts. Revesz emphasized the spatial nature of haptics and its possibilities for apprehending an object from all sides. His theories and experiments with blind persons have had important implications for the development of aids for the blind, such as tactile maps. Perspective cues, which work so well in drawings presented to the eyes (lines vanishing to the horizon, as shown in figure 3.2; occlusion; and background fading), do not work well in raised-line drawings presented to the hands. Recognition of three-dimensional models of objects with the hands, in contrast, is very good.

18.2.6 James Gibson

Gibson contributed in subtle but important ways to the field of psychophysics, and haptics in particular. He was interested in fostering a more ecological approach to research in sensory processes and perception, an approach that takes into account all properties of an environment that may have relevance to a person with particular intentions within that environment. He argued that perceptual psychologists should study recognition of objects rather than such "intellectual" processes as memory or imagination, or such low-level phenomena as stimulus response. Gibson proposed that perception is not simply a process of information-gathering by the senses and subsequent processing by perceptual centers, but the result of a hierarchical perceptual system whose function depends on active participation by the perceiver. For example, the visual system includes not only the eyes and visual cortex but also the active eye muscles, the actively positioned head, and even the mobile body. The haptic system, in addition to the tactile and kinesthetic sensors and somatosensory cortex, includes the active muscles of the arms, hands, and fingers.

Gibson, like Katz, stressed the importance of intentional movement in haptic perception. He preferred to think of active touch as a separate sense. Even when a subject has no intention of manipulating an object, he/she will choose to run his/her fingers over the object when left to his/her own devices. Certainly the fingertips are to the haptic sense as the fovea centralis is to the visual sense: an area with a high concentration of sensors, and thus particular acuity. The fingers may be moved to place the highest concentration of sensors on the area of interest. Movement may be used to produce vibration and transient stimuli, which we know to be important from the experiments of Katz.

Gibson pointed to yet another reason for exploratory movement of the hand: to "isolate invariants" in the flux of incoming sensory information. Just as the image of an object maintains identity as it moves across the retina, or the sound of an instrument maintains identity as its changing pitch moves the stimulus across the basilar membrane, so an object maintains its identity as its depression moves across the skin. The identity even persists as the object is moved to less sensitive areas of the arm, and it is felt to maintain a fixed position in space as the arm glides by it. These facts, central to Gestalt theory, were underlined by Gibson and used as a further basis for understanding active touch. The exploratory movements are used to produce known changes in the stimulus flux while monitoring patterns that remain self-consistent. Thus, active touch is used to test object identity hypotheses—in Gibson's words, to "isolate the invariants." Remember from chapter 3 that common fate is a very strong principle for grouping, according to Gestalt theorists, and certainly it seems plausible that a subject will choose to exploit common fate when given the opportunity to do so.

Gibson also demonstrated that a subject passively presented with a haptic stimulus will describe an object in subjective terms, noting the sensations on the hand. By contrast, a subject who is allowed to explore actively will tend to report object properties and object identity. Under active exploration, he/she will tend to *externalize* the object, or ascribe percepts to the object in the external world. For example, when a violin bow is placed on the palm of a subject's passive hand, he/she will report the sensations of contact on the skin, whereas a subject who is allowed to actively explore will readily identify the object and report object properties rather than describe sensations. Furthermore, when a string is bowed, the contact is experienced at the bow hairs and not in the hand.

If we were to attempt to extend Gibson's ideas regarding active touch and active ocular scanning to audition, the question arises: What is active listening? What is the fovea of the ear? Although we cannot move our pinnae like a cat, we certainly can move our head to modify auditory stimuli to our ears. But one could also argue that there exists a kind of internal auditory fovea, or mechanism for choosing a direction in which to concentrate attention. If you concentrate your attention on a particular area in your environment, you will notice more auditory sources in that area. Alternatively, certain pitch or timbre ranges can be singled out with concentration.

18.2.7 The Present

Today the field of haptics has many proponents in academe and industry. After having been taken for granted in perceptual psychology, and considered subservient to vision and audition for so long, haptics is finally enjoying a resurgence of interest.

From our present vantage point in history, we can identify reasons for the earlier lack of research interest in haptics. Certainly the haptic senses are more complex than the auditory or the visual, in that their function is coupled to movement and active participation by the subject. And further, the availability of an experimental apparatus for psychophysical study in haptics has been lacking until now—something that corresponds to the computer screen for vision and the loudspeaker or headphones for audition. That apparatus is called the *haptic interface.* It is a specially engineered device that, in response to motions imparted by a human user, can impart reaction forces. The reaction forces are produced by motors under computer control. A haptic interface is a human–computer interface device like a mouse and a monitor screen. Unlike a mouse or computer monitor, however, a haptic interface is simultaneously used for information input and output. Through a haptic interface, human subjects may explore virtual objects. Since the virtual objects are computer-programmable, properties of these objects can be varied more easily than can those of real-world objects.

Current leaders in haptics research include Roberta Klatzky and Susan Lederman, who are often cited for their work on *exploratory procedures,* motor patterns that are used by subjects to ascertain certain object properties. For example, when asked about an object's texture, subjects will glide or rub their fingers over the object, whereas when asked about shape, they will follow contours with fingertips or enclose the object between their hands. It seems that certain patterns of movement maximize the availability of certain information. Klatzky and Lederman have also conducted experiments on the recognition of object representations that have demonstrated poor apprehension of form in two dimensions but good apprehension in three dimensions. The work of Klatzky and Lederman is providing the empirical evidence to back up the ideas of Katz, Revesz, and Gibson on active touch.

Many open questions remain in haptics. We are still not sure if we have an answer to the question that Aristotle raised: What is to haptics as sound is to hearing and color is to seeing? As is apparent from experiments with active and passive touch, the notion of haptic sensation cannot be divorced from the notion of manipulation. Furthermore, the spatial and temporal sensitivity of the haptic sensors is not fully understood. Much research, especially using haptic interfaces, will likely lead to new results. As never before, psychologists and mechanical engineers are collaborating to understand human haptic perception. Results in the field have important implications for virtual reality: the effective design of virtual objects that can be touched through a haptic interface requires a thorough understanding of what is salient to the haptic senses. Furthermore, the design of electronic musical instruments requires research into such topics as active and passive touch and sensory equivalence.

18.3 The Sensors

As we have seen, the designation of the *organ* of touch is a subject open to debate. The gathering of haptic information involves the integration of many faculties, one of which is movement production. The description of the haptic sensors by themselves, however, can be laid out neatly. In this case we may stop our investigation at the level of nerve impulses, and avoid raising questions about higher-level perceptual processes. The following are some of the research techniques that have produced the present knowledge of the haptic sensors.

Knowledge about the structure and function of the various nerve endings that convert thermal or mechanical stimuli into impulses is the product of recent histological (anatomical) and physiological research. Knowledge is still limited, however, because the receptor structures are difficult to isolate from the skin. But perhaps isolation from the skin is counterproductive, since the mechanical properties of the skin and the mechanical integration of sensor and skin largely determine the function of each sensor. A second research technique for haptics is mechanical modeling and simulation of the sensors and skin. Noting that mechanical modeling of the cochlea has contributed to auditory research, haptics researchers hope to gain an understanding of mechanical energy transduction through skin and sensor structures by observing the behavior of models (a much simpler venture than histological observation). A third important technique is microneurography, in which nerve impulses emanating from a single sensor are monitored by using a tiny tungsten fiber inserted into a nerve bundle while various mechanical stimuli are presented to the corresponding site on the skin. In this manner, the receptive field and the response characteristics of a particular receptor type may be mapped out.

If we look beyond the nerve impulses and attempt to find associations between particular receptor types and reported sensations, results are a bit more sketchy. There do not appear to be any clear delineations by sensor type of the haptic percepts. Probably the most promising technique used to associate sensors with sensations is microneurography performed on alert human subjects. While a particular mechanical stimulus is presented to the skin, neural responses are recorded and the subject is asked to report sensations. Alternatively, the nerve fiber may be stimulated electrically with a tungsten fiber. In that case, the subject typically reports the same tactile sensation, localized to the same site where the sensor was stimulated mechanically. Such subject responses may be used to confirm a correspondance between mechanical stimulus, recorded nerve signal, and percept.

In the next sections, the sensors located in the skin (cutaneous sensors) and those located in the muscles, tendons, and joints are described. Very roughly, the cutaneous sensors mediate the tactile senses, and the sensors in the muscles, tendons, and joints mediate the kinesthetic senses. This distinction is rough, however. For example, the skin moves when joints move.

18.3.1 The Cutaneous Sensors

The cutaneous sensors include free nerve endings and a number of specialized nerve endings responsible for transducing warmth, cold, pain, and mechanical energy.

THERMAL SENSORS

Since the fingers are generally warmer than environmental objects, thermal conductivity plays a large role in thermal sensitivity. The rate at which heat is conducted away from the fingers will determine why a metal object feels colder than a glass object, and a glass object feels colder than a wooden object, even though all three objects are at room temperature before contact. It has long been known that there are separate cold and warmth sensors, for certain sites on the skin are sensitive to cold and certain sites to warmth. This can be shown with a simple temperature-controlled metal probe placed at various sites on the skin. The punctilious nature of the each of the cutaneous sensors must be taken into acount when designing stimuli for psychophysical experiments.

MECHANORECEPTORS

Let us concentrate our study on the four distinct structures, called the mechanoreceptors, responsible for transducing mechanical energy. Individually, they are known as Meissner's corpuscles, Ruffini endings, Merkel's disks, and the Pacinian corpuscles. These sensors lie at various depths in the dermal tissue or at the dermal–epidermal interface, as shown in figure 18.2. In addition to the morphology of the sensors themselves, it is interesting to note that each is integrated into its surrounding tissue in a unique fashion. For example, Meissner's corpuscules are loosely encased at their base and connected with fibrils on top, while the Ruffini endings are tightly integrated all around. Differences in their integration into surrounding tissue presumably have to do with differentiation in function.

The neural response to all four mechanoreceptors dies out if the mechanical stimulus (usually a motion input) is discontinued. Relative movement is required between skin and object in order to sense aspects like texture. Microneurography studies show that the firings of two types of mechanoreceptors die out quickly and are called rapidly adapting (RA), while the firings of the remaining two last longer and are called slowly adapting (SA). Today it is believed that Pacinian corpuscles and Meissner's corpuscles are the rapidly adapting units, and Ruffini endings and Merkel's disks are the slowly adapting units.

Another means to classify the sensors is by receptive field. Generally, the sensors that are located deeper in the skin have larger sensitive areas. It appears that the Pacinian corpuscles are the vibration sensors. They are capable of sensing vibrations well into the audio range. The Ruffini endings respond most vigorously to skin stretch. Table 18.1 shows some characteristics of the four types of mechanoreceptors.

Table 18.1 Field of sensitivity, frequency range, and supposed sensed parameter, by receptor type

RECEPTOR	FIELD	TYPE	FREQUENCY RANGE	SENSED PARAMETER
Meissner	3–4 mm	FAI	10–60 Hz	skin stretch
Merkel	3–4 mm	SAI	DC–30 Hz	compressive stretch (curvature)
Pacinian	>20 mm	FAII	50–1000 Hz	vibration
Ruffini	>10 mm	SAII	DC–15 Hz	directional skin stretch

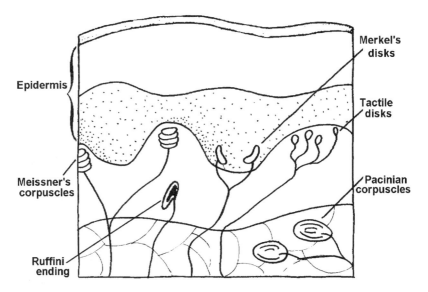

Figure 18.2 A schematic section of human skin, showing the mechanoreceptors. (Drawing courtesy of Jon Forsyth.)

The concentration of the cutaneous sensors varies a great deal over the body. The concentration in the thumb, forefinger, and lips is quite high, while on the torso it is relatively low. There are about 17,000 sensors on each hand—and 15,000 receptors in each cochlea, and 130,000,000 receptors in each eye. The entire body surface is mapped through neural connections to the somatosensory cortex, which lies on the top surface of the brain, running from ear to ear. The sensory homunculus shown in figure 18.3 has each body part sized according to its amount of associated gray matter, and thus has oversized lips, hands, and fingers.

Figure 18.3 Mapping of the surface of the body to the somatosensory cortex by means of the sensory homunculus. (Drawing courtesy of Jon Forsyth.)

18.3.2 The Kinesthetic Sensors

To complete our picture of the suite of sensors that mediate the haptic sensations, there remain the kinesthetic sensors: muscle spindles in the muscles and Golgi organs in the tendons.

The muscle spindles are instrumented fibers among the bundles that make up a muscle body. Muscle spindles consist of so-called alpha fibers wrapped around flower sprays that lie on the surface of the muscle fiber. The spindles are thought to mediate muscle stretch, rate of change of stretch, and perhaps effort. They are particularly interesting sensors because they involve both efferent (from the brain) and afferent (to the brain) nerves (recall the efferent and afferent nerves in the cochlea, discussed in chapter 1). As with the efferent connections in the cochlea, the efferent connections to the muscle spindles are thought to facilitate active gain control (signals from the brain to the muscle spindles can act to suppress signals coming back to the brain). Efferent signals perhaps cause the muscle fiber around which the afferent fibers are wrapped to tense up independently of the other fibers of the muscle, and thus change spindle sensitivity.

The Golgi organs in the tendons are thought to mediate tendon tension. Pacinian corpuscles are also found in the joints, and are thought to pick up vibration associated with the energy of impacts transmitted through the skeleton. The Golgi organs have little to do with proprioception (sensations of position), according to recent findings. Instead, the muscle spindles are thought to be responsible for proprioception and kinesthesia.

18.3.3 Efference Copy

Efference copy is yet another means of acquiring kinesthetic information. Efference copy refers to the idea that one part of the brain can be made aware of the motion of a limb by receiving a copy of the efferent signal issuing from the motor command center of the brain. Thus, even if the muscle spindles, skin stretch sensors, and Golgi organs associated with a particular limb fail to fire, the perceptual centers tracking that limb would be aware of motion because they would have received a copy of the outgoing motion command. One good demonstration of efference copy was first pointed out by Helmholtz. It presumes the existence of a visual perceptual center processing the information coming from the eye in such a way as to keep the perceived environment from moving relative to the body. The perceptual center must account for movement of the image across the retina as the eye moves relative to the environment. By efference copy, this visual perception center receives a copy of the commands given to the eye muscles, thereby knows where the eye is, and can compensate smoothly for the eye movement. If the eye is moved by some other means, say, by gently pressing on the side of the eyeball with a finger, there is a motion of the eyeball for which there is no efference copy, and the perception of the environment moves. Efference copy, then, is a kind of sense without a sensor.

18.4 Interlude: The Haptic Senses in Musical Performance

Musical instruments, by design, vibrate so as to produce sound. But they also vibrate so as to produce haptic sensations. Take, for example, the vibrations of the left-hand finger of a cellist during note onset, as shown in the spectrogram of figure 18.4. Comparison of the vibration frequencies with the data from table 18.1 reveals that certain vibrations will indeed be apparent to the player through the haptic senses. In general, the onsets of notes are particularly rich in low-frequency energy, and thus are candidates for haptic events. Almost all instruments produce mechanical vibration in the 10–1000 Hz range during such note changes, even when the note fundamental is well above 1000 Hz.

Let us make some conjectures about what kind of information is carried by the vibrations felt by a player in his/her fingers, palms, or lips. How can a player make use of haptic information?

A brass instrument player can feel the register jumps in the horn at the embouchure (the mouthpiece). Changes in the pressure or air

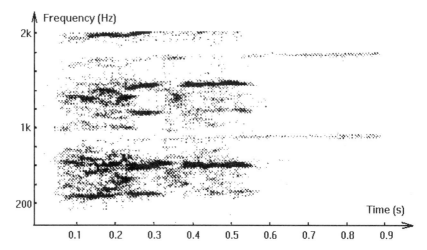

Figure 18.4 Vibration spectrum on the finger of the left hand of a cellist during a note onset. Broadband transients persist for about 0.5 second before a stable note at 880 Hz settles in. (Courtesy of Chris Chafe, CCRMA.)

flow rate through the embouchure during register jumps or note changes are also apparent to sensors in the vocal tract and even the diaphragm. It seems likely that brass players use these haptic cues to determine if the note is properly settled and stable in the instrument, as shown by Perry Cook (1996).

A string bass player can actually tune the instrument to a nearby instrument in the bass section of an orchestra by haptically monitoring the vibrations in his/her instrument. This rather specialized technique becomes useful when the sounds of low and long unison tones are masked to the ears by the sounds of the rest of the orchestra. It does not depend on frequency discrimination of the haptic sensors, since, as we have learned, vibrotactile frequency discrimination is poor. Instead, the bass player will monitor beats in the vibration amplitude that arise in the body of the instrument as it vibrates with its own note and, through air and floor conduction, with the note of an adjacent bass. (Recall the discussion in chapter 5 on how sums of slightly mistuned sine waves exhibit beating.)

From your own musical experience, whatever your instrument, you can probably identify a number of aspects in which the feel of your instrument provides information valuable to your expressive goals. It is hard to imagine playing an instrument successfully with numb fingers or lips. You probably have strong opinions about the make and model of your instrument that are based not only on the tone but also on the feel. For example, if you are a pianist, you appreciate the feel and control of a well-regulated action.

These comments regarding the utility of haptic feedback to a musician's artistic goals bring up another point. We have been speaking mainly about the haptic sensory system as one that supports awareness of the environment, but haptics also play a large role in the process of manipulating that environment. After all, playing a musical instrument is not simply a sensory process, it is a manipulation process. Does the feel of an instrument have anything to do with the ease with which it is played, the ease with which it may be learned, and ultimately its expressive potential? In the next chapter, we will investigate the role of haptics in playing or learning to play a musical instrument.

References

Aristotle (350 B.C.). *De Anima (On The Soul)*. Translated by Hugh Lawson-Tancred. New York: Penguin Books, 1986.

Askenfelt, A., and E. V. Jansson. (1992). "On Vibration Sensation and Finger Touch in Stringed Instrument Playing." *Music Perception,* 9 (3): 311–315.

Burdea, G. C. (1996). *Force and Touch Feedback for Virtual Reality.* New York: Wiley.

Cook, P. (1996). "Hearing, Feeling, and Playing: Masking Studies with Trombone Players." In B. Pennycook and E. Costa-Giomi, eds., *Proceedings of the 4th International Conference on Music Perception and Cognition,* pp. 513–518. McGill University.

Durlach, N., and A. Mavor, eds. (1994). *Virtual Reality: Scientific and Tehnological Challenges,* chap. 4. Washington, D.C.: National Academy Press.

Gibson, J. J. (1966). *The Senses Considered as Perceptual Systems.* Boston: Houghton Mifflin.

Heller, M. A., and W. Schiff, eds. (1991). *The Psychology of Touch.* London: Lawrence Erlbaum.

Katz, D. (1925). *The World of Touch.* Translated by Lester E. Krueger. London: Lawrence Erlbaum, 1989.

Klatzky, R. L., and S. J. Lederman. (1995). "Identifying Objects from a Haptic Glance." *Perception and Psychophysics,* 57 (8): 1111–1123.

Klatzky, R. L., J. M. Loomis, S. J. Lederman, H. Wake, and N. Fujita. (1993). "Haptic Identification of Objects and Their Depictions." *Perception and Psychophysics,* 54 (2): 170–178.

Lederman, S. J., and R. L. Klatzky. (1993). "Extracting Object Properties by Haptic Exploration." *Acta Psychologica,* 84, 29–40.

Schiff, W., and E. Foulke, eds. (1982). *Tactual Perception: A Sourcebook.* Cambridge: Cambridge University Press.

Vallbo, A. B., and R. S. Johansson. (1978). "The Tactile Sensory Innervation of the Glabrous Skin of the Human Hand." In G. Gordon, ed., *Active Touch. The Mechanism of Recognition of Objects by Manipulation: A Multidisciplinary Approach,* 29–54. Oxford: Pergamon Press.

White, B. W., F. A. Saunders, L. Scadden, P. Bach-y-Rita, and C. C. Collins. (1970). "Seeing with the Skin." *Perception and Psychophysics,* 7, 23–27.

19 *Haptics in Manipulation*

Brent Gillespie

19.1 Introduction

In chapter 18, we saw that in order to gather haptic sensory information most effectively, humans produce relative movement between their fingers and an object under scrutiny. Touch accompanied by movement was given the name "active touch" or "haptic exploration." In this chapter, movement takes on a different role: it is produced to influence or manipulate an object. Sometimes we touch objects to sense their motion; on other occasions we touch objects to move them. In changing our focus from haptic exploration to manipulation, movement production and haptic sensing swap roles: movement takes on the role more closely associated with the human's intention, and haptic sensing takes on the supporting role. Note that even when an object is being manipulated, information is available to the haptic sensors. For example, while an object is being moved, sensors on the fingers sense its resistance to motion. This sensory information collected during manipulation can be quite valuable for carrying out certain manipulation tasks or for planning subsequent manipulation strategies.

While a manipulation task is being carried out, the haptic senses may be used to determine whether or not the task is proceeding as desired. The haptic sensors allow pertinent information to be fed back to the centers in the brain responsible for manipulation, so that updates may be made in the outgoing commands if necessary. Alternatively, if the responses of a particular object to various manipulation inputs are known ahead of time, a manipulation task may be carried out without feedback information. Learning the responses, or characterizing that object, however, would undoubtedly have involved the haptic senses.

In this chapter, we will distinguish between sensory information used while carrying out a manipulation task and sensory information used subsequently, to select or plan manipulation strategies. For the investigation of both situations, we shall use concepts from the field of feedback control. In particular, we shall interpret a musician playing an instrument as a feedback control system. Although a proper study of feedback control is part of an engineering curriculum rather than of psychology, our brief foray into the subject will help clarify the utility of haptic information for manipulation. We cite the rich history of cross-fertilization between the fields of control theory and psychology.

We begin our investigation with a close look at the flow of information across a mechanical contact between human and object. Insofaras that manipulation can be considered an information-providing process, while haptic sensing can be considered an information-gathering process, a mechanical contact supports simultaneous information flow in both directions. Examples from the field of telerobotics are used to further elaborate on the concept of information flow during manipulation. Thereafter, feedback control will be introduced. In particular, we interpret a musician controlling an instrument as a feedback control system. Certain musical tasks are interpreted as applications of tracking control, while others are interpreted as applications of adaptive control. Finally, our consideration of the role of haptics in skill acquisition will lead us into a brief review of anticipatory control and learning theory.

19.2 The Mechanical Contact: A Two-Way Street

Let us begin by zeroing in on the physical contact between musician and instrument. Physical contact is essential to the transmission of information to the haptic sensors, except in such cases as radiant heat transfer or, say, puffs of air. In general, it is energy transmitted through the contact that deforms the skin or causes joints to move and, thus, sensors to respond.

In physics, a full description of the interaction between two objects that contact at a point requires that two variables be tracked: the interaction force and the position of the contact point. Once a time history of position has been recorded, both velocity and acceleration histories are also available, since these are time derivatives of the position history. Simple electronic sensors will do the job: a load cell placed between the contacting bodies may be used to record the interaction force while, say, an optical sensor may be used to record position. Given time histories of these two variables, the energy flow between the objects is fully determined, since power is force times velocity.

Force, velocity, position, and so on are the variables that an experimenter or engineer would measure, but are these the variables tracked by the haptic sensors and haptic perceptual system? Is a musician really aware of force and position histories after depressing a piano key, for example? If not these, then what aspects of mechanical interaction actually carry haptic information? Remember Aristotle's question: What is to the haptic senses as sound is to hearing, and color is to seeing?

One theory put forth by James Gibson regarding the encoding of haptic information holds that it is the relationship between force and motion that carries information for the human haptic system. This idea suggests that, rather than separate histories of force and motion, one is aware of degrees of stiffness (the relationship between force and position), damping (the relationship between force and velocity), and mass (the relationship between force and acceleration). Amounts of stiffness, damping, or mass in the "give" of an object are better candidates for the name "object feature" or, in Gibson's words, "object invariant" than are force and motion histories. These are more closely related to the object's identity or makeup. Other researchers have suggested that properties that are salient to the haptic system are other measurables, such as energy flow or effort. Perhaps the carrier of information is context-dependent. These questions are active areas of research.

19.3 Force and Position Control: Examples from Telerobotics

To further explore the concept of haptic information in relation to measurable variables, let us turn to the field of telerobotics. *Telerobots* allow remotely located objects to be manipulated by a human. Telerobotic devices have been in use since the 1950s for handling hazardous materials. The first telerobots consisted of grippers at the remote site, directly coupled through mechanical linkages to a handle in the hands of a human operator. The gripper is typically called the slave and the handle, the master. In the 1960s, electronic sensors were incorporated into the handle for sensing the user's commands, and motors were incorporated into the gripper for executing those commands. Although electronics afforded many advantages, this enhancement to the telerobot was actually, in a certain sense, a step back. For without the direct mechanical coupling, the person operating the handle cannot sense the contact forces that develop between the gripper and an object in its grip. These electronically coupled telerobots are called *unilateral,* in that commands are fed to the remote site but haptic data are not fed back to the user.

The Claw, depicted in the computer-animated movie *Toy Story,* and often seen as a coin-operated toy-vending machine in grocery stores and drugstores, is a unilateral telerobot. The master on this device is usually a set of control buttons, and it is not isomorphic to the slave. Commands are sent electronically to the slave from the master, but forces are not reflected back—one cannot feel the grip force. The only feedback information for grip force available to the operator is the deformation of the captured toy, as seen with the eyes.

Now imagine a Claw gripper outfitted with a force sensor, and an isomorphic (clawlike) handle outfitted with a motor. In such case, when the Claw bumps up against an object, the handle can be made to present that interaction force to the user by activating the handle motor according to the remotely sensed force. When contact is made with a toy, that fact could be detected haptically at the handle. With this enhancement, the toy-retrieving Claw would be called a *bilateral telerobot.* Information flows in both directions. We might expect that one's skill at retrieving toys with a bilateral Claw would far exceed the skill levels achieved in drugstores across the country.

Indeed, bilateral telerobots have been shown to allow much more dexterous manipulation than unilateral ones. With a high-fidelity bilateral telerobot, one can even achieve what is called telepresence: the operator at the handle cannot haptically detect the separation between the master and slave. The user imagines himself/herself operating directly in the remote environment.

So long as the force and motion between slave and object are high-fidelity replications of the force and motion at the master, the user can be fooled—no matter what the particular variables may be to which the human haptic system attends. A high-fidelity bilateral telerobot will reproduce the same relationship between force and motion at the master as that at the object and the slave, thus carrying the relevant object property information (as Gibson suggests). Given, however, that high-fidelity replication is expensive, the challenge is to achieve telepresence for the lowest price, and an improved understanding of the human haptic system is needed to accomplish that.

Let us make a final comment before leaving the telerobotic example. Our bilateral telerobot at present features a slave that is controlled to reproduce the position sensed at the master, and a master that is controlled to reproduce the force sensed at the slave. Since we essentially already have both the slave and the master outfitted with motors and with force and position sensors, we can reverse the flow of force and position signals. The slave can be controlled to reproduce the force sensed at the master while the master can be controlled to reproduce the position sensed at the slave. In theory, the operation and capabilities of such a telerobot would not differ from those of the first. Note, however, that we cannot make both signals flow in the same direction. The slave cannot be made to simultaneously reproduce both the force and the position sensed at the master, or vice versa. Such a proposition would violate principles of cause and effect.

In the following sections, we shall ignore the issue of whether a human is aware of force or motion, or of a relationship between the two, considering this simply an implementation detail in telerobotics and an open question in haptics research. Instead, we will simply refer to information flow.

19.4 Feedback Control

The term *feedback control* is applicable whenever the control or influence on a particular object is derived by using information from a sensor that monitors the behavior of that object. Two entities can always be identified in a control system: the *controller* and the object under control (often called the *plant*). The controller must have at its disposal an *actuator* (for exerting influence over the plant) and a *sensor* (for sensing changes in the plant). Figure 19.1 shows a typical feedback control system, with the components labeled according to standard engineering practice. The error signal is computed as the difference between input and the sensed plant behavior. The controller operates on the error signal to produce a command signal. The goal of the controller can be stated simply: minimize the error. Often the controller simply amplifies the error (multiplies the error by a gain) to produce the command signal. The commanded effort exerted on the plant by the actuator drives the output closer to the input, continually reducing the error. With a suitable gain setting in the controller, the output may be expected to track the input. The input may be interpreted as a *desired* output. Thus this scheme is called a tracking controller.

We are interested in interpreting a musician controlling his instrument from this viewpoint. Let us arrange the musician and instrument in a feedback control block diagram, along with the muscles, ears, and haptic sensors, as shown in figure 19.2. The musician is the controller; the muscles, the actuator; the instrument, the plant;

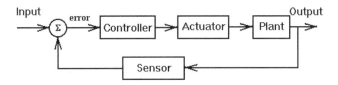

Figure 19.1 A generic feedback control system.

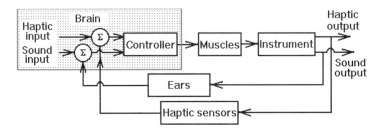

Figure 19.2 The musician and instrument in a feedback control system, showing haptic and audio feedback paths.

and the ears and haptic sensors, of course, the sensors. The correspondence between the elements of a generic feedback control system and our musician/instrument system is simple and direct. The function of the controller, we presume, is performed in the brain. We also presume that the generation of the desired responses and the computation of the error signal occur in the brain. The single forward path denotes the human transmission of mechanical energy, through the limbs and muscles, to the instrument. This transfer of energy takes place through the mechanical contact at the instrument controls (keys, mouthpiece, bow, etc.). Two feedback paths are drawn, one for each of the sensory modalities through which a musician is aware of the instrument's behavior: audio and haptic.

Figures 19.1 and 19.2 are functional block diagrams, showing information flow as inputs and outputs. In the corresponding physical system, there is a single mechanical contact between player and instrument (say, at a fingertip) and a medium shared between player and instrument (the air) through which sound waves may travel. The human transmits information (encapsulated in mechanical energy) to the instrument through the contact point, and the instrument transmits audio information back through the air as sound. In addition, the instrument transmits haptic information back through the contact point at which information was transmitted *to* the instrument. In the block diagrams, this single contact point is represented by two information signal lines: one in the forward path and one in the feedback path. We recognize that there is in fact no inconsistency, since the mechanical contact supports bidirectional information flow, as discussed above. We also see that there is good reason for the location of haptic sensors on the "haptic information output" organs of the body—the arms, hands, and fingers.

Figure 19.2 suggests the following interpretation. By comparing the instrument's actual sound output against a desired sound output (internally conceptualized), the performer can make comparisons and modify subsequent manipulations of the instrument in order to produce new sounds that more closely match the desired sounds. Alternatively, a musician may compare the mechanical information arriving in the haptic feedback path against a desired haptic response, then modify subsequent manipulations to minimize that difference.

A specific example of the use of audio feedback can be found in the tuning of an instrument. The actual pitch is compared against the desired pitch to produce a commanded position of a tuning peg or mouthpiece. The desired pitch may also be a function of time, in which case the commanded position will continually change so that the output tracks the desired pitch. To come up with a good example of the use of haptic feedback is a bit more challenging. One example might be the control of the position of a trombone slide or a finger on a fingerboard. An experienced musician knows what desired position corresponds to a desired pitch, and possibly uses his/her kinesthetic senses in a feedback loop to control that position. A more likely and direct method for pitch control, however, is audio feedback. After all, if the musician knows his/her instrument well enough to generate the desired position based on the desired pitch, he/she may also know enough about the mechanical response of his/her limb and instrument to generate a desired hand position trajectory that accounts for the instrument's response, and does not depend on haptic feedback. (This is called open loop control or anticipatory control, and will be considered in section 19.5.)

Suppose you have an unfamiliar musical instrument in your hands, and you have a musical phrase you would like to produce with this instrument. Without any knowledge of the instrument, the task at hand includes selecting an appropriate manipulation strategy. You must start by manipulating the instrument, monitoring its output, and comparing that output against the response you desire. If at first the match between actual and desired response is poor, you try again. And try with a different strategy. By varying your manipulation strategy, and observing the variations in the instrument's response, both audio and haptic, you may determine how to modify your manipulation so as to produce something closer to your desired response. Basically, you will begin to build a correspondence between manipulation strategies and responses. Now you are using adaptive control. You are adjusting parameters in the controller on the basis of auditory and haptic feedback. You are adaptively changing the dependence of your command on the error, using the trends observed in the error signal over your sequence of attempts.

Finding the *letoff* in a piano key (the position in the key depression at which the jack is disengaged from the hammer) is a useful trick for playing soft notes requiring haptic feedback. The letoff level of each piano must be found by feel.

Suppose you are a pianist who wants to achieve a certain repetition rate of a single note on a piano with a particular loudness. Keeping a desired rate and loudness in mind, you command the muscles of your arm and fingers to move through a particular motion path, with a particular speed, posture, and agonist/antagonist muscle tension. The key and the various elements of the piano action move in response, propelling the hammer toward the string. The hammer strikes the string, causing a note of a particular loudness to be produced by the piano. You repeat the strike. Aside from hearing the note and judging the loudness, you feel how easily the key goes down each time, how "heavy" or "light" the action feels. You feel aspects of timing in the kickback of the key after each note strike. For subsequent strikes, you may or may not change some aspect of how you hit the key, depending on the match between the desired or expected feel and the actual feel of the piano. Thus the feel of the piano contains information that is useful in choosing a *manipulation strategy* for a desired repetition rate.

19.5 Anticipatory Control

In the manipulation of musical instruments that are familiar, one can predict the response to a given input. Thus, there is no need to use feedback control. One can use control without feedback, called *open loop control* or *anticipatory control,* wherein the musician anticipates an instrument's response to a given manipulation. From among many possible manipulations, one is chosen that is expected to give the desired response, according to the controller's best knowledge or guess. Anticipatory control is closely related to *ballistic control.* In ballistic control, not only the feedback, but also the feedforward path, is cut before the manipulation task is complete. In the case of a ball aimed at a target and thrown, for instance, we have no control over the ball's trajectory after it leaves our hand. Both anticipatory control and ballistic control require that the human be familiar with the behavior of an environmental object or system, under a variety of input or manipulation strategies.

An object that is unfamiliar might be either completely foreign or classifiable into a group of similar objects. If it is similar to another object, especially in terms of size, simple scaling of the candidate manipulation/response interaction set (or model) would probably be appropriate. Scaling of an already available candidate input/output pair can be considered a case of using an internal model. Evidence for the existence of internal models is found in a manipulation experience with which you are probably familiar. When grasping and lifting a cup, you may be surprised to have the cup rise off the table faster and higher than expected, only to realize that the cup is empty. The grasp and lift manipulation was chosen and planned for a full cup. Occasionally, the anticipatory control strategy chosen is not the most appropriate.

The most important reason that humans and animals use anticipatory control rather than feedback control is that adequate time is not available for feedback control. There are significant delays in the arrival of sensory information, partly because of the slow conduction of impulses along nerve fibers. Likewise, the execution of commands by muscles is accompanied by delays. Human response times, which include both sensory delays and command delays (the subject must register perception by pushing a button) are on the order of 180 milliseconds. Yet many musical events are faster. Take, for example, a fast trill, 8 to 10 Hz. With less than 100 milliseconds per cycle, the musician must issue commands almost a full cycle ahead of schedule. Actuation based on a comparison between desired and feedback information is not possible.

No wonder it takes years to learn a musical instrument. The musician must characterize his instrument, that is, learn the mapping from input manipulation to audio and haptic response, then either invert this model or otherwise learn to choose appropriate inputs for each desired response. Learning can be considered in part the process of building internal models.

19.6 Hierarchical Control

It is well accepted that the human motor control system is organized hierarchically. Hierarchic organization is a pervasive theme in cognitive, sensory, and motor biology. There are low-level systems responsible for carrying out lower-level tasks, and high-level systems responsible for supervising. Control loops are closed at both low levels and high levels in the nervous system. Examples of low-level control loop closure can be found in the spinal reflexes. For example, the incipient slip of an object in one's grip will be prevented by grip-tightening muscles triggered from the spinal cord by afferent signals issuing from mechanoreceptors at the contact patch.

Motor programs are believed to reside in the cerebellum, at the back and base of the brain. Neuronal connections whose formations depend on learning a particular movement pattern have been found in the cerebellum. The basal ganglia at the center of the brain also play a role in motion production, as evidenced by the loss of certain voluntary movements experienced by persons with injuries there.

19.7 Learning Theory

Feedback is used in learning as well as in control. Through feedback one may develop the internal models necessary for anticipatory control. Learning theory is a large field. Here we introduce a few of its main components, with motor control as our focus and the development of musical skills as an example. Three principal means for effecting performance improvement (learning) have been proposed: method selection, component strengthening, and chunking.

19.7.1 Method Selection

Virtually any task can be accomplished in various ways. *Method selection* assumes that some methods for executing a given task are better than others, and selecting the better method results in performance improvement. Method selection is the learning process in which teachers may involve themselves most actively. The whole educational system is premised on this method of learning.

19.7.2 Component Strengthening

Component strengthening refers to the improvement in task performance (according to a given measure) resulting from pure repetition.

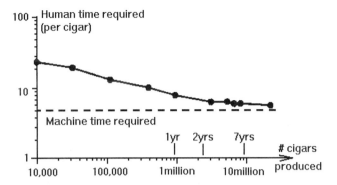

Figure 19.3 Speed of human cigarmaking as a function of practice. (From E. R. F. W. Crossman, "A Theory of the Acquisition of Speed Skill," *Ergonomics,* 2, 1959.)

According to scientific testing, the familiar adage "Practice makes perfect" really is true. For example, the improvement realized by human assemblers of cigars over the course of seven years is shown in figure 19.3. Improvement continues in manual labor indefinitely, although the rate of improvement does decrease.

19.7.3 Chunking

Chunking is the name given to the process of breaking down any task into smaller subtasks. A simple example will illustrate the meaning of chunking. Given the five eighth notes of figure 19.4(a), a subject asked to play the phrase over and over again on a given instrument, as fast as possible, might decide to play the sequence in any one of the three manners suggested by the subfigures (a), (b) and (c). The subject might group all notes separately, as shown in (a), or group the middle three notes into a single set, and leave the two outer eighth notes in sets by themselves, as shown in (b). Alternatively, the musician might choose to group in eighth-note pairs, as in (c). On most instruments, chunking method (b) will produce the fastest possible sequence. Although the performance might otherwise sound the same in all three cases, the actual maximum speed could differ. Various internal conceptualizations by the performer can simplify the task to varying degrees.

Chunking also plays a role in the effectiveness of practicing one part at a time. How the individual parts are chunked will have an impact on the performance when the parts are reassembled to form the whole. Practice itself may also be chunked. Any experienced musician or athlete knows that distributed practice works better

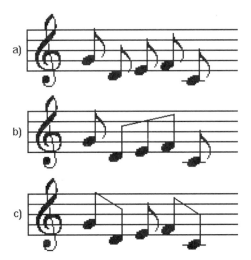

Figure 19.4 A pattern of eighth notes (a) subject to two chunking strategies (b) and (c).

than the same practice time spent all at once. This may be due to fatigue and the need for muscles to recover, rebuild, and strengthen, but quite possibly the motor programs that govern movement also need time to recover, rebuild, and strengthen.

19.8   Summary: The Utility of Haptic Feedback

In chapter 18 and this chapter, we have presented examples of haptic exploration and manipulation with haptic feedback from the playing of musical instruments. Naturally, we have concentrated on the musician while discussing the relationship between musician and instrument. Let us now focus on the instrument and even bring the instrument designer into the picture. For now, having studied feedback control and anticipatory control, we appreciate the importance of the feel of an instrument. Motor control is a faculty that depends on haptic feedback. Before anticipatory control can be used, the internal models of the instrument must be built, using audio and haptic feedback. For the instrument designer, this means that the feel of a particular instrument design is as much a criterion for judgment as the sound. The superior instrument is the one that is most easily or effectively controlled by the musician. Moreover, the relationship between the feel and the sound is very important.

The instrument design challenge is most apparent now that electronic synthesis has become a popular method of sound production. There is no longer a naturally enforced coupling between the feel and the sound of an instrument, as was the case in acoustic instruments, in which both the sound and the feel depend on the physics of a mechanical-to-acoustical energy conversion. With electronic sound production and mechanical/electrical modulation, the feel and the sound need not be related through the physics of the same device.

The present state of affairs in the design of electronic musical instruments can be likened to the period in the development of telerobots that preceded the bilateral telerobot. Most electronic instruments today are "unilateral," in that the feel at the master (the handle or key) has little or nothing to do with the physics governing the interaction between the slave and the remote environment (the sound production physics).

An interesting tool for the study of these questions is haptic interface technology. A keyboard in which each key is outfitted with a motor and a motion sensor can realize programmable feel while a synthesizer offers programmable sound. Arbitrary relationships between the feel and the sound can be explored. Those relationships between the sound and feel that are intuitive (in that they are reminiscent of physical devices) may have advantages over those that are nonintuitive, but this remains an open question. Figure 19.5 shows

Figure 19.5   A six-key musical keyboard with force feedback capability. (From Gillespie, 1996.)

a motorized keyboard designed for this kind of research. We anticipate the arrival of keyboards and other synthesizer interfaces with programmable feel on the market in the foreseeable future.

References

Geldard, F. A. (1972). *The Human Senses.* Second edition. New York: Wiley.

Gibson, J. J. (1962). "Observations on Active Touch." *Psychological Review,* 69, 477–491.

Gillespie, R. B. (1996). "Haptic Display of Systems with Changing Kinematic Constraints: The Virtual Piano Action." Ph.D. dissertation, Stanford University.

Lederman, S. J., and Klatzky, R. L. (1997). "Haptic Aspects of Motor Control." In F. Boller and J. Grafman, eds., *Handbook of Neuropsychology,* vol. 11, 131–148. New York: Elsevier.

Magill, R. A. (1989). *Motor Learning: Concepts and Applications.* Dubuque, Iowa: Wm. C. Brown.

Powers, W. T. (1973). *Behavior: The Control of Perception.* Chicago: Aldine.

Sheridan, T. B. (1992). *Telerobotics, Automation, and Human Supervisory Control.* Cambridge, Mass.: MIT Press.

20 *Perceptual Fusion and Auditory Perspective*

John Chowning

Ligeti spent six months at Stanford (January–June 1972). He came as a guest composer having no knowledge of the work in computer music that we had been pursuing over the previous eight years. At that time we were a small part of the Stanford Artificial Intelligence Laboratory, with no support other than limited access to the computer; thus we were required to work nights and weekends. Ligeti's first visit to the lab led to far-ranging discussion of the capabilities offered by the computer in projecting sound in space, transformations of timbre, the fine control of pitch and time, and precisely constructed tuning systems. On his return to Europe he spoke to his colleagues of the work he had seen in computer music in California. Ligeti became an advocate for the medium. His understanding and vision were great indeed. They still are.

20.1 Introduction

Loudspeakers controlled by computers form the most general sound-producing medium that exists, but there are nonetheless enormous difficulties that must be overcome for the medium to be musically useful. Music does not come easily from machines. This is true whether the machine is a musical instrument of the traditional sort or a computer programmed to produce musical sound. In the case of musical instruments, years of training are required of the performer and instrument builder, and in the case of the computer, substantial knowledge of digital processing, acoustics, and psychoacoustics is required of the composer/musician. It is with this newest instrument, the computer, that we confront new problems with solutions leading to insights that transcend the medium, increase our knowledge, and enrich our experience in the grandest sense. It is important to note that the precision required in constructing the sounds that led to the topics discussed in this chapter was not available before

First authored as *"Music from Machines: Perceptual Fusion & Auditory Perspective"* for Ligeti

1957, when computers were first programmed to produce sound by Max V. Mathews at the Bell Telephone Laboratories.

Two issues are addressed in this chapter:

1. The auditory system's sensitivity to minute fluctuations, a significant characteristic that is little known but that has important implications

2. Auditory perspective, with some insight regarding the multidimensionality of perceived loudness.

Much of what is discussed surrounds phenomena that are well known to musicians and scientists, such as periodic waves, vibrato, and loudness. In the course of this chapter we question the common understanding of some of these phenomena. What is of interest pertains to subtleties of perception that require a more comprehensive understanding of these phenomena. For example, *periodic* is a term frequently used by scientists and engineers to describe a large class of signals whose component parts fall in the harmonic series, but in fact signals in nature are not periodic, and the human auditory system knows this to be so.

20.2   Perceptual Fusion and Quasi Periodicity

20.2.1   The Limits of Perfection

We may have thought that one of the purposes of both the performer and the instrument builder is to reach ever greater degrees of perfection, that the finest instrument and the finest performer can be superseded by an even finer instrument and performer. The great violins of the seventeenth and eighteenth centuries might be replaced by new, superior instruments having strings of ever greater constancy in mass, played by performers whose bow arms, perhaps through better training, could maintain more consistent pressure and more consistent velocity while in contact with the string. Curiously, there are degrees of perfection in acoustic signals beyond which the auditory system responds in quite surprising ways. It can become confused with regard to what instrument or source produced the sound or, in the case of simultaneously occurring sounds, it can become confused with regard to the assignment of the constituent parts or partials to their proper sources. Faced with such perfection, the auditory/cognitive system can exercise a kind of *aesthetic rejection*. It

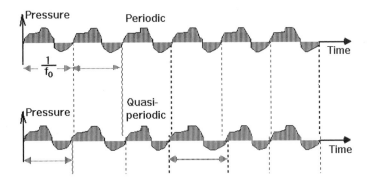

Figure 20.1   Pressure variations typical of sound. There are small period-to-period variations in the quasi-periodic waveform.

is interesting, and perhaps fortunate, that such degrees of perfection are well beyond the capabilities of both acoustic instrument builders and human performers, now and probably forever. This order of perfection exists only in sound generated electronically, especially by means of digital devices such as computers and synthesizers.

20.2.2   Periodicity and Quasi Periodicity

A perfectly regular recurrent pattern of pressure change in time is *periodic.* A recurrent pattern of pressure change in time that has small variations in period and/or pressure is *quasi periodic* (figure 20.1).

Acoustic waves that appear to the auditory system to be periodic, having undetectable variation, are little known in nature but can be produced by loudspeakers whose signals have been generated electronically. Quasi-periodic waves, however, are typical in nature. The auditory system is extraordinarily sensitive to quasi periodicity because it is able to detect a variation in period of a small fraction of a percent. These small, continuous variations are imposed by nature in the form of random pitch, and in many cases an additional variation is consciously imposed by the performer in the form of vibrato and/or tremolo.

Random pitch variation occurs even when there is no vibrato imposed by the performer. This variation is caused by small imperfections in both the performer and the instrument. In the case of a singer, there are small variations in pressure of the air from the lungs as it is forced through the vocal folds, small changes in muscle tension of the vocal folds themselves, and non-linearities resulting from turbulence at the vocal folds that couple with the acoustic wave in the vocal tract. The set of harmonics composing the waveform are modulated in frequency by a common random variation pattern, also referred to as *jitter*. The period-to-period random fluctuations of the harmonic amplitudes are called *shimmer*.

Vibrato is a more or less regular variation in pitch that results from a small modulation of string length, length of the air column, or tension of a vibrating reed or lips. Singers produce vibrato by a variation in tension of the vocal folds. *Tremolo* is a similar variation, but one of loudness, resulting from a variation of bow pressure and/or velocity in the case of strings, and air pressure in the case of winds. Singers produce a tremolo by varying the breath pressure through the vocal folds. (Organ pipes and recorders are constrained to tremolo modulation alone because of their sound-producing mechanisms, whereas most other instruments, including the voice, are capable of both.) Both kinds of modulation, but especially vibrato, serve a variety of musical, acoustic, and perceptual functions.

20.2.3   Source Identification

In 1980 experiments were performed that, for the first time, revealed the special significance of small amounts of variation in pitch. The experiments were based on modeling the voice of a singer (the only musician who is the instrument, its builder, and its performer). A soprano tone lasting 15 seconds was synthesized in three stages, as seen in figure 20.2

Stage 1   A sinusoid at the frequency of the fundamental, $f_0 = 400Hz$
Stage 2   Harmonics are added appropriate to a sung vowel, $2f_0 \ldots nf_0$
Stage 3   A mixture of random pitch variation and vibrato is added to the total signal.

Stages 2 and 3 evolve continuously from the previous stage. At stage 2, all of the spectral information is present that is required for the singing voice. However, not only is the character of the human voice unidentifiable during stage 2, but the added harmonics do not cohere with the fundamental as an entity. Not until the random deviation and vibrato are added at stage 3 do the harmonics *fuse*, becoming a unitary percept and identifiable as a voice. Without the variation in pitch, the sound of the simulated singer (whose control over pitch has reached perfection) does not have a *source signature*

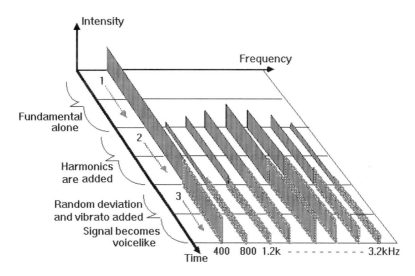

Figure 20.2   Building a soprano tone piece by piece: (1) a single sinusoid, then (2) the harmonics are added, then (3) random and periodic frequency deviation. Only at this last stage does the tone sound like a soprano singer.

or contain information that is essential to her identification as a female singer.

Perceptual fusion is dependent upon a wave or signal being in a condition of quasi periodicity where component partials, through common motion or variation in the pitch space, define themselves as "belonging together." The random frequency (and/or amplitude) variation seems to be present in all sources, while the particular pattern of variation differs according to the source class.

20.2.4   Source Segregation

The fusion of the constituent partials of a sound is a requirement for the auditory system to *segregate sources* or perceive sources as being separate from each other. If we were to listen to the experiment shown in figure 20.2, with the addition of two more sinusoids at 500 Hz and 600 Hz, followed by their associated harmonics, we would expect to hear a purely tuned triad having pitches at 400 Hz, 500 Hz, and 600 Hz. At stage 2, the triad is not easily heard because the partials of all three groups form a harmonic series over a missing fundamental of 100 Hz. At stage 3, however, the triad is clearly heard as sung by three singers. The mix of periodic and random vibrato applied to each group of harmonics is slightly different, causing them to cohere. This allows the auditory system to segregate the three different sources.

20.2.5 The Chorus Effect and Spectral Smearing

What would occur if in the previous experiment all three fundamentals were at the same frequency? Through stages 1 and 2, an increase in loudness would be the only perceived difference. At stage 3, however, a different pitch variation is introduced in each of the three groups, thus *smearing* the spectrum because of the complex random beating that occurs between all proximate harmonics. Source segregation occurs, and the three voices appear to be singing in unison, but as a chorus (figure 20.3).

In complex acoustic contexts where there are multiple sources, as in a chorus, each source has its unique random pattern that differs in detail from all others to a degree detectable by the ear. If there were no imperfections in the source causing quasi periodicity, perceptual fusion would not occur and a listener could neither identify its nature (*source identification*) nor hear parts (*source segregation*). Nor could the listener recognize that there is more than one source per part (*chorus effect*). Thus, the auditory system is utterly dependent upon acoustic imperfections.

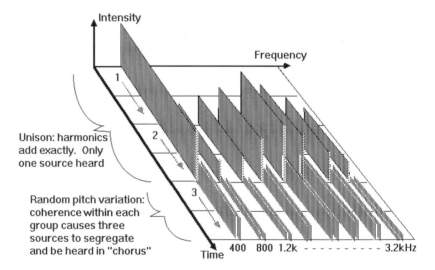

Figure 20.3 Building three sopranos piece by piece. Three unison sinusoids, then the harmonics, then finally random and periodic frequency deviations. If the frequency deviation functions are different for the three synthesized sources, segregation occurs and the three voices are heard.

20.2.6 More About Vibrato

In addition to being an expressive device, vibrato serves a variety of acoustic, perceptual, and musical functions. It can complement the natural random pitch variation, which is of critical importance to source identification and source segregation. The timbral richness (identity) of a source is enhanced by even a small amount of vibrato because partials oscillate under resonant envelopes, causing a complex, asynchronous amplitude modulation. In the context of a soloist playing with an ensemble, instruments having a limited dynamic range (such as the violin) use vibrato to help segregate their sound from that of the ensemble that otherwise masks the solo instrument. This is analogous to the visual system's ability to segregate an object hidden in a background only when the object moves. Finally, vibrato frequency and depth are used expressively to support pitch and dynamics in the articulation of a musical line.

20.2.7 Periodicity and Symmetry

The auditory and visual systems seem to treat periodicity and symmetry in a similar manner, but in different degrees. The eye does not immediately detect the quasi periodicity in figure 20.4 without the aid of lines indicating the periods (as in figure 20.1), nor does the eye detect the one building of the three that is least symmetrical about the center axis. However, the auditory system can readily detect a fraction of a percent of deviation from periodicity, as noted above.

Both the auditory and the visual systems become inattentive, or in a sense turn off, when periodicity/symmetry is perceived over even a rather short time, and thus fail to extract critical information. This is especially true in the case of the auditory system.

The making of music by using machines demands that attention be given to the requirements of the perceptual system. Unlike acoustic instruments, electronic instruments do not have the inherent imperfections in sound production upon which the auditory system depends.

20.3 Auditory Perspective

The perception of sound in space remains a critical issue in music composed for loudspeakers, whether prerecorded or from real-time digital synthesizers. In the simplest case a listener localizes the

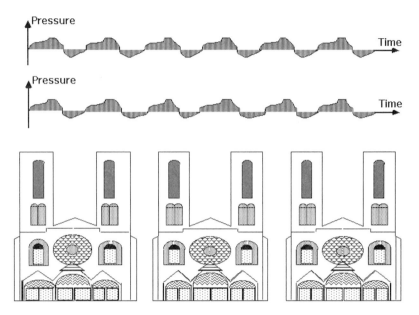

Figure 20.4 Seemingly identical things are actually quite different on close inspection. To see this, measure the periods of the waveforms or the spacings of the windows on the buildings.

emanating sound from points defined by the position of the loudspeakers. In all other acoustic settings the listener associates a sound source with horizontal and vertical direction and a distance. The auditory system seems to map its perceived information to the higher cognitive levels in ways analogous to those in the visual system. Acoustic images of wide breadth are reduced to a point source at great distances, as one would first experience listening to an orchestra at a distance of 20 m and then at 300 m. This is equivalent to converging lines and the vanishing point in visual perspective. Sounds lose intensity with distance just as objects diminish in size. Timbral definition diminishes with distance of a sound from a listener just as there is a color gradient over large distance in vision.

Therefore *perspective* is as much a part of the auditory system as it is of the visual system. It is not surprising that the two systems have evolved in a way that avoids conflict of sensory modes in comprehending the external world, since many visually perceived objects can also be sound sources. Identifying these sources and their locations can be especially important to survival: the mother's voice, the growl of a lion, or the approach of a fast-moving automobile. While not always perceived with great precision, the position of sound in space, *auditory perspective,* is composed of important acoustic and psychoacoustic dimensions.

20.3.1 Loudness

Commonly thought to be the exact perceptual correlate of physical intensity, loudness is a more complicated percept involving more than one dimension. In order to reveal this, we can imagine the following experiment.

A listener faces two singers, one at a distance of 1 m and the other at a distance of 50 m. The closer singer produces a **pp** tone, followed by the distant singer who produces a **ff** tone. The tones have the same pitch and the same timbre, and are of the same duration. The listener is asked which of the two tones is the louder (figure 20.5). Before speculating about the answer, we should consider the effect of distance on intensity.

Sound emanates from a source as a spherical pressure wave (we are ignoring small variances resulting from the fact that few sources are truly points). As the pressure wave travels away from the source, the surface area of the wave increases with the square of the distance (the area of a sphere increases with the square of the radius). The intensity at any point, then, decreases according to the inverse square law: $1/d^2$ (figure 20.6).

The distance in the experiment is 50 m, which results in a decrease of intensity of $1/50^2$ or $1/2500$ the intensity of the same **ff** tone

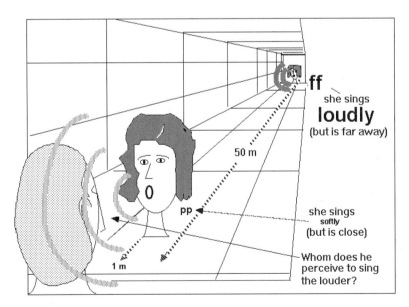

Figure 20.5 Perception of distance and auditory perspective. Sound coming from a loud singer far away could be identical in amplitude to the sound coming from a soft singer close by. How do we manage to figure it out?

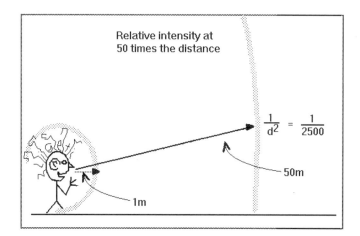

Relative intensity at
50 times the distance

$$\frac{1}{d^2} = \frac{1}{2500}$$

50m

1m

Figure 20.6 Intensity falls off as the square of the distance.

sung at a distance of 1 m. The listener, however, is asked to judge the relative loudness where the closer tone is **pp** rather than **ff.** Let us suppose that the intensity of the **pp** is *1/128* that of the **ff.** The greater of the two intensities then is the closer **pp,** and by a large amount. If loudness is indeed the perceptual correlate of intensity, then the answer to the question is unambiguous. However, the listener's answer is that the second tone at 50 m is louder even though the intensity of the closer tone is about 20 times greater. How can this be so?

20.3.2   Spectral Cues

In the definition of the experiment above, it is stated that the timbre of the two tones is the same. The listener perceives the tones to be of the same timbral class: soprano tones that differ only in dynamic or vocal effort. As was shown in figure 9.4, in natural sources the spectral envelope shape changes significantly as the pitch and energy applied to the source change. As the pitch increases, the number of partials in a spectrum decreases and the spectrum changes shape. In other words, the centroid of the spectrum shifts toward the fundamental. The spectral envelope changes shape, favoring the higher component frequencies as musical dynamic or effort increases. The centroid shifts away from the fundamental.

Figure 20.7 represents a generalization of harmonic component intensity and spectral envelope change as a function of pitch, dynamic (effort), and distance. Because of the high dimensionality involved, a representation is shown where two-dimensional spaces (instantaneous spectra) are nested in an enclosing three-dimensional space. The positions of the origins of the two-dimensional spaces are projected onto the "walls" of the three-dimensional space in order to see the relative values. Nesting the spaces allows visualization of dimensions greater in number than three, an otherwise unimaginable complexity. Our ability to assemble the enormous collection of spectra resulting from a single instrument class along the loudness and pitch dimensions, then designate it a "soprano" or "violin" continuum, is a considerable accomplishment of the perceptual/cognitive systems. It would be even more so were we to consider the additional dimensions of articulation. Timbral continuity, then, first depends upon perceptual fusion (signal coherence) and source identification, and second it depends on placing the tone in the perceptual timbre space.

Now we begin to see the difference in overall intensity and spectral envelope between the tone that is soft and close and the tone that is loud and far. We also understand how the listener in the experiment was able to make a judgment regarding loudness that controverts the dominant effect of intensity on perceived loudness. Knowing the difference in timbral quality between a loudly or softly

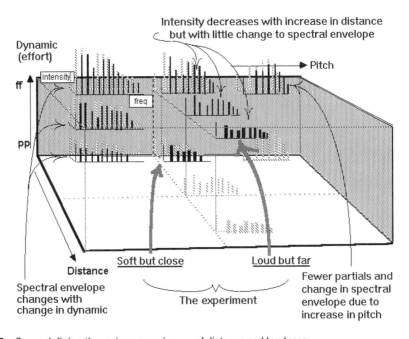

Figure 20.7 Space defining the various experiences of distance and loudness.

sung tone, reflecting vocal effort, the listener apparently chose spectrum over intensity as the primary cue. But what if the two tones in the experiment were produced by loudspeakers instead of by singers, and there were no spectral difference as a result of difference in effort? The answer is probably still the distant tone, even though its intensity is the lesser of the two, if there is reverberation produced as well.

20.3.3 Distance Cue and Reverberation

The *direct* signal is that part of the spherical wave that arrives uninterrupted, via a line-of-sight path, from a sound source to the listener's position. *Reverberation* is a collection of echos, typically tens of thousands, reflecting from the various surfaces within a space and arriving indirectly from the source to the listener's position. The intensity of the reverberant energy in relation to the intensity of the direct signal allows the listener to interpret a cue for distance. How does our listener in the experiment use reverberation to determine that the distant tone is the louder?

If, in a typical enclosed space, a source produces a sound at a constant dynamic, but at increasing distances from a stationary listener, approximately the same amount of reverberant energy will arrive at the listener's position. At the same time the direct signal will decrease in intensity according to the inverse square law (figure 20.8).

If at a distance of 5 (figure 20.8), a sound is produced having six times the intensity of a softer sound at distance 2, then the reverberant signal increases by the same factor. It is for this reason that the listener does not confuse the location of the source at a distance of 5 with that of a source at a distance of 2 whose direct signal intensity is approximately the same. The listener in the experiment determined that the reverberant energy associated with the distant loudspeaker was proportionally greater than the reverberant energy associated with the softly sounding, nearby loudspeaker. This led him to infer that there was greater intensity at the source.

A sound having constant intensity at the source will be perceived by a stationary listener to have constant loudness as its distance increases from 1 to 2 to 3, and so on. As seen in figure 20.8, it is the constant intensity of the reverberant energy that provides this effect of *loudness constancy* when there are no spectral cues. A similar phenomenon occurs in the visual system. *Size constancy* depends

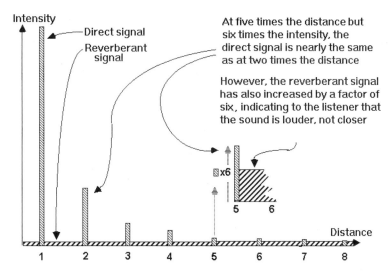

Figure 20.8   Direct-to-reverberant ratio as a function of distance. Reverberant component is roughly constant, but direct sound obeys inverse square law.

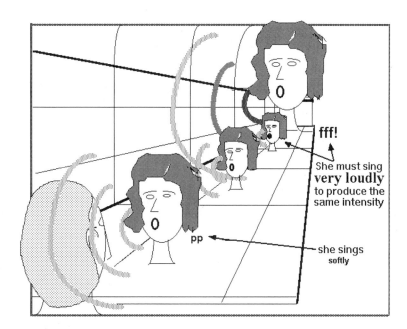

Figure 20.9   Perception of distance and auditory perspective. The sound coming from a loud singer far away could be identical to the sound coming from a soft singer close by. But spectral brightness gives a clue as to how much effort the loud singer is using.

upon perspective. It allows judgments to be made about size that do not necessarily correlate with the size of the retinal image. In figure 20.9, we can see what is required to produce constant image size at the retina and constant sound intensity for the listener. The distant image is the same size as the close image.

Just as the distant singer must sing much louder to produce the same intensity as the nearest singer, so must she also become bigger in order to produce the same size image on the retina of the listener/viewer. It must be noted that *loudness constancy* is complicated in a way that *size constancy* is not. Few images in the visual world are expected to increase or decrease in actual size in a short period of time, thus facilitating the perceptual task. Auditory sources are commonly expected to vary in loudness in short times, especially in music, where many different loudnesses can occur in quick sequence without confusing the listener.

Auditory perspective is not a metaphor in relation to visual perspective, but rather a phenomenon that seems to follow general laws of spatial perception. It is dependent upon loudness (which is subjective), the physical correlates of which we have seen include spectral and distance cues, in addition to intensity. Further, the perception of loudness can be affected in a subtle but significant manner by the *chorus effect,* and by vibrato depth and rate.

The listener in the experiment used all the information available—spectral and distance cues in addition to intensity—to make a determination of loudness at the source. In the absence of spectral cues, the distance cue sufficed. Were there no reverberation present in the latter case, then intensity alone would be the cue, and the answer to the question would be that the closer of the two is the louder.

20.4   Conclusion: Computer Instruments and Computer Composition

Computers can be programmed with some care to extend the dimensions of loudness beyond intensity, thereby providing the composer with a control of loudness vastly more subtle, and more musical, than that provided by intensity alone. However, only recently have synthesizers offered the composer spectral and intensity change as a function of effort (key velocity), and distance as a function of constant reverberant signal in relation to a varying direct signal. The latter has been possible since the first spring and plate reverberators became available. The musical importance of these dimensions of loudness cannot be overemphasized, yet their use in either general-purpose computers or synthesizers is still not widespread.

The issues surrounding perceptual fusion, including quasi periodicity and source identification, segregation, and chorus effect, can be fully addressed only with computers and large general-purpose synthesizers. To be sure, there may be reasons of economy why generally available synthesizers cannot provide such capabilities. However, there may also be some insensitivity to the importance of perceptual domains in which musicians (and listeners) find their reality.

Finally, the issues of perceptual fusion and auditory perspective are of general interest because they bear upon the basis of music perception. The domain of sounds to which these issues are relevant is not constrained to those similar to natural sounds, but may include all imaginable sounds. In fact, the understanding and exploration of these issues suggests somewhat magical musical and acoustic boundaries that cannot be part of our normal acoustic experience, yet can find expression through machines in ways that are consonant with our perceptual/cognitive systems.

References

Bregman, A. S. (1990). *Auditory Scene Analysis: The Perceptual Organization of Sound.* Cambridge, Mass.: MIT Press.

Chowning, J. M. (1971). "The Simulation of Moving Sound Sources." *Journal of the Audio Engineering Society,* 199, 2–6.

———. (1980). "Computer Synthesis of the Singing Voice." In Johan Sundberg, ed., *Sound Generation in Winds, Strings, and Computers,* 4–13. Stockholm: Royal Swedish Academy of Music.

Dodge, C., and T. Jerse. (1985). *Computer Music.* New York: Schirmer Books.

Gardner, M. (1969). "Distance Estimation of 0° or Apparent 0°-Oriented Speech Signals in Anechoic Space." *Journal of the Acoustical Society of America,* 45: 47–52.

McAdams, S. (1984). *Spectral Fusion, Spectral Parsing, and the Formation of Auditory Images.* Technical Report STAN-M-22. Stanford University, Dept. of Music (CCRMA).

Moore, F. R. (1983). "A General Model for Spatial Processing of Sounds." *Computer Music Journal,* 7(3): 6–15.

Moore, F. R. (1990). *Elements of Computer Music.* Englewood Cliffs, N.J.: Prentice-Hall.

Zwicker, E., and B. Scharf (1965). "A Model of Loudness Summation." *Psychological Review,* 72, 3–26.

21 Passive Nonlinearities in Acoustics

John Pierce

21.1 Introduction

It is through nonlinearities that traditional musical instruments, such as violins and wind instruments, produce sustained tones (McIntyre et al. 1983; Smith 1986). The string or tube of such an instrument has nearly harmonic modes of oscillation. Excited and then left to themselves, such modes will oscillate with exponentially decreasing amplitudes. The bow or the breath can continually supply energy through a nonlinear process, so that the normally passive instrument produces a sustained tone.

This is not, however, the sort of nonlinearity discussed in this chapter. Here we are concerned with those nonlinear processes that do not add energy to the overall system of modes. We will talk about systems that are excited initially by a nonlinear process such as plucking a string, striking a gong, or clashing cymbals together. The nonlinearities we consider redistribute energy among modes of oscillation, so that the shape of the spectrum changes as the overall oscillation decays in energy. This change of spectrum is heard as an essential part of the characteristic musical sound.

21.2 A Few Examples

In initially seeking examples of such nonlinearities, I turned to a book by Neville H. Fletcher and Thomas D. Rossing (1991). Figure 21.1 is a subband decomposition for a tam-tam, a flattish Chinese gong. The figure shows the buildup and decay of vibrations in various frequency bands during the first 0.4 second after striking. In some bands the buildup occurs well after striking, while the band marked 162 Hz is falling in magnitude. It seems clear that energy is being transferred from some lower-frequency modes that are excited directly by striking to higher-frequency modes whose amplitudes rise later.

Figure 21.2 shows the sound spectra of cymbals immediately after striking, 50 milliseconds after striking, 1 second after striking, and

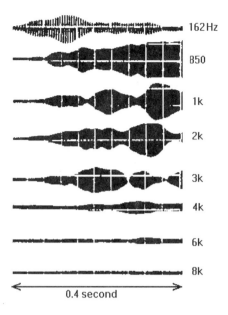

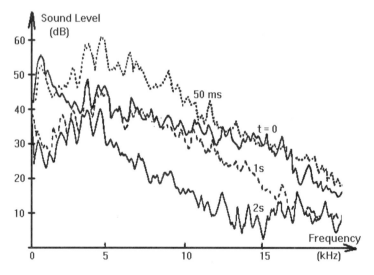

Figure 21.1   Buildup and decay in various frequency bands for a tam-tam during the first 0.4 seconds. (From Fletcher and Rossing, 1991.)

Figure 21.2   Spectra of cymbals immediately after striking (t = 0) and 50 ms, 1 s, and 2s later. Note the buildup of higher frequencies at 50 ms and later, and the eventual decay of higher frequencies. (From Fletcher and Rossing, 1991.)

2 seconds after striking. By 50 milliseconds after striking, a good deal of energy at lower frequencies has been transferred to a frequency range around 5 kHz. Thereafter the spectrum peaks at around 5 kHz, and by 2 seconds has decayed at higher frequencies.

If we were to inspect the individual amplitude trajectories for the partials of a grand piano note, we would see that some curves rise while others fall. The modes of the string come in pairs close in frequency, one for oscillation up and down, the other for oscillation left and right. Are the rises and falls in the curves due to beating between such modes? Or could they involve small passive nonlinearities?

Rossing and Fletcher also refer to the sitar, an Indian stringed instrument, and note that "the curved bridge leads to both amplitude and frequency modulation due to rolling and sliding of the string." Electronic sitars are now available, and a clear modification of timbre (through a modification of spectrum) is heard after plucking.

It is easy to demonstrate the excitation of higher modes of a string after plucking by means of the system shown in figure 21.3. Here the string is stretched between a rigid support, R, at the right and an inclined support of springy material, S, at the left. We note that pushing the string either up or down bends the spring support inward, causing the movable end of the string to move downward. Thus, if the string oscillates with a frequency f, the end of the string will move up and down with a frequency $2f$. This causes the string to oscillate with a frequency $2f$ in the up–down direction. If we pluck the string and listen, we will hear the emergence of a second harmonic, followed by the emergence of higher harmonics. This system is similar to one investigated by K. A. Legge and Neville Fletcher in 1984.

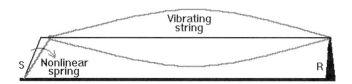

Figure 21.3   A string is supported at one end by an inclined springy flap that moves in the same direction (inward) whether we push the string up or down. If the string oscillates at a frequency f, the spring will move up and down with a frequency $2f$, and the harmonics build up.

21.3 Passive Nonlinearities

Nonlinearities in systems such as gongs, strings, and columns of air must be *passive nonlinearities*. After initial striking or plucking, there is no source of energy. In physical systems, energy is lost continually, and the oscillation decays and vanishes. In computer models of physical systems, or in programs intended to generate waveforms, we may omit losses, so that oscillation can continue forever. Passive nonlinearities can change the spectrum, but not the total energy of the oscillation that the program produces.

The value or potential value of nonlinearities in computer sound-generating programs has been recognized. Many proposed methods of introducing nonlinearities add to or subtract from the total energy of the system. The introduction of such nonlinearities causes the system to oscillate at some unexpected and undesired frequency. Criteria for stability may be difficult to formulate and to evaluate.

Through the use of passive nonlinearities we can avoid any possibility of rendering the system unstable. How can we assure that nonlinearities will indeed be passive? We could represent the waveform-generating program as a network of springs and masses, or of capacitors and inductors. Using such elements, we can design a network that will have the desired modes or frequencies of oscillation. We will initially omit friction or resistors, and our modes of oscillation will be lossless. We can use delays if we wish, as in the Karplus–Strong formulation of vibrations on a string (Karplus and Strong 1983; Jaffe and Smith 1983).

To introduce passive nonlinearity, we use nonlinear capacitors or inductors in electronic circuits, or nonlinear springs or masses in physical systems. The energy stored will be zero at zero voltage, at zero current, at zero deflection, or at zero velocity. The energy stored will be different for a positive and a negative voltage, for a positive and a negative current, for a positive and a negative deflection, or for a positive and a negative velocity.

A simple and effective nonlinear circuit element is a capacitance that has one constant value for any negative voltage and a different constant value for any positive voltage. In further discussions we will confine ourselves to this simple element.

Figure 21.4 shows a simple consequence of a different capacitance for positive and negative voltages. The (simulated or programmed) electric circuit consists of a capacitor and an inductor. If the capacitance is the same for a positive and a negative voltage, the waveform is as shown in (a).

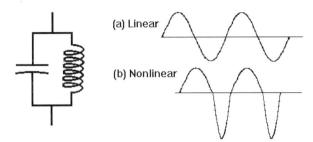

Figure 21.4 Oscillations (right) of the capacitor–inductor circuit shown at the left. If the capacitance is equal for positive and negative voltages, the oscillation will be sinusoidal (a). If the capacitance for negative voltages is 1/4 that for positive voltages, the oscillation will be as shown in (b). The energy stored for the peak positive voltage is the same as the energy stored for the peak negative voltage.

Suppose we make the capacitance 1/4 as great for negative as for positive voltages. For negative voltages the frequency is doubled and the period is halved. For a constant energy, the greatest negative voltage must be twice the greatest positive voltage. The waveform for this nonlinear capacitance is as shown in (b).

Figure 21.4 shows that the effect of passive non-linearities can be great. However, what we really seek to do is transfer energy among many modes of a nearly linear system, as is illustrated in figure 21.5. The left-hand side represents the modes of a truly linear system. The total voltage of all modes is applied to a nonlinear capacitor at the upper right. The complicated current that flows through this nonlinear capacitor transfers energy among the modes of the almost linear system.

21.4 Digital Simulation of Passive Nonlinearities

The value of nonlinearities in computer sound-generating programs has been recognized. But most means of adding nonlinearities in simulations change the energy of the system. This is pointed up by Xavier Rodet (1993) in his paper about simulating nonlinear systems.

There is, however, a class of nonlinearities that are passive, and do not change the energy of the system. This is true of actual physical systems, such as the gong and cymbals in figures 21.1 and 21.2. If such systems are lossless, their oscillation persists with unvarying energy, although the waveform and spectrum change with time. Small losses cause the system energy to decay slowly.

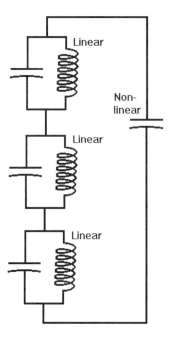

Figure 21.5   A circuit element whose capacitances are different for positive and negative voltages (upper right) can be used to couple the modes of a linear network (at the left).

The author and Scott van Duyne (1997) designed a system in which one reactive element has different values for positive and for negative amplitudes. Suitable systems are those in which the interchange of smaller and larger values is made as the voltage or current crosses zero. This could be a capacitance that is greater or less for positive and negative voltages, or an inductance that is greater or less for positive or negative currents. A mechanical system that satisfies this requirement is shown in figure 21.6. The nonlinear spring requires different amounts of force to displace it in either direction.

This obviously meets the criterion of passivity. The overall oscillation in a system including such an element will have a spectrum and a waveform that vary with time, but the nature of the system conserves energy. Even a relatively small variation in time will give a liveliness, a musical quality that many real acoustic systems exhibit. A large variation in time will model highly nonlinear systems, such as gongs and cymbals.

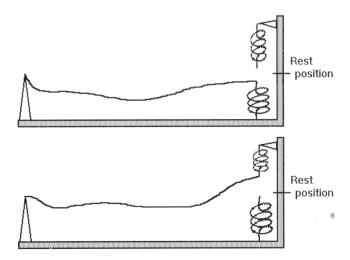

Figure 21.6 A vibrating string coupled to a nonlinear spring.

21.5 Summary

Linear computer models can be used with fair to good success in simulating the resonant qualities of stringed and wind instruments. By use of passive nonlinearities, features of sounds of instruments such as gongs and cymbals can be obtained by using the nonlinearity in connection with an essentially linear model of other vibrating structures. With linear models of the modes of stretched strings, interesting sounds with gonglike properties can be obtained by adding passive nonlinearities. New efficient models allow these to be added to simulations without adding significantly to the total computation. The overall effect and value of adding passive nonlinearities to present linear models has not been explored. I hope that this chapter provides the impetus to begin such explorations.

References

Fletcher, N. H., and T. D. Rossing. (1991). *The Physics of Musical Instruments*. New York: Springer-Verlag.

Jaffe, D., and J. Smith. (1983). "Extensions of the Karplus–Strong Plucked-String Algorithm." *Computer Music Journal*, 7 (2): 56–69.

Karplus, K., and A. Strong. (1983). "Digital Synthesis of Plucked-String and Drum Timbres." *Computer Music Journal*, 7 (2): 43–55.

Legge, K. A., and N. H. Fletcher. (1984). "Nonlinear Generation of Missing Modes in a Vibrating String." *Journal of the Acoustical Society of America*, 76, 5–12.

McIntyre, M. E., R. T. Schumacher, and J. Woodhouse. (1983). "On the Oscillation of Musical Instruments." *Journal of the Acoustical Society of America*, 74 (5): 1325–1344.

Pierce, J. R. and S. A. Van Duyne. (1997). "A Passive Nonlinear Digital Filter Design Which Facilitates Physics-Based Sound Synthesis of Highly Nonlinear Musical Instruments." *Journal of the Acoustical Society of America,* 101 (2): 1120–1126.

Rodet, X. (1993). "Flexible yet Controllable Physical Models: A Nonlinear Dynamics Approach." In *Proceedings of the International Computer Music Conference,* pp. 48–55. San Francisco.

Smith, J. O. (1986). "Efficient Simulation of the Reed-Bore and Bow-String Mechanisms." In *Proceedings of the International Computer Music Conference,* The Hague.

22 Storage and Reproduction of Music

John Pierce

22.1 Introduction

Music does not go on forever, like the babbling of a stream (though some New Age music seems to). A song or music for a dance has a beginning and an end point. Simple music is memorable—or, rather, memorizable. Many people who have heard a popular song many times can sing it, and more can recognize it. Musicians can remember and reproduce longer pieces of music. Thus, memory is one way of perpetuating music, often with some changes.

Musical scores go beyond human memory. What they have to tell us can perpetuate music as long as the score lasts and is understood, and as long as there are skilled musicians to play from the score.

Music is reproduced even more exactly by machines that play and replay music, such as music boxes, player pianos, and modern MIDI (musical instrument digital interface) player pianos. It appears that such machines were made in classical times, though none survive. Such mechanoacoustic machines seem to offer the most exact reproduction of music. The reproduction does not depend on the memory, skill, or interpretation of a performer. Nor is an environment of noise, reflections, and reverberation built into these music machines.

The invention of the telephone by Bell in 1876, and of the phonograph by Edison in 1877, brought something entirely different on the scene. Those inventions made possible the re-creation, well or ill, of the actual sound waves themselves, rather than re-creation of sounds by men or by machines playing instruments. Today we all experience transmitted musical sound (radio, TV) and recorded musical sound (tapes, compact discs) more often than we hear live musical sound. Yet the re-creation and replaying of music persists, in actual playing from scores and in the playing of various electronic instruments, usually via MIDI, from sequencers of one sort or another.

The variety of ways that we have for reproducing music raises a number of problems. If a musician plays from memory, the music he/she reproduces may change somewhat with time and circumstance. Further, there is a limit to what a musician can remember. What a musician produces in playing from a score differs according to his/her skill and interpretation. There seems no limit to the number of scores available, except perhaps in terms of cost. Today we would tend to measure that cost in the number of bits (binary digits) that are necessary to reproduce the score.

A machine that plays music has some monetary cost itself. It also has some cost of storage of music to be played, such as player piano rolls or the computer memory or disk space necessary for a sequencer to control a synthesizer with digitally stored scores. Recorded music has a built-in environment as well as the environment in which it is played. It also has a cost in bits of storage far higher than the cost of providing a score to a musician or playing instructions to a machine. What can be said about the problems of reproducing music is endless. The following material elaborates on some considerations and aspects of storing and reproducing sound and music.

22.2   Scores

Musical notation, such as that of figure 22.1, can tell those who can read it a great deal about how a composition should sound. The places of the notes on the staffs, the key signature (in this case, two flats), and the clef marks describe the pitches to be produced. The forms of the notes—*quarter, eighth,* and so on—together with the *time signature* (in this case "common" or 4/4) and the *tempo* (in this case allegro), describe the note durations. The score of figure 22.1 tells us something about timbre by specifying the instruments to be used (in this case organ, two oboes, violins, cello, and bass). The name of the composer can be helpful (in this case Handel), and so can the name of the piece (Organ Concerto in F Major).

Other scores have signs indicating intensity or loudness, such as *pp, mf,* or *ff.* There are indications for crescendos and diminuendos. Marks associated with notes can indicate style of playing, such as staccato or marcato.   A score can give a great deal of information to a skilled performer.

What it can scarcely give is what the contemporary listener expects in the interpretation of a score. Some late nineteenth-century

Organ Concerto Op. 4 No. 4

G. F. Handel

Figure 22.1 A score is an effective representation of a composition, but a player is needed to bring the music "back to life."

and early twentieth-century interpretations of scores exist either as primitive sound recordings or as player piano rolls. Some of these indicate that there have been large changes in interpretation. Indeed, different interpretations of scores are found among skilled performers of our time.

As to the inherent cost of scores, we can say that producing a master copy by classical means is costly. When the score is produced through some computer-aided process, as in Leland Smith's computer program SCORE, we can measure the number of bits per measure or per page. This number of bits is small compared with the number of bits for a compact disc recording of the same music. Smith has added to SCORE means for playing the music scored with computer-generated sound. However, a skilled human player is needed to re-create from the score what the composer intended, or what the audience will approve of.

22.3 Mechanical Instruments

Mechanical instruments can record and play music in a limited way. Replayings are indistinguishable to the ear. Mechanical instruments antedate modern musical notation. It appears that such instruments were built in classical times, and they are mentioned in texts of the Middle Ages. It is said that Leonardo da Vinci constructed a mechanical instrument late in the fifteenth century, a spinet and two drums played by protrusions on a rotating cylinder. In the fifteenth century, mechanically played carillons were placed in clock towers.

The barrel organ, familiar in my youth from the organ grinder and his monkey, is one of the most persistent of mechanical instruments. In it a rotating wooden cylinder with protruding brass staples or pins opens valves and plays pipes or free reeds. Barrel organs were known as early as the seventeenth century and were common in the nineteenth century. Haydn, Mozart, and C. P. E. Bach wrote pieces for them. More elaborate machines, differently named and with a wider range of sounds, were constructed to imitate the orchestra. Beethoven wrote a piece for such a machine (*Wellington's Victory*). The music box was invented later than the barrel organ, at the close of the eighteenth century. Some later music boxes had disks with cut and bent protrusions that were replaceable, like phonograph records.

Of all the mechanical instruments, the player piano was the most musical. The essentials of the player piano were patented as early as 1860, but successful instruments were not produced until some 20 years later. In the first player pianos the playing mechanism was separate from the piano, and struck the piano keys. By the turn of the twentieth century the mechanism was integrated into the piano. Controls were provided for intensity and tempo, so that the player could, to a degree, interpret the piece. Pianos with recorded control of intensities of notes were first produced around 1905, and several piano companies were producing them by 1914.

Today, devices such as the Yamaha DiscClavier are MIDI pianos that can reproduce every nuance of a performance recorded on a floppy disk. Or they can perform edited versions of the player's performance. The only thing missing is the audience noise. The MIDI piano is attractive because it can exactly reproduce the sound of a fine instrument as played by a skilled musician. Like a live performance, the actual sound is affected by the room or hall in which the instrument is played. But it is the sound of an actual instrument in a room, not a sound recorded in one room and reproduced in another.

It is easy to make a useful if limited comparison between the amounts of storage sufficient for a DiscClavier and for a compact disc. The MIDI interface is sufficient for driving a DiscClavier, because it is more than is necessary to record and transmit keyboard information. MIDI has a bit rate of 31,250 bits per second. CD-quality recording of two 16-bit channels at 44,100 samples per second per channel gives 11,411,200 bits per second. This is about 45 times the MIDI rate.

There are keyboard instruments other than the piano, including the harpsichord and the organ, and digital keyboards of one sort or another. These also can be played in exact reproduction of a performance by a skilled performer. However, the sounds of most musical instruments involve features of performance that cannot be imitated exactly from recordings of what a musician does in a performance.

22.4 Imitation Instruments

Before going on to sound recording, it seems appropriate to consider briefly what we might call imitation instruments. By this I mean electronic hardware or software that can be used to give the effect of actual physical or electronic instruments. Various attempts have been made to imitate the crucial features of vocal and instrumental sounds.

The vocoder, an artificial speaking machine devised by Homer Dudley in 1939, is shown in figure 22.2. At the transmitting end, an attempt is made to classify the sound as either voiced or unvoiced. If voiced, an estimate is made of the pitch. The spectrum of the sound is measured by the outputs of a modest number of band-pass filters. At the receiving end, the sound is synthesized by controlling the gains of band-pass filters in accord with the outputs observed at the transmitting end. The filters are excited by either a noise or a pitched signal, in accord with the analysis at the transmitting end. Vocoders of this form have been used in secrecy systems. They can produce intelligible but unnatural speech. The output is primitive. They do allow one to replace the buzzy sound source with other excitation functions, so that the chuffing of a locomotive can be made to speak. This is sometimes called *cross-synthesis*.

A somewhat different vocoder, the Linear Predictive voCoder (LPC), has been widely used in computer music. In linear prediction, the spectral analysis is not represented directly as a bank of filters. Rather, the representation is a prediction of the next sample

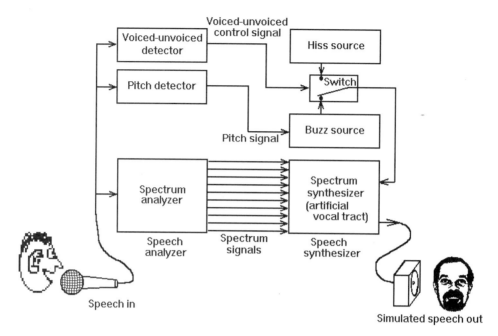

Figure 22.2 The channel vocoder. Filters decompose the voice for coding, transmission, and reconstruction. Systems like this are used for security as well as communication. (Modified after Dudley, 1939.)

amplitude by a linear sum of a few past sample amplitudes. Nine is a typical number of past sample values used in LPC. This is equivalent to an all-pole filter representation of the filtering effect of the vocal tract. An excitation function can be obtained at the transmitting end as the difference between the actual signal and the predicted signal, and can be transmitted in some reduced or approximated form.

Linear prediction has been used successfully to reduce the number of bits per second required to transmit a voice signal of telephone quality (Schroeder 1985). The speech quality is better than one might expect. This appears to be because the ear's sensitivity to spectral error is small during rapid transitions, when linear prediction error tends to be large. LPC spectral error is least during slow or no transitions. Beyond this, it appears that in good LPCs, quantizing noise is masked by spectral prominences in the actual signal. As we will see later, such an effect has been exploited more recently as a means for producing a high-quality recorded sound without reproducing the actual waveform with 16 bit per sample accuracy.

Another vocoder, the phase vocoder, has been widely used in computer music as a means for modifying voice and other musical sounds. The phase vocoder does not in itself modify sounds. It represents a sound as the sum of a number of smoothly overlapping, equally spaced frequency bands. The waveform in each band looks like a sine wave whose amplitude and phase change with time. If one replaces the sine waves in all bands with sine waves that go up and down twice as many times a second, all frequencies in the combined signal are doubled, and the pitch of the signal goes up an octave.

Xavier Serra and Julius Smith (Serra 1989; Serra and Smith 1990) describe a related system for imitating and modifying the sound of any solo musical instrument. The basic approach is illustrated in figure 22.3. The waveform of the instrument is represented by two parts: a deterministic or predictable part, and a stochastic or noisy part. The deterministic part is derived from successive spectral analyses of the sound. As indicated in figure 22.4, spectral peaks that move slowly and continuously in frequency are interpreted as deterministic, and are resynthesized as sinusoidal partials that change smoothly and slowly in frequency and amplitude. This deterministic resynthesis is subtracted from the initial waveform to give the remaining stochastic waveform. Adding this stochastic waveform to the deterministic waveform is guaranteed to give the original waveform.

Serra found that the stochastic waveform tends to be small compared with the overall waveform, and often it is concentrated in the attack and other special portions of the overall sound. Moreover, he found in many cases that in resynthesis, the stochastic portion of

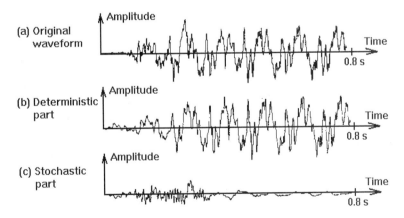

Figure 22.3 Original piano attack waveform (a) is decomposed into (b) deterministic and (c) stochastic (or noisy) components. (Courtesy of Xavier Serra, CCRMA.)

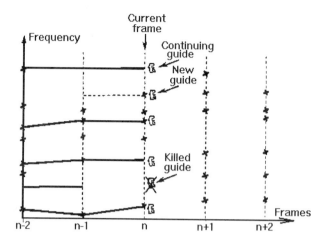

Figure 22.4 The deterministic component is taken as that for which spectral peaks persist. (Courtesy of Xavier Serra, CCRMA.)

the waveform could be replaced by a noise with roughly the same spectrum. This means that the noise portion of the waveform has a different waveform in every resynthesis. Serra used this approach successfully in resynthesizing a number of musical sounds, both unmodified and modified. Reductions in the number of bits per second necessary to resynthesize musical tones were not striking. Later researchers found that satisfactory resynthesis was not always assured by applying Serra's procedure as described.

22.5 Listening to Sounds

A recording such as a compact disc produces the same waveform every time it is played. This does not mean that we hear the same sound that we would have heard in a performance in a concert hall, or even in a recording studio. What we hear depends on where the microphones are placed during recording, and on what reverberation there is in the concert hall or studio. Further, it depends on the reverberation of the room in which the recording is played back, and on where we are with respect to the two stereo speakers.

In recording popular music, two stereo channels are commonly derived from a number of single-channel microphones placed near performers. Often, recordings are made in which the performer plays while hearing previously recorded sounds. These multiple recorded tracks are processed and combined. The overall sound of the stereo compact disc that we buy first exists when the final recording of the processed channels is played and heard.

In recording classical music, two channel signals are derived from a two-channel microphone, or from two or more microphones. A piece may be recorded multiple times, as many various sections. In the final recording to which we listen, errors or noises are replaced with appropriate material. Thus, there is much editing even in the production of classical recordings.

If we covered the walls, floor, and ceiling of a recording studio with microphones, and if we fed the multitude of microphone signals to loudspeakers covering the walls, floor, and ceiling of a "hearing" room, we could reproduce or at least approximate the pattern of sound waves present in the recording studio. There have been attempts and proposals to go in this direction. Most people seem satisfied with a "good" home stereo system and "good" commercial recordings, but affordable *home theater* systems may add more speakers to our listening rooms in the future.

What we can and should ask of our playback equipment is that it be linear up to a sufficient level, and that the component parts, the amplifiers and the speakers, be sufficiently flat in frequency transmission. Generally, the high-frequency speakers should be close to walls in order to avoid appreciable reflections near the speaker elements. It appears that it is all right to use a single woofer, whose location is not critical. The equipment will have various frequency and relative level adjustments. Above all, the reproducing equipment should sound good to the user. Compact discs give us two stereo channels that can reproduce pleasing music. However, the sound field in the living room is bound to be different from that in a concert hall.

One of the chief advances in stereo recording is attaining compact disc quality with fewer than the present number of compact disc bits per second per channel. The approach is not to try to reproduce the waveform of the sound that is picked up, but to produce a waveform with fewer bits that human hearing cannot detect as differing from the waveform derived from the microphones.

22.6 What We Cannot Hear

What we can hear varies with frequency and intensity. What we cannot hear also varies with frequency and intensity. The curves of figure 22.5 (Zwicker, 1990) are constant loudness curves. At 1000 Hz the compact disc standard of representing sample amplitudes by 16 bits takes us about 90 dB above the threshold of hearing, to a constant loudness curve that is almost horizontal at lower frequencies.

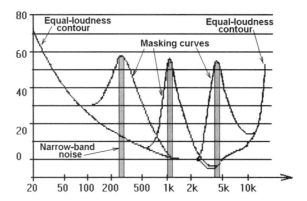

Figure 22.5 An equal loudness curve and the threshold of hearing for three masking curves. (Adapted from Zwicker, 1990.)

At 30 Hz the threshold of hearing is 60 dB above that at 1000 Hz. One bit corresponds to 6 dB; 60 dB corresponds to 10 bits. Thus, at 30 Hz it requires only about 16 − 10 = 6 bits to take us from the threshold of hearing to the 90 dB constant-loudness curve, while at 1000 Hz it requires 16 bits.

It should be satisfactory to encode both the low-frequency and the high-frequency components of the sound wave with fewer than 16 bits. We can accomplish this by filtering the signal into various frequency bands and using the appropriate number of bits for each frequency band. Such a technique has been understood for years (Jayant and Noll 1984). It was used for bit-rate reduction in the Phillips DCC (digital compact cassette) system.

Beyond this, masking of one sound by another can reduce the number of bits needed to give the ear all that it can hear. Figure 22.5 shows both the threshold of hearing in the absence of any signal and the elevation of that threshold by the presence of narrowband noise at 250, 1000, and 4000 Hz.

Let such a narrowband noise represent a strong spectral component of a sound wave. We see that such a strong component can raise the threshold of hearing over a considerable range of frequencies above and below that of the strong component. This raising of the threshold of hearing through masking by strong components of sound may cause other, weaker components to lie below the elevated threshold of hearing. It may, on the other hand, reduce the number of bits necessary to encode weak components satisfactorily.

All of this is taken into account in the MUSICAM system proposed by Phillips in the Netherlands, as explained by Houtsma (1992). The signal is divided into 32 equal bandwidths, each about 700 Hz wide.

The overall spectrum is evaluated every 24 milliseconds. Based on the threshold of hearing in the presence of masking, bit allocations for the signal in each subband are made according to the following rules:

1. If the amount of energy in a subband falls below the masking threshold, the signal is allocated 0 bits.
2. In all other subbands, enough bits are allocated to yield a level of quantization noise just below the masking threshold.

The source of the quantization noise lies in the fact that the digital representation of the signal amplitude in any band is not exact. Approximately, if N bits are used to represent the signal, the quantization noise will be less than the largest signal represented by nearly 6N dB. This is 90 dB down for N = 16 bits, but only 30 dB down for 5 bits. The quantizing noise need only be lower than the masking threshold.

More elaborate encoding schemes, such as that of Dolby (Bosi and Davidson 1992), explicitly take into account time domain aspects of masking: *backward masking* (softer signals before a louder sound are masked) and *forward masking* (softer signals after a louder sound are masked). Backward masking works on time scales of just a few milliseconds, while forward masking can take place for hundreds of milliseconds (recall the discussion on reverberation in chapter 3).

The performance of an overall system depends on the particular music encoded. It appears that degradation is undetectable for 5 to 6 bits per sample (in place of 16), and that good sound can be obtained with fewer bits per sample. Such encoding results in a distorted waveform, but the distortion is undetectable (or nearly undetectable) by the human ear.

The adoption of some standard encoding of this general sort seems inevitable. Work toward standards is going on at the international Radio Communication Bureau and the Moving Picture Expert Group (MPEG), and in the United States, under the auspices of the Federal Communications Commission.

Once a standard or standards are adopted, does this mean that we will not be able to play old recordings? Probably not. Complicated digital circuits are cheap when they are mass-produced. A way to make money is to introduce new formats. However, it seems likely that some players will accommodate old as well as new recordings, alerted to the format by a header. It also seems likely that the actual recordings will be made with 16 or more bits per sample, and that bit-saving recordings will be derived from such data.

22.7 In Retrospect

Representations of musical compositions are intended to allow re-creation of the composition through playing it by a human performer, or by mechanical or electronic means (player piano, Disc-Clavier). The DiscClavier and other keyboard instruments allow a reproduction of the sound of the instrument, without environmental noise, reflections, or reverberation, from a recording of a reasonable number of bits per second.

The voice and other nonkeyboard instruments cannot yet be imitated satisfactorily through the use of synthetic instruments, though synthetic instruments can produce musically useful outputs mimicking those of nonkeyboard instruments.

An alternative is to capture the sound of a performance and somehow reproduce that sound. These appear to be clear alternatives, but they can be mixed, as we see in the old "music minus one" records, and in musical interactions among performers and machines, which usually have an improvisatory element.

In listening to stereo recordings of classical music, what we hear is not what we would hear in a concert hall or recording studio. What we hear depends both on microphone placement in recording and on the inherent limitations of two-channel systems. It depends on the acoustics of the room in which the recording is played, as well as on the qualities of the amplifiers and speakers.

In stereo and multichannel recording, a persistent problem is the large number of bits per second required to reproduce the waveform. It appears that a considerable reduction in the bits-per-second requirement can be obtained by using a criterion not of reproducing the exact waveform but, rather, of producing a new waveform that the ear cannot distinguish from the original.

References

Bosi, M., and G. Davidson. (1992). "High Quality, Low-Rate Audio Transform Coding for Transmission and Multimedia Applications." Paper presented at the 93rd convention of the Audio Engineering Society, San Francisco, October 1–4.

Dudley, H. (1930). "Remaking Speech." *Journal of the Acoustical Society of America,* 11, 169–177.

Groves Dictionary of Music. (1954). London: MacMillan. Very helpful in connection with subjects such as barrel organs, player pianos, mechanical instruments, and music boxes.

Houtsma, A. J. M. (1992). "Psychophysics and Modern Digital Audio Technology." *Phillips Journal of Research,* 47, 3–14.

Jayant, N. S., and P. Noll. (1984). *Digital Coding of Waveforms.* Englewood Cliffs, N.J.: Prentice-Hall.

Schafer, R. W., and J. D. Markel, eds. (1979). *Speech Analysis.* New York: IEEE Press.

Schroeder, M. R. (1985). "Linear Predictive Coding of Speech: Review and Current Directions." *IEEE Communications Magazine,* 23, 54–61.

Serra, X. (1989). "A System for Sound Analysis/Transformation/Synthesis Based on a Deterministic plus Stochastic Decomposition." Ph.D. dissertation, Stanford University.

Serra, X., and J. O. Smith. (1990). "Spectral Modeling Synthesis: A System Based on a Deterministic plus a Stochastic Decomposition." *Computer Music Journal,* 14 (4): 12–14.

Zwicker, E., and H. Fastl. (1990). *Psychoacoustics, Facts and Models.* Berlin: Springer.

23 Experimental Design in Psychoacoustic Research

Daniel J. Levitin

23.1 Introduction

Experimental design is a vast topic. As one thinks about the information derived from scientific studies, one confronts difficult issues in statistical theory and the limits of knowledge. In this chapter, we confine our discussion to a few of the most important issues in experimental design. This will enable students with no background in behavior research to complete a simple research project. The student will need to consult statistical and experimental design texts (listed in the references at the end of this chapter) in order to answer specific questions that are not covered here.

This chapter is intended for undergraduate and beginning graduate-level students who are enrolled in a psychoacoustics course, or who are interested in learning about psychoacoustics research through independent study. It assumes no prior knowledge of statistics, probability, experimental design, or psychology. A central component of the psychoacoustics course as it has been taught at Stanford since 1990 is the term project. Typically this is in the form of a psychoacoustic experiment using human subjects to test a hypothesis or demonstrate a principle in psychoacoustics or auditory perception. The term project affords students the opportunity to participate firsthand in psychoacoustics research, and it encourages them to become engaged with a rich and interesting history of behavioral research.

Experimental psychology is a young science. The first laboratory of experimental psychology was established just over 100 years ago. Consequently, there are a great many mysteries about human behavior, perception, and performance that have not yet been solved. This makes it an exciting time to engage in psychological research—the field is young enough that there is still a great deal to do, and it is not difficult to think up interesting experiments. The goal of this chapter is to guide the reader in planning and implementing experiments, and in thinking about good experimental design.

A "good" experiment is one in which variables are carefully controlled or accounted for so that one can draw reasonable conclusions from the experiment's outcome.

23.2 The Goals of Scientific Research

Generally, scientific research has four goals:

1. Description of behavior
2. Prediction of behavior
3. Determination of the causes of behavior
4. Explanations of behavior.

These goals apply to the physical sciences as well as to the behavioral and life sciences. In basic science, the researcher's primary concern is not with applications for a given finding. The goal of basic research is to increase our understanding of how the world works, or how things came to be the way they are.

Describing behavior impartially is the foremost task of the descriptive study, and because this is never completely possible, one tries to document any systematic biases that could influence descriptions (goal 1). By studying a phenomenon, one frequently develops the ability to *predict* certain behaviors or outcomes (goal 2), although prediction is possible without an understanding of underlying causes (we'll look at some examples in a moment). Controlled experiments are one tool that scientists use to reveal underlying causes so that they can advance from merely predicting behavior to understanding the *cause* of behavior (goal 3). *Explaining* behavior (goal 4) requires more than just a knowledge of causes; it requires a detailed understanding of the mechanisms by which the causal factors perform their functions.

To illustrate the distinction between the four goals of scientific research, consider the history of astronomy. The earliest astronomers were able to *describe* the positions and motions of the stars in the heavens, although they had no ability to *predict* where a given body would appear in the sky at a future date. Through careful observations and documentation, later astronomers became quite skillful at *predicting* planetary and stellar motion, although they lacked an understanding of the underlying factors that *caused* this motion. Newton's laws of motion and Einstein's special and general theories of relativity, taken together, showed that gravity and the contour of the space–time continuum cause the motions we observe. Precisely how gravity and the topology of space–time accomplish this still remains unclear. Thus, astronomy has advanced to the determination of causes of stellar motion (goal 3), although a full *explanation* remains elusive. That is, saying that gravity is responsible for astronomical motion only puts a name on things; it does not tell us how gravity actually works.

As an illustration from behavioral science, one might note that people who listen to loud music tend to lose their high-frequency hearing (description). Based on a number of observations, one can predict that individuals with normal hearing who listen to enough loud music will suffer hearing loss (prediction). A controlled experiment can determine that the loud music is the cause of the hearing loss (determining causality). Finally, study of the cochlea and basilar membrane, and observation of damage to the delicate hair cells after exposure to high-pressure sound waves, meets the fourth goal (explanation).

23.3 Three Types of Scientific Studies

In science there are three broad classes of studies: controlled studies, correlational studies, and descriptive studies. Often the type of study you will be able to do is determined by practicality, cost, or ethics, not directly by your own choice.

23.3.1 Controlled Studies ("True Experiments")

In a controlled experiment, the researcher starts with a group of subjects and randomly assigns them to an experimental condition. The point of *random assignment* is to control for extraneous variables that might affect the outcome of the experiment: variables that are different from the variable(s) being studied. With random assignment, one can be reasonably certain that any differences among the experimental groups were caused by the variable(s) manipulated in the experiment.

A controlled experiment in medical research might seek to discover if a certain food additive causes cancer. The researcher might randomly divide a group of laboratory mice into two smaller groups, giving the food additive to one group and not to the other. The variable he/she is interested in is the effect of the food additive; in the language of experimental design, this is called the "independent variable." After a period of time, the researcher compares the mortality rates of the two groups; this quantity is called the "dependent variable" (figure 23.1). Suppose the group that received the additive tended to die earlier. In order to deduce that the additive caused

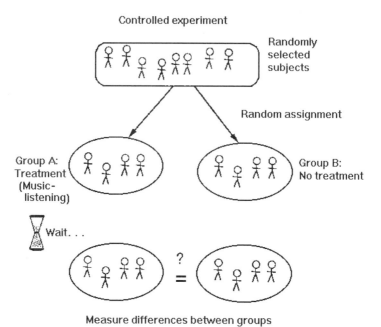

Controlled experiment

Randomly selected subjects

Random assignment

Group A: Treatment (Music-listening)

Group B: No treatment

Wait. . .

?
=

Measure differences between groups

Figure 23.1 In a controlled experiment, subjects are randomly assigned to conditions, and differences between groups are measured.

the difference between the groups, the conditions must have been identical in every other respect. Both groups should have had the same diet, same feeding schedule, same temperature in their cages, and so on. Furthermore, the two groups of mice should have started out with similar characteristics, such as age, sex, and so on, so that these variables—being equally distributed between the two groups—can be ruled out as possible causes of the difference in mortality rates.

The two key components of a controlled experiment are *random assignment* of subjects, and *identical experimental conditions* (see figure 23.1). A researcher might have a hypothesis that people who study for an exam while listening to music will score better than people who study in silence. In the language of experimental design, music-listening is the *independent variable,* and test performance, the quantity to be measured, is the *dependent variable.*

No one would take this study seriously if the subjects were divided into two groups based on how they did on the previous exam—if, for instance, the top half of the students were placed in the music-listening condition, and the bottom half of the students in the silence condition. Then if the result of the experiment was that the music listeners as a group tended to perform better on their next exam, one could argue that this was not because they listened to music while they studied, but because they were the better students to begin with.

Again, the theory behind random assignment is to have groups of subjects who start out the same. Ideally, each group will have similar distributions on every conceivable dimension—age, sex, ethnicity, IQ, and variables that you might not think are important, such as handedness, astrological sign, or favorite television show. Random assignment makes it unlikely that there will be any large systematic differences between the groups.

A similar design flaw would arise if the *experimental conditions* were different. For example, if the music-listening group studied in a well-lit room with windows, and the silence group studied in a dark, windowless basement, any difference between the groups could be due to the different environments. The room conditions become confounded with the music-listening conditions, such that it is impossible to deduce which of the two is the causal factor.

Performing random assignment of subjects is straightforward. Conceptually, one wants to mix the subjects' names or numbers thoroughly, then draw them out of a hat. Realistically, one of the easiest ways to do this is to generate a different random number for each subject, and then sort the random numbers. If n equals the total number of subjects you have, and g equals the number of groups you are dividing them into, the first n/g subjects will comprise the first group, the next n/g will comprise the second group, and so on.

If the results of a controlled experiment indicate a difference between groups, the next question is whether these findings are generalizable. If your initial group of subjects (the large group, before you randomly assigned subjects to conditions) was also randomly selected (called *random sampling* or *random selection,* as opposed to *random assignment*), this is a reasonable conclusion to draw. However, there are almost always some constraints on one's initial choice of subjects, and this constrains generalizability. For example, if all the subjects you studied in your music-listening experiment lived in fraternities, the finding might not generalize to people who do not live in fraternities. If you want to be able to generalize to all college students, you would need to take a representative sample of all college students. One way to do this is to choose your subjects randomly, such that each member of the population you are considering (college students) has an equal likelihood of being placed in the experiment.

There are some interesting issues in representative sampling that are beyond the scope of this chapter. For example, if you wanted to take a representative sample of all American college students and you chose American college students randomly, it is possible that you would be choosing several students from some of the larger colleges, such as the University of Michigan, and you might not choose any students at all from some of the smaller colleges, such as Bennington College; this would limit the applicability of your findings to the colleges that were represented in your sample. One solution is to conduct a *stratified sample,* in which you first randomly select colleges (making it just as likely that you'll choose large and small colleges) and then randomly select the same number of students from each of those colleges. This ensures that colleges of different sizes are represented in the sample. You then weight the data from each college in accordance with the percentage contribution each college makes to the total student population of your sample. (For further reading, see Shaughnessy and Zechmeister 1994.)

Choosing subjects randomly requires careful planning. If you try to take a random sample of Stanford students by standing in front of the Braun Music Building and stopping every third person coming out, you might be selecting a greater percentage of music students than actually exists on campus. Yet truly random samples are not always practical. Much psychological research is conducted on college students who are taking an introductory psychology class, and are required to participate in an experiment for course credit. It is not at all clear whether American college students taking introductory psychology are representative of students in general, or of people in the world in general, so one should be careful not to overgeneralize findings from these studies.

23.3.2 Correlational Studies

A second type of study is the *correlational study* (figure 23.2). Because it is not always practical or ethical to perform random assignments, scientists are sometimes forced to rely on patterns of co-occurrence, or correlations between events. The classic example of a correlational study is the link between cigarette smoking and cancer. Few educated people today doubt that smokers are more likely to die of lung cancer than are nonsmokers. However, in the history of scientific research there has never been a controlled experiment with human subjects on this topic. Such an experiment would take a group of healthy nonsmokers, and randomly assign them to two groups, a smoking group and a nonsmoking group. Then the experimenter would simply wait until most of the people in the study have died, and compare the average ages and causes of death of the two groups. Because our hypothesis is that smoking causes cancer, it would clearly be unethical to ask people to smoke who otherwise would not.

The scientific evidence we have that smoking causes cancer is correlational. That is, when we look at smokers as a group, a higher percentage of them do indeed develop fatal cancers, and die earlier, than do nonsmokers. But without a controlled study, the possibility exists that there is a third factor—a mysterious "factor x"—that both causes people to smoke and to develop cancer. Perhaps there is some enzyme in the body that gives people a nicotine craving, and this same enzyme causes fatal cancers. This would account for both outcomes, the kinds of people who smoke and the rate of cancers among them, and it would show that there is no causal link between smoking and cancer.

In correlational studies, a great deal of effort is devoted to trying to uncover differences between the two groups studied in order to identify any causal factors that might exist. In the case of smoking, none have been discovered so far, but the failure to discover a third causal factor does not prove that one does not exist. It is an axiom in the philosophy of science that one can prove only the presence of something; one can't prove the absence of something—it could always be just around the corner, waiting to be discovered in the next experiment (Hempel 1966). In the real world, behaviors and diseases are usually brought on by a number of complicated factors, so the mysterious third variable, "factor x," could in fact be a collection of different, and perhaps unrelated, variables that act together to cause the outcomes we observe.

An example of a correlational study with a hypothesized musical cause is depicted in figure 23.2. Such a study would require extensive interviews with the subjects (or their survivors), to try to determine all factors that might separate the subjects exhibiting the symptom from the subjects without the symptom.

The problem with correlational studies is that the search for underlying factors that account for the differences between groups can be very difficult. Yet many times, correlational studies are all we have, because ethical considerations preclude the use of controlled experiments.

Correlational experiment

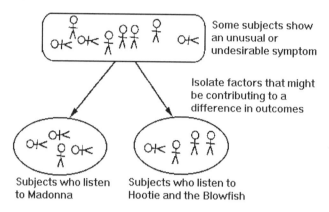

Some subjects show
an unusual or
undesirable symptom

Isolate factors that might
be contributing to a
difference in outcomes

Subjects who listen
to Madonna

Subjects who listen to
Hootie and the Blowfish

Two possible conclusions:

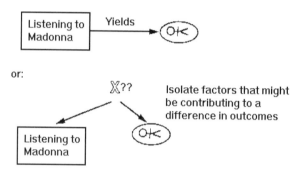

Isolate factors that might
be contributing to a
difference in outcomes

Figure 23.2   In a correlational study, the researcher looks for a relation between two observed behaviors—in this case, the relation between untimely death and listening to Madonna recordings.

23.3.3   Descriptive Studies

Descriptive studies do not look for differences between people or groups, but seek only to describe an aspect of the world as it is. A descriptive study in physics might seek to discover what elements make up the core of the planet Jupiter. The goal in such a study would not be to compare Jupiter's core with the core of other planets, but to learn more about the origins of the universe. In psychology, we might want to know the part of the brain that is activated when someone performs a mental calculation, or the number of pounds of fresh green peas the average American eats in a year (figure 23.3). Our goal in these cases is not to contrast individuals but to acquire some basic data about the nature of things. Of course, descriptive studies can be used to establish "norms," so that we can compare

Descriptive study

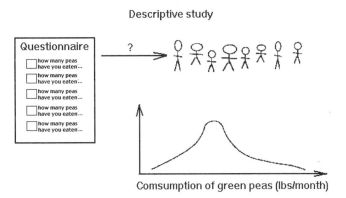

Comsumption of green peas (lbs/month)

Figure 23.3 In a descriptive study, the researcher seeks to describe some aspect of the state of the world, such as people's consumption of green peas.

people against the average, but as their name implies, the primary goal in descriptive experiments is often just to describe something that had not been described before. Descriptive studies are every bit as useful as controlled experiments and correlational studies— sometimes, in fact, they are even more valuable because they lay the foundation for further experimental work.

23.4 Design Flaws in Experimental Design

23.4.1 Clever Hans

There are many examples of flawed studies or flawed conclusions that illustrate the difficulties in controlling extraneous variables. Perhaps the most famous case is that of Clever Hans.

Clever Hans was a horse owned by a German mathematics teacher around the turn of the twentieth century. Hans became famous following many demonstrations in which he could perform simple addition and subtraction, read German, and answer simple questions by tapping his hoof on the ground (Watson 1967). One of the first things that skeptics wondered (as you might) is whether Hans would continue to be clever when someone other than his owner asked the questions, or when Hans was asked questions that he had never heard before. In both these cases, Hans continued to perform brilliantly, tapping out the sums or differences for arithmetic problems.

In 1904, a scientific commission was formed to investigate Hans's abilities more carefully. The commission discovered, after rigorous testing, that Hans could never answer a question if the questioner did not also know the answer, or if Hans could not see his questioner. If was finally discovered that Hans had become very adept at picking up subtle (and probably unintentional) movements on the part of the questioner that cued him as to when he should stop tapping his foot. Suppose a questioner asked Hans to add 7 and 3. Hans would start tapping his hoof, and keep on tapping until the questioner stopped him by saying "Right! Ten!" or, more subtly, by moving slightly when the correct answer was reached.

You can see how important it is to ensure that extraneous cues or biases do not intrude into an experimental situation.

23.4.2   Infants' Perception of Musical Structure

In studies of infants' perception of music, infants typically sit in their mother's lap while music phrases are played over a speaker. Infants tend to turn their heads toward a novel or surprising event, and this is the dependent variable in many infant studies; the point at which the infants turn their heads indicates when they perceive a difference in whatever is being played. Suppose you ran such a study and found that the infants were able to distinguish Mozart selections that were played normally from selections of equal length that began or ended in the middle of a musical phrase. You might take this as evidence that the infants have an innate understanding of musical phraseology.

Are there alternative explanations for the results? Suppose that in the experimental design, the mothers could hear the music, too. The mothers might unconsciously cue the infants to changes in the stimulus that they (the mothers) detect. A simple solution is to have the mothers wear headphones playing white noise, so that their perception of the music is masked.

23.4.3   Computers, Timing, and Other Pitfalls

It is very important that you not take anything for granted as you design a careful experiment, and control extraneous variables. For example, psychologists studying visual perception frequently present their stimuli on a computer using the MacIntosh or Windows operating system. In a computer program, the code may specify that an image is to remain on the computer monitor for a precise number of milliseconds. Just because you specify this does not make it happen, however. Monitors have a *refresh rate* (60 or 75 Hz is typical), so the "on time" of an image will always be an integer multiple of the refresh cycle (13.33 milliseconds for a 75 Hz refresh rate) no matter what you instruct the computer to do in your code. To make things worse, the MacIntosh and Windows operating systems do not guarantee "refresh cycle accuracy" in their updating, so an instruction to put a new image on the screen may be delayed an unknown amount of time.

It is important, therefore, always to verify, using some external means, that the things you think are happening in your experiment are actually happening. Just because you leave the volume control on your amplifier at the same spot doesn't mean the volume of a sound stimulus you are playing will be the same from day to day. You should measure the output and not take the knob position for granted. Just because a frequency generator is set for 1000 Hz does not mean it is putting out a 1000 Hz signal. It is good science for you to measure the output frequency yourself.

23.5 Number of subjects

How many subjects are enough? In statistics, the word "population" refers to the total group of people to which the researcher wishes to generalize findings. The population might be female sophomores at Stanford, or all Stanford students, or all college students in the United States, or all people in the United States. If one is able to draw a representative sample of sufficient size from a population, one can make inferences about the whole population based on a relatively small number of cases. This is the basis of presidential polls, for example, in which only 2000 voters are surveyed, and the outcome of an election can be predicted with reasonable accuracy.

The size of the sample required is dependent on the degree of homogeneity or heterogeneity in the total population you are studying. In the extreme, if you are studying a population that is so homogeneous that every individual is identical on the dimensions being studied, a sample size of one will provide all the information you need. At the other extreme, if you are studying a population that is so heterogeneous that each individual differs categorically on the dimension you are studying, you will need to sample the entire population.

As a "rough-and-ready" rule, if you are performing a descriptive psychoacoustic experiment, and the phenomenon you are studying is something that you expect to be invariant across people, you need to use only a few subjects, perhaps five. An example of this type of study would be calculating threshold sensitivities for various sound frequencies, such as was done by Fletcher and Munson (1933).

If you are studying a phenomenon for which you expect to find large individual differences, you might need between 30 and 100 subjects. This depends to some degree on how many different conditions there are in the study. In order to obtain means with a relatively small variance, it is a good idea to have at least five to ten subjects in each experimental condition.

23.6 Types of Experimental Designs

Suppose you are researching the effect of music-listening on studying efficiency, as mentioned at the beginning of this chapter. Let's expand on the simpler design described earlier. You might divide your subjects into five groups: two experimental groups and three control groups. One experimental group would listen to rock music, and the other would listen to classical music. Of the three control groups, one would listen to rock music for the same number of minutes per day as the experimental group listening to rock (but not while they were studying); a second would do the same for classical music; the third would listen to no music at all. This is called a *between-subjects* design, because each subject is in one condition and one condition only (also referred to as an *independent groups* design). If you assign 10 subjects to each experimental condition, this would require a total of 50 subjects. Table 23.1 shows the layout of this experiment. Each distinct box in the table is called a *cell* of the experiment, and subject numbers are filled in for each cell. Notice the asymmetry for the *no music* condition. The experiment was designed so that there is only one "no music" condition, whereas there are four music conditions of various types.

Testing 50 subjects might not be practical. An alternative is a *within-subjects* design, in which every subject is tested in every condition (also called a *repeated measures* design). In this example, a total of ten subjects could be randomly divided into the five conditions, so that two subjects experience each condition for a given period of time. Then the subjects switch to another condition. By the time the experiment is completed, ten observations have been collected in each cell, and only ten subjects are required.

Table 23.1 Between-subjects experiment on music and study habits

CONDITION		ONLY WHILE STUDYING	ONLY WHILE NOT STUDYING
Music	Classical	subjects 1–10	subjects 11–20
	Rock	subjects 21–30	subjects 31–40
No music		subjects 41–50	

The advantage of each subject experiencing each condition is that you can obtain measures of how each individual is affected by the manipulation, something you cannot do in the between-subjects design. It might be the case that some people do well in one type of condition and other people do poorly in it, and the within-subjects design is the best way to show this. The obvious advantage to the within-subjects design is the smaller number of subjects required. But there are disadvantages as well.

One disadvantage is *demand characteristics.* Because each subject experiences each condition, they are not as naive about the experimental manipulation. Their performance could be influenced by a conscious or unconscious desire to make one of the conditions work better. Another problem is *carryover effects.* Suppose you were studying the effect of Prozac on learning, and that the half-life of the drug is 48 hours. The group that gets the drug first might still be under its influence when they are switched to the nondrug condition. This is a carryover effect. In the music-listening experiment, it is possible that listening to rock music creates anxiety or exhilaration that might last into the next condition.

A third disadvantage of within-subjects designs is *order effects,* and these are particularly troublesome in psychophysical experiments. An order effect is similar to a carryover effect, and it concerns how responses in an experiment might be influenced by the order in which the stimuli or conditions are presented. For instance, in studies of speech discrimination, subjects can habituate (become used to, or become more sensitive) to certain sounds, altering their threshold for the discriminability of related sounds. A subject who habituates to a certain sound may respond differently to the sound immediately following it than he/she normally would. For these reasons, it is important to counterbalance the order of presentations; presenting the same order to every subject makes it difficult to account for any effects that are due merely to order.

One way to reduce order effects is to present the stimuli or conditions in random order. In some studies, this is sufficient, but to be really careful about order effects, the random order simply is not rigorous enough. The solution is to use every possible order. In a *within-subjects* design, each subject would complete the experiment with each order. In a *between-subjects* design, different subjects would be assigned different orders. The choice will often depend on the available resources (time and availability of subjects). The number of possible orders is *N!* ("n factorial"), where *N* equals the number of stimuli. With two stimuli there are two possible orders (2! = 2 × 1); with three stimuli there are six possible orders (3! = 3 × 2 × 1); with six stimuli there are 720 possible orders (6! = 6 × 5 × 4 × 3 × 2 × 1). Seven hundred twenty orders is not practical for a within-subjects design, or for a between-subjects design. One solution in this case is to create an order that presents each stimulus in each serial position. A method for accomplishing this involves using the Latin Square. For even-numbered N, the size of the Latin Square will be N × N; therefore, with six stimuli you would need only 36 orders, not 720. For odd-numbered N, the size of the Latin Square will be N × 2N. Details of this technique are covered in experimental design texts such as Kirk (1982) and Shaughnessy and Zechmeister (1994).

23.7 Ethical Considerations in Using Human Subjects

Some experiments on human subjects in the 1960s and 1970s raised questions about how human subjects are treated in behavioral experiments. As a result, guidelines for human experimentation were established. The American Psychological Association, a voluntary organization of psychologists, formulated a code of ethical principles (American Psychological Association 1992). In addition, most universities have established committees to review and approve research using human subjects. The purpose of these committees is to ensure that subjects are treated ethically, and that fair and humane procedures are followed. In some universities, experiments performed for course work or experiments done as "pilot studies" do not require approval, but these rules vary from place to place, so it is important to determine the requirements at your institution before engaging in any human subject research.

It is also important to understand the following four basic principles of ethics in human subject research:

1. *Informed consent.* Before agreeing to participate in an experiment, subjects should be given an accurate description of their task in the experiment, and told any risks involved. Subjects should be allowed to decline, or to discontinue participation in the experiment at any time without penalty.

2. *Debriefing.* Following the experiment, the subjects should be given an explanation of the hypothesis being tested and the methods used. The experimenter should answer any questions the subjects have about the procedure or hypothesis. Many psychoacoustic experiments involve difficult tasks, leading some subjects to feel frustrated or embarrassed. Subjects should never leave an experiment feeling slow, stupid, or untalented. It is the experimenter's responsibility to ensure that the subjects understand that these tasks are inherently difficult, and when appropriate, the subjects should be told that the data are not being used to evaluate them personally, but to collect information on how the population in general can perform the task.

3. *Privacy and confidentiality.* The experimenter must carefully guard the data that are collected and, whenever possible, code and store the data in such a way that subjects' identities remain confidential.

4. *Fraud.* This principle is not specific to human subjects research, but applies to all research. An essential ethical standard of the scientific community is that scientific researchers never fabricate data, and never knowingly, intentionally, or through carelessness allow false data, analyses, or conclusions to be published. Fraudulent reporting is one of the most serious ethical breaches in the scientific community.

23.8 Analyzing Your Data

23.8.1 Quantitative Analysis

MEASUREMENT ERROR

Whenever you measure a quantity, there are two components that contribute to the number you end up with: the actual value of the thing you are measuring and some amount of measurement error, both human and mechanical. It is an axiom of statistics that measurement error is just as likely to result in an overestimate as an underestimate of the true value. That is, each time you take a measurement, the error term (let's call it *epsilon*) is just as likely to be positive as negative. Over a large number of measurements, the positive errors and negative errors will cancel out, and the average value of epsilon will approach 0. The larger the number of measurements you make, the closer you will get to the true value. Thus, as the number of measurements approaches infinity, the arithmetic average of your measurements approaches the true quantity being measured. Suppose we are measuring the weight of a sandbag.

Formally, we would write:

$n \rightarrow \infty, \bar{\varepsilon} = 0$
where $\bar{\varepsilon}$ = the mean of epsilon

and

$n \rightarrow \infty, \bar{w} = \mathrm{w}$
where $\bar{w}$ = the mean of all the weight measurements and w = the true weight.

When measuring the behavior of human subjects on a task, you encounter not only measurement error but also performance error. The subjects will not perform identically every time. As with measurement error, the more observations you make, the more likely it is that the performance errors cancel each other out. In psychoacoustic tasks the performance errors can often be relatively large. This is the reason why one usually wants to have the subject perform the same task many times, or to have many subjects perform the task a few times.

Because of these errors, the value of your dependent variable(s) at the end of the experiment will always deviate from the true value by some amount. Statistical analysis helps in interpreting these differences (Bayesian inferencing, meta-analyses, effect size analysis, significance testing) and in predicting the true value (point estimates and confidence intervals). The mechanics of these tests are beyond the scope of this chapter, and the reader is referred to the statistics textbooks mentioned earlier.

SIGNIFICANCE TESTING

Suppose you wish to observe differences in interval identification ability between brass players and string players. The question is whether the difference you observe between the two groups can be wholly accounted for by measurement and performance error, or whether a difference of the size you observe indicates a true difference in the abilities of these musicians.

Significance tests provide the user with a "p value," the probability that the experimental result could have arisen by chance. By convention, if the p value is less than .05, meaning that the result could have arisen by chance less than 5% of the time, scientists accept the result as statistically significant. Of course, p < .05 is arbitrary, and it doesn't deal directly with the opposite case, the probability that the data you collected indicate a genuine effect, but the statistical test failed to detect it (a power analysis is required for this). In many studies, the probability of failing to detect an effect, when it exists, can soar to 80% (Schmidt 1996). An additional problem with a criterion of 5% is that a researcher who measures 20 different effects is likely to measure one as significant by chance, even if no significant effect actually exists.

Statistical significance tests, such as the analysis of variance (ANOVA), the f-test, chi-square test, and t-test, are methods to determine the probability that observed values in an experiment differ only as a result of measurement errors. For details about how to choose and conduct the appropriate tests, or to learn more about the theory behind them, consult a statistics textbook (e.g., Daniel 1990; Glenberg 1988; Hayes 1988).

ALTERNATIVES TO CLASSICAL SIGNIFICANCE TESTING

Because of problems with traditional significance testing, there is a movement, at the vanguard of applied statistics and psychology, to move away from "p value" tests and to rely on alternative methods, such as Bayesian inferencing, effect sizes, confidence intervals, and meta-analyses (refer to Cohen 1994; Hunter and Schmidt 1990; Schmidt 1996). Yet many people persist in clinging to the belief that the most important thing to do with experimental data is to test them for statistical significance. There is great pressure from peer-reviewed journals to perform significance tests, because so many people were taught to use them. The fact is, the whole point of significance testing is to determine whether a result is repeatable when one doesn't have the resources to repeat an experiment.

Let us return to the hypothetical example mentioned earlier, in which we examined the effect of music on study habits using a "within-subjects" design (each subject is in each condition). One possible outcome is that the difference in the mean test scores among groups was not significantly different by an analysis of variance (ANOVA). Yet suppose that, ignoring the means, every subject in the music-listening condition had a higher score than in the no-music condition. We are not interested in the size of the difference now, only in the direction of the difference. The null hypothesis predicts that the manipulation would have no effect at all, and that half of the subjects should show a difference in one direction and half in the other. The probability of all 10 subjects showing an effect in the same direction is $1/2^{10}$ or 0.0009, which is highly significant. Ten out of 10 subjects indicates *repeatability.* The technique just described is called the *sign test,* because we are looking only at the arithmetic sign of the differences between groups (positive or negative).

Often, a good alternative to significance tests is estimates of *confidence intervals.* These determine with a given probability (e.g., 95%) the range of values within which the true population parameters lie. Another alternative is an analysis of *conditional probabilities.* That is, if you observe a difference between two groups on some measure, determine whether a subject's membership in one group or the other will improve your ability to predict his/her score on the dependent variable, compared with not knowing what group he/she was in (an example of this analysis is in Levitin 1994a). A good overview of these alternative statistical methods is contained in the paper by Schmidt (1996).

Aside from statistical analyses, in most studies you will want to compute the mean and standard deviation of your dependent variable. If you had distinct treatment groups, you will want to know the individual means and standard deviations for each group. If you had two continuous variables, you will probably want to compute the *correlation,* which is an index of how much one variable is related to the other. Always provide a table of means and standard deviations as part of your report.

23.8.2 Qualitative Analysis, or "How to Succeed in Statistics Without Significance Testing"

If you have not had a course in statistics, you are probably at some advantage over anyone who has. Many people who have taken statistics courses rush to plug the numbers into a computer package to test for statistical significance. Unfortunately, students are not always perfectly clear on exactly what it is they are testing or why they are testing it.

The first thing one should do with experimental data is to graph them in a way that clarifies the relation between the data and the hypothesis. Forget about statistical significance testing—what does the pattern of data suggest? Graph everything you can think of—individual subject data, subject averages, averages across conditions—and see what patterns emerge. Roger Shepard has pointed out that the human brain is not very adept at scanning a table of numbers and picking out patterns, but is much better at picking out patterns in a visual display.

Depending on what you are studying, you might want to use a bar graph, a line graph, or a bivariate scatter plot. As a general rule, even though many of the popular graphing and spreadsheet packages will allow you to make pseudo-three-dimensional graphs, don't ever use three dimensions unless the third dimension actually represents a variable. Nothing is more confusing than a graph with extraneous information.

If you are making several graphs of the same data (such as individual subject graphs), make sure that each graph is the same size and that the axes are scaled identically from one graph to another, in order to facilitate comparison. Be sure all your axes are clearly labeled, and don't divide the axis numbers into units that aren't meaningful (for example, in a histogram with "number of subjects" on the ordinate, the scale shouldn't include half numbers because subjects come only in whole numbers).

Use a line graph if your variables are continuous. The lines connecting your plot points imply a continuous variable. Use a bar graph if the variables are categorical, so that you don't fool the reader into thinking that your observations were continuous. Use a bivariate scatter plot when you have two continuous variables, and you want to see how a change in one variable affects the other variable (such as how IQ and income might correlate). Do NOT use a bivariate scatterplot for categorical data. (For more information on good graph design, see Chambers et al. 1983; Cleveland 1994; Kosslyn 1994).

Once you have made all your graphs, look them over for interesting patterns and effects. Try to get a feel for what you have found, and understand how the data relate to your hypotheses and your experimental design. A well-formed graph can make a finding easy to understand and evaluate far better than a dry recitation of numbers and statistical tests can do.

23.9 Sources of Ideas for Experiments

There are many ways to generate ideas for an experiment. One is to begin with a theory about how one thing should affect another (such as how music might affect study habits). Another source of ideas is observation, such as the observation that people who listen to a particular type of music get sick.

One of the best sources for ideas is studies published in scientific journals. By reading about someone else's research, you get a clearer idea of what some of the research problems are. A good article clearly lays out the theoretical issues, provides a background of research on the topic, and reports on studies designed to test certain aspects of the problem. Sometimes the researcher tackles only part of the problem, paving the way for someone else (maybe you) to come along and perform additional studies. Sometimes, after reading a report carefully, you might think that the researcher has overlooked an important control or drawn conclusions that are unwarranted. The search for alternative explanations of an experimental result is one of the more exciting aspects of scientific research—it is a bit like trying to solve a logic problem or a brain teaser. Was the assignment of subjects truly random? Were the experimental conditions the same, and if not, could the differences have affected the outcome? Reading published studies has another advantage. It helps you to understand and appreciate the types of issues that workers in the field consider important.

Two of the better journals for psychoacoustic research are the *Journal of the Acoustical Society of America* and *Perception & Psychophysics*. Other journals publish articles on a wider variety of research topics. The following is a list of recommended journals, and their focus. The first five journals are published by the American Psychological Association.

Psychological Bulletin—Review articles on topics of broad interest to psychologists, summarizing and analyzing the body of research to date on a given topic.
Psychological Review—Primarily theoretical papers and in-depth reports of multipart experiments of general interest.
Journal of Experimental Psychology: General—Reports on experiments of general interest.
Journal of Experimental Psychology: Human Perception & Performance—Reports on experiments of more specialized research on perception and human performance.

Journal of Experimental Psychology: Learning, Memory, & Cognition—Reports on experiments of more specialized research on learning, memory, and other higher cognitive tasks.

Psychonomic Bulletin & Review—Similar to *JEP: General* or *Psychological Review*, but featuring experimental and theoretical papers; published by the Psychonomic Society.

Music Perception and *Psychology of Music*—Reports on experiments in music perception and cognition.

Psychological Science—Features reports of interesting experiments on a variety of topics, similar to *JEP: General* or *Psychonomic Bulletin & Review;* published by the American Psychological Society.

Current Directions in Psychological Science—Features brief reports of interesting experiments, usually without in-depth coverage of methods and statistical analyses; also published by the American Psychological Society.

Science, Scientific American, and *Nature*—Articles of general interest or importance covering all topics in the natural sciences, life sciences, behavioral sciences, and some engineering; those on psychoacoustic studies are generally excellent, but few are reported in any single year, and they do not typically report in detail on experimental methods or analyses.

Once you have an idea for a topic, it is important to perform a literature search. By reading previous reports on the topic in which you are interested, you can see what experiments have been done on your topic. It is possible someone had the same idea as you, and has already run the experiment. What is more likely, though, is that someone had an idea similar, but not identical, to yours, and you can learn a great deal by reading about how he/she approached the problem. This can also be a good source of guidance for experimental design.

A good place to start a literature search is "PsycINFO," an on-line database available through many university libraries. It indexes over 1,200 journals in psychology and associated fields, with coverage from 1984 through the present. Its sister database, "PsychLit," is available on CD-ROM at many university libraries, and offers expanded coverage going back to 1978; book chapters as well as journal articles are included. Once you find an article or book chapter related to your topic, you can use its bibliography to direct you to other papers.

23.10 Special Considerations in Psychoacoustic Research

Particular problems that arise in psychoacoustic research are unique to the field and should be considered when designing an experiment.

1. *Perceived loudness is frequency dependent.* That is, given two auditory signals at different frequencies and with equal power (or amplitude), there will be systematic and predictable differences in their perceived loudness as a function of frequency. The Fletcher–Munson curves (Fletcher and Munson 1933), reproduced in most acoustic textbooks, illustrate the way in which loudness varies with frequency. If your experiment involves presenting tones of different frequencies to your subjects, you will need to remove perceived loudness as a variable. The most rigorous way to do this would be to compute equal loudness curves for each subject and adjust the power of your signal accordingly. A more common (and practical) solution is simply to vary the loudness of different signals randomly. This effectively removes loudness as a source of variance in your data.

2. *Reverberation.* In studies of perceived durations or locations of different tones, the room in which you are playing the signals can add a significant amount of delay to the signal, thus affecting subjects' judgments. One solution is to conduct the experiments in an anechoic chamber. A more practical solution is to use headphones to present the stimuli. Be certain to use "over-the-ear" headphones that encompass the entire ear, so that the sound is less likely to escape into the room and reverberate.

3. *Hysteresis.* Hysteresis refers to the failure of a system to return immediately to its original state following stimulation. Hysteresis effects are not confined to psychoacoustic work but appear in studies involving all psychophysical domains. In acoustic studies, there are two possible sources of hysteresis effects: the physical equipment being used to create sound and the human auditory system. Analog physical equipment, such as oscillators, do not always produce the same output with identical settings of the dial; this is a result of hysteresis and "slop" in the physical components. Similarly, the human auditory system does not always return to its resting state following the presentation of a given stimulus. Suppose that the subject's task is to tune a variable oscillator to match a tone he/she has held in memory. A subject who adjusts the oscillator upward from a low tone might settle in on a different frequency than if he/

she adjusted the oscillator downward from a high tone. Furthermore, there may be a range of frequencies that sound the same to the subject. We might talk about this as "slop" in the setting of the oscillator. It is important, therefore, in experiments in which the subject makes adjustments of some sort, that you average across several trials, and that you measure with adjustments from both above and below the target point.

4. *Echoic memory.* In studies of auditory memory and perception, it is often necessary to ensure that a given stimulus tone is masked, or erased, from the subjects' short-term memory, in order that the judgment of the subsequent tone is not influenced by memory of the first. The most effective way to erase memory of a pitch is to play a sequence of random tones. More specific details about auditory masking are in Butler and Ward (1988).

23.11 Checklist: The Ten Stages of a Research Project

Research is a collaborative process. Do not be afraid to discuss your ideas with other people, even if you are not clear about them. A research project is not like a closed-book exam in which you are not allowed to get help. On the contrary, it is an opportunity for you to interact with people who can be collaborators in the process of reasoning through a scientific problem, and who share your intellectual interests and curiosities. Accordingly, the following checklist emphasizes the importance of talking to people—fellow students and instructors—throughout the process of conducting a study.

1. *Get an idea.* You may already have one, or you can consult previously published reports, because many papers include a section called "directions for future work."
2. *Perform a literature search.*
3. *Talk to people.* By this stage of the project, you have an idea of what you want to study, and colleagues can help you to figure out if (a) the idea is theoretically interesting, (b) it has been done (you might have missed it in your literature search), and (c) the experiment is actually "do-able," that is, you can study the problem using the time, methods, and resources that are available to you.
4. *Set up a time line.* Most students undertaking their first independent project dramatically underestimate the amount of time it will take. Setting up computer programs or apparatus to present stimuli and to analyze data can involve some setbacks. The actual experiments

may not run smoothly. The subjects may not show up for the scheduled session. And so on. It is important to consult with your research adviser to come up with a reasonable estimate of how long the study will take, and to create a time line of completion dates for each phase of the project.

5. *Design the study.* Often you can use the procedures in a previous study to get ideas for equipment, conditions, and stimuli to use. During this phase of the project, specify how many subjects you will use, what their task(s) will be, and how you will measure and record their responses.

   Once you have designed the study, and before you have tested any subjects, it is a good idea to begin writing your paper. At this point in the project the literature review is fresh in your mind, so you can easily write the introduction and methods sections, as well as the references section. A brief account of the hypotheses being tested and the procedures used will be needed for human subjects approval. A description of the proper format of a research paper is beyond the scope of this chapter, but examples can be easily found in the journals listed earlier, or in the *Publication Manual of the American Psychological Association* (American Psychological Association 1994).

6. *Run a pilot study.* Now that the study is designed, run a *pilot study* with a few subjects just to see how everything works. This gives you a chance to test the equipment, practice what you will say to the subjects, and be sure that the task makes sense to the subjects. It also lets you see how long the experiment will take. Analyze the pilot data to see if they make sense. For a quarter-long course like the psychoacoustics course at Stanford, a pilot study is often as far as the students can go, but it forms the foundation for further work.

7. *Run the study.* Be sure to keep accurate records for each subject: the date and time the subject was tested, the subject's name, age, sex, and so on. Be sure to ask the subjects about any variables that might affect their performance. In a hearing study, do any of your subjects have a cold? In a vision study, do any of your subjects wear glasses?

8. *Analyze the data.*

9. *Talk to people.* After you have performed your analyses, it is a good idea to talk to fellow students and advisers again. Do your findings suggest follow-up studies? Do they suggest an explanation due to experimental artifacts? Have you overlooked an important analysis?

10. *Write up the results.* A good report will include an introduction to the problem, a discussion of previous studies on the topic (you

should have done all this in step 4), and a lucid presentation of your findings. In the results and discussion sections, discuss the data qualitatively. Discuss what you think they mean. Also discuss possible alternative explanations for your findings, and tests that might be done in the future to control for artifacts. Be careful in your report not to draw conclusions that are not supported by the data, and not to overgeneralize your findings.

23.12   Coda: An Example of a Class Study

Anne Stern was an undergraduate student taking the psychoacoustics course at Stanford CCRMA in 1993. In addition to being an interesting and clever experiment, her final project clearly illustrates some of the design issues we have reviewed. Anne's question was this: If one were to ask people to sing a musical note with no further instructions, what note would they sing? Across a large number of people, will the productions tend to cluster around middle C? Around A? Or will the notes be uniformly distributed? Her idea was to stop people in White Plaza (a central point on the Stanford campus, between the bookstore and the Coffee House) and ask them to sing the first tone that popped into their heads, using the syllable "la." This is an interesting question for memory researchers, who wonder whether we have an internal template for musical tones, and it is an interesting question for music psychologists. This concluding portion of the chapter is a class discussion of her project, presented in dialogue form.

Daniel Levitin: What are some of the things she needs to think about in designing the experiment?

Student: Different vocal ranges?

Daniel Levitin: Right—people are going to have different vocal ranges. We can ignore octaves, as they do in absolute pitch research. Because, really, what we are interested in is *pitch class,* or *chroma.* What else?

Student: They might have just heard some music, and that could influence the tone they sing.

Daniel Levitin: Yes—White Plaza often has live bands or a boom box playing, and this could skew the results; if subjects' productions cluster around a tone, it could be because they were all influenced by some external source.

Student: The method of recording and playback might be variable
. . . the tape recorder speed could change as the batteries wear down.

Daniel Levitin: Right—this is a very important point. The ideal way to
record would be digitally; this way, we can be sure that the pitch
stays constant even if the motor fluctuates. What else might we want
to control for?

Student: Students in White Plaza might not be representative of students in general . . . there might be a particular type of student who
goes to White Plaza, and they may differ systematically from other
students.

Perry Cook: Also the time of day is a confound—people who sing at
10 in the morning might sing a different pitch than they would sing
at 4 in the afternoon, when their vocal folds are warmed up.

Daniel Levitin: Both of these are important. Ideally, you would like to
pick student numbers at random from a bin, so that you knew nothing about the person ahead of time. There is always the problem in
psychological research that you have not selected people in such a
way that you can generalize your findings. Most of the research done
in the Psychology Department at Stanford, whether it's on coopera-
tive attitudes, memory, social behaviors, or decision-making, is done
on Introductory Psychology students. Now it is possible that Introductory Psychology students are representative of students in general on campus, but it is also possible that they are not. In fact, it
turns out that students enrolled in Introductory Psychology at Stanford tend to be more depressed than students in general. This may
or may not have an effect on your experiment.

Well, Anne collected her data, and here is what she found (Figure 23.4).

Daniel Levitin: Notice that the modal response was to sing B, and nobody sang G. The research question is whether there is a preferred
tone, or whether these results are uniformly distributed. What do
you think, just by looking at it?

John Pierce: Uniform.

Daniel Levitin: That's right. Even though nobody sang G and more
people sang B than any other tone, these minor variations from uni-
formity are what we might expect by chance with such a small sample. By performing the Rayleigh test—a goodness-of-fit test—we can
conclude that the distribution we observed is more likely to have
arisen from a uniform distribution than a unimodal distribution

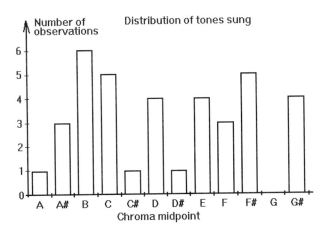

Figure 23.4 Data on tone production from Anne Stern's class project.

with G as the mode. [For details on the Rayleigh test, see Levitin 1994b.] In other words, suppose we hypothesize that the true state of the world is that the distribution of tones is uniform. What the statistics are telling us is that this distribution, even with its non-uniformities, is likely to have arisen as a result of sampling error, not as a result of the state of the world being different than we think it is.

Student: What would happen if you had a larger number of subjects?

Daniel Levitin: If our statistical inferencing is correct, if we had 10 times as many subjects, the frequencies of tones produced in each category should start to even out.

John Pierce: In a rather different experiment, Diana Deutsch found a difference between English people and Americans in their perception of ambiguous Shepard tones (Deutsch 1991, 1992). And so one might, in an experiment like this, ask what country the subjects came from.

Daniel Levitin: Yes—that would have been an important control in this study. Anne might have restricted her subjects to Americans, or she might have asked them about their country of origin.

I like this study as a course project because it addresses an interesting question, it allowed Anne to gain experience in a number of different techniques, and it was possible to do a good job on the study in the few weeks that she had.

John Pierce: It's important to note the difference between *demonstrations* and *experiments*. A demonstration, such as of the *precedence effect* or of *auditory streaming,* is something you prepare and play for a large number of people, most of whom perceptually experience the effect. For the purposes of this class requirement, demonstrations are an acceptable project. If you find some way of demonstrating an effect, either one that was unknown or one that was previously known, and you can demonstrate it in a way that is very clear and overwhelming, that represents a significant contribution.

Daniel Levitin: Diana Deutsch's tritone paradox is an example of a demonstration.

Brent Gillespie: Another important point in experimental design is to ask a research question in terms of a hypothesis that is falsifiable. You want to be able to run an experiment that can disconfirm a very specific hypothesis.

Daniel Levitin: Yes. The best situation is if you can design an experiment such that either way the data come out, you have an interesting finding. Anne's study is an example of that—whether she found a uniform distribution or a unimodal distribution, either result is interesting. A less interesting study is one in which you have something interesting to report only if the data come out one particular way.

Perry Cook: How do you decide what kind of response you want from your subjects, forced-choice or free-response?

Daniel Levitin: As the names imply, in a *forced-choice* experiment, the subject knows all the possible responses and just chooses one; in *free response,* the subject answers without any specific guidance from the experiment or the experimenter. In a *memory study,* or in a *psychophysical identification* study, you often want to use free response in order to get an unbiased answer. But forced-choice responses are easier to code (or evaluate) because the responses are constrained. There's no easy answer to this question, and psychoacousticians debate about this all the time.

John Pierce: This is tough stuff. I want to convey to all of you that you should consult with us on your project so that we can steer you away from undertaking too much. Students usually tackle too big a problem to do in a term project. Demonstrations show that some things are so true, that people can be convinced in an informal way. You said earlier that it is not difficult to think up good psychology experiments, but I think it is very difficult to think up ones that are worth doing and can be handled within your demands for subject time, variety, and methodological cautions. This is why I like demonstrations. And Anne's study is good because it is simple to state and test.

Daniel Levitin: It is important for you to think about experiments early in the term, so that you can change your mind if need be, and still have time to do something worthwhile.

Acknowledgments

This chapter benefited greatly from comments by Perry Cook, Lynn Gerow, Lewis R. Goldberg, John M. Kelley, and John Pierce. During the preparation of this chapter, I received direct support from an ONR graduate research fellowship (N-00014-89-J-3186), and indirect support from CCRMA and from an ONR Grant to M. I. Posner (N-00014-89-3013).

References

American Psychological Association. (1992). "Ethical Principles of Psychologists and Code of Conduct." *American Psychologist, 47,* 1597–1611.

American Psychological Association. (1994). *Publication Manual of the American Psychological Association.* Fourth edition. Washington, D.C.: American Psychological Association.

Butler, D., and W. D. Ward. (1988). "Effacing the Memory of Musical Pitch." *Music Perception, 5* (3), 251–260.

Chambers, J. M., W. S. Cleveland, B. Kleiner, and P. A. Tukey. (1983). *Graphical Methods for Data Analysis.* New York: Chapman & Hall.

Cleveland, W. S. (1994). *The Elements of Graphing Data.* Revised edition. Summit, N.J.: Hobart Press.

Cohen, J. (1994). "The Earth Is Round (p < .05)." *American Psychologist, 49,* 997–1003.

Cozby, P. C. (1989). *Methods in Behavioral Research.* Fourth edition. Mountain View, Calif.: Mayfield Publishing Co.

Daniel, W. W. (1990). *Applied Nonparametric Statistics.* Second edition. Boston: PWS-Kent.

Deutsch, D. (1991). "The Tritone Paradox: An Influence of Language on Music Perception." *Music Perception, 84,* 335–347.

Deutsch, D. (1992). "The Tritone Paradox: Implications for the Representation and Communication of Pitch Structure." In M. R. Jones and S. Holleran, eds., *Cognitive Bases of Musical Communication.* Washington, D.C.: American Psychological Association.

Fisher, N. I. (1993). *Statistical Analysis of Circular Data.* Cambridge: Cambridge University Press.

Fletcher, H., and W. A. Munson. (1933). "Loudness, Its Definition, Measurement and Calculation." *Journal of the Acoustical Society of America, 72,* 82–108.

Glenberg, A. (1988). *Learning from Data: An Introduction to Statistical Reasoning.* San Diego: Harcourt, Brace, Jovanovich.

Hayes, W. (1988). *Statistics.* Fourth edition. New York: Holt, Rinehart and Winston.

Hempel, C. G. (1966). *Philosophy of Natural Science.* Englewood Cliffs, N.J.: Prentice-Hall.

Hunter, J. E., and F. L. Schmidt. (1990). *Methods of Meta-analysis: Correcting Error and Bias in Research Findings.* Newbury Park, Calif.: Sage.

Kirk, R. E. (1982). *Experimental Design: Procedures for the Behavioral Sciences.* Second edition. Pacific Grove, Calif.: Brooks/Cole.

Kosslyn, S. M. (1994). *Elements of Graph Design.* New York: Freeman.

Levitin, D. J. (1994a). "Absolute Memory for Musical Pitch: Evidence from the Production of Learned Melodies." *Perception & Psychophysics,* 56 (4), 414–423.

———. (1994b). *Problems in Applying the Kolmogorov-Smirnov Test: The Need for Circular Statistics in Psychology.* Technical Report #94-07. University of Oregon, Institute of Cognitive & Decision Sciences.

Schmidt, F. L. (1996). "Statistical Significance Testing and Cumulative Knowledge in Psychology: Implications for the Training of Researchers." *Psychological Methods,* VI (2): 115–129.

Shaughnessy, J. J., and E. B. Zechmeister. (1994). *Research Methods in Psychology.* Third edition. New York: McGraw-Hill.

Stern, A. W. (1993). "Natural Pitch and the A440 Scale." Stanford University, CCRMA. (Unpublished report).

Watson, J. B. (1967). *Behavior: An Introduction to Comparative Psychology.* New York: Holt, Rinehart and Winston. First published 1914.

Zar, J. H. (1984). *Biostatistical Analysis.* Second edition. Englewood Cliffs, N.J.: Prentice-Hall.

Appendix A: Suggested Lab Exercises

Overview

Lab 1   Frequency Domain Aspects of Sound Localization

Sine wave localization, sound shadowing, head-related transfer functions (HRTFs), horizontal plane, function of pinnae, medial plane with keys, auditory scene analysis

Lab 2   Synthesis & Stimuli I: Decibels and Sine Waves

Measuring equal-loudness curves, additive synthesis, finding highest audible frequency, time domain versus frequency domain, decibels

Lab 3   Synthesis & Stimuli II: Critical Bands and Masking

Masking, band-limited noise, critical bands, two-interval forced-choice experiments

Lab 4   Psychoacoustic Measurements

Just-noticeable differences (JNDs) of frequency and loudness, missing fundamental, pitch perception, tone pulses, sum and difference tones

Lab 5   Temporal Aspects of Sound Localization

Simultaneity, precedence effect, Clifton effect, cocktail party effect, echoes from walls, echolocation

Lab 6   Voice Acoustics

Tubes and formants, impulse response, average speaking pitch, velum position, larynx height

Lab 7 and beyond   Project Discussion and Work

Note: By lab 7, students are usually working on their projects, so lab 7 and lab times of the remaining weeks are spent discussing and refining experiments, testing other students, etc.

Lab 1   Frequency Domain Aspects of Sound Localization

This lab will deal with one of the three main ways that signals at the ears are used by the brain to create a mental image of the environment. The three aspects are the following:

1. Timing information (which gives the angular location of sound sources)
2. Amplitude (interaural helps give angular location, absolute helps give distance).
3. Filtering of sound—which will be explained through experiments and demonstrations in this lab.

I.   Wavelengths of Sound

Experiment: Measure the wavelength of a standing wave by ear. Use a synthesis program to generate a sine wave for this experiment. Create a standing wave by placing two speakers opposite each other. Then listen for two maximums or two minimums in space, by moving your head to various locations between the two speakers. Use a sine wave frequency of A440.

II.   Sine Wave Localization

Experiment: Determine which speaker a sine wave is coming from. Synthesize sine waves of 110, 440, and 1760 Hz. Be sure to use a smooth envelope (it should rise and fall smoothly over more than a second or so). Place two speakers a few feet apart (say 10 feet), a few feet in front of you (say 10 feet). Play these sine waves randomly in each speaker, for yourself and for other students. See if you can determine which speaker the sine waves are coming from. It might be easier to synthesize a total of six stereo files, one for each frequency in the left speaker only, and in the right speaker only. That way you play the six files in random order. Try to do this experiment in both a relatively reverberant room and a relatively dead room.

III. Sound Shadowing, Head-Related Transfer Functions (HRTFs), Horizontal Plane

Experiment: Place an obstacle in front of a speaker (about 5–10 feet away) and play sine tones of different wavelengths. Note that the low frequencies are less affected by the obstacle than the higher frequencies, by comparing by ear the loudness behind the obstacle against the loudness with an unobstructed path to the speaker. Try obstacles of different sizes and shapes.

IV. Function of the pinnae: localization on the median plane (front vs. back, above vs. below).

Experiment: Have someone sit in a chair while another person jingles keys in three positions around the seated person's head: (1) in front of the head, (2) above the head, (3) behind the head. Each position should be the same distance from the head. First have the seated person close his/her eyes and try to detect the keys in the three positions. Observe how well the position of the keys is determined. Now have the seated person fold his/her ears (pinnae) down and have him/her detect the position of the keys again. Is there any difference in ability to detect the position of keys? Why are keys used? What other sound sources would be better or worse?

V. Auditory space

Experiment: Outside, in front of a building, close your eyes and listen around you for as many things as possible. Do the same experiment again, but this time try to focus on a small region of space at a time, sweeping through the horizontal plane.

Lab 2   Synthesis and Stimuli I: Decibels and Sine Waves

I. Decibels

This section of the laboratory should be demonstrated and verified by using a decibel meter to read the sound levels of various types of music and sound effects being played in a room.

Why are decibels used to measure loudness? One reason is that the ear can hear a wide range of amplitudes, and it is not convenient to relate those on a nonlogarithmic scale. For example, if the softest sound audible was 1 unit of intensity, the threshold of pain (which is 120 dB) would be 10^{12} units of intensity, or 1,000,000,000,000 units of intensity louder.

Decibels are comparisons of two different intensities (energy) or amplitudes based on the following formula:

dB = 20 log10(amp/reference amp)

or

dB = 10 log10(intensity/reference intensity).

The reason for the two different equations is that intensity is proportional to amplitude squared, and by the properties of logarithms, log I = log A2 = 2 log A. So you should see how the two equations relate to each other.

The table below shows U.S. limits on permissible daily occupational noise exposure and more conservative limits suggested by OSHA for avoidable exposure. Some other countries allow only a 3 dB level increase for each halving of exposure time.

Maximum 24-Hour Exposure

SOUND LEVEL (DBA)	OCCUPATIONAL	NONOCCUPATIONAL
80	—	4 hr
85	—	2 hr
90	8 hr	1 hr
95	4 hr	30 min
100	2 hr	15 min
105	1 hr	8 min
110	30 min	4 min
115	15 min	2 min
120	0 min	0 min

The dBA values above have a special weighting based on the inverse of the equal-loudness curve you will measure in this lab: sine waves of different frequencies that have the same perceived loudness have the same dBA value. This is not true for the regular dB scale, as you can see in your graph of equal loudness, where the functions are not flat over all frequencies.

A source for tables and graphs involving loudness, and other useful musical information, is:

Hall, Donald E. (1991). *Musical Acoustics.* Second edition. Brooks/ Cole Publishing, Pacific Grove, Calif.

II. Measuring Your Own Equal Loudness Contours.

Experiment: Synthesize tones in octaves, A55, 110, 220, . . . 3520 at various amplitudes that differ by 10 dB. Start by listening through headphones to the A880 tone at one level. Without touching any volume controls, and still listening through headphones, determine which amplitudes sound equally loud at other frequencies of A (work outward—440, 220, 110, . . . , then 1760, 3520). Plot the amplitudes of the equally loud tones as a function of frequency. Repeat for a different level of A880. Compare your plots against the Fletcher–Munson contours.

Lab 3   Synthesis and Stimuli II: Critical Bands and Masking

Introduction

This lab demonstrates how one sound can mask (perceptually cover) another. You will investigate masking with both individual sine waves and bands of noise. Using additive synthesis of sinusoids, and the synthesis of noise bands from this lab, you can re-create most classic psychoacoustic experiments. We will also give an example of a two-interval forced-choice experiment that will be used extensively in lab 4 and perhaps in your own experimental projects.

I. Masking of Sine Waves by Other Sine Waves

EXAMPLE 1
Synthesize a sound called example 1, with base frequency 300 Hz and partials:

{1, 0.6},{2, 0.3},{3, 0.15},{4, 0.07},{5, 0.03},{6, 0.01}.

(These pairs are of the form {partial frequency ratio, partial amplitude}.)
Use a spectrum analysis tool to verify that your synthesized sound is as you expect.

EXAMPLE 2

Synthesize a sound called example 2, with just one partial:

{6, 0.01}.

The frequency of this single sine wave will be 300 × 6 = 1800 Hz.

Listen to example 2, then play example 1 again. Can you hear the highest partial?
Alternate listening to each sound file a few times.

EXAMPLE 3

Synthesize a sound file called example 3, the same as example 1 but with the highest partial taken out:

{1, 0.6},{2, 0.3},{3, 0.15},{4, 0.07},{5, 0.03}.

Is there any difference between example 3 and example 1?

EXAMPLE 4

Now move the highest harmonic an octave higher, so that it is equivalent to the twelfth harmonic of the fundamental (which is partial 1). (Increasing a harmonic by an octave is the same as multiplying the harmonic number—6, in this case—by 2.) Call this sound example 4.

{1, 0.6},{2, 0.3},{3, 0.15},{4, 0.07},{5, 0.03},{12, 0.01}.

Now the highest partial is easily heard in the combination, even though it has the same amplitude as partial 6. Listen to and compare example 1 with example 4. Is there a difference in the sound? How would you explain the differences between the differences of (examples 1 and 3) and (examples 1 and 4)?

EXAMPLE 5

Actually, there is a difference between example 1 and example 3. If you synthesize a sound that slowly elides from example 1 into example 3, you can hear the highest harmonic disappear from the sound.

II. Masking by Noise Bands

Just like sine waves, noise can mask sounds.

Here we suggest using some examples from the compact disc Phillips 1126-061, "Auditory Demonstrations," by Houtsma, Rossing, and Wagenaars (approx. $27+tax).

CRITICAL BANDS BY MASKING (TRACK 216)
2000 Hz tone masked by spectrally flat (white) noise of different bandwidths

0. Unmasked test tone
1. Broadband noise (all frequencies from 20 to 20,000 or so)
2. Noise with bandwidth of 1000 Hz; that is, noise goes from 1000 Hz to 3000 Hz
3. Noise with bandwidth of 250 Hz
4. Noise with bandwidth of 10 Hz.

CRITICAL BANDS BY LOUDNESS COMPARISON (TRACK 7)
A noise band inside one critical band will sound less loud than a noise band spanning more than one critical band.

III. Synthesizing Noise Bands

Using inverse FFT synthesis, we can control noise quite exactly. Synthesize and compare the following noise band examples:

Bandnoise: a noise envelope that is 0.0 from 0 to 200 Hz, rises linearly to an amplitude of 1.0 at 350 Hz, falls linearly back to 0.0 at 500 Hz, and is 0.0 for the remainder of the spectrum
White noise: a noise envelope that is 1.0 for all frequencies
Pink noise: a noise that exhibits a $1/f$ amplitude response.

IV. Two-Interval Forced-Choice Experiments

A two-interval forced-choice paradigm is very useful in perceptual experiments. It is useful for determining the minimum amount that two "samples" must be different from one another in order for them to be distinguished from one another. Understand? It will be demonstrated here.

With a two-interval forced-choice experiment you can determine the JND (just-noticeable difference) for a particular type of perception. We might ask the question "What is the smallest increase in frequency for a tone to change pitch?" Or, in the reverse sense, "What is the largest change in frequency between two sine tones such that they sound like the same frequency?"

Think of two extreme cases for testing this:

1. There is no difference between the two frequencies
2. There is an octave difference between the two frequencies.

If I play for you octaves from case 2, with the highest and lowest notes in a random ordering, and then ask you to tell me which one was higher, you would probably have no trouble in telling me which tone was higher. Thus, your correct identification rate would be 100%, because you could give me the right answer.

Now suppose I play identical tones from case 1, and I ask you to tell me which sound is higher in pitch. They of course sound the same to you, but you must choose one of the two sounds. Now suppose one of the sounds is 0.00000000000000000000001% higher than the other. You can't tell the difference, but I can, because I created the two sounds. Therefore, you will have a 50% correct answer rate for case 1. Do you see why? It is because you are essentially guessing.

As the difference in frequency increases, you will become better able to identify the difference. There will be a fuzzy area between a correct answer rate of 50% and of 100%. The JND is defined as the point at which you can reliably tell the difference between two stimuli. The standard point is at a 75% correct identification.

Experiment: Synthesize some sine wave sound files with frequencies A440, 441, 442, 443, 444, 445, . . . Present pairs of these (one 440 and one other), in random order, to a subject and have him/her tell you which of the tones is higher. Keep track of correct responses. After presenting each pair four or more times, you should have enough data to begin determining the 75% correct identification point. Repeat this using complex spectra such as example 1 from section I, above. Are your results different?

Lab 4   Psychoacoustic Measurements

I.   Minimum Cycles to Determine Pitch

Synthesize a number of windowed sinusoidal pulses to determine the minimum number of cycles needed for such a sound to sound pitched. Useful parameters for this experiment are the following:

1. The frequency of the oscillations in the sound
2. The number of oscillations of frequency 1 in the click
3. The loudness of the click, from 0 to 1.0.

Question: What is the minimum number of cycles of a sine wave needed to perceive a pitch (correctly)? This experiment works well with a person with perfect pitch.

II. Pitch Perception and Fusion

Synthesize a number of sounds on middle C containing the following partials:

a. One partial at frequency f_0
b. One partial at frequency $2f_0$
c. One partial at frequency $3f_0$
d. A sound with two harmonic partials, $f_0 + 2f_0$
e. A sound with all three harmonic partials of equal amplitude
f. A sound as in e but with 0.2% vibrato at 6Hz
g. A sound as in e but with 0.5% vibrato at 6Hz
h. A sound as in e but with 1.0% vibrato at 6Hz.

Play the files in this order: a, b, c, a, d, e, f, g, h.
Observe how the highest partial is more or less audible, depending on modulation.

III. Missing Fundamental

Synthesize a number of sounds on middle C containing the following partials:

a. {1,0.5},{2,0.25},{3,0.16},{4,0.13},{5,0.1},{6,0.08},{7,0.07},{8,0.06}, {9,0.06},{10,0.05}
b. {2,0.25},{3,0.16},{4,0.13},{5,0.1},{6,0.08},{7,0.07},{8,0.06},{9,0.06}, {10,0.05}
c. {3,0.16},{4,0.13},{5,0.1},{6,0.08},{7,0.07},{8,0.06},{9,0.06},{10,0.05}
d. {4,0.13},{5,0.1},{6,0.08},{7,0.07},{8,0.06},{9,0.06},{10,0.05}.

Listen to these, and note that the pitch is still evident. Try removing various partials and see what patterns still yield a sense of the same fundamental.

IV. Measuring JNDs for Intensity and Frequency

Recall from the last lab the procedure for measuring the JND with a two-interval forced-choice test.

Measure your JND for the following:

1. The intensity of a sine wave at 100 Hz
2. The intensity of a sine wave at 1000 Hz
3. The intensity of a sine wave at 10,000 Hz
4. The intensity of broadband noise (white noise)
5. The frequency of a sine wave at 100 Hz
6. The frequency of a sine wave at 1000 Hz
7. The frequency of a sine wave at 10,000 Hz.

You should work in pairs, or find another person to give you the samples in a random ordering, because you will be influenced if you know what the difference actually is. Have the subject listen to the first sound and second sound in random order to determine which of the two bursts of sound in each sound file is louder, and record the answers. The JND is located at the point where the subject is about 75% right.

V. Non-linearities in the Ear

Sum and difference tones: if we input two sine tones into a non-linear system, the output is more than the sum of outputs resulting from the inputs alone. For a short discussion of sum and difference tones, see Murray Campbell and Clive Greated, *The Musician's Guide* (1987), 62–67.

Design a demonstration of this, using synthesized sine tones.

VI. Binaural Beats

Beats are not just physical results of the canceling and addition of waveforms. The brain can synthesize beats from two slightly different frequencies even if they are presented separately into the two ears.

Synthesize a stereo sound with a 300 Hz sine tone in one ear and a 303 Hz sine tone in the other ear. Listen to this sound in headphones.

Lab 5 Temporal Aspects of Sound Localization

I. Measuring the Speed of Sound

Connect two microphones separated by about 20 feet to your computer's stereo microphone input jack. While recording the stereo signal from both microphones, create a noise near microphone 1. Examine the sound file to find the difference in timing when the sound entered the two microphones. Try this with different microphone spacings.

II. Precedence Effect
Demonstrate the precedence effect, using the example from the compact disc (track 23) from this book. Then synthesize some files with the same signal on both channels, but with different delays between the left and right channels. Listen using headphones, and see how small time differences can make big differences in the perceived location.

III. Clicks
Synthesize pairs of clicks spaced 0.0, 0.001, 0.005, 0.01, 0.02, 0.03, 0.04, 0.05 seconds. Play these and observe the points when there are perceptual shifts.

Synthesize pairs of stereo clicks (one on left, then one on right) and see how different the spacing must be to determine which click (left or right) comes first. Repeat these two procedures, but using clicks of different pitch heights. Do this by using one click consisting of three cycles of 300 Hz, and one of three cycles of 450 Hz. Can you now determine time orders at smaller time delays?

IV. Echoes from Walls, and Human Echolocation
Take a walk, with a long tape measure, around an area with lots of buildings and flat surfaces. Find out how far from a wall you must be to perceive the echo from a hand clap. Close your eyes and see if you can use hand claps to determine where walls are located around you. See if you can use the sounds of your feet scraping to determine where obstacles are located around you.

Recall some of the time discriminations of the ear:

Binaural azimuth about 20 ms (the precedence effect)
Clicks around 2 ms (high-to-low, low-to-high discrimination)
Musical tones around 20 ms
Playing together 30–50 ms
Echoes (clapping, voice) 50–60 ms.

Lab 6   Voice Acoustics

I.   Modal Resonance Peaks (Formants)

Modal resonance peaks in the transfer function of a system are called "formants." To investigate resonant formants experimentally, find a narrow (1-inch diameter or so) tube about 4 feet long, and sing through it. As you sweep your voice frequency slowly up and down, you will find frequencies that are reinforced, or easier to sing, and others that seem difficult to sing. The easy frequencies are the modal frequencies, or peaks in the transfer function. Measure as many of these as you can (use falsetto voice for high modes), using a spectrum analysis application or a pitch detector. You can measure many resonances at once by slapping your hand onto the end of the tube (keep it there once you've slapped it) and recording the sound at the other side. Use a spectrum analysis program to compare the resonances you found using your voice with those you found by recording the impulse response, and try to explain any differences.

II.   Average Speaking Pitch

Carry on a conversation with a lab partner, and try to observe the average pitch in his/her speech. Pick a typical sentence, and have him/her say it a few times. Try to pick a word within that sentence that represents the average pitch used in that sentence. Record the sentence on your computer, pick out the word that represents the average pitch, and do a spectrum analysis on it to measure the frequency of the fundamental. Form a class average and standard deviation for males and females, and try to explain any results that deviate too much from the averages.

III.   Getting in Touch with Your Hidden Articulators

The velum is a small flap of skin in the back of the throat that is responsible for controlling the amount of sound and air which is allowed to enter the nasal passages. If you say the sound "ng" (as in sing), with the back of your tongue as far back as possible, it will be resting on your velum, and all of the sound will come from your nose. Try it with a lab partner and observe the vocal quality change as you move the velum.

Control of larynx height allows human speakers to change the effective length of the vocal tract, thus giving a perception that the speaker has a smaller, larger, or variable-sized head. The voices of the many cartoon characters (like Dudley Doright) have a characteristic high tenor quality, produced by raising the larynx. Large, intimidating vocal qualities like that of *Star War's* Darth Vader are produced with a lowered larynx height. When we talk to babies or pets, we often shorten our larynx and talk high and fast to show approval or excitement, and we lengthen our larynx to show disapproval. A good singer or professional actor with flexible control over the voice can produce a large range of sounds and voices by varying, among other things, the height of the larynx. Try modulating your larynx height when speaking to a lab partner. Now try to do it without also changing your speaking pitch. (It's hard but possible.)

IV. Spectrum Analysis of Speech

Use a spectrum analysis program to look at a few seconds of speech and some singing. See if you can begin to recognize the spectral shapes of common vowels and consonants.

Appendix B: Questions and Thought Problems

These questions are designed to get you thinking, then remembering, then motivated to look things up. Some of the answers are in this book; others require you to use references at the ends of the chapters. Some problems may not have answers known to researchers in psychoacoustics. You could be the first one to come up with a solution.

1. The ear
   Describe in your own words the anatomy of the cochlea and how it works to enable us to hear sounds and to analyze their frequency composition.
   Discuss how the basilar membrane works.
   What is the function of the inner hair cells?
   What is the function of the outer hair cells?
   How long does it take a sound wave to travel from the oval window to the round window through the fluid in the scala vestibuli and scala tympani?
   Which end of the basilar membrane has the highest amplitude vibrations for high-frequency sounds?
   Which end has the highest amplitude vibrations for low-frequency sounds?
   What are the main types of deafness and what are their causes?
   What is the pinna?
   What function does the pinna serve in directional hearing?
2. More on the ear
   What is the eighth nerve, and how are sound waves represented by signals in this nerve?
   About how many neurons are in the eighth nerve? Where do they originate? Where do they end?
   What is the approximate maximum rate of firing of a neuron in the eighth nerve?
   How do you think we perceive the pitch of sounds?
   Discuss how you think sound waves are represented by neural signals. Why is it unlikely that sound waves are encoded by the inner ear in a manner similar to the way that music is encoded on a compact disc?

The ear canal is roughly a cylinder 22 mm long and 7 mm in diameter. What is the first resonance frequency of the ear canal? Show your calculations. Remark on where this resonance is located on the equal-loudness curve.

3. Up the auditory chain

   In what structures in the brain are signals from the left and right ears compared?

   How accurate are the comparisons in time and in intensity? What uses do we make of these comparisons?

   If the neurons carrying the signals are firing every 2 ms, what is the accuracy as a percent of the firing interval?

   What is meant by tonotopic organization of the auditory cortex?

4. Waves, waves, waves!

   What is a traveling sound wave?

   What is a standing wave?

   What is a standing wave in a room?

   How fast does sound travel in air? in water? in steel? on a violin string? (This could be a trick question. Does sound travel on a violin string? Do traveling waves travel on a violin string? Traveling waves of what? Are the waves on a violin string transverse or longitudinal?)

   What is a surface wave and where do you normally observe it?

   What is a standing wave on a violin string?

   If you look at a vibrating violin string, how can you tell whether it has a standing wave or a traveling wave?

5. What is a decibel? You are asked to participate in a listening test in which you hear two sounds. The first sound is at 70 dB SPL. Describe how loud the second sound will be relative to the first sound if its intensity is

   71 dB . . . 80 dB . . . 70.1 dB . . . 0 dB . . . 140 dB . . . (should you trust this experimenter?) . . . 5 dB.

   You and a friend are talking 10 ft apart in an open field. You walk away from your friend. When you are 20 ft away, how many dB has his voice intensity decreased? How many dB has his voice decreased when you are 50 ft away? You repeat the same test in an auditorium. Are the answers the same? How will the ratio of direct to reflected (reverberant) sound change with distance in the field? in the auditorium?

6. Masking

   What is meant by the term "masking"? What is the musical importance of masking?

In a listening test, the masking signal is a band-pass noise with the band going from 300 Hz to 350 Hz and the maskee is a flute note.

The flute plays a one-octave scale starting from middle C. Which notes of the scale will be most strongly masked? Which will be least masked?

Which is stronger, masking of low frequencies by high frequencies or masking of high frequencies by low frequencies?

What is forward masking? What is backward masking? (Serious points will be subtracted for saying that backward masking is the embedding into rock recordings of time-reversed subversive satanic messages.)

7. You want to buy a new power amp and loudspeakers. You have some money, but not lots of extra money, and many other uses for your money, so you don't want to make any mistakes in choosing the speakers. The store has two different amps and three kinds of speakers that you can afford. It has a $1000 speaker that is more efficient than a $500 speaker, but otherwise is acoustically identical. In other words, if you turn up the amp, the $500 speaker sounds as good as the $1000 speaker. Six friends are willing to help you choose. How will you decide? Design a listening test involving your friends to help you decide. What are some obvious factors to be careful about to avoid biasing your decision with unimportant factors? By the way, within limits, people (especially your friends) prefer louder music. How will you decide between a more expensive amp + cheaper speakers versus a cheaper amp + more expensive speakers? How long will the listening test take? Can you do it in the music store?

8. Name five speech articulators and five famous voices or sounds associated with them. Ex.: Lips → Roger Rabbit: "PPPPPlease!!?"

9. Give an explanation for helium-affected speech. That is, when we inhale helium and talk, our voices sound higher in pitch and our heads sound smaller. Is anything odd here, given our understanding of the linear source-filter model of speech?

10. Contrast the guitar and the voice, discussing such things as the guitar body resonator versus the vocal tract tube, and the guitar string source versus the vocal folds.

11. Buglers can play harmonics from the series f_1, $2f_1$, $3f_1$, etc. Given what we know about the vocal tract tube being generally closed at the vocal fold end and open at the lip end, and the resulting series of resonances, what's up with the bugle? Discuss other profound differences between a voice and a bugle.

12. Questions from the animal kingdom

    Why are dolphins able to produce and perceive sounds in the range of 20–150,000 Hz, while people can only hear in the range of 20–20,000 Hz? Discuss why or why not it might be useful for dolphins to have this extra range, and why or why not it might be useful to have ears like ours.

    Can giraffes talk (or articulate sounds in a "vocal" sense)? If they could, would we be able to understand their "speech"?

    Why do ducks quack? Specifically, why don't they say something else, like "hello," or "bark," or "psychoacoustics"?

13. Standard telephone lines transmit only frequencies from roughly 250 Hz to 4000 Hz. How is it that we can understand speech over this channel? Why don't we hear voices higher than normal, since the fundamental will often not be transmitted?

14. What determines the pitch of a sound wave with many harmonic components?

15. Show for the one-dimensional case (sound propagating down a tube), the two-dimensional case (sound propagating between two parallel planes), and the three-dimensional case (sound propagating in free space) how the peak pressure of a sound wave varies with distance from the source. Use the conservation of energy principle (no energy is created or destroyed). Give your answers in both linear and decibel units.

16. Humans, even if only allowed to "touch" surfaces with a pencil, are still good at discerning various textures (without looking). How do they do it? Would their results be any different with a sharpened pencil or a blunt one? Would their results be any different if they could touch only with the eraser end? Suggestion: try it first, then write about it.

17. Any experienced keyboardist can tell the difference between a digital piano and a real piano. Differences lie in the areas of sound, feel, and sound/feel relationship. What do we mean by the sound/feel relationship? With a DiscClavier** and a MIDI synthesizer, design an experiment to test the importance of this sound/feel relationship. (A DiscClavier is a MIDI-compatible player piano. Music can be made on this instrument by playing it or by sending MIDI commands to it from a computer or synthesizer. Furthermore, it can output MIDI commands, so you can play a synthesizer from its keyboard.)

18. You are running listening tests to determine the just noticeable differences (JNDs) for various simple but (possibly) musically impor-

tant factors. The tests are two-interval forced-choice tests in which the subject must say (or guess) which of two sounds has more of the factor. In each of the following cases, what average percent correct answers would you expect from your subjects? For each case give a reason for your choice.

case 1 200 Hz 60dB SPL tone	vs.	201 Hz 60dB SPL tone
case 2 200 Hz 10dB SPL tone	vs.	201 Hz 10dB SPL tone
case 3 200 Hz 60dB SPL tone	vs.	200 Hz 61dB SPL tone
case 4 200 Hz 60dB SPL tone	vs.	200.1 Hz 60db SPL tone
case 5 200 Hz 60dB SPL tone	vs.	200 Hz 62dB SPL tone
case 6 200 Hz 10dB SPL tone	vs.	200 Hz 12dB SPL tone
case 7 Sung note, 6 Hz vibrato	vs.	Sung note, 7 Hz vibrato
case 8 Sung note, 1st formant = 200 Hz	vs.	Sung note, 1st formant = 210 Hz

19. The "phoneme restoration effect" describes the perceptual ability of humans to "fill in the gaps" when pieces of speech are removed, and replaced with silence or noise. An example might be "Whe . . . are you . . . ing?" Discuss what Gestalt grouping principles might be at work here (test them all, and eliminate the ones that probably don't apply). Then discuss what higher-level linguistic perceptual processes might be at work as well. Name one other example of a stimulus that demonstrates this principle.

20. You are conducting an experiment on auditory thresholds for the Department of Defense, Office of Naval Research. You have been asked to determine if the average person can hear the difference between the sound of a specific non-American ship engine and an American ship engine as transmitted through water.

To run this experiment, you obtained tape recordings of each type of engine, made with underwater microphones. The non-American tapes were stolen during the Gulf War, and the American tapes were given to you by the Office of Naval Research. In your experiment, you're planning to teach your subjects the difference between the two engine sounds by playing each tape for them in its entirety, while showing them a sign that identifies each tape as it's being played.

Following this training, you plan to test them by playing an excerpt from each tape in strict alternation: American, non-American, American, non-American, etc. Each subject will be instructed to tell you which engine he/she thinks he/she is hearing. To recruit your subjects, you stand in front of the Stanford Hospital Allergy and Asthma Clinic and ask people randomly if they will participate in your experiment in exchange for two front row tickets to the thrash metal band Victoria's Festering Pustule.

Provide a critique of this experimental methodology.

21. In creating musical tones by computer synthesis, and in testing theories about scales and consonance, why are the partials used not made equal in amplitude?

22. Concerning the pulse experiments described in chapter 5 (figure 5.3), make a sensible estimate of the highest frequency at which waveform c would give the same pitch as waveforms a and b.

23. The Phlegminian delegates have arrived on Way-Deep Space 11, and you, the linguistics officer, have been called in to help program the automatic translator for discussions. Their vocal tracts are about 30 cm long, and closed at both ends, but they can breathe our air by absorbing it through a membrane in their necks. Calculate the positions of their first three formants (assuming cylindrical tubing shape), and estimate the ranges of the first three formants. Should we consider more formants?? Discuss some of the difficulties and ramifications of such a vocal tract configuration.

24. Although figure 16.2 doesn't show it clearly, there is a measurable component of vocal pitch deviation at about 1.2 Hz. This component is not affected by auditory feedback. Where might be the cause of this?

25. Why do clarinets exhibit principally odd harmonics? Why is this not generally true of voices? Discuss the differences between your voice and a clarinet.

26. In one paragraph, give an example of the usefulness of haptic cues from a musical instrument.

27. An acoustician is standing in a rectangular auditorium 200 ft long, 50 ft wide, and 90 ft high. The walls, ceiling, and floor are hard reflective surfaces. The acoustician is standing 75 ft from the back of the hall and 20 ft from the left side. He claps his hands. Describe the first 10 echoes he will hear. Assume that the echoes reflect perpendicular to the walls. Which of these is the acoustician likely to hear as a distinct echo and why? What is the experimenter likely to hear after the first 10 echoes?

28. Make a Cartesian graph (an X axis and a Y axis), and label the Y axis "Pitch," going from fixed at the bottom, through discrete at the middle, to continuous at the top. Label the X axis "Spectrum," going from fixed at the left side to variable at the right side.

Fill in the graph with as many instruments and sound-producing things as you can think of. Here are two for free: the voice goes in the upper right corner (continuous pitch, variable spectral shape), and a car horn goes in the lower left corner (fixed pitch and spectral shape). Write a short sentence justifying each instrument you put on the grid. Big points for finding and justifying instruments that fit in the middle regions.

Now discuss the haptic interfaces of each of these instruments.

Appendix C: Sound Examples on CD

Chapter 1

1. Beats: pairs of equal-amplitude sines at 400+500, 400+490, 400+480, 400+470, 400+460, 400+450, 400+440, 400+430, 400+420, 400+410

2. Risset's musical beats example

a. Basic 100 Hz tone of seven harmonics, with amplitudes $1/f$

b. Seven such tones with fundamentals 100, 100.1, 100.2, 100.3, 100.4, 100.5, and 100.6 Hz

c. Seven equal-amplitude sinusoids with frequencies 700.0, 700.7, 701.4, 702.1, 702.8, 703.5, 704.2 Hz. This is a synthesis of the seventh harmonics of example 2b.

3.

a. High sines mask low: 500 Hz tone at 0 dB with lower tones at −40 dB, 300, 320, 340, 360, 380, 400, 420, 440, 460, 480 Hz

b. Low sines mask high: 500 Hz tone at 0 dB with higher tones at −40dB, 1700, 1580, 1460, 1340, 1220, 1100, 980, 860, 740, 620 Hz

Chapter 2

No sound examples

Chapter 3

- Size constancy audio examples are in chapter 20 sound examples.

4. Temporal inversion examples

a. Arpeggiated chord on the piano with three clearly defined tones

b. Same sound as above, but reversed. How many notes do you hear? Can you hear the order of note releases?

c. Brick tapped with a hammer (twice)

d. Same sound backward (twice)

e. Speech forward with reverb

f. Speech with reverse reverb (voice was reversed, then reverb applied, then resulting sound was reversed)

g. Voice with lots of forward reverb

h. Voice with lots of backward reverb

5. Bregman perceptual completion examples

a. Sinusoid going up and down in pitch, with pauses at the top

b. Gaps in previous example are filled with noise. Now the sine wave sounds continuous, but is just obscured by the noise bursts

c. Musical example with gaps (Dan Trueman, Hardanger Fiddle)

d. Musical example with gaps filled by noise bursts

6. Common fate example. When separate frequency modulation functions are applied to the odd versus even harmonics of a tone, two sounds are heard. (After Steven McAdams.)

• More common fate examples are in chapter 20 sound examples.

• For examples of singing without vibrato, the listener is directed to recordings by the Bulgarian Women's Choir.

Chapter 4

7. Building a sawtooth by harmonics

a. top down

b. bottom up

• Equal loudness contour examples are in the sound examples of chapter 6.

8. Waveforms with 12 equal-amplitude sinusoids using cosine/Schroeder/random phase, at fundamental frequencies of 880, 440, 220, 110, 55, and 27.5 Hz

9. Phase vocoder examples: time stretched/pitch shifted speech

Chapter 5

10. Bright versus dull spectra

a. Human vowels "eee" and "ooo"

b. Trombone and french horn notes

11. Adding harmonic partials of equal amplitudes. We hear a strengthening of the pitch frequency with each additional harmonic. We also hear a high pitch associated with the small wiggles in the waveform

a. at 55 Hz

b. at 440 Hz

12. Tone bursts from figure 5.1

a. Four periods of 13.5, 27.5, 55, 110, 220, 440, 880, 1760, 3520 Hz

b. 10 periods of 13.5, 27.5, 55, 110, 220, 440, 880, 1760, 3520 Hz

c. 25 periods of 13.5, 27.5, 55, 110, 220, 440, 880, 1760, 3520 Hz

13. Wiggly waveforms from figure 5.3, tunes played near 55 and 440 Hz
   a. 12 successive harmonics with amplitudes 1.2, 1.1, 1.0, . . .
   b. 6 successive harmonics with amplitudes 1.2, 1.0, 0.8, . . .
   c. Harmonics 7–12 with amplitudes .4, .8, 1.2, 1.2, .8, .4
14. Tone bursts from figure 5.4; 4000 Hz tone used in all examples
   a. 300 bursts/second for waveform a
   b. 300 bursts/second for waveform b
   c. 300 bursts/second for waveform c
   d. 400 bursts/second for waveform a
   e. 400 bursts/second for waveform b
   f. 400 bursts/second for waveform c
   g. 160 bursts/second for waveform a
   h. 160 bursts/second for waveform b
   i. 160 bursts/second for waveform c
15. All versus odd harmonics. Tone with 12 successive harmonics followed by tone with 6 odd harmonics at frequencies 880, 440, 220, 110, 55, and 27.5 Hz.
   • Shepard tone examples are included in chapter 10 sound examples.
   • Risset tone sound examples are included in chapter 10 sound examples.

Chapter 6

16. Equal loudness examples
   a. Equal amplitude sinusoids at 55, 82.5, 110, 165, 220, 330, 440, 660, 880, 1320, 1760, 2640, 3520, 5280 Hz. Listen to this series at a number of levels
   b. Same sinusoids adjusted in amplitude to follow the equal loudness contour at 90 dB SPL, 50 sones loudness level.
17. Which is twice louder, 5 dB or 10 dB? Tone pair on 500 Hz, second tone 5 dB louder. Same tone pair, second tone 10 dB louder.
18. Complex sounds composed of partials. Which sounds louder?
   a. A single sine wave at 1000 Hz
   b. A tone of the same power, consisting of sine waves at 500, 1000, 1500, 2000, 2500, and 3000 Hz
   c. A tone of the same power, consisting of sine waves at 500, 1100, 1773, 2173, 2717, and 3141 Hz

Chapter 7

19. Waveforms from figure 7.1
    a. 12 equal-amplitude sinusoids
    b. 12 sinusoids, 3 dB/octave rolloff
    c. 12 sinusoids, 6 dB/octave rolloff
    d. 12 sinusoids, 9 dB/octave rolloff
    e. 12 sinusoids, 12 dB/octave rolloff
20. Holy tones 1–9, from figure 7.4
21. Violin without body, violin with body (Dan Trueman, violin)

Chapter 8

22. The cocktail party effect
    a. Two speakers, one location
    b. Two speakers, two locations
23. Precedence effect
    a. Same voice on both speakers
    b. Same voice, phase inverted on both speakers
24. Sines plus noises in binaural (after Moore) (use headphones)
    a. Sines plus noise, in phase
    b. Sines in phase, plus noise out of phase
    c. Sine and noise, one ear only
    d. Sine one ear, noise in phase, both ears
25. Reverberation (Dan Trueman, violin)
    a. Music without reverberation
    b. Same music with reverberation
26. Binaural recording, jingling keys (use headphones)
    a. Left to right
    b. Center front to center above head
27. Gaussian pulse trains
    a. Average 33 pulses/second
    b. Average 67 pulses/second
    c. Average 125 pulses/second
    d. Average 250 pulses/second
    e. Average 500 pulses/second
    f. Average 1000 pulses/second
    g. Average 2000 pulses/second
    h. Average 4000 pulses/second

Chapter 9

28. The source-filter model of the voice
   a. A single click of glottal closure
   b. Single clicks on different vowels
   c. A periodic glottal source
   d. c through "ahh" filter
   e. c through "eee" filter
   f. c through "ooo" filter
29. Spectral tilt as function of vocal effort
   a. Loud singing
   b. Soft singing
   c. a and b normalized to same power
30. Source/filter consonants
   a. Noise source
   b. Filtered "fff"
   c. Filtered "sss"
   d. Filtered "shh"
   e. Filtered "xxx"

Chapter 10

31. Grouping by timbral similarity: trumpet tones alternating with a vocal tone and a steel drum sound
32. Segregation examples (after Bregman)
   a. High and low pitch played in succession; easy to follow as single line
   b. High-low-high pattern repeated ever faster until there are two streams of pitches
   c. Slow alternation between notes a minor second apart. Note that it is easy to think of the sound as a single line
   d. Same as c, but the interval is wider
   e. Same interval as c, but faster
   f. Same interval as d, but faster
   g. Same as c, even faster. Do you hear one or two lines?
   h. Same as d, even faster. Do you hear one or two lines?
33. Apparent motion in music: yodeling
34. Interleaved melodies
   a. Example from figure 10.4
   b. Same as a, increasing distance between melodies each time
   c. Separation of a by volume
   d. Separation of a by timbre

e. Two new melodies, increasing distance

f. Separation of e by volume

g. Separation of e by timbre

35. Warren loop

36. Wessel loops

a. Arpeggio with same timbre for all notes. Single perceived line arpeggiating upward

b. Increase in the timbral difference from a. Now it is easy to hear two lines arpeggiating downward.

37. Musical example of interleaved melodies

• Bach Violin Partita in D minor (Meesun Hong, violin)

• Shepard tones are in chapter 13 sound examples.

Chapter 11

38. Formant shifts with head size and pitch

39. Vowel sounds associated with five vocal tract shapes, two of which are unreasonable

40. Normal, emphasized, and sinusoidal vowels

41. Examples of flanging

42. Singing with and without the singer's formant

Chapter 12

43. Ambiguous speech sounds

a. goo, doo, boo

b. a played backward. Note how much easier it is to hear the transitional vowels

44. Inserting silence into speech

a. Say

b. a with 10 ms of silence inserted between /s/ and /e/ sounds

c. a with 20, 40, 60, 80, 100, 120, 140 ms of silence

45. Reasonable vs. ridiculous speech: yah yah, yah, faster and faster and . . .

46. Ara ala becomes arda alga with increasing amounts of silence inserted between the consonant and the final vowel. Inserted times are 0, 10, 20, 40, 60, 80, 100, 120, 140 ms

47. Gray ship, with editing silences and becomes gray chip, great ship, etc.

Chapter 13

48. Scales with equal steps on the mel scale
   a. Down the chromatic mel scale
   b. Diatonic mel scale in the midrange
   c. Diatonic mel scale in high range
   d. Diatonic mel scale in low range
49. Mel scale music
   a. Tune in middle mel scale pitches
   b. a tune in lower mel scale
   c. Original Bach tune
   d. Mel scale version of c
50. Risset-like tones
   a. Pitches are rising by major sevenths, but can be heard going down chromatically
   b. Pitches are falling by sevenths, but chroma is rising by a major scale.
51. Height only
   a. Height only, without chroma change, noise
   b. Height only, without chroma change, string timbres
   c. Height only, no change of chroma, sine tones
   d. One more noise example
52. Shepard tritone paradox
   a. Tritone can be heard as going up or down
   b. Diminished thirds going upward give the context of "upwardness"
   c. a repeated. Now likely to be heard as going upward
   d. Diminished thirds going downward give context of "downward"
   e. a repeated
53. Scrambled/stretched melodies
   a. Familiar song with pitches placed in random octaves
   b. Same song with melodic shape (up and down) preserved in choice of next octave
   c. Song in original correct pitch height
   d. Another song, octave scrambled
   e. d stretched, but shape preserved
   f. d in correct melodic spacing
54. Risset's ever-rising glissando
55. Original version of Shepard tone with discrete scale steps
56. Tempo illusions
   a. Ever faster patter from a Risset composition
   b. Example of fast trills from a Ligeti piece

57. More Shepard examples
  a. Variation on the Shepard tones, where fifth up, fourth down pattern is endlessly repeated
  b. Close canon in endless rise

Chapter 14

58. Stretched scale/partials examples
  a. A few bars of a hymn played with normal scale and harmonic partials
  b. hymn played with stretched scale but normal harmonic partials
  c. hymn played with stretched scale and stretched partials
  d. hymn played with normal scale and normal partials (repeat of a)
59. Musical intervals with sines, versus complex waves
60. Nonlinear beating between sinusoids as described in section 14.5
61. C major triads in temperaments
  a. Just temperament
  b. Mean tone in C
  c. Just temperament
  d. Equal temperament
  e. Just temperament
  f. Mean tone in C
  g. Mean tone in C♯
  h. Mean tone in C
62. Pierce scale examples

Chapter 15

63. Categorical perception, a wren warbling (three different "utterances")
64. Probe-tone studies, diatonic scale
  a. Diatonic scale up, with no octave
  b. First probe tone to play after a
  c. Same as a
  d. Second probe tone to play after c
65. Probe-tone studies, musical context
  a. Cadence without arrival on tonic
  b. Probe pitch that is remote from intended end of cadence of c
  c. Same as a
  d. Probe pitch that is third of a
66. Stretched scales

a. C scale in which all intervals are wide, so that the octave C is actually a C♯

b. Probe tone C, which is actual starting note of a

c. Repeat of a

d. Probe tone C♯ an octave below to match end of a

67. Equalized scale

68. Gamelan orchestra examples

a. Gamelan musical example

b. Sample tune in Bali tuning

c. Probe ending to b

d. Repeat of b

e. Another probe ending to b

69. One more probe-tone example

a. Melody in Western scale

b. Probe ending to a

c. Repeat of a

d. Another probe ending to a

Chapter 16

70. Synthesized singer

a. No vibrato

b. With random and periodic vibrato, and singer scooping slightly upward at the beginning of each note

71. Normal to ridiculous articulations

a. Vocal

b. Trumpet playing

Chapter 17

No sound examples

Chapter 18

No sound examples

Chapter 19

No sound examples

Chapter 20

72. A periodic tone, followed by a quasi-periodic tone
73. Building a soprano tone. First a G-pitched sinusoid, then harmonics are added, followed by vibrato.
74. Like 73, but on B pitch
75. Like 73, but on D pitch
76. Mixture of 73, 74, and 75, but with different vibrato functions on each "voice"
77. FM synthesis example that transforms a bell to three voices, then back to a bell timbre. The three voices are drawn out by applying separate vibrato functions to them.
78. Perception of distance and effort
    a. Successive vocal tones, where amplitude is turned down with each note. Relation of harmonics remains constant, like turning down volume on stereo.
    b. Same sequence as a, but high end of spectrum is successively lowered, as would happen for decreasing effort.
    c. Same as b, but additionally the ratio of reverberation to direct sound is held constant, so voice sounds like it is getting quieter in a fixed location.
    d. Same as a, but the ratio of reverberation to direct sound is increased, so voice sounds farther and farther away.

Chapter 21

79. String sounds by Scott A. VanDuyne
    a. Plucked string with no nonlinear effect, followed by four plucked string sounds with gradually increasing nonlinear effect
    b. More extreme nonlinear string sounds
80. Membrane (drum) sounds by Scott A. VanDuyne. Without, followed by with, non-linearity. Then a variety of different excitations and amounts of non-linearity

Following the audio examples on this CD, there is a data segment that includes ANSI C code for generating many of the sound examples on the CD. There are also a number of MIDI level 0 files for performing experiments/demonstrations in real time. The authors hope that these code and data files are useful to those wishing to do their own experiments.

Index